UNDER COVER

JEREMY ROBSON

UNDER COVER

A POET'S LIFE IN PUBLISHING
... AND ALL THAT JAZZ

AN ANECDOTAL MEMOIR

JEREMY ROBSON

Biteback Publishing

First published in Great Britain in 2018 by
Biteback Publishing Ltd
Westminster Tower
3 Albert Embankment
London SE1 7SP
Copyright © Jeremy Robson 2018

Jeremy Robson has asserted his right under the Copyright, Designs and Patents Act 1988
to be identified as the author of this work.

ISBN 978-1-78590-409-7

10 9 8 7 6 5 4 3 2 1

A CIP catalogue record for this book is available from the British Library.

Set in Adobe Caslon Pro

Printed and bound in Great Britain by
CPI Group (UK) Ltd, Croydon CR0 4YY

To Carole
And for our daughters, Deborah and Manuela
And our grandchildren, Lauren, Sam and Caitlin

CONTENTS

1

A FINE AND PRIVATE PLACE

It began with a warning, which I should perhaps have heeded. I must have been in my very early twenties at the time, earnestly writing what I thought were poems and vaguely contemplating going into publishing. Knowing this, an uncle of mine, Kenneth Snowman, whose books on Carl Fabergé were published by Faber, arranged for me to talk to one of the company's founding directors with whom he was friendly.

Morley Kennerley, a tall and courteous American, received me warmly in Faber's famous Russell Square offices, where I swore I could feel the breath of T. S. Eliot in the air. I don't remember Mr Kennerley's exact words as he delivered his cautionary message, but I still have the warning letter he sent me after our meeting. 'Remember', he wrote, 'that to be a poet in publishing is rather like trying to be a virgin by night and a prostitute by day.' It was many years before I was to fully appreciate the wisdom of his words, the poetry drying up as the publishing became all-consuming. I wonder now whether he ever gave the same advice to the great TSE.

Looking back, I realise that, ever the chameleon, I seem to have had several publishing lives (and two poetry ones), and if others are sometimes confused by the various names I've sheltered under, then I must confess I often am too: Robson Books, JR Books, the Robson Press... and who knows what's yet to come? But what's in a name!

Truth to say, as far as a life in publishing was concerned, nothing was ever really planned and nothing could have been further from my mind when I left school. A future in the law was on the cards then.

The school I went to, Haberdashers', now housed in lovely grounds in Elstree, was then in the rather less salubrious neighbourhood of Cricklewood (though it pretentiously called itself Haberdashers' Aske's *Hampstead* School). Many of the masters seemed to me to be relics of the war, and they were the ones who had to shout and whack to get attention. There was also a youngish master, a tall, gangly Australian we called Aussie Ostrich, who came in for a year to try to teach us maths and seemed to be cut from the same cloth.

Perhaps it was his first job, but he couldn't for the life of him control the class, who would break into a riot of conversation the moment he entered, so not a lot of maths was learned. Clearly he'd complained about us to the head of the junior school, Mr Cooper, and as a result would suddenly round on this or that unfortunate boy, shouting, 'Go down to Mr Cooper and get a hiding!', as he must have been instructed to do. Now, a hiding from Mr Cooper would not be fun. I can vividly recall him walking through the door of the school's indoor swimming pool and, on seeing a round mark on the recently painted white wall, asking in his dangerously quiet way who was responsible, all the while chewing menacingly on the transparent arms of his glasses. A boy gallantly owned up to throwing a tennis ball against the wall. He was sorry, he hadn't meant to make a mark. But his protests were in vain, and the ice-cold Mr Cooper marched him out of the pool to his office. When the tearful boy returned five minutes later, he had six long, deep stripes on his behind. The mark of Cain, indeed. Perhaps appropriately, Mr Cooper used to take us for religious instruction and once, rather surprisingly, he decided we should discuss Andrew Marvell's 'To His Coy Mistress'. Something made me ask him naively how a mistress could be coy. There was silence and much chewing on the spectacles, and only later did I realise how dangerously close to the flame I had flown. I shudder whenever that man's face surfaces in my mind.

For some reason, a doctor would appear every so often to examine us and we'd have to line up and drop our trousers in turn while he made a grab for our no-longer-private parts. If it was to test our reactions, I must have passed with honours, given the record speed with which I pulled away. Or perhaps he was just preparing us for life. Now and again I certainly had the impression that there were some masters who would have willingly stood in for the doctor.

I remember my terror on my first day in the senior school, when the French master, Mr Barling, greeted us by warning that if anyone was late for his lessons he would wind the offender in and out of the radiators. Far too anxious then to appreciate that he was a man of humour, I stared at those radiators, wondering how he would do it. Nothing in my five relatively carefree years at Haberdashers' Prep School had prepared me for this. Needless to say, none of us was ever late. Despite the introduction, I came to rather like and admire Taffy Barling, a superb teacher whose French was far superior to the others in his department, who all spoke a version that often sounded more like Franglais than the real thing. When they gave us a *dictée*, it was a matter of guessing what the words were in the text they were reading out and hoping you'd guessed right. Just as valuable to the school, Mr Barling was a first-class rugby coach who'd played for Wasps, and he'd race up and down the touchline as we played, screaming instructions. Rugby was never really my game, and I missed the football I'd played enthusiastically in earlier years.

It's said that one inspiring teacher can change your life, and Mr W. A. Nicholas, who taught English to the senior forms, did mine. If not publishing, he certainly put poetry, and the magic and importance of it, into my mind. Not only was he suave and handsome in his black velvet jacket, with a caustic wit no one wanted to be on the receiving end of, he had that rare gift of making literature seem both vital and exciting. Everyone tried to live up to the standards he set.

For his part, Mr Nicholas was lucky to have a batch of exceptional boys to work with – most, I have to say, in the class above me, in all senses of the word. Among these was Leon Brittan, already then passionate about politics and a keen debater. Leon, of course, was to become Home Secretary under Margaret Thatcher, the youngest Home Secretary since Winston Churchill. I can't claim great friendship with Leon, but we did play fives together on what was for him a rather painful occasion, since he smashed his hand against the fives court wall, and I remember him dancing up and down and rubbing his hands together. I always found him a gentleman in all respects, and it was shameful that he had to end his life under a shadow that should never have been there.

Brittan was one of a group of brilliant sixth-form boys who would often eat at lunchtime in a deli of sorts on nearby Cricklewood Broadway, where the food was rather more palatable than that on offer in the school canteen. I often joined them, hovering on the edge of their enlightening conversation. I kept in touch with Leon spasmodically after leaving school and from time to time he'd invite me to send a recent poem, always responding in a generous and not too critical way, whatever reservations he may have had. We met again some years later in Jerusalem at a small party given by another ex-Haberdasher and regular at those lunchtime forays, Leslie Sebba, now a professor of law at Jerusalem University. At the time, Leon, not yet an MP, was staying in Leslie's flat and since the party was taking place in what was to be his bedroom, he had little option but to join in, spending part of the evening dancing with my wife, Carole. Dancing, apparently, like fives, was not his strongest suit!

Among the other outstanding Haberdashers of that time were Steven Rose, now an eminent professor of biology and neurology, and Michael Lipton, also a professor, specialising in rural poverty in developing countries. Their paths never directly crossed mine, but those of the Oxford economist Peter Oppenheimer and the iconoclastic theatre director Michael Kustow did to some extent. Peter, who had taken up Russian at school (unusual in those days), married one of Boris Pasternak's nieces, and coincidently one of Pasternak's sisters, Lydia Pasternak Slater, took part in the first of the poetry and jazz events I arranged in the early '60s. It was the vivacious Peter who, when Carole and I visited him in Oxford, played us the 'Reading of the Will' sketch from a 1965 American comedy LP called *You Don't Have to Be Jewish*... Samuel B. Cohen has died and the family are assembled to hear his lawyer read out (amidst gasps, sobs and applause) details of his lavish bequests: 'To my son Sheldon, one million dollars, tax-free; to my daughter Jayne (with a 'y'), the same; to my wife Miriam, two million dollars, tax-free, and everything that is not already in her name, including the Picasso at the back of the store.' Finally the lawyer comes to the last named person, solemnly intoning:

'And to my brother-in-law Louis, who lived with us all his life, always smoked the finest cigars – mine – never did a day's work, who always said I'd never mention him in my will… Hello, Louis!' It still makes me laugh.

Mike Kustow and I were both to become involved in Arnold Wesker's Centre 42 arts festivals, for which I directed the poetry events, but more of that later. Among other things, Kustow became an associate director of both the National Theatre and the Royal Shakespeare Company, and director of the Institute of Contemporary Arts, where we gave a concert.

All these boys were very much at the centre of the school's intellectual life, dominating the debating society and also a literary society called the Christmas Islanders. Looking back through the school magazine, *Skylark*, I was amused to see that in 1952 Leon Brittan actually spoke for the socialists in a mock election (what would Lady T have said about that!), while a few years later Steven Rose was calling Nye Bevan, Minister of Health in the post-war Attlee government, a 'playboy Welsh crooner'. The other of the famous five, Michael Lipton also seemed to be hyperactive in the debating society and in 1952 he was selected by the BBC 'in a competitive audition' to speak in a special broadcast to America on foreign affairs.

They were also all bastions of the school dramatic society. On a lighter level, Kustow and Oppenheimer devised a school revue called *Prank* for which they wrote witty sketches, Peter and Mike starring along with two very attractive and talented girls, Jeannette Weitz and Pamela Walker. We didn't appreciate it then, but our headmaster, Dr T. W. Taylor (known as 'Spud'), must have been quite liberal for those times, in that he allowed the girls to take part in the revue, which created quite a stir among the tittering boys in the audience.

The fact that Dr Taylor had five daughters may well have had something to do with his relative broadmindedness, which seems also to have extended to religion: apart from the morning prayers in the large school hall, where the names of those ex-Haberdashers who had 'given their lives for their country' were displayed in gold on wooden panels along the walls, he arranged for Jewish prayers to be held at the same time. In fact, he attended these so frequently that some began to call him 'our Jewish headmaster', which he certainly was not. He seemed an aloof and shy man, but later I learned that his first name was Tom, which made him seem much more human. Distant as he was, rumour had it that he knew the names of so few boys that he would write 'Persevere' on reports at random.

Years later I was reminded of that old, cold school hall where the external O and A level exams were held when I happened to hear an episode of *Desert Island Discs* with the contentious art critic Brian Sewell, who recalled sitting in that very hall himself, taking art A level, which he said was rather frowned upon. Sewell described how a particularly philistine science teacher who was overseeing the proceedings paced up and down, his shoes loudly tapping the floor as if in disapproval and disturbing Sewell's concentration. As he spoke, I could see the hall before my eyes and recalled the exams I had anxiously sat there myself, and I also knew exactly who the master was, although he was not named. Sewell was someone I would have loved to publish, and I did come very close to signing up his outrageously frank autobiography, having a number of long and friendly conversations with him on the phone in which I gave him the assurance he asked for that we would not cut or censor it. That was the book in which he revealed that he'd had well over a thousand male lovers, giving much juicy detail… Then, just a couple of years ago, when he was already quite ill, Sewell took up my offer to write a short, controversial book on the art world for a series we had started, but alas his strength began to wane before he had got very far, and he had to abandon it. He had seemed to relish the idea of going out with a provocative bang.

Remarkably, four other Haberdashers' boys were later to play important parts in my publishing life. At just under seven feet tall, Michael Rivkin loomed largest. Always in trouble, he was too big for the school in every sense and on one memorable occasion he lost his rag with a teacher he'd accused of picking on him, rising to his full height and smashing his fist down in anger on a wooden desk, splitting it into flying pieces. Even the master had to laugh. I have another vivid memory of Michael standing a girl on a table at a party so he could dance cheek to cheek with her. We were close friends, and it was

Michael, by then a high-flying property tycoon, who later proposed that I start my own publishing company and guaranteed the necessary finance. At Michael's prompting also, Jeremy Morris, my valiant tennis partner in many school matches, who'd qualified as an accountant after studying law at Cambridge, came on board to look after the finances for our first few years, which was invaluable. (I remember Jeremy being an extremely fast runner at school – not a bad thing for an accountant to be.) Third up was the quick-minded and outspoken Jeffrey Pike, who, like Michael, had become very successful. Jeffrey was to prove himself a real friend when, sensing the personal strain Carole and I were under after some twenty-five years of independent publishing, he made it his generous business to help find a publishing partner for us. Lastly there was Laurence Orbach, son of Maurice Orbach, then a Labour MP, and brother of Susie Orbach, the psychotherapist and writer. Laurence founded the Quarto publishing group I was eventually to join (as JR Books) for some three years.

But back to the two girls who appeared in the school revue and really brought it to life, both of whom went on to greater things. Under the stage name of Fiona Walker, Pamela has appeared in numerous theatre and TV roles and in a number of films including *Far from the Madding Crowd* with Julie Christie. Despite her obvious talent, Jeannette (now Kupfermann) never really wanted to pursue an acting career, though she did land a few small film roles before going to LSE to study anthropology, and later making her mark as a writer and feature journalist. At LSE she did return briefly to the boards, playing Blanche in *A Streetcar Named Desire*, and at one point she even became Miss Air France, appearing bikini-clad on posters. Jeannette married the American painter Jacques Kupfermann about a month after Carole and I married, and the four of us spent many Sunday evenings together eating pasta and watching movies. Jacques died too young, and Jeannette wrote a sensitive and helpful book about widowhood, *When the Crying's Done*, which we published.

In the heady and innocent days of the school revue and after, Jeannette appeared rather bohemian for a north-west London girl, and I sensed that the popular French novelist Françoise Sagan and the

Left Bank singer Juliette Gréco were more her role models than the academics she was later to follow. (Did the firebrand Sagan really say, 'A dress makes no sense unless it inspires men to take it off you'?) It was through Jeannette, who sometimes came jiving at the 100 Club with me, that I became friendly with the Beat poet Pete Brown. Come Saturday night, Pete always knew of a party somewhere, and the fact that he hadn't been invited rarely stopped him. My chums and I would readily follow in his wake, and Jeannette and her attractive friend Jackie were often already there. At those parties there was always a lot of bold talk as the booze went down, but talk it generally remained, though it was often highly amusing, for even then Pete, who liked to hold court, was something of a comedian. Passionate about the great jazz saxophonist Coleman Hawkins, and modelling himself on the American Beat poets, he seemed to talk in riffs, bouncing his inventive verbal improvisations onto the heads of his inebriated listeners, whose critical senses were by then more than a little inhibited.

I remember driving him home in my battered little old car one night from God-knows-where to his parents' house on the Hendon Way, spilling a very drunk Pete into the arms of his mother, who more or less accused me of poisoning her collapsing son, exclaiming, 'Drink couldn't do this to my Pete!' But it could, Mrs Brown, it could! That car, a cramped black Morris, cost £40, and whenever you put your foot on the brake you had to pray at the same time for the car to stop. Fortunately, I was the one driving that night, not Pete.

With the poet and songwriter Pete Brown, who always knew where the parties were.

As well as continuing to write his special brand of often very funny performance poetry, the talented Pete went on to become a highly successful songwriter, co-writing with Jack Bruce the lyrics to some of Cream's biggest hits. He's also had various bands of his own over the years, including the Battered Ornaments, with whom he sang, and he continues to perform.

On the subject of battered ornaments, the school magazine reminds me that in 1952, weighing in at seven stone, seven pounds, I actually won the junior school boxing competition. To all those who know my gentle ways, this may come as a surprise, but I can only say that my father was responsible. He was born and brought up in Leeds, but sadly I have only a few memories of my paternal grandparents – my Ortho-dox Russian grandfather Max, with his black rabbinical beard, and my kindly and good-looking Polish-German grandmother Emilia, who, when she was not washing clothes and wringing them out through a wooden contraption in the kitchen, would rattle off Chopin pol-onaises on an old upright in the dusty sitting room. I stayed with them occasionally when very young in their old rambling house in Chapeltown, and loved to turn the handle of that wringer, pretending I was driving one of the trams that crisscrossed Leeds at that time. My grandfather had a rather imposing shop in town which specialised in repairing and selling watches and jewellery, and in all the photos I have of him he is formally dressed in a wing collar. He was, by all accounts, for all his Orthodoxy, a flamboyant character, having one of the first cars in Leeds and at one time buying an aeroplane and an extremely large house – and not just any large house, but Potternewton Hall, an eighteenth-century manor house with thirteen acres of land, where the Duchess of Cambridge's great-grandmother was born and grew up. However, it seems that his wife refused to live there, and he sold it a year later, apparently at a loss. For all the distance in time, I can distinctly recall the morning he descended the long, winding staircase of his Chapeltown house and startled me by raising his hands above my head and, in a scene out of the Bible, solemnly blessing me with Hebrew words I did not then understand. Was I Esau or was I Jacob, the pretender? I wonder.

My paternal grandfather in the doorway of his shop in Leeds
– quite an adventurer, despite his religious orthodoxy.

It was in Leeds that my father experienced anti-Semitism at first hand, not only in the streets, where it was rampant, but later at medical school, where one day the consultant announced to the students around him, while looking at my father, 'I don't like foreigners on my wards.' The same consultant later told my father that as long as he had anything to do with it my dad would never qualify, so he took off for London and sat his finals there. Before that, though, he'd learned to box, sparring from time to time with Harry Mason, who was also brought up in Leeds and became the British welter- and lightweight champion. I must add here, as a tailpiece to this story, that my father's younger brother Leo (father of my cousin, the knowledgeable and extremely witty journalist David Robson) had similar experiences at the same hospital. A brilliant surgeon, Leo was in line to succeed the then consultant when the latter retired, but he was bypassed. Disillusioned, Leo, the mildest and most easy-going of men, gave up medicine, moved to Harrogate and took up dentistry.

Because of his experiences, my father felt it important that I should learn to defend myself, so I joined the boxing club at General Motors, around the corner from where we lived in Colindale, and where he was the medical officer, and I continued to box at school. It stood me in good stead when I found myself fighting the class bully in the semi-finals of the school championship. It was a ferocious fight and to my amazement I was given the verdict – perhaps because he was a rather hit-and-miss fighter (who luckily missed more than he hit), and I'd learned to box in a more orthodox way, jabbing and moving and counter-punching. Afterwards that boy gave me a wide berth, so my dad definitely had a point. I gave up boxing after a year or two when I realised the boys we fought from nearby schools were becoming dangerously large!

Apart from the girls in the school revue (and one or two others), tennis was a major distraction in my senior school years, and the only thing I really excelled at, captaining the team. For some reason tennis was considered a sissy game by certain masters and I often wondered how they would fare over five sets on the Centre Court. There's no doubt that far too much of my time was spent on the tennis court when I should have been studying. Once again my father, a keen but very average tennis player, was partly responsible, taking me to tournaments whenever possible. At that time you didn't have to fight or queue all night for tickets for Wimbledon, Queen's Club, or the other main tournaments in order to see the leading players, as many of them would play at local tournaments where you could get in easily and often find yourself brushing shoulders with them as they strolled, unchaperoned, to whichever court they were scheduled to play on next. Those were the days when our top-ranked player, Bobby Wilson, who was just four years older than me and whom I'd watched in awe in the Junior Middlesex Championships, would travel to Wimbledon by bus with his wooden rackets and his mother, gallantly reaching the quarter-finals four times as the nation held its breath. One memorable year we hit gold when my father, who had evolved an effective way of treating tennis elbow, was called in on the eve of Wimbledon to treat the world's leading women's player, the big-serving American Louise Brough, who had hurt her elbow. Brough won Wimbledon four times (three in succession in 1948, '49 and '50) and so the press were all over my dad as he set to work, successfully treating her at our local club – which meant there was no shortage of Wimbledon tickets for us that year!

Haberdashers' tennis team, 1956. The very tall Michael Rivkin, our original backer, is directly behind me. I was the captain in those days!

I hadn't realised just how deeply those early tennis years had entered my psyche until very recently, when I was given two Wimbledon programmes from the early '50s. Remarkably, the competitors then were all amateurs, yet those names, sprinkled through the gentlemen's singles draw, were like royalty to me, though many are hardly remembered now except perhaps by devotees of my generation – players like Victor Seixas, Ted Schroeder, John Bromwich, Gardnar Mulloy, Pancho Gonzalez (my idol, whose matches against the small, fiery, bandy-legged Pancho Segura were among the most marvellous I've been privileged to watch), Frank Sedgman and the film-star-handsome Budge Patty, who, in the days before tie-breaks, played what was then the longest match in the history of Wimbledon, losing 6–8, 18–16, 6–3, 6–8, 10–12 to Jaroslav Drobný, with me courtside, savouring every stroke, every rally. And that was just the men. In the ladies' singles, Louise Brough, Margaret duPont, Doris Hart, Shirley Fry and Maureen Connolly ('Little Mo') topped the list, and while those early programmes devoted several pages to photos of the men, there is not a single photo of a woman – despite (or perhaps because of) the appearance a few years earlier of 'Gorgeous' Gussie Moran, who raised establishment eyebrows with her (relatively) short skirt and her frilly lace knickers. And I had the luck to be courtside once again when she made her startling first appearance!

No doubt fired by all this, every Sunday morning I'd set off early to play with my close friend Anthony Stalbow, who was fortunate enough to have a court in the gardens of his parents' flat in Highgate. We'd first met at our local club when we were thirteen, playing in an American tournament. This was mixed doubles and you drew for your partner, sticking with him or her throughout as you played a set against all the other pairs in turn. When our turn came to play against each other, and no doubt wanting to impress, Tony and I pulled out all the stops, un-gallantly 'poaching' too many shots from our not-altogether-brilliant (not even glamorous) partners. Luckily, Tony's vivacious Israeli mother, who *was* glamorous, was watching and she invited me to come and play on their court with my erstwhile opponent. So started our great friendship, which continues to this day. We were kindred spirits, and both of us were to win junior tournaments and play for the Middlesex under-18 team. And both of us were so shy that whenever the rather attractive girl whose family also lived in the apartments appeared in the garden with some friends, we would creep stealthily away to avoid an encounter. How we ever managed to get ourselves girlfriends at that stage of our lives is a wonder, but somehow we did. And how heart-churning those early amours were!

> It always seemed like love,
> but who can say?
> How innocent those days,
> the fumblings behind that
> broken fence, the constant fray.

Tony Stalbow and I were privileged to have a series of lessons with Don Tregonning, a young member of the Australian squad who went on to coach the Danish national team, including Kurt Nielsen, a future Wimbledon finalist. He taught us to start our backhand swing low down and to come up through the ball – none of the wrist bending of today. And he and his Wimbledon partner Peter Cawthorn would hit bullets at us as we stood at the net trying to parry them. As well as free Slazenger rackets, I was also given free tennis coaching by the county and had a series of lessons on the Green Park public courts from Frank Wilde, twice a Wimbledon doubles finalist in the late 1930s. I was surprised to read in the notebooks of that fine writer Frederic Raphael that he too had taken lessons with Wilde – something we talked about fifty or more years later when I came to publish some of Freddie's novels and his Cambridge memoir, *Going Up*.

When we were in our fifties, Tony and I came together again on court to win the Veteran Doubles title at the same club where we'd met umpteen years earlier, and where we'd won the junior tournament in successive years. The cup we were now presented with was ambiguously inscribed 'VD Champions'. When I tried to impress my teenage daughters, pointing to our names newly engraved on the clubhouse board, the only comment I got was, 'How pathetic!'

Sic transit gloria mundi.

2

A LAW UNTO ITSELF

In his cordial letter to me from Faber, gently edging me away from thoughts of a publishing career, Morley Kennerley had gone on to remind me that T. S. Eliot had written his finest poems while working in a bank. Whatever the uncertainties in my young life at that time, of one thing I was sure: a banking career was not for me. Instead, without much thought I found myself hurtling like a lemming in the direction of the law, becoming articled to B. A. Woolf and Co., a small but dynamic firm with offices in Lincoln's Inn Fields, just around the corner from the Law Courts in the Strand. The rather Dickensian offices consisted of just two large rooms, with old files spilling out of cabinets and piled up along the walls. One room, overlooking the square, was occupied by the firm's principal, David Lewis; the other by two young solicitors, Michael Roscoe and Raphael Teff, a managing clerk, Mr Fields, a super-efficient typist/secretary – and me, perched behind a tiny desk facing the window at the back of the room and trying to make myself invisible.

Small the company might have been, but there was nothing small about David Lewis, whether in stature, personality, reputation or intellect. A sometimes excitable man who didn't suffer fools gladly, he always seemed to be a step ahead of everyone else. No wonder he had a number of high-flying clients who relied on his agile mind and obvious erudition. David Lewis kept his sharp eyes on everything, and when the morning post arrived, the two young solicitors would traipse into his office with me in tow. There we would stand in front of his huge desk while he went through and discussed any letters or documents relating to matters one or other of them was handling, questioning them carefully and making suggestions as to how best to proceed. Since I wasn't directly in the firing line, I would find these morning sessions stimulating, but I sensed it was rather different for my two colleagues, though they both admired Lewis greatly. He was like a GP of the old school, and was equipped and ready to handle all kinds of cases, whether personal or corporate.

Raphael Teff was quiet and scholarly, Michael Roscoe rather more extrovert. I think they must have quickly recognised that I wasn't cut out for the law, though I'm not sure I realised that myself for quite some while. Nevertheless, they were both amazingly patient and did their best to guide and help me through. In those days there were no computers, nor even word processors, so everything had to be typed, and if in drafting a lease or document you made a mistake or changed your mind – as I invariably did – it all had to be typed again. Incredible now to think of the amount of work this entailed.

The dapper Mr Fields, as English as they come, was a mine of information, a man of considerable experience and knowledge on whom everyone seemed to rely. He must have seen them come and go over the years, and I always sensed a touch of irony in the way he looked at me. Yet he too was courteous and helpful, if a little formal, never addressing me by my first name. His small moustache was always perfectly trimmed.

David Lewis's brother Leonard was an eminent QC whom David would consult from time to time and brief when one of their cases was coming before the courts. Every bit as vibrant as David, and just as brilliant, Leonard Lewis seemed rather intimidating to a rookie like myself, but listening to him in his chambers as he debated various points with David was eye-opening, and both would go out of their way to briefly explain for my benefit the background of whatever they were discussing. They were busy men, but generous to me with their time.

Sometimes I would have to accompany Michael or Raphael to appear before a Master of the High Court. Masters, I discovered, were a kind of procedural judge who, in the early stages of a case, dealt with all aspects of an action, from its issue until it was ready to go before a trial judge. There was one particularly daunting Master who seemed to relish cross-examining the young solicitor before him, always trying to pick fault with the documents that he was being asked to approve. I felt sorry for my understandably nervous colleagues as we walked towards the Law Courts to face the Master in his cold, stony room, and I dreaded the day it would fall to me to make that journey to the scaffold.

There was one major case David Lewis was handling. I no longer remember the name of the client he was acting for or what the case was about (insider dealing?) but I do vividly recall the weeks I had to spend in the library of the Law Society, noting down the day-by-day price of a particular share over a six-month period. It seemed an interminable task, and I never understood what the brothers Lewis were looking for, nor whether my findings helped or hindered their case. But it was an insight into the kind of detail that was required and for the first time I began to seriously question whether I was suited to such a demanding profession. Having read the cases of Marshall Hall and other famous lawyers in preparation for my plunge into the law, and doubtless having watched too much television, I imagine I was expecting something rather more glamorous than spending day after day in a dusty library that was as silent as the tomb.

As the months went by, I became increasingly unhappy and withdrawn. Michael Roscoe, with whom I'd become friendly, would often take me to lunch, and one day he confided, 'Jeremy, we're all worried about you, you look so miserable. Please, please think carefully about the law, and whether it's for you.' That rather took me aback. Raphael, it seemed, was also concerned, but his approach was less direct. No doubt sensing my growing literary interests, he began to casually mention poems that he'd been reading, which surprised me (perhaps he'd seen me scribbling away at the back desk when I thought no one was looking). He was particularly enthusiastic about Eliot's 'The Love Song of J. Alfred Prufrock'.

I'd read some Eliot at school, and in fact *Murder in the Cathedral* had been an A-level set text. I could recite reams of it, but I'd never read Prufrock closely. Now, reading it again as a result of Raphael's subtle prompting, I found it a revelation – the language, the imagery, the conversational tone, the striking conceits:

> Let us go now you and I
> When the evening is set out against the sky
> Like a patient etherised upon a table…

Those spellbinding opening lines – written in 1920 yet so modern – went round and round in my head as I gradually started to write, and I now recognise that the voice of Eliot was in almost every line I wrote in those teething days. I was shocked later to discover what many have justly seen as anti-Semitic lines in several of Eliot's poems, notably in 'Burbank with a Baedeker: Bleistein with a Cigar', with the oft-quoted lines, 'The rats are underneath the piles / The Jew is underneath the lot'.

Shocking indeed, and the lawyer Anthony Julius pulled no punches when he wrote, 'He [Eliot] did not reflect the anti-Semitism of his times, he contributed to it, even enlarged it.' Even if I'd been aware of this then, I don't think it would have diminished my appreciation of Eliot's poems, nor has it since. Strangely, I have never felt as tolerant about Ezra Pound and his Fascistic activities, but then I have never been as captivated by his poems.

The poet Emanuel Litvinoff wrote his own powerful response in a poem called 'To T. S. Eliot', which ends:

> Let your words
> tread lightly on this earth of Europe
> lest my people's bones protest.

I heard him read that chilling poem years later at the launch of an anthology we both had poems in, but there was a famous occasion at the Institute of Contemporary Arts in 1951 when Litvinoff read the poem and Eliot walked in just as he was starting, to the horror of many people there, including Stephen Spender, who protested. But the poet Dannie Abse, who was sitting behind Eliot, heard him mutter, 'It's a good poem, a very good poem.'

* * *

Things were coming to a climax, and I was becoming more and more depressed. Then, one evening as I was travelling home on a bus from Finchley Road Station, I suddenly found it hard to climb down the stairs. By the time I'd limped home I could hardly move. Alarmed, my father somehow got me up to my room, while my mother watched anxiously. Stretched out on my bed at last, I could barely move at all – it was a kind of paralysis, both frightening and agonising, and the various pills my father gave me had no real effect. I remained like that for three worrying weeks, and the visits of my friends did little to raise my spirits. Obviously worried, and acutely aware of how the mind can control the body, my father decided to ask a physician he knew and respected to visit me.

Dr Aleck Bourne was one of the most distinguished gynaecologists of his day, famous for winning a landmark case after performing an illegal abortion on a fourteen-year-old rape victim, having alerted the police to what he was about to do. He was subsequently charged and acquitted at trial. However, my father had not called on him for his gynaecological skills, but because he was an amateur sculptor and interested in all the arts. Thus it was a kind of social visit, and Dr Bourne sat by my bed as we talked about painters we admired, and about poetry. Afterwards he told my parents that in his opinion I should be encouraged to give up law, since my interests and ambitions were plainly elsewhere. After a long discussion, the die was cast: I would abandon all thoughts of a legal career – and abracadabra, from the moment that decision was made I began to move more easily and the pain quickly vanished.

Over the years, the humane and worldly Dr Bourne and I exchanged letters and he encouraged me to send him my early poems. From time to time he would invite me to dine with him and his wife in their flat above his Harley Street consulting rooms. He'd done me a greater service than he could possibly have realised, and how wise and understanding it was of my father to have called on him.

One thing's for sure: that is the only time in my life I've been treated by a gynaecologist!

*   *   *

Having informed the not-altogether-surprised David Lewis of my decision to give up law, I now had to think what I really wanted to do. Write poems, yes, and I was doing that more and more, but I would also have to earn a living, as I was being gently reminded. Some evenings I would wander up to Hampstead Village and sit in a café to ponder my future, scribbling away, trying to look like a poet even though on the evidence of what I'd written to date I was far from being one. At that stage my parents had an attractive live-in help from what was then Yugoslavia, whose room was at the top of the house, a few tempting steps up from mine, which was off a half-landing (my parents and younger brother David were on the floor below). One night I made the exciting discovery that a friend of hers, a slim, blonde English girl, sometimes stayed over with her, creeping out in the morning before my unsuspecting parents and brother woke up (David, nine and a half years younger than me, still slept the sleep of the innocent, though he later more than made up for it!). Rather taken by the fact that I wrote, or was trying to write, poetry, the friend suggested I come round to her flat in West Hampstead of an evening to write – an invitation I was not slow to accept. However, once she'd told me her doctor had warned her that if a man so much as hung his trousers on the back of her door she would fall pregnant, I beat a hasty retreat. What had that to do with poetry? You may well wonder.

I'd done well in English at school, and the more I thought about it, the more journalism seemed a reasonable possibility as a career, so I contacted our local paper, the *Hampstead and Highgate Express*, and the editor, John Parkhurst, was kind enough to say I could work there for six weeks – work experience, we'd call it now. No money, of course, but that really didn't matter. The *Ham and High* was considered one of the finest local papers in the country, and I was thrilled to have this opportunity. I later learned that Parkhurst had kept the paper going through the war years, a period that enabled more women to become journalists and receive equal pay long before the vast majority of professions.

He was friendly and encouraging and even more so was his chief reporter, Gerald Isaaman, who took me under his wing. I couldn't have had a better mentor, for Gerry, who became editor in 1968 and remained at the helm for a remarkable twenty-five years, is a walking encyclopaedia of anything and anybody to do with the Hampstead area. It was under his editorship that the *New York Times* described the paper as 'the only local paper with a foreign policy'. These days, having moved out of London, Gerry writes regular features and reviews with great knowledge and flair for the arts pages of the *Camden New Journal*.

Through Gerry, whose continuing friendship and support I greatly value, I got a real taste of what it is like to be a working journalist. I loved the buzz of the *Ham and High* office, the constant clack of the typewriters, the reporters rushing in and out, the gossip, the sense of excitement on press day. I was sent to review plays and art exhibitions, accompanied journalists on their not-always-pleasant assignments, especially when there'd been a death or an accident. I went to local meetings, the odd sport event, and shows of all kinds in schools and halls, always doing my best to look cool and not show just how raw and nervous I was. I even reviewed some books but was never let loose on the famous writers and personalities in the area.

Then I got my big break, for with Easter came the Fair on Hampstead Heath, and I was given the job of writing a lengthy feature article about it. This was my opportunity to show just how well I could write, but as I look at the yellowing cutting now I don't think I'd give myself many marks out of ten. How pretentious, how embarrassing it is. Under the heading 'So Noisy, Yet So Happy at the Fair', I tried to capture the atmosphere, the characters behind the various stalls, the noise, the fun, the smell of hamburgers, the dust, the excited yells of the oh-so-attractive girls in the bumper cars, but it was way, way over the top. And of course, being in the shadow of Keats House, I couldn't resist bringing the great poet in. 'The poetry of earth is never dead,' he wrote, and I quoted his lovely lines towards the end of the article as a sort of grand finale. Whatever they really thought, everyone on the paper muttered nice things and the piece appeared just as I wrote it, under my byline. I bought lots of copies.

For all my faults and faux pas, at least I hadn't done what my new idol Dylan Thomas had when working on his local paper in Wales. Sent one day to review a new play, the young Dylan had got rather delayed in a pub, as was his wont, but that hadn't stopped him from handing in a review even though he hadn't been anywhere near the theatre – which, as his editor sternly told him, was a pity, since a fire had broken out, the theatre had burnt down, and of course there had been no performance.

ENTER THE GOONS

Apart from the Pete Brown parties, Saturday nights frequently found me and my friends at one north London home or another, dancing in a sitting room cleared of its furniture to the steady beat of the Glenn Miller Orchestra (oh, the nostalgia of 'In the Mood' and 'Moonlight Serenade') or the irresistible allure of the evergreen Frank Sinatra, whose *Songs for Swingin' Lovers!* album went with us everywhere, along with a portable Dansette record player. Luckily for me, one of my lifelong friends, Anthony Harkavy, played great jazz piano, so he was always in demand to perform at parties, and I was never far behind. In later life, as a lawyer, he was to skilfully advise and steer me through various sticky publishing situations and negotiations, even getting an advance back from the notoriously unreliable Jeffrey Bernard, whom I had unwisely contracted to write a book on his friend, the legendary jockey Lester Piggott.

Anyone who saw the entertaining play *Jeffrey Bernard Is Unwell*, or who read his columns in *The Spectator* on which it was based, will need no reminding that, besides his drinking, Bernard was proud of his ability to charm unwitting publishers into advancing him money for books he never wrote. So, after various unfruitful meetings in his flat in Great Portland Street and numerous un-kept promises, we finally decided enough was enough. As a very small publisher we simply couldn't afford to finance his drinking habits. Serving a writ on Bernard, which in the end we were obliged to do, was not an easy matter, but it was finally served – appropriately enough in a Soho pub, and doubtless not with the beverage he was expecting. Did any other publisher ever get their advance back from him, I wonder? It may have been a publishing first!

I also have to thank Anthony for sitting down one morning a couple of years ago at the inviting upright piano in St Pancras Station and playing that lovely old jazz number 'Georgia on My Mind'. As he played, with his back to the gathering crowd, a group of tall teenage boys made their way towards the piano, touching it lovingly before turning away. As they did so, I noticed they all wore large white hearing aids behind their ears. It was a heart-stopping moment that led me to write a poem called 'Jazz at St Pancras', which ends:

> Clearly, those boys had heard a melody
> we could not, and suddenly the
> station was no longer cold, and there
> was more than music in the air.

When we weren't standing around a piano, or partying with Pete, we were listening to the bands of Humphrey Lyttelton or Chris Barber at the 100 Club in Oxford Street, or to the purist clarinet of Cy Laurie at his club opposite the Windmill Theatre in Piccadilly. I always loved the voice of Ottilie Patterson, who sang with the Barber band and was to marry its leader. For me, her 'Careless Love' was one of the Seven Wonders, and her voice still thrills me these many decades on, as indeed does the clarinet of Barber's star performer, Monty Sunshine, attacking the testing, set-piece solo in the classic jazz number 'High Society'.

It was at the 100 Club that the Skiffle King, Lonnie Donegan, came into his own, not only playing in the early Barber band but having a featured solo spot when the main band took a break. 'Rock Island Line' was the number we all wanted to hear, a song I first stumbled on when an excited salesman in a record shop in Golders Green Road ardently recommended it – yes, there were such shops in those days, and we were regular customers.

The pioneering Lyttelton band was a main attraction then and was to remain popular right up to Humph's death in 2008. As I tried to pluck up enough courage to ask one of the many long-haired beauties who lined the walls to jive, I little thought that I would one day become the proud publisher of this famous Old Etonian trumpeter.

Going to the 100 Club – drug-free, I imagine, in those days – seemed daring at the time, a kind of rite of passage, and I tried to relive those days in more recent years when Humph and his devoted manager (and later partner) Susan da Costa would invite me to hear the band at the Bull's Head in Barnes – the music rather more mainstream then than the Dixieland fare I seem to remember from my youth, but every bit as potent and transporting. And on one memorable occasion, for the launch at a club in Dover Street of Humph's book, *It Just Occurred to Me...*, not only did the band turn up to back him on a couple of numbers, but we were treated to the wonderful voice of Elkie Brooks. Carole and I became close to the dynamic Elkie and her husband Trevor when, a few years after Humph's death, we published her frank autobiography *Finding My Voice*, and indeed she would jokingly call me her 'brother'.

Elkie Brooks joins Humphrey Lyttelton at the launch party for his book It Just Occurred to Me...

* * *

If, earlier, I held my father Joe responsible for my early boxing activities, I must also credit (and thank) him for my meeting and later involvement with the Goons, which all started with the arrival of that

Arch Goon Spike Milligan in my father's consulting rooms. I must have been around fifteen or so then, and *The Goon Show* was at the height of its popularity. At the time there were other popular radio comedy shows such as *Take It From Here*, *Hancock's Half Hour* and *Round the Horne* but, brilliant though these were, the innovative, surrealist humour of *The Goon Show* was startling. As well as writing most of the show's scripts, Spike also performed in it every week alongside the multi-voiced Peter Sellers and Harry Secombe, with two musical interludes featuring the Ray Ellington Quartet and Max Geldray, the virtuoso jazz harmonica player.

Having to write, rehearse and perform in a new episode every week for weeks on end took its toll on Spike, as he confessed in an interview years later: 'The pressure and the tension of keeping up the standard drove me mad. I dedicated my whole life to it, seven days a week … I gave my sanity for that show. It was terrifying, sheer agony. It wrecked my first marriage, and it wrecked my health.' He was counting on my father, to whom he had been recommended by his GP, to help him through his various crises. I should explain that my dad had become a leading medical practitioner of hypnosis, using it as a psychiatric aid to get to the bottom of particular problems. At that time hypnosis was looked on with a degree of suspicion by the medical establishment, but my father (who was always strongly against the use of hypnosis for non-medical purposes, such as entertainment) had remarkable success with it in a number of areas, including asthma, nail-biting, stammering, insomnia, sexual problems, smoking, depression and childbirth. I myself had a wisdom tooth out under hypnosis, with no pain at all and everything healing more swiftly than the dentist thought possible. After my father died, I found a thick file of touching letters from patients thanking him for his patience, understanding, kindness and care, and testifying to the effectiveness of his treatment. There were also many similar letters from doctors who had referred patients to him.

My father rarely listened to the radio and had no real idea who Spike was when he first came to see him, though he knew from my mother that he was famous. Being a blunt Yorkshireman, that fact cut little ice with him, and when Spike's opening sally was, 'I don't trust doctors and I don't trust you,' my father simply responded that he wasn't there to prove himself and pointed to the door. 'I think we can get on,' said an impressed Spike, stopped in his tracks, and thus began a lifelong friendship of great trust and affection, with my dad coming to the rescue on a number of occasions when Spike hit one of his frequent bad spots. There were periods when he was in our house almost every night, and over the years our home became a haven for him, my mother's table coupled with my father's medical skills proving an appealing combination.

I have memories from that time, too, of dropping off Barry Humphries and an attractive lady friend somewhere in West Hampstead. That was long before Dame Edna became a sensation, and I can only imagine he'd come to us with Spike for tea. Through my later involvement with *Punch* magazine and friendship with its editor, Alan Coren, we published *Punch on Australia*, which Barry edited. As I'd never really got to know him, when my father died in 1990 I was immensely touched to receive a phone call out of the blue from Barry saying he just wanted to tell me how sorry he was to hear the news and how much he'd liked my dad.

* * *

The Goon Show was recorded on Sunday nights at the BBC's Camden Theatre before a live audience, and tickets were like gold dust, with crowds jostling on the steps of the theatre, pressing to get in. Often I was lucky enough to have two tickets, and the extra one was sometimes a winning card in wresting a date from a reluctant girl. At school everybody imitated the show's famous characters – and the voices of Eccles, Moriarty, Bluebottle, Henry Crun and Neddie Seagoon echoed round the playground and school corridors.

It's hard to convey the power of radio in those days, and to what extent *The Goon Show* permeated the lives of so many. None of my friends would miss an episode, or the repeat, and those recordings were wondrously exciting, the audience warm-up sessions every bit as enthralling as the show itself. Once the large orchestra, under its director

Wally Stott (later known as Angela Morley), was seated, Peter Sellers
and Harry Secombe would enter stage right to huge applause from
the theatre audience, which usually included a number of well-known
showbiz personalities. Harry would somehow loosen Peter's trousers
so that they fell to his ankles, before launching into a high-pitched
version of 'Falling in Love with Love', his fabulous voice spiralling
to the Gods. Then Peter, his trousers now safely up, would move through
the ranks of the orchestra to the drums, whereupon Spike would enter
with his trumpet, and Dixieland mayhem would ensue. After that we
were sometimes treated to a number from Max Geldray and the Ray
Ellington Quartet. Eventually the straight-faced announcer Wallace
Greenslade would somehow get everyone under starter's orders, and
they were off.

I became very friendly with Max Geldray and his pretty young partner, Barbara. I often visited them at their home in Highgate, listening
to records and just talking, for Max loved to talk. Sometimes he would
actually play for me, putting on a recording of one of the big bands
and playing along with it – as well as his tremendous sense of rhythm,
he had a phenomenal ear. A pioneer of the chromatic harmonica, Max
was one of the first players to adapt the instrument to the demands
of swing music. Born in Amsterdam, he'd formed his own band at an
early age before joining the famous big band of Ray Ventura in Paris,
appearing with many of the stars of the day. I enjoyed hearing him
recall his days in Paris and friendship with the legendary gypsy guitar-
ist Django Reinhardt, and how they'd meet up late at night in the cafés
of Montmartre, playing together until the small hours. There was one
story I hadn't heard before, about the famous Quintette du Hot Club
de France, which featured Django and the great jazz violinist Stéphane
Grappelli. One day they were invited to perform at a nudist camp's
annual ball. When the organisers tried to persuade them to appear in
the nude as a courtesy to the guests, who'd be similarly unclad, they
had demurred – until the fee was trebled. The big night came. Duly
unclothed, they started playing as the curtains opened – to reveal the
cheering audience fully and formally dressed in black tie and dinner
suits, the ladies in long dresses. A student prank.

Max Geldray, the great harmonica virtuoso and Goon Show *regular.*

Great though he was as a jazz musician, Max was no actor, and his English, while good, wasn't perfect. Spike, who had a cruel streak, loved to give him comic lines to read on air for the simple joy of hearing him stumble over them in his soft, hesitant voice. I was rather in awe of the mercurial Milligan in those teenage years, though he was always extremely friendly and interested in whatever I was doing. He never talked down to young people, and there was something of the eternal child in him, for all his quicksilver brilliance, which is perhaps why he was able to write comic verse that was so popular with young readers. As Spike became as much a family friend as a patient of my father's, from time to time he'd invite us to parties at his house in Holden Road in Finchley, or to dip in the large inflatable pool in his garden. The trouble was, you never knew what mood Spike would be in, or when he'd suddenly turn tail, bid everyone good night, and vanish to his room. Sometimes he would send telegrams with instructions to his then wife, June, who of course lived in the same house! Once, he was accused of shooting at his neighbours' dog because its constant barking unnerved him. There was the time, too, when he walked into an undertaker's, lay down on the floor and cried 'Shop!' But when Spike was up, he was very, very up, the Irish stories and inventive wit flowing like the red wine he liked to drink. (Mention of red wine reminds me that Spike could also be generous: when Carole and I celebrated a special wedding anniversary, he sent us a bottle of wine with a note saying, 'Enjoy this with a good meal.' It was a bottle of Chateaux Margaux, bottled in 1964, the year of our marriage, and worth several hundred pounds. It was a long time before we could bring ourselves to open it.)

For all his down moods, Spike liked to have people, especially young people, round on Guy Fawkes Night, which was always fun with a large bonfire and barbecue. At one of those parties I recall seeing a rather reserved Kenneth Tynan (the great make-or-break theatre critic of his day, and reputedly the first person to say 'fuck' on British television) and his then wife Elaine Dundy, author of the bestselling *The Dud Avocado*. Years later, remembering them sitting sedately on the edge of the Milligan settee, I was amazed to read how this venerated critic would enjoy flagellating the understandably reluctant Dundy.

At another Milligan Bonfire Night party, this time at Monkenhurst, the beautiful old mansion Spike had moved to in 1974, Carole and I fell into conversation with the singer Lynsey de Paul and her then partner James Coburn, the American film star. Lynsey (whom Spike always affectionately called Lynsey the Small) came to live opposite us some years later, by which time we had formed our publishing company, Robson Books. I would find her name cropping up more and more (often libellously!) in books I was offered about the music industry, particularly in one by the notorious impresario Don Arden, who, exasperated by her behaviour, passed her over to his daughter, Sharon Osborne, to manage. In time, she too gave up, and I had to quietly tone down a number of potentially damaging remarks about Lynsey in Arden's book. Among other things he wrote that no married man was safe walking past Lynsey's house, a remark I couldn't help remembering whenever I cautiously passed her door on my way home of an evening. For all the trouble the prickly Lynsey sometimes caused her neighbours, she deserved a far happier end than the cruel one she suffered, dying of a suspected brain haemorrhage shortly after moving from the area, and only a few weeks since we'd had a friendly chat at a ceremony to unveil a statue of Spike in the grounds of Stephens House, Finchley, where he loved to walk.

At that event, held in September 2014, Michael Parkinson recalled being in the middle of broadcasting a show from LBC when an assistant rang to say there was a man in reception calling himself 'Mr Spike Milligan, the well-known typing error'. 'Send him up,' said a wary Michael, and in walked Spike in his dressing gown saying he'd been listening to the show and it was so boring he thought he'd better drop in and liven it up!

Lynsey de Paul did me one great favour in introducing me to Tom Conti, who lived around the corner from us both and who, so Lynsey told me, was writing a book. I'd always greatly admired Tom, ever since he'd starred in Frederic Raphael's *The Glittering Prizes*, the unmissable TV series about a Cambridge generation – and he had, indeed, just finished a book, a novel called *The Doctor*. Fiction was not normally our territory, but I was nevertheless interested and arranged to meet Tom at his house. Cautious at first, he asked me searching questions about our company and publishing in general, eventually agreeing to email me the manuscript. As I left, I noticed a grand piano in the living room with Beethoven scores on it, and Tom explained that he'd trained as a classical pianist before taking up acting. Perhaps the fact that we published the great Alfred Brendel helped to swing things our way.

Tom Conti with the singer-songwriter Lynsey de Paul at the launch of his novel The Doctor.

I was about to go on holiday and took Tom's book with me. Prodigiously researched, *The Doctor* ranged from the plains of Africa to the operating theatre of a London hospital, and I turned the pages quickly as I followed the many twists of the ingenious plot. There was only one problem: it didn't have a satisfactory ending, with everything left, surreally, in the air. I wondered how I was going to tell him, but I needn't have worried, for the minute I got back to the office my assistant said, 'Do you realise you didn't print out the last forty pages of the manuscript you took away?' I crept off and read them at once, and everything tied up perfectly. Chekhov said that if you plant a gun in a drawer in the first act of a play, you must make sure it goes off in the last. In Tom's book it certainly did!

He was wonderful to publish, and I enjoyed the literary lunches I drove him to, not just for his speech (he always shunned the mike – with that rich voice he didn't need it), but for the signing session afterwards, when I'd watch the queues of women of a certain age wanting a photo with him as well as a signed book, some asking jokingly, 'Can I be your Shirley Valentine?' (A reference to the film in which he'd played a seductive Greek taverna owner, with whom the middle-aged Liverpool housewife, Shirley Valentine, has a romance.) As a result of Tom's book, which, incidentally, the BBC recorded despite the sex scenes, we became friendly with him and his multi-talented wife Kara, whose one-woman shows, performed in the theatre-like lounge of their house as well as in public venues, we have greatly enjoyed. Her dramatic portrayal of the art deco portraitist Tamara De Lempicka is especially memorable.

*   *   *

If I was shy of Spike, I was even more so of Harry Secombe whenever I went backstage after a recording, though no one could have been friendlier or warmer. Harry was always considered the sober member of the team, and was often called on to make the peace when Spike had gone off the rails for one reason or another – whether with the producer, the BBC censor, the people responsible for the unusual sound effects that were such an integral part of the show, or whoever.

Where Spike went, Peter Sellers often followed, and it wasn't long before he too came knocking on my father's door. He'd been hypnotised before, and hadn't been impressed when he heard a voice saying as he came round, 'Be sure to pay my secretary in cash on your way out.' But Spike must have reassured Peter he would be in safe hands, and he and my dad hit it off from the start, Peter eventually becoming almost as friendly with my parents as Spike.

Peter had bought a lovely country house, Chipperfield Manor, in Hertfordshire, complete with swimming pool and tennis court, and it wasn't long before we were invited on Sundays to join his circle. Oddly, I never remember Spike being there, but Peter's cronies always were – Graham Stark, David Lodge, Max Geldray and also Peter's agent Dennis Selinger ('The Silver Fox'). A shy and reserved man, forever hiding behind one voice or another, Peter seemed only comfortable with this inner circle of friends he'd known for years, though I do remember the Boulting brothers being there once, as well as Stanley Kubrick and Richard Attenborough. Peter was proud of his house and liked to show it off – and why not? He'd come from a humble show-business background and had made it the hard way, though he never seemed secure. It was said he changed houses as often as he did cars, which were his passion. On one occasion, detecting a slight squeak or rattle in his car, he summoned his actor mate Graham Stark in the early hours of the morning to come over at once and help him detect it. What Graham hadn't expected was to be asked to climb into the boot with a torch while Peter drove around the neighbourhood – slowly at first, with the boot ajar, but when a sports car cut him up he responded by putting his foot down on the accelerator, causing the boot to slam shut... Graham had to remain in there amidst the fumes until, forced to stop at a red light, Peter suddenly remembered he was locked in the boot and let him out!

Of more interest to me then was the fact that Peter's lovely wife Anne liked to play tennis, and playing tennis was one of the few things I could do well in those teenage years. So while Peter entertained his court, Anne and I would rally on another court at the end of the garden. It seemed like heaven.

One memorable Sunday, when Peter was in the middle of filming *The Millionairess*, he announced that he had a special guest – and in sailed his co-star Sophia Loren, all elegance and sophistication, wearing a lovely light summer dress and hat and cutting a swathe through the other guests, who were sitting around in their shorts and swimming costumes, more than a little stunned. I stared in silent wonder, thinking I must be dreaming, for such visions belonged on the silver screen, not in someone's garden. In that film Peter played the part of an Indian doctor and he and Sophia performed a song together in which the flirtatious 'patient' Loren sang, 'Oh doctor, I'm in trouble,' and Peter, flustered by her advances, responded in his best Indian accent, 'Oh, goodness gracious me.' (Lyrics by the esteemed Herbert Kretzmer, whom we were to publish many years later.)

That brief encounter with the staggeringly beautiful Loren was a one-off for us, but Peter's infatuation with her was eventually to lead to the break-up of his marriage to the long-suffering Anne. My father quickly found himself in the firing line when, a week or so after the swimming party, the doorbell in our house rang and there was a visibly distressed Peter on our doorstep, wearing a turban and the full Indian regalia in which he'd been filming all day. 'I need your help, Joe,' he proclaimed without waiting to be led into the privacy of my father's consulting room. 'Sophia's in love with me and I'm in love with her.'

Years later, after Peter's death, my father told me how he'd tried to reason with him, warning that it would break up his marriage and devastate his children, telling him not to be a silly boy and that the worldly Sophia, who was married to Carlo Ponti, the director who had discovered her, would be up and away and out of his life once the film was finished. Not, I imagine, what Peter wanted to hear. But my father was a blunt speaker and he was soon proved right.

Much has been written about this so-called 'affair', but those close to Peter (we've published books by two of them) always maintained that while Loren liked him and found him amusing, it was a one-sided infatuation and never a physical relationship. But who knows? What I do know is that one night my father was summoned to Chipperfield Manor, where he did his best to mediate and help mend the fences that Peter had insensitively knocked down. But, as is well known, there was no happy ending to this part of the story and eventually Anne and Peter split up, she going on to marry the architect Ted Levy, and he remarrying three times.

* * *

From time to time I would go to the recordings of another hugely popular show that I also loved, *Educating Archie*, which starred the ventriloquist Peter Brough and his dummy Archie Andrews. If that doesn't sound like a very promising line-up, let me add that the show attracted an average of fifteen million listeners (many coming to think of Archie as a real person, he seemed so lifelike on air), and that the show featured an incredible list of future stars, including Tony Hancock, Julie Andrews, Benny Hill, Beryl Reid, Bruce Forsyth, Warren Mitchell and Max Bygraves. The latter had the programme's most popular catch-phrases: 'I've arrived and to prove it, I'm here', and 'That's a good idea... *son*' – pronounced slowly with a strong emphasis on the 'son'. There were huge cheers from the audience whenever Max declaimed them, and they became part of the lingua franca of the day.

Another comedian who was a regular in the show, and whose ability to do a huge variety of comic voices helped to bring it to life, was Dick Emery. It was through Spike that Emery became a regular on my father's couch and in our home, and it was through Dick that I got tickets for *Educating Archie* recordings. Later, he had his own popular television show in which he appeared in a host of hilarious guises, among them Hetty, the man-mad spinster; the Bovver Boy, a young aimless heavy; Lampwick, the doddering but proudly independent relic of World War I; Mandy, the well-endowed flirt, naughty but nice ('Ooh, you are awful – but I like you'); and many other colourful characters. He was to become a cult figure, but at that time he was very much second billing, despite his huge talent. Even at my young age, I could sense Emery often had his down moods, despite his very attractive lady friend, Vicki. I used to love watching Dick skilfully warming up the audience, telling them that he'd just come from a sick bed – 'My girlfriend's got the flu' – and continuing with one of the few jokes I've ever remembered, about two old Chelsea Pensioners reminiscing about the war. ''Ere,' says one, 'do you remember them pills they used to give us during the Boer War to stop us thinking about women?' 'Yes,' says the other one, 'of course I do.' 'Well,' continues the first, 'I think mine are just beginning to work.'

4

POLY BOUND

M y brief spell at the *Ham and High* led me to feel that journalism might be the way ahead. Looking around, I discovered that the Regent Street Polytechnic (now Westminster University) had a one-year course in journalism, so I applied and somehow managed to scrape a place. But it was now June and the course didn't start until the autumn. As I had several free months, I enrolled for a summer course at the Alliance Française in Paris with a view to brushing up my hesitant French, and was delighted when Tony Stalbow decided to join me. For some reason he couldn't get away until after the course had started, so I went on ahead.

One night I was sitting alone in a café in the Place St Germain, nursing a glass of red wine and struggling with a rather difficult novel by Henry de Montherlant that was recommended on the course, when a smartly dressed woman of a certain age, also alone, sat down opposite me. Noticing the book I was wrestling with, she began to say something about de Montherlant and his attitude to women. I did my best, but she was speaking quietly and at great speed so I couldn't grasp the point she was trying to make, though it was clear she had strong views on the subject. Eventually she gave up and turned her attention elsewhere. Later, I realised that this was perhaps another of the many catches I'd already managed to drop in the course of my short life, so I went back the next night, but she was nowhere to be seen. Doubtless she'd gone to another café and struck up conversation with someone altogether more responsive. 'Happiness writes in white ink on a white page,' wrote de Montherlant. I wonder what my mysterious lady would have made of that!

In Paris, and trying my best to look like a poet.

Summer in Paris can be hot, and the summer of 1959 was very hot. Having studied French literature for A level, I'd formed a strong attachment to the French poets and I'd also read a fair amount about the writers who'd converged there before and after the war. So, naturally, with books by Sartre and de Beauvoir in my bulging pockets, I made a beeline for the famous cafés I knew they'd all frequented – the Café de Flore, where they'd settle down to work, rarely addressing a word to one another, and where Juliette Greco had made her startling entrance, and then the nearby Deux Magots in the Place St Germain, where they would go later to converse with those they had previously ignored. A strange daily ritual. I found it invigorating to be there, sipping coffee, making notes, scribbling away, lines of Baudelaire, Lamartine, Hugo and de Vigny swirling around my head, as well as the more modern ones of another Café de Flore regular, Jacques Prévert, whose poem 'Barbara' I have always loved, which starts:

> Rapelle-toi Barbara
> Il pleuvait sans cesse sur Brest ce jour-là.

The romance of Paris was overwhelming.

I had a memorable 'first' in Paris, though not of the kind normally associated with that romantic city – Venice had had the privilege of hosting that particular performance. No, this was a religious matter: I'd been raised in a traditional (though not overtly Orthodox) Jewish home and brought up to eat only kosher meat. But as I sat down resolutely in a restaurant near the Place de la République, I eyed the steak frites on the menu and decided my moment of liberation had come. Scraping the butter off quickly with my knife (you are not meant to mix milk and meat, and old habits die hard), I took my first bite, then another, and another. Nothing happened. No thunderbolts, no applause, the earth didn't move. Nothing would ever be the same again. Mind you, to this day I have been unable to eat such forbidden delights as pork, or rabbit, or shellfish. That would still seem to me a kind of betrayal of my heritage. Come to think of it, the earth didn't exactly move in Venice either, probably just as well given the city's fragile infrastructure. No wonder really, since it wasn't exactly a romantic affair, but a night out with my Venetian friends whose hospitality I was enjoying and whose Saturday nights often took in a 'social' visit to one of the city's high-class bordellos (then licensed but subsequently abolished). As I put it in a poem, 'Postmark Venice', a few years later:

> Why, they've even closed Rosina's
> since '59, leaving a legend: Hemingway
> in Harry's Bar would have raged.

In my recollection, I was far too nervous and overcome by the jaded surroundings, overpriced liquor and fake jollity to have moved a pillow, let alone the earth. At the time, I prided myself on the fact that I virtuously declined the offer of a return visit the following week. As I saw it, the first occasion had been a kind of professional assignment, an experience no red-blooded would-be writer could possibly have ducked, but to go back for an encore would have been an indulgence. How prissy! For all that, I recall, afterwards, strolling cock-a-hoop with the others past lines of empty gondolas and, under an indifferent Venice moon, joining their loud chorus of 'O Sole Mio'. It always amused me in subsequent years, when I met up again with my now respectably married Venetian friends, how they would hush me up immediately if I even hinted at the name of the legendary Rosina.

But back to Paris, where I'd come to improve my French, not to come to terms with my Jewish heritage. Once Tony arrived, we started going to the Alliance in the mornings, but not for very long. We found it all rather intimidating – perhaps because we were almost the only males in the class (something we should have relished!). But the girls were so tall and sophisticated and all seemed so aloof, we couldn't imagine what they'd want with two young English boys. Besides, there was plenty else to do: exhibitions to see, afternoons spent swimming in a pool along the Seine, evenings listening to jazz in Le Caveau de la Huchette, where the bands of André Reweliotty and Claude Luter held sway. I remember hearing the great Sidney Bechet too, his soprano saxophone pointing at the sky, enormous rings flashing from his fingers. There was hot American jazz to be savoured in the cafés of Pigalle, and much else that was hot besides. We also had friends to look up, girls we'd met in London who invited us to various parties, and the fact that they'd heard we were in Paris seemed to encourage friends from London to visit us. So much for improving our French!

That didn't stop us soaking up the atmosphere of the famous bookshop, Shakespeare and Company, founded by Sylvia Beach in 1919, a shop that became a second home to many writers including Ernest Hemingway, F. Scott Fitzgerald, Ezra Pound and James Joyce. Indeed, it was Beach who bravely published Joyce's *Ulysses*. Way in the future the day would come when I would nervously give a reading there myself. The bookshop, and indeed Le Caveau jazz club, was just around the corner from the rather grotty hotel we'd found in the Rue de la Harpe, a place (to quote Eliot) of 'restless nights in one-night cheap hotels / and sawdust restaurants with oyster shells'. But it was an exciting area, especially given the occasional gunshot that would explode in the night, bringing everybody to the windows of the narrow street.

One weekend we made a surreptitious foray to Lausanne, where we had Swiss friends, including an ex-girlfriend of mine I'd met when she was in London studying English. It had been an intense involvement, and she had, in many ways, been a lifesaver during my low law days, as we talked and talked into the small hours. But we had very different backgrounds and with her return to Lausanne (where her father was chief of police!), despite a long-running exchange of express letters, the party was really over. Or was it? Ever the romantic, and never wanting things to end, I had persuaded Tony to make the long rail journey with me from Paris, just to be sure. I vaguely recall a long boozy night with my ex and a group of friends in a restaurant high in the hills above the town, with the enthusiastic singing of songs we didn't know, and as the evening progressed it becoming increasingly clear that my ex was going to remain strictly ex. It all ended rather dramatically when her would-be new beau, who was evidently disturbed by my presence and had been drinking heavily since we arrived, suddenly staggered very unsteadily to his car and drove off furiously into the night, causing more than a little alarm. Still, it had been a kind of adventure, and as we took the train back to Paris we managed to convince ourselves that we'd had a good time, even that it had been good for our French. For my part, I was glad to have the past well and truly behind me... or was I?

Inevitably, we visited the notorious Madame Arthur nightclub in the Rue des Martyrs, where dolled-up tarty women who were actually men pranced about in *plumes et paillettes* (less sexy than it sounds), singing, dancing and flirting with the audience in a Folies Bergère-style cabaret act. People seemed to love it, but I found it an uncomfortable experience and rather sad. I'd have swapped it any day for the real thing at the Folies, or at the more risqué Crazy Horse (yes, we tried those too).

A lingering memory of that short time in Paris is of several visits to a major exhibition of Chaim Soutine's work. For some reason I responded strongly to that great Jewish artist who, brought up in an extremely Orthodox environment in a Russian village, where the painting of the human form (graven images) was taboo, had turned to the carcasses hanging in the windows of butcher shops for his models and

inspiration. Having arrived in Paris, he'd been able to study at the Ecole
Nationale des Beaux-Arts, where among his few friends was the painter Amedeo Modigliani. Soutine's life, like Modigliani's, was tragically
short, and when, on my first visit to Israel, I was wandering one night
through the streets of Tel Aviv, I was immensely moved to come across
Soutine Street and Modigliani Street converging on each other. How
imaginative, I thought, as the romantic in me surfaced once again.

Now when I reread those French poets I so loved, I can see how
their emotionally charged verses would have held such appeal for a
wide-eyed young man on the loose in Paris. I think of Lamartine's 'Le
Lac', with its imploring lines:

> O temps! suspends ton vol, et vous, heures propices!
> Suspendez votre cours:
> Laissez-nous savourer les rapides délices
> Des plus beaux de nos jours!

or Samson's cry in de Vigny's 'La Colère de Samson':

> Et, plus ou moins, la Femme est toujours Dalila.

How many thwarted young men must have identified with that sexist
outburst, I wonder, and how many women must have thought the
reverse!

Could we get away with such inflated language in English? I rather
doubt it. One only has to compare those lines from 'Le Lac' with
Andrew Marvell's more sophisticated 'But at my back I always hear
/ time's wingèd chariot hurrying near' to highlight the difference. Yet
the emotive power of Lamartine's poem is so French, so affecting, so
memorable, as are the songs of the incomparable chansonniers Bras-
sens, Barbara, Brel, and such stars as Piaf, Aznavour and Chevalier.
How marvellous that we can savour them all, pour ourselves a glass of
fine French wine, and drink to *la différence!*

*   *   *

The Regent Street Poly was as near to university as I would ever get, and I've often regretted the forces that took me in the false direction of the law when I could have been closeted somewhere reading English. I seem to have spent my life since then trying to catch up and cover up the enormous gaps in my knowledge. On the other hand, my life and so-called career, unexpected and unplanned as it has been, have proved rewarding, and perhaps would have turned out very differently if I'd been smothered by academic strictures. Who can say?

The Poly (part of the School of Modern Languages) was not in the rather grand main Regent Street building but in nearby Great Titchfield Street, off Oxford Circus, in a somewhat makeshift building. The students were a mixed but lively and convivial bunch, not all of them English. Mark Colley, a tall, intelligent student from Rhodesia, became the sports editor of a major newspaper in Johannesburg. There was also a friendly, rather earnest student from Pakistan, older than most of us, called Tarikul Alam, who will feature in the story a little later. Once again the girls seemed to outnumber the boys, so I had little to complain about. It was refreshing to be in a relatively creative environment with students who were mostly bright and ambitious.

The two people I became closest to – both of whom remain friends, and both of whom we subsequently published – were Anne Hooper and Jeff Powell. After a distinguished career in journalism, the very attractive and vivacious Anne was to become a bestselling author of over seventy books and a well-known sex therapist, with her own newspaper column and radio programme where she would speak with authority and wisdom. Her biggest success was probably *Anne Hooper's Kama Sutra*, which we didn't publish and which I'd eye with envy when it appeared week after week on the bestseller lists. What we did successfully publish was her *How to Make Great Love to a Man* (her equally well-known therapist partner Phillip Hodson wrote a matching book for us, *How to Make Great Love to a Woman*, which seemed only fair!). In the days before Amazon, when book clubs were an important outlet for publishers, I remember taking these titles to the editor of the Doubleday Book Club in New York, and from her excited reaction to Anne's name I could appreciate just how successful she'd become,

for the editor was willing to take the books sight-unseen. I didn't think
it wise to tell her that in Anne's books very little went unseen.

My Regent Street Poly friend, the bestselling sex writer and counsellor Anne Hooper,
with her equally well-known therapist partner Phillip Hodson.

Jeff Powell struck out in a different direction, starting on the *Waltham-*
stow Journal, and graduating to sports editor before becoming an ace
sports writer for the *Daily Mail*. During his long and continuing
career on the *Mail*, Jeff has covered twelve World Cups and countless
world title fights, winning various awards along the way, including
that of Lifetime Achievement. His dramatic and colourful accounts
of the big sports events have brought him close to many of the great
sporting figures of our time. He can proudly claim to have been the
only British journalist invited to Muhammad Ali's 70th birthday party,
and his friendship with Bobby Moore led him to write a bestselling
biography of the footballing legend for which we found ourselves in a
bidding war against a well-known publisher, and which I'm pleased to
say we won. Jeff has always had an eye for a good deal, and this proved
an excellent one for us both.

Among the other students I remember was Penny Valentine, who became an influential critic of pop and soul music, championing Aretha Franklin before she was famous and becoming the favourite interviewer of both the Beatles and the Rolling Stones, as well as press officer for Elton John's record label. There was also a rather sultry dark-haired beauty called Wendy whom I was rather taken by. However, the only favour she offered was free tickets for the Academy Cinema in Baker Street, where her mother was the manager. For me and half the class, that is. The mother of another girl called Susie Moreland was the influential director of the Institute of Contemporary Art, and as a result Susie got me into to a number of talks and readings there. It was around this time, at the ICA, that I first heard the poet Adrian Mitchell read – a dynamic performance of poems with biting political attack and much wit – quite different from anything I'd learned at school. I couldn't have imagined that within a year or so I'd be giving a number of readings with this iconic champion of the left.

The lecturers at the Poly had very different styles. The urbane Frank Huggett, who'd worked on the *Daily Telegraph* for many years, had an amusing line in wry, cynical humour, while Ray Boston, who hailed from the *Mirror*, had an altogether racier and more direct style, bravely covering up a slight stammer with a whistle whenever he was stuck for a word. The bright red socks he always wore (which may or may not have reflected his political views) were the subject of much mirth. Both lecturers were somewhat informal in their approach and treated us more like friends than students. I enjoyed my year there, and the course certainly produced some good journalists, even if I wasn't among them. Pete Brown, who went to the Poly the year after me, recalls Frank Huggett saying rather sarcastically, 'Some people think that when they leave here they will become poets.' I appreciate the irony of that humorously intended remark as much as Pete!

Messrs Huggett and 'Red Socks' Boston would set us tasks, send us to cover various events, then go through the pieces we wrote, pointing out where we had fallen down, suggesting how they could be improved, other angles we might have taken. They explained how the different papers worked and what was expected of their writers, taught us how

to proofread and made us sub each other's work, write arresting headlines and striking lead-ins to our stories. We visited newspapers, went
on a three-day course at the London School of Printing and Graphic
Arts, for which we got certificates, and were given talks on the British
constitution and valuable lectures from a barrister on various aspects
of media law, including libel, which were useful to me in years to come.
We even had regular lessons in shorthand from a small, elderly lady,
but I must confess that I could never get the hang of this mysterious
language. I eventually found it so daunting that I would often dodge
her classes to go to an exhibition in nearby Bond Street, writing an
unwanted review of it as if I'd been sent by a paper. All grist to the
mill, I suppose. If only I'd had the money to pick up one or two of
the early Bacons I remember seeing and admiring – relatively inexpen-
sive then – this story might have taken a different turn.

Sometimes, when I felt particularly restless, I'd stray further afield to
browse in Better Books in Charing Cross Road, a fine literary bookshop which stocked the small poetry magazines of the time. I'd eye
them hungrily, dreaming that one day I'd find poems of my own within
their alluring covers. It was there I bought my cherished copy of Allen
Ginsberg's *Howl*, whose opening lines stir strongly in my head even to
this day: 'I saw the best minds of my generation destroyed by madness'.
How wild, how full of energy, how full-on! The small, square paperbacks with their distinctive black and white covers (of which *Howl* was
one), published by Lawrence Ferlinghetti's City Lights in San Francis-
co, were magical. Gregory Corso, William Carlos Williams, Kenneth
Rexroth… the list is legendary. At Better Books, too, I bought copies
of *The Evergreen Review*, Jack Kerouac's *On the Road* and Ferlinghetti's
own landmark collection, *A Coney Island of the Mind*. All a lot more
exciting than shorthand! Some years later I went with my future wife
Carole to hear Ginsberg reading in Hampstead, to find him sitting
cross-legged on the floor, facing the audience and hitting a large iron
bell with a metal rod repeatedly and monotonously for some minutes
until an increasingly agitated Carole turned to me and said, 'If he does
that once more, I'll scream.' Fortunately, he stopped, and started to read.

Unquestionably, the lectures I found most stimulating were by the head of the English literature department, David Waldo Clarke, a tall, beautifully spoken, elegant man who rather resembled Graham Greene, one of the authors he was passionate about. He was also keen on Hemingway, Evelyn Waugh and James Joyce, discussing the work of these authors in fine detail, analysing their style and the structure of their books, encouraging us to write short stories in their various styles. Given my passion for the American West and the fact that I'd spent hours of my childhood queuing at the local Odeon for the latest Roy Rogers film, perhaps the thing that endeared me most to the excellent Waldo Clarke was that he wrote popular Westerns on the side under a pseudonym. Who would have imagined it? Perhaps to balance this, he also wrote respectable books on English usage. He was particularly generous to me, spending considerable time commenting on the poems I shyly showed him, not slow to recognise the obvious Eliot influence, and always sharp but encouraging in his observations and criticism.

Not a student at the Poly but far more forthright, and spot-on in everything she said, was Valerie Barnett (as she was then), a highly intelligent and perceptive girl who was really a friend of a friend and reading English at Reading University. We had a sort of literary friendship, and when she asked me to send her some poems I readily complied. Her long, detailed reply took my poems to pieces line by line, image by image, thought by thought, as she was being trained to do. Her letter started: 'I don't quite know what I expected but I certainly didn't expect this. BUT – OK, here we go…' And away she went. Someone once said the price of reading other people's poems was praise, a maxim she certainly didn't subscribe to. I picked myself up, dusted myself down and started all over again. When we met again in 2014, Valerie had become a highly successful children's writer for Simon & Schuster under her married name, Valerie Mendes, and was launching *Larkswood*, her first historical novel for Orion. She was also the mother of the director Sam Mendes. And I'm relieved to say that the warm words she sent me after reading my newly published book of poems *Blues in the Park* were generous in the extreme – all the more appreciated since I knew she was still a lady who didn't mince her words. I don't recall what I sent her all those years ago, and hopefully she doesn't either. But she'd taken the poems seriously, and that meant a lot to me at the time.

But back to the Poly. We started our own magazine called *Slant*, which I edited, with Anne, Jeff and a pretty girl called Fleur Whitehurst with whom Jeff was rather smitten, as assistant editors. By the time we produced our last edition (selling price: sixpence), we also had a diary editor. Most of the students contributed and there was a wide variety of material – short stories, articles, criticism, poems. In the first edition there is even an article by a Mr S. Milligan entitled 'How to Make a Foon', which he must have given me as a favour. It begins, 'The editor of this well-known English newspaper has asked me to write 1,000 words on How to Make a Foon … with what I've just written that leaves me about 965 words to go.' He goes on to advise readers that it would be wise to buy a Geiger counter before continuing, 'such as you will find in any American's home. These can be bought from Surplus Army Stores, or indeed from the surplus army itself.' The article ran on over several pages in the same Milliganesque vein. We were thrilled to have it.

Apart from contributing my own poems to *Slant* (and who could stop me!), I was elated to have several accepted by the main, rather smartly printed Polytechnic magazine across the road in Regent Street, and three in a Scottish literary magazine called *Gambit* – a breakthrough for me. Reading those three poems now, I see that they are shorter than previous ones, the imagery more exact, less abstract, and that at last the tone was moving away from that of the Master.

The party was coming to its end, and we all took our final exams and probably all left with the same certificate. Nothing was too demanding. I even managed to pass shorthand, and can only surmise the examiner must have been either short-handed or short-sighted. Anne Hooper, who has vivid memories of the Poly, tells me that at the end of the year we were all given what she calls 'a proper reporting assignment', that she 'panicked like mad', and that I said, 'Leave it to me,' marched her into the nearest telephone box 'and called a friend'. We'd then presented the piece we wrote as a joint project, which was accepted by Ray Boston.

All we had to do now was find a job.

5

TO HULL AND BACK

It wasn't *The Times*, it wasn't *The Guardian* or the *Daily Telegraph* or the *Mail* or even the *Mirror*, and how or why I ended up there, I can't imagine. *Faute de mieux*, I think the French expression is. But there I was walking down Borough High Street to take up my new job as assistant editor of *Modern Refrigeration* – far down the High Street and long before Borough Market turned the area into a rather swinging place. I suppose at the time I was relieved to have survived the interview and been offered the job, but I suspected that most of my fellow students had gone to rather more glamorous places and were writing dramatic front-page stories, their names writ large. In reality, though, nearly all of them were cutting their teeth on local papers, on which I'd already served a kind of brief apprenticeship.

The owner and editor of the monthly trade magazine I'd joined was a small, spruce man whose bow tie never seemed to wobble even when he became animated, which wasn't often. I never once saw him with his jacket off, and I suppose that however hot the weather the thought of all those refrigerators kept him cool. He was courteous and well-mannered and went out of his way to make me feel at home, walking me round and introducing me to all and sundry. The scrutinising eyes made me think of my first day at school. I'd rarely felt so shy.

I can't pretend to have found the world of refrigeration overwhelmingly exciting, but I did my best to sub and rewrite the copy and press releases that landed on my desk, which was in the same room as the editor's and meant I was under constant observation. Some were rather technical, but still I smiled and tried hard to show interest. The editor was passionate about his subject, naturally enough, and would wax lyrical about the latest models as the details arrived in the post. I believe his father had started the magazine at the turn of the century, so it was in his blood. He certainly knew everyone in the industry and everyone knew him: the phone never stopped ringing and invitations seem to pour in. Despite his small stature, as far as refrigerators and refrigeration were concerned, he was Mr Big. It amazed me, but still, come lunchtime, I'd find myself pacing up and down the High Street wondering whether giving up law had been such a wise move after all.

Then something wonderful happened. I received a letter from the literary editor of *Tribune*, Elizabeth Thomas, asking me to contact her. She'd heard about me, she said, via Spike Milligan, a close friend of Michael Foot, who, though no longer the editor, was still involved with the paper. He knew she was looking for someone to review poetry and had passed the word on, and Spike knew of my interests and ambitions. Mrs Thomas wondered whether I might like to review some books for her. Would I not!

In those days, *Tribune*, founded in 1937, had a respectable circulation and considerable influence, and I soon learned that Elizabeth Thomas doubled as assistant to Michael Foot, who'd just been re-elected to Parliament. Later, when he became leader of the Labour Party, she became his special adviser. Already a hero of mine, he had been *Tribune*'s editor from 1948 to 1952, following in the steps of Aneurin Bevan. Elizabeth, for her part, was following in those of George Orwell, who'd become literary editor of the paper in the early 1940s, as well as writing a series of columns entitled 'As I Please'. It was a distinguished heritage. In a flash, my life was to change, and I immediately accepted Elizabeth's invitation to the *Tribune* office in the Strand to meet her. What a delightful woman she was: tall, attractive, with fine features, sharply intelligent, and a great deal softer than the glasses she wore made her seem at first meeting. She was most encouraging and we appeared to hit it off. I returned to the office with a pile of books in my bag and a smile on my face.

It didn't take me long to get going. My first *Tribune* review, a critical study of Wilfred Owen by D. S. R. Welland, appeared on 14 October 1960, and in it I thank Dr Welland for his 'painstaking study' of Owen's work. I was particularly interested to see how, as far as poetry was concerned, he divided the war into two phases – the first, in which soldiers in active service took time off to daydream and rhapsodise about their homes, the girls they'd left behind, the French countryside, etc., the war being incidental to the poetry rather than integral; then, in the second phase, the crusade quality of the war evaporating, with all the bestiality and horror coming to the fore in the powerfully realistic poetry of Owen, Rosenberg, Graves and Sassoon.

My review, which I thought the whole world must have read, seemed to have gone down well enough with Mrs Thomas, for two weeks later I was reviewing Auberon Waugh's *Foxglove Saga*, calling it – rightly or wrongly – an 'average novel'. The fact that Waugh gave up novel writing because he was sick of being compared with his father Evelyn may have proved my judgement right. Many years later he would invite me to lunch with the aim of enticing me to publish some material from the *Literary Review*, which he edited. Perhaps the whole world (Waugh at any rate) had not been reading my reviews after all.

After this, in quick succession came Aldous Huxley's *Collected Essays*, a book by André Gide, a biography of Gabriel Rossetti. Then, for the first time, I was given a batch of poetry books to review, and quite quickly I was established as *Tribune*'s poetry reviewer. I was in my element, especially as I was starting to get my own poems accepted by various publications – *Ambit, Envoi*, the *New Statesman* and others. More importantly, I'd become friendly with Elizabeth Thomas and urged her to publish more new poetry in the paper, which she readily did, and eventually we started a regular series of *Tribune* poetry readings together.

What was refreshing about Elizabeth was that her door was always open to young writers and – unlike many of the literary editors of other papers – she wasn't a literary snob, though her standards were high. For that reason people were willing to write for her, despite the low fees. She was generous in her praise of others and unfailingly modest – one would never have guessed that she'd won a scholarship to Girton

College, Cambridge, obtaining a First in Classics. Her interest in politics had come at an early age, when she joined the Fabian Society. Encouraged by *Tribune's* editor, Richard Clements, the coverage she gave to books, new exhibitions and plays was remarkable for a paper of its size, especially one that was ostensibly a political publication. She even commissioned an excellent artist, Cecily Ben-Tovim, to illustrate the theatre reviews, which livened up the page no end. At that time *Tribune* was very much like a family, and a number of the MPs who contributed would regularly convene at the office, the colourful Ian Mikardo among the most vociferous of them. At Christmas there was always a jolly party at the editor's house.

I started to develop the idea of arranging a poetry event in Hampstead, but for the moment there was the day job to cope with, and the editor of *Modern Refrigeration* must surely have noticed my restlessness and growing lack of enthusiasm. Things came to a head when I was asked to go to Hull to report on the opening of a large cold store, an enormous refrigerated depot where meat and fish were kept in readiness for distribution to the trade. In my mind, Hull was more associated with Philip Larkin than with cold stores (Hull's other famous export, Maureen Lipman, had not yet come into my life), but there was no dodging the assignment. There was just one problem: I had managed to wheedle a date out of a great-looking girl on the evening of the store's opening and I wasn't going to miss out on that. So to Hull I swiftly went, listened to most of the interminable speeches, and then hot-footed it back to London without waiting for the reception or interviewing anyone. As it happened, the train was delayed, and by the time it crawled into London my date had flown. Poetic justice, perhaps.

When I arrived rather shamefacedly at the office next morning, I was greeted by an angry editor, his bow tie for the first time just a little bit skew-whiff. Not surprisingly, he'd had a strong complaint from the directors of the cold store. 'This can't go on,' he said. 'It reflects very badly on me.' 'I quite understand,' I replied, my boxing training having taught me that it's always best to land the first blow. 'I can see that I'm not really cut out for this and I think we should call it a day. I'm sorry to have disappointed you,' and with that I was off to poetry new. I felt a little guilty, since, apart from sending me to Hull on the wrong day, he'd been nothing but decent to me. Still, the die was cast.

* * *

I may have been on some kind of mini-rollercoaster, but I was also out of a job. But first things first. At this point, and more or less out of the blue – perhaps via Pete Brown – I was invited to read in Oxford at an event arranged by *New Departures*, the avant-garde literary magazine I've never been avant-garde enough to appear in, which was (and still is) edited by Michael Horovitz. It takes real courage and commitment and not a little chutzpah to keep a magazine of this kind going these days. I admire Mike for it, as I also admired a remarkable man I met at around the same time, Miron Grindea, who for many years kept going his own very different magazine, *ADAM International*. The ambiguous title was an acronym for Arts, Drama, Architecture and Music. When he died in 1995, Grindea was actually working on the 500th edition of *ADAM*, which at the time was said to be the longest-running literary magazine. Born in Romania and educated in Paris at the Sorbonne, Miron was an intellectual of the old school, a true cosmopolitan who spoke several languages, often in the same sentence. A ball of fire, he seemed able to entice famous writers and thinkers from around the world to contribute just for the honour of being in *ADAM*. As interested in the visual arts and music (his wife Carola was a pianist) as he was in literature, he managed to persuade Cocteau, Picasso, Chagall and other artists to provide original pictures for his covers – gratis – always beginning his approach almost on his knees with the supplicating address '*Cher maître*', and not letting go until he got what he wanted. T. S. Eliot, Robert Graves, Bertrand Russell, André Gide, Graham Greene, George Bernard Shaw, Max Beerbohm, W. H. Auden – the list of his conquests was endless.

I well remember an early Saturday morning phone call from Miron in which he told me excitedly that he'd had a vision in the night that I was to be his heir apparent. What he really meant was that he wanted me to write letters, bring in contributors, help him raise money, and perhaps even store the magazine! In other words, it was a dogsbody he was after, not an heir, and even at my young age I was wise enough to decline his apparently flattering proposal. Later, he did publish several poems of mine, so he must have forgiven me.

Another stoic I met at around the same time was Jacob Sonntag, founder and editor of the *Jewish Quarterly*. In personality and interests, he was very different from Grindea, looking to 'literary journalism in the best tradition of Central and Eastern Europe' for his inspiration rather than the literary salons and ateliers of Paris. But as well as political and intellectual issues, his door was always open to the arts, including poetry. Indeed, to mark the 50th edition of his magazine in 1966, he invited me to present an anthology of Anglo-Jewish poetry within its pages, in which I featured sixteen poets as well as critical articles and a discussion on the theme of Anglo-Jewish poetry ('Is there such a thing'?), to which several non-Jewish poets contributed original articles. Sonntag died in 1984, but the magazine continues to appear regularly.

The *New Departures* reading in Oxford I'd been invited to participate in wasn't a grand affair but held in the upstairs room of a flat in a road leading into the High Street. It was packed, though, and when my turn came I somehow stumbled through the ten minutes I'd been allocated. It must have been one of the first times I'd read in public, and I've always been grateful to Michael Horovitz for the opportunity. I'd driven myself up to Oxford and come the Cinderella hour I felt it time to head back to London, especially since I was involved in another reading there the next day. As I walked down the stairs I was followed by a tall, dark-haired girl. Catching up with me, she said she'd enjoyed my poems and could she ask me some questions as she was reading English and it would help her studies. I politely explained that I was about to drive home, but she was not to be shaken off, following me to the car and asking if we could talk there for a few minutes. I could hardly say no, and in she climbed.

It was only then that she revealed her true intentions, which, as she bluntly put it, were to 'have' all the poets who'd read. Flattered as I was to have been chosen to open the batting, we were hardly into the first over when I decided I was going to be the odd poet out that night. She wasn't *that* attractive, the car was tiny, it had been a long and smoky evening in a stifling room, and I was tired. That, at any rate, is what I told myself as I made my excuses, bundled her out, and pressed my foot down hard on the accelerator. Another catch dropped, no doubt, but deliberately this time.

Welcome to the Swinging '6os, I thought, as I sped towards London.

* * *

The following night's reading was in Soho at the Partisan, the radical left-wing coffee bar in Carlisle Street, established in 1958 by the Marxist historian Raphael Samuel. In its heyday all manner of writers, academics, politicians, poets and showbiz personalities would be found there. The actual coffee bar was on the ground floor and downstairs was a large cellar where talks, exhibitions and screenings were held, and where our reading was to take place.

Naturally, it was exciting to be reading at a place with such a fascinating history and, just about recovered from my Oxford adventures of the previous night, I turned up in good time with some friends, as prepared as I could be. How could I have envisaged that the evening was to bring into my life someone who was to be a dear and inspiring friend for over fifty years? The other poets reading were Bernard Kops, the Finnish poet Anselm Hollo, Michael Horovitz, Peter Brown and Dannie Abse. I didn't then know Hollo's work, though I knew he had a considerable reputation in Finland and a growing one in England, where he now lived, working at the BBC and writing in English. I knew of Bernard Kops from his seminal play, *The Hamlet of Stepney Green*, as well as from various poems I'd read in magazines. One exuberant poem in particular, 'Shalom Bomb', has always stuck in my mind with its celebration of love and life:

… I want a laughter bomb
filled with sherbet fountains, licorice allsorts, chocolate kisses, candy floss,
tinsel and streamers, balloons and fireworks, lucky bags,
bubbles and masks and false noses.
I want my bomb to sprinkle the world with roses.

Poet, playwright, novelist, Bernard was born in the East End in 1926, left school at thirteen and never seems to stop writing, nor to have lost for a moment his infectious optimism and enthusiasm for life and poetry. How admirable! He was friendly that night, and he is warm and friendly now when we bump into him in Waitrose with his wife Erica, who features in so many of his poems. Seeing this lovely, close couple arm in arm as they enter the shop always adds a spring to my step. And the poems and plays, he tells me, are still flowing.

Then in his late thirties, Dannie Abse was a poet whose work I knew and admired, and I'd also read his picaresque autobiographical novel *Ash on a Young Man's Sleeve*, in which, with great humour and tenderness, he recalled growing up in Wales in the 1930s with his re-markable brothers: Leo, the future firebrand MP, and Wilfred, who was to become an eminent professor of psychiatry. But it was the fine poems in his most recent volume, *Tenants of the House*, that first drew me to Dannie. As I entered the Partisan, there he was, a thick mane of hair over his broad, handsome face, his smile welcoming and gentle, wisdom in his eyes. He introduced himself charmingly, and said the words I was to hear a hundred times over the years: 'Jeremy, you read first.' What could I do but obey? I did my best, but Dannie clearly *was* the best, as the *Jewish Chronicle*, which for some reason covered the event, justly recorded in a feature article. But they were kind to me, too, sort of. Having talked about the other poets, the reviewer went on: 'Far more orthodox in appearance was Jeremy Robson, who, at twenty-two, already shows maturity and promise. He was the only poet present who was formally dressed – that is, minus a chunky-knit sweater.' Reading that review the following Friday, I lost no time in going out to buy myself one. Next time out I was going to look the part!

After the reading, Dannie came up to me and gave me a piece of paper with his phone number, suggesting I should ring and go over for a coffee. Meadway 1961, the year of the reading. I'd never forget it.

6

POETRY RETURNS
TO HAMPSTEAD

From the heady heights of the Partisan basement it was now time to come down to earth and find myself another job, and this, after much searching, I finally did, moving from the cold world of refrigeration to the rather hotter one of a popular weekly magazine called *Tit-Bits*. The first magazine in his successful publishing empire, *Tit-Bits* had been founded in Manchester in 1881 by George Newnes, who had financed it by opening a vegetarian restaurant, quickly moving the operation to London as the circulation soared. The first really popular magazine of its day, it paved the way for the *Daily Mail*, whose founder, Alfred Harmsworth, wrote for *Tit-Bits*, while Arthur Pearson, who later launched the *Daily Express*, worked on it for five years. A number of popular writers contributed over the years too, including Isaac Asimov, P. G. Wodehouse and Rider Haggard, whose adventure novels were serialised in the magazine.

The *Tit-Bits* offices were situated in a side street off the Strand, with Covent Garden just behind, a far cry from the then barren Borough High Street. I was given a place in the editorial office, alongside three other journalists, all a good deal more experienced than me, and a chief sub who sat in the centre of the room overseeing the editorial side of things and issuing directives.

It was a lively enough office, and the paper ran short stories, articles on film stars, competitions, interviews, cartoons, bits of gossip and so-called sexy photos. The photos – usually of scantily clad young ladies running out of the sea, the waves bubbling around their feet – were brought in by a man in a black mac, selected by the chief sub, and then usually landed on my desk. I had the exciting job of writing captions below them, full of innuendo and *double entendre*. As I invented away, I remembered Ray Boston saying it was harder to write for a popular paper like the *Mirror* than for an upmarket daily. I began to see what he meant – you had to be creative! My other big job was to look after the weekly horoscope, and here I have to admit that I was shamelessly creative with the copy. If you were hoping for a handsome stranger to cross your path, or you wanted to know whether this was the week to make a big decision – romantic, financial or otherwise – you only had to turn to me. I wonder how many people's destinies I changed. Apart from that, it was a question of cutting stories down to size, writing the lead-ins or thinking up racy headlines as I wandered around Covent Garden during my lunch break.

As I mentioned earlier, I'd been thinking about arranging a poetry reading locally, and now, in between the tits and bits, I turned my mind to it. I believed there were many exciting poets writing, and that there was a large young audience to be won over. I wanted to prove it in as lively a way as possible. At first, my idea was to arrange something in a Hampstead coffee bar, but then I began to think more ambitiously, with a view to involving jazz musicians alongside the poets. Several of my friends were ready to help me, particularly one from my early teenage years, Edward Gold, who offered to look after the general administration, especially the finances – always my blind spot. That made all the difference, so, taking a deep breath, we got on to the Hampstead Town Hall, enquired about the availability and cost of hiring it, and managed to convince them that it would be an orderly, important cultural event, and committed ourselves. It seemed like a small undertaking, but it turned out to be quite a major one, with posters and leaflets to be produced, publicity to be drummed up and tickets to be sold.

However, before we could even begin I had to recruit the poets and musicians. I was lucky to have learned from the *Tribune* illustrator Cecily Ben-Tovim that her brother Arnon, a doctor, played alto saxophone and led his own group. Arnon, whom I soon heard and thought excellent, loved the idea. I wanted the music to be disciplined and not to dominate the proceedings and we saw eye to eye immediately. We even discussed setting various poems to music. Given the nature of the event, Arnon decided to expand the group, adding two professional musicians to what he described in the programme as 'a motley collection of designers, medics, admen, and teachers who'd started to play jazz in their carefree college days'. The two musicians he enlisted were his sister, Atarah Ben-Tovim, a classical flautist, and the jazz trumpeter Buddy Bounds, so we ended up with an octet. Now I had to find the poets. Jon Silkin, the respected editor of the literary magazine *Stand*, was one of the first I approached, and he readily agreed to come down from Leeds for the event. Then, remembering the dynamic reading I'd heard at the ICA when I was at the Poly, I took a deep breath and contacted Adrian Mitchell, and he also agreed. So too did Pete Brown and Anselm Hollo.

At this point, fate lent a hand in the form of a note from Boris Pasternak's sister, Lydia Pasternak Slater, following a review I'd written of a new translation of her brother's last poems. She'd liked what I'd written and invited me to a reading of Boris's poems she was giving in Kensington. The venue in question was large and cold with a high stage, but there was a reasonable turnout. It was a pretty formal occasion, with solemn introductions and some classical music too. Lydia read movingly from her own superb translations of her brother's powerfully haunting poems. In fact, they didn't seem like translations – the true test. The last two lines of one she read, 'Hamlet', stay in my mind (the last line being a Russian proverb):

> I am alone; all round me drowns in falsehood:
> Life is not a walk across a field.

As it transpired, there wasn't much opportunity to talk after the reading as Mrs Slater was rushing to get a train to Oxford, but I wrote to her straight away inviting her to read at Hampstead. Her response came in a four-page letter, again thanking me for my review and going on to say how bad most of the translations of Boris's work generally were, 'praised by people who knew no Russian and have no idea how the poems sound in the original, nor what Boris's style really was'. As for the Hampstead reading, she was understandably wary, asking many questions – about the length, who else was taking part, was it a private affair or would there be an audience, would it be advertised, would she be able to get the 11 p.m. train from Paddington and so on. Above all she made it clear that she would not take part in anything overtly political, since this might be an embarrassment to relatives in Russia. I hastened to reassure her, and she responded immediately on a card that she'd be happy to read. Those cards of Lydia's (and I was to receive a number in due course) were rather special, since on one side there was always a reproduction of one of her distinguished father Leonid's magnificent portraits. One of the first Russian painters to label himself an Impressionist, Leonid Pasternak painted many of the great writers of his day. A close friend of Tolstoy's, he'd also illustrated editions of *War and Peace* and *Resurrection*.

Encouraged by her response, I looked out the note Dannie Abse had given me at the Partisan. Plucking up courage, I dialled his number. Dannie's response was to invite me round for a coffee. So the next Saturday morning I found myself walking, rather nervously, towards 85 Hodford Road, where I was welcomed not only by Dannie but by his wife Joan, and was eventually introduced to their three very lively children – Keren, the oldest, who was probably about eight, Susanna, around five, and David, who could only have been about three. Many years later Dannie signed a book to me and Carole in which he scored through the word 'friends' from the inscription he was writing and touchingly wrote, 'well, family really, except that we never quarrel'. I could never imagine the Abse family quarrelling, or anyone quarrelling with them, especially with Joan, whom we came to love every bit as much as we did Dannie – such an erudite, modest, gentle, caring, beautiful woman whose wise judgement Dannie always depended on. In one of his books he humorously recalls his young son David earnestly saying to a friend as he pointed to a shelf full of his father's books, 'You see all those books over there? My mother typed them' – as indeed she had. But Joan was far from being simply Dannie's 'typist': she was also a writer and an art historian whose outstanding 1980 biography of John Ruskin was acclaimed on both sides of the Atlantic, and is still a key work.

Dannie was in a particularly good mood that Saturday, having just heard that his play *House of Cowards* had won the prestigious Charles Henry Foyle award. Still, forever a little cautious where poetry was concerned, he wanted to know who else was reading, but when I told him Jon Silkin, Adrian Mitchell and Lydia Pasternak Slater would be in attendance he was reassured, getting out the small pocket diary he always carried in his top pocket and putting down the date. Did I mention the jazz, I wonder? Probably not. What I didn't realise was that anything Dannie did on Saturdays was governed by where Cardiff City were playing, for he never liked to miss a home match and arranged his poetry-reading schedule around the Bluebirds' fixture list. They must have been playing away. My luck was in.

So we had the cast... Although not quite. We were in deep so why not go even deeper, I thought, and on an impulse I approached Spike Milligan and asked him whether he would be willing to read some of his witty children's verse. He readily agreed. My next inspired thought was to cheekily title the evening 'Poetry Returns to Hampstead'. Team Hampstead then set to work, sending out press releases, leaving leaflets around the area, putting up posters in the windows of any shop that would take them, including Ian Norrie's long-gone and sadly missed High Hill Bookshop, and selling tickets. Edward Gold was unstinting in his help, and Anne Hooper and other friends joined in too, stuffing envelopes, arranging with a local café, the Loft, to provide refreshments for the audience during and after the interval, and helping with the publicity. Those Poly years couldn't be allowed to go to waste!

The provocative title, the line-up and the unusual combination of Spike, Pasternak and jazz seemed to catch people's imagination and the press took it up in an exciting way. Meanwhile, the musicians would come over whenever possible and we would rehearse the programme, and Pete Brown and I even worked with Arnon on combining a couple of poems with the jazz.

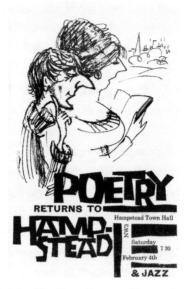

Cecily Ben-Tovim's striking Poetry Returns to Hampstead programme cover.

4 February 1961. Finally the day had come, and we didn't know what had hit us. The Town Hall was completely sold out, there were long queues, with people fighting to get in – and a moment of real panic when Spike phoned to say he didn't feel well enough to make it. Pleadingly I told him about the crowds, that Dennis Dobson, the publisher of his *Silly Verse for Kids*, was waiting for him, that he couldn't let down so many people (let alone me!), and eventually he took pity on me and relented, though warning he'd have to keep it short and get away smartly. Anything, Spike, anything! Looking back, I'm convinced he'd just had a fit of nerves, having seen all the publicity and never having read his poems in public before.

The amazed poets arrived, the musicians began to play, while Edward struggled valiantly to control the crowds at the door. Dannie Abse, used to the usual fare of rather sedate, pious poetry readings, was perhaps even more taken aback than Lydia Pasternak. Here is part of his account of the night:

> I set out for the Town Hall not expecting a particularly large audience.
> So when I saw in the distance an extraordinarily long queue stretching

between the Odeon and the Town Hall I briefly wondered what popular film was being shown that night in the cinema. Then I observed the queue was facing the wrong way. When I struggled through the crowds on the steps of the Town Hall, a man tried to close the doors as he barked irritably, 'Full up.' By the time I managed to enter the Town Hall that first Poetry and Jazz Concert had commenced.

Dear Dannie. I don't suppose he ever imagined he'd be taking part in several hundred more of these concerts in the coming years… and willingly.

Given that this was indeed a 'first', it's a wonder the concert proved so successful, but the atmosphere was electric and all the poets responded wonderfully, as did the musicians. There couldn't have been a greater contrast between the styles and indeed the poems of those who braved it on the stage that night. For my part, I did my best not to let the side down, reading a few of my own fledgling poems, including one with jazz. It was an exhilarating mix of the serious, the moving, the satirical, the quietly lyrical, the dramatic and, of course, the humorous, for there (thank the good Lord) was Spike to end the evening, resplendent in green corduroy trousers and a plum-coloured sweater. He'd spent most of the evening in the wings quietly savouring the atmosphere. Anne Hooper recalls that when I introduced him he staggered in from below the stage with a lit match in his hand, pretending the lights had gone out. I don't remember that, but I do recall his opening lines when he finally made it onto the stage: 'I thought I'd begin by reading some of Shakespeare's sonnets. But then I thought, "Why should I? He never reads any of mine."' The place erupted, and Spike took off, reading one comic poem after another with great aplomb, dropping his papers all over the stage, Gooning, improvising, timing it all like the master he was, relishing the occasion. If he'd really been ill earlier, this was patently the medicine he'd needed.

The response of both the press and the public was astonishing. In a review headed 'Full House for the Poets of Hampstead', *The Observer* called it 'a live and brave evening'; *Tatler*, which covered it photographically over three pages, proclaimed it 'a triumphant evening for poetry'; while in a leader the *Hampstead and Highgate Express* was effusive in its praise, calling it 'a splendid and alive occasion we hope will be repeated again and

again'. I cherish, too, a lively account in the *Bolton Evening News*, whose
London correspondent captured the mood of the evening perfectly:

> Incredible is the only word to describe the wild scenes of arty frustration
> enacted outside Hampstead Town Hall on Saturday night when 300
> young people found themselves unable to gain admittance to – of all
> things – a poetry reading. Mad bangings on the stout municipal door
> went on for nearly an hour after the programme inside the hall began
> before a packed audience of nearly 500 people of all ages.

The writer ended by quoting one girl as saying, 'To think that I wasted
seventeen years in Chorlton-cum-Hardy.'

Letters began to pour in, both from those who were there and from
many who couldn't get in. One lady echoed the thoughts of many
when she wrote, 'Although there was much I didn't understand, it has
certainly changed my attitude to contemporary poetry.' There were
also letters from various poets, including a surprisingly generous one
from Nathaniel Tarn, a normally aloof person. 'As a member of the
audience,' he wrote, 'I should like to congratulate you on this – socio-
logically – remarkable feat of drawing and keeping such a large crowd
engrossed for such a length of time.' He went on to say how much he
liked the way we'd mixed the generations and brought in humour, too.
He also thought the jazz had livened up the proceedings. Who could
ask for more? To me, the whole evening was like a dream, and if I didn't
have all these cuttings I'd find it hard to believe it really happened. I
also have many precious photos: Spike on the crowded steps being
'arrested' by the police … Dannie signing books in the interval … a
bearded Jon Silkin sitting studiously at the edge of the stage … Adrian
Mitchell looking down from a balcony … Lydia Pasternak stately and
poised as she read … Cecily Ben-Tovim drawing in the wings … Pete
Brown and the band in full blast … and a very young me, introducing
it all (and wearing a sweater this time!). Would I have the nerve to
do it all now? I very much doubt it.

*   *   *

Spike was elated, and in no hurry to rush away after the event, coming to the party we'd arranged and being among the last to leave. There's no doubt that the evening had excited his imagination. 'We must do it again,' he said, 'perhaps somewhere larger' – and that's how we came up with the idea of trying to arrange a follow-up concert at the Royal Festival Hall. I had no idea about the feasibility, the costs, and whether there would be a free date in the foreseeable future – nor, indeed, whether they would have us. Looking back and going through the old file I still have, marked RFH, I must have been more than a little crazy. I couldn't possibly have foreseen the amount of work this would entail, especially as I had a full-time job and no possibility in those pre-mobile days of making personal calls during office hours. I was also continuing to review and write for *Tribune* almost every week. Still, Spike had responded enthusiastically to my suggestion, promising to help publicise the event and share the responsibility – the fact that he had a new book of verse about to come out no doubt helped. But, above all, the continuing positive response to Hampstead was simply too exciting for someone as headstrong as me to ignore.

Thus, on 3 March 1961 a contract was signed between the London County Council (for the Royal Festival Hall) and the Hampstead Contemporary Poets (the fancy name we'd come up with to give ourselves the necessary appearance of respectability as far as the RFH was concerned). On our side the signatories were a Mr S. Milligan and me. We had to pay £75 on signing the contract, and a further £145 a month later, with a percentage of the ticket sales on top after we'd had receipts of £500 – rather like a publishing contract, really. The date set for the concert was Sunday 11 June 1961, in the afternoon. There was just one problem – the hall held over 3,000 people! There was nothing for it but to weigh in, and this my enlarged team of helpful friends did with great enthusiasm, Edward Gold once again handling the administrative side of things: quite a task. Whatever it took, we had to get the required number of bums on all those seats. In retrospect it all seems rather like an episode of *The Apprentice*.

In the midst of all this organisation I took part in an unusual event in the Holland Park studio of the painter Jan Le Witt, which was arranged to tie in with an exhibition of his paintings at the Grosvenor Gallery. Le

Witt had been in the audience at Hampstead together with John Smith, a poet who was later to become involved with our concerts, writing a number of poems for jazz settings. Enthused by the Hampstead reading, Jan (with John Smith's encouragement) decided to hold an evening of poetry and music in his large studio, during which he would also display some paintings. Calling it 'A Triangle of Muses', he invited a string trio to play Beethoven and Mozart, and five poets. His own striking paintings completed the artistic triangle. After all that, there was jazz from 'Arnon Ben-Tovim and friends', and a 'Rampatunda' cocktail, the mystery ingredients of which I never discovered. The evening was indeed a strange cocktail, but highly civilised, and together with Bernard Kops, John Smith, Muriel Spark and a young American poet called Edward Brash, I read a few poems. As well as a rather snooty Auberon Waugh, the invited audience included the art historian Sir Herbert Read, who was quoted in a paper as saying, 'I don't like jazz awfully, but it does liven up the proceedings.' And indeed, on this occasion, as always, it did.

In May, there was a rather less rarefied evening at 'Mayfair's Plush Phoenix Jazz Club', where, together with Spike ('appearing in person'), I read some poems. Coincidentally, the guest soloist that night, playing with the resident quartet, was the startlingly brilliant Jamaican jazz saxophonist Joe Harriott. I didn't meet Joe that night, but our paths would cross many times in the future. Indeed, he still owes me £50!

Meanwhile, arrangements for the RFH concert were moving apace. I'd long admired the lyrical poetry of Laurie Lee, so I wrote to him explaining the background and inviting him to read. To my delight, he agreed, and so, for the first time – but by no means the last – I was able to watch him take a small yellow book from his pocket and announce to the captivated audience in his quiet Gloucestershire burr, 'This is my life's work,' before leading into 'Day of These Days', or another of his entrancing poems, lacing each of them with a brief anecdote. Laurie, whom I always thought of as the Pied Piper, was to become one of the most regular readers in the many concerts to come and we shared a lot of memorable experiences. Finally, two more superb jazzmen were added to the line-up: drummer Laurie Morgan and the saxophonist Dick Heckstall-Smith.

As before, we printed leaflets and posters, but on a much larger scale. Friends and contacts took batches of these and distributed them as widely as possible. Lydia Pasternak Slater (whose surprised response to my latest mad venture had been to exclaim, 'We'll be reading to each other!') volunteered to leave leaflets and put posters up in various Oxford colleges, and Leon Brittan offered to do the same in Cambridge, asking me for a big poster to put up in the Union, though, ever the realist, he wrote, 'But I don't know whether you can expect many to come from Cambridge as it is May Week and people will be reluctant to budge.' He ended his letter – which I rediscovered in my RFH file – by asking me to give him a ring once the term ('my last one incidentally') was over 'as I haven't really seen you since your poetry career got under way'. We also wanted to have all the poets' books on sale, which meant contacting their publishers, arranging delivery, setting up a stand and arranging for someone to man it. It was important, we felt, for people to be able to read the poetry they had just heard, which would hopefully lead them to explore poetry more widely.

We decided to produce a rather more elaborate programme than last time, hoping to attract advertisers – easier said than done, as Edward, who wrote dozens of letters, quickly discovered. But we scored some successes, including a leaflet insert from the Jazz Book Club, and full pages from Guinness, the *Ham and High* and EMI (Parlophone Records). We also landed several smaller ones. The EMI advert had come about through the legendary Beatles producer George Martin, who, in an exciting development, had agreed to record the concert. We placed a hundred posters on the Underground, advertised in a few select places, and sent out press releases far and wide. Everything was strikingly designed by Arnon's pianist, Peter Taylor. As with the first concert, the press seemed intrigued by our unlikely concoction and both Spike and I were called on to give a number of interviews, Spike pulling out all the stops. Things really looked up when I was asked to appear on an ITV programme called *Sunday Break* to read with the band, and then we were given an enormous boost when the *Daily Mail* ran an interview with Spike in which they included a few witty verses from his forthcoming *A Dustbin of Milligan*. Spike ended the interview by saying, 'Unlike Shelley I was not drowned in Italy. But I am one of the

Lake poets. Some of my best poetry has been written under water.' By that, of course, as the interviewer rightly surmised, he was referring to the gentle inspiration of a red liquid called Burgundy.

On the day of the concert, a more serious piece by Christopher Booker in the *Sunday Telegraph* gave us additional welcome publicity. In it, he rehearsed the history of the Hampstead sell-out and ended by saying that the instigators now 'found themselves in just a few months tackling a venture that would give pause even to a hardened promoter of professional wrestling'. I must say I hadn't thought of it like that. Probably I was still too green and carried away by enthusiasm to feel as anxious as I should have been. Alongside Booker's piece was a photo of Spike, me and our bass player Neil Barton (plus bass) outside the RFH in front of a large poster for the concert. It was a nerve-jangling time, and when Peter Sellers asked for three tickets to be reserved in his name, I felt – not being a wrestling promoter – that I'd landed myself with something I might well regret. It wasn't just the organisational responsibility; there was the little matter of standing up and reading before 3,000 or more people without falling flat on my face. My feelings were well expressed in a typed note I sent Lydia Pasternak Slater which began, 'I'm sorry if this letter is a little bit jerky but that's how I feel and how I will feel until June 12th!'

Published in the Sunday Telegraph *on the morning of our Festival Hall concert, this gave the sales a welcome boost.*

Well, we did it. The hall was full, all our expenses were met, and the pattern was set for a great many more poetry and jazz concerts featuring a strong and varied line-up of poets and outstanding musicians. Naturally, in such an enormous hall the concert had a different feel from the first one, and there wasn't the same element of surprise, for us anyway. But it was every bit as thrilling and memorable, and as far as poetry readings in this country went, a landmark. Perhaps the now defunct *Daily Herald* summed it up best in its headline: 'The day 3,000 people listened to … POETRY!' The paper went on to say, 'The poets went to the Royal Festival Hall yesterday, read their poems, and 3,000 people gave them the reception normally reserved for the great names of music. I call that a piece of history.' For those who may have wondered, as a few did, what Spike Milligan was doing in the middle of a programme of basically 'serious' poetry, the political and literary weekly magazine *Time and Tide* provided a fitting response: 'The zany, cataclysmic satire of Goonery is not so far removed from the anti-nuclear burden of most young poets; we all have our own way of shouting in despair. Milligan listened gravely as the poets read to a breathless 3,000.'

The Guardian especially seemed to be intrigued by the occasion, running a full-page picture story, followed the next week by a rather earnest piece about poetry and music which also referred to a concert that had taken place in the RFH's Recital Room a few days after ours. Called simply Jazz Voices, that concert, to which I went, involved speakers from London University and a small jazz group, with settings of poems under the direction of a pianist/composer called Michael Garrick, who had written all the music. That was to prove a fortunate coincidence.

7

ON THE ROAD

Michael Garrick's Jazz and Voices programme was a revelation, and at the end of the performance something seemed to tug at my sleeve and lead me to introduce myself to him. I've always felt it was a kind of 'Dr Livingstone' moment, for me certainly, but for Michael also, to judge from his warm account of our meeting in his autobiography, *Dusk Fire*. At any rate, he seemed well aware of the concert we'd given the previous week, and welcomed the opportunity to meet. As well as speakers from London University, the concert I'd just enjoyed featured Michael's own quartet alongside a quintet which included a harp and cello – a rather different kind of programme from ours, perhaps, but Michael's special talent – his empathy with the poems he'd set, together with his superb musicianship and his ability to compose striking melodies – was immediately obvious.

We arranged to meet, and did so several times over the coming months. I gave him a few poems I felt might work well with jazz, and he came back quickly with a couple of sensitive settings. As it happened, Arnon Ben-Tovim, who'd done so much to make our first events such a success, had indicated that he wouldn't be able to devote the necessary time to future concerts, especially if they involved travelling. His hands were more than full with his job (he became a prominent child and family psychiatrist). Thus, when in due course we received an invitation from the director of the Belgrade Theatre, Coventry, I asked Michael if he would like to provide the music. We went on to give well over 300 poetry and jazz concerts together over the next decade or so – at universities, theatres, arts festivals, schools, town halls and the like all over the country.

While I too had a day job to contend with, it was not one that was as testing or responsible as Arnon's, and I was able to combine my fairly routine job at *Tit-Bits* with future thoughts and plans for what came to be called Poetry and Jazz in Concert. At the same time I was reviewing ever more frequently for *Tribune*, and trying to write and publish poems.

During the lull between the Festival Hall and the next concert, my life was greatly enriched by my growing friendship with Dannie Abse. Through his older brothers, Dannie had been immersed from an early age in the politics and intellectual issues of the day – the civil war in Spain, the rise of Fascism, the work of Freud. He opened my eyes to many things. Although a practising doctor (for many years he worked as a radiologist at the Royal Air Force clinic in London), Dannie lived and breathed poetry. For some eight years he'd edited a poetry magazine called *Verse*, which first appeared in the winter of 1947. An offshoot of the magazine was the controversial anthology *Mavericks*, which he co-edited with Howard Sergeant, editor of the poetry magazine *Outposts*. Their aim was to provide a counterbalance to the fashionable so-called Movement Poets featured in the recent *New Lines* anthology edited by Robert Conquest.

As Abse and Sergeant made clear in their introductions to *Mavericks*, they weren't trying to create a new group or attach labels but simply to provide a platform for some of the younger poets who'd been overlooked and who, in Dannie's words, 'were unafraid of sensibility and sentiment, who are neither arid nor lush'. In his letter to Sergeant, which formed part of the introduction to the anthology, Dannie went on: 'I can think of a number of young poets who are not writing mere exercises but working from the heat of personal predicament and common experience; who remember perhaps Dryden's "Errors like straw upon the surface flow; / He who would search for pearls must search below."' In his response, Sergeant pointed out that even Kingsley Amis, the archetypal Movement Poet, had admitted, 'The trouble with the newer poets, including myself, is that they are often lucid and nothing else – except arid and bald.' Quite a self-indictment!

It was fascinating for me to hear Dannie's personal account of those stirring times, and I was interested to be introduced via their anthology to poets whose work I had not yet encountered. A few of them were to feature in future poetry and jazz concerts along with several arresting poets I had reviewed. Since Dannie knew some of them, he was able to steer me to those whose work not only read well on the page (essential) but who were also good readers of their own work (just as essential). Dannie would also reminisce about the Cosmo restaurant in Swiss Cottage, and the writers, poets, artists, refugees and colourful characters who converged there in the years after the war, talk, talk, talking and verbally wrestling until closing time – some, like Elias Canetti, who won the Nobel Prize for Literature in 1981, to become famous. For a while, it had become Dannie's regular haunt, living as he then did just around the corner.

While I worked on in London during the summer of '61, Dannie sensibly went on holiday. But holidays for Dannie were never quite that. Also, it seems, the poetry and jazz concerts had excited him, and he referred to them half-jokingly in a letter he sent me from Devon:

I've looked around Salcombe but there's no place here as big as the Festival Hall, which is a pity because Tennyson's ghosts round the creek and are across the bar. We are perched high up over South Sands with a marvellous view 'so beautiful it seems a fake'. All around, through trees, views of bays, cliffs and the sea, all drizzling sunlight. The wild flowers here – meadowsweet, fuchsia, Jack-by-the-Hedge, eyebright, blackberry blossom – a whole list in fact to make up a poem by Edward Thomas. I try to work for a couple of hours each day but however much I stare no poems float up. If I don't write I feel quite guilty. One has to offer something in exchange for the scenery.

'Are you finding the hours tame after the tensions of TV and the Festival Hall?' Dannie went on to ask, ending his welcome letter by reminding me of our forthcoming date at the Belgrade Theatre in Coventry (as if I needed any reminding!) and wishing me 'all that is good, and odd'.

Before the Coventry concert, which was scheduled for the following February, I was given an unexpected personal boost when I was invited by the Writers Club to be the first poet in a series of 'Penny Poets' they were launching. This was a small, one-page publication – a single sheet – with (in my case) four poems on it and selling for one penny. Four poems for a penny! (I've squirrelled a few copies away, so perhaps by now they will have doubled in value.) There was a 2,500 print run. No money in it for anyone, but that wasn't the point. The club had various branches, meeting fortnightly, and the project was being funded out of members' subscriptions with the aim of introducing the work of young poets to a wider audience at a more or less giveaway price. At any rate I was truly thrilled to have been chosen as their first poet and it seemed a fitting end to what had been a tumultuous year.

* * *

The Belgrade Theatre concert took place on 18 February 1962, and once again Spike Milligan had agreed to take part, alongside Christopher Logue, Adrian Mitchell, Dannie Abse, Laurie Lee and me. Michael Garrick led the music, which for the first time featured the stupendous Shake Keane. Born in St Vincent, Shake, to quote *The Times*, was 'the most brilliant trumpet and flugelhorn player of his generation'. A large figure of a man, Shake was dynamic, exciting to listen to, full of humour, and, having studied English literature at London University, he had a great love of poetry, which he wrote himself (hence his nickname, short for Shakespeare). In later concerts, when the fiery alto saxophonist Joe Harriott joined the line-up, the jazz was simply sensational. Shake and Joe (a pioneer of free-form jazz) were in harmony with what we were doing and intrigued to be involved in something they thought novel and fresh. When in due course Shake went off to join a German band, Ian Carr, another tremendous horn player, came on board, and often with him saxophonist Don Rendell. All stars.

Joe Harriott, it must be said, was a loner and never easy to control, and once in full solo flight it was sometimes hard for Michael to rein him in. Shake Keane, who was as close to Joe as anyone and perhaps the only musician he truly felt to be his equal, spoke of Joe's 'noble arrogance, the way he sat, the way he played'. The attack of Joe's playing was mesmerising, so it was easy to forgive his occasional rampages, which always added to the excitement of the occasion. As Joe once said, measuring himself against the legendary American saxophonist Charlie Parker, 'There's them over here can play a few aces too.' Fittingly, those words are inscribed on Joe's headstone. Michael Garrick paid ready tribute to Joe and Shake in his autobiography:

> When we worked together I didn't have to write any marks of expression on the lead sheet … the way they played was fantastic. They each had a beautiful sound instantly recognizable from the first note. Their playing was unique with warmth and maturity. They were also black in an alien society, determined their voice should be heard … I didn't fully realise what a lucky lad I was to have them play the music I wrote.

I believe that all the poets who read alongside them were also lucky lads to have the exciting and informal setting the jazz provided in which to read their poems, and all recognised this. Conversely, the musicians appreciated the quality of the poetry read, the different personalities of the poets reading and the showcase it gave their music. It made for an intoxicating combination, and a number of barriers were sent flying. Did audiences come for the poetry or for the jazz? It didn't really matter. That they came, and in large numbers, is what mattered, and that they went away with both music and poetry in their heads, and perhaps some books under their arms. Above all, almost everything read or played was original, poets reading their own work, musicians playing their own music – or at least Michael Garrick's. For as well as setting a few of my poems and Adrian Mitchell's (and later, too, poems by Vernon Scannell, John Smith and Thomas Blackburn), Michael composed original numbers for the band, including his beautiful 'Wedding Hymn', which he always played after Dannie Abse's poem 'Epithalamion', and he'd programme an appropriately lyrical number to follow Laurie Lee's poems. Occasionally, though, Shake liked to play 'She's Like a Swallow' as a solo next to Laurie's poems, a lovely slow number that allowed him to display the beauty of his tone. Laurie loved it. He also loved it when Joe Harriott, with his wicked sense of humour, immortalised 'She's Like a Swallow' by shifting the 's' from the end of 'she's' to the end of 'like'!

If Joe had his wild moments, several of the poets had theirs too. There was the time when the bird-like Stevie Smith hurled a book at a photographer who was annoying her with his persistent clicking (was she raving or clowning?), and the night at Southampton University when Thomas Blackburn, who seemed to have a personal war with religion, halted mid-poem to harangue an unfortunate clergyman who happened to be sitting in the front row. The unpredictable Tom, whose deep voice and dark, compelling poems would hold audiences riveted, could sometimes become the victim of his own demons. And it's hardly surprising there were demons, since, as he recalled in a memoir, when he was at boarding school, his father, a vicar, sent him a clip of steel to wear at night to deter nocturnal erections and prevent the loss of vital bodily fluids. The casting-off of these and other childhood repressions and impositions led to the wickedly handsome Tom running riot with the ladies when he got to Cambridge, landing him in considerable trouble. I think it was after a reading at Southampton that Tom and Dannie found themselves having to share a room in student digs. As there was only one bed, they'd agreed to toss for it, and when Dannie won Tom exclaimed indignantly, 'You're not going to take advantage of the toss are you, Dannie?'

But for all Tom's ravings, nothing was more dramatic than the occasion at the Arts Theatre in Cambridge when the blind poet John Heath-Stubbs, having been led onto the stage, gradually turned around as he was reciting in his sonorous voice until he ended up facing the back of the stage, which startled the audience into a breathless silence. The image of John standing there in the spotlight, tall and gaunt, his arms outstretched and raised to the heavens, was like something out of a Greek drama.

There was, too, the time when a disgruntled Christopher Logue arrived in Bristol by train with Dannie for a concert at the university. Seeing that there wasn't a car to meet them at the station, instead of sharing a cab with Dannie he turned around in a huff and took the next train back to

London. No reading from him that day! Socialism, and poetic egos, it seems, come in various shades. I'm reminded of when Edith Sitwell (no socialist!) was asked what fee she required to read to a certain literary society. She named her figure, and then added, 'But double that if I have to have dinner with members of the committee afterwards!'

* * *

To our relief, the Belgrade Theatre was packed that Sunday afternoon. It was the first time Christopher Logue had read with us, though in the light of the above we should perhaps have been relieved that he turned up. For all that, he was never anything but friendly to me over the years. I was a great admirer of the poetry and jazz recording he'd made with the Tony Kinsey Quintet, on which he read his own adaptations of delicate poems by Pablo Neruda. One love poem in particular, 'Blue Lament', in which the poet looks back at a lost love, still moves me with its simple lyricism and deep feeling, beautifully read by Logue, whose deep-throated, crystal-clear voice adds to the effect, as does Kinsey's subtle musical arrangement around the words. That afternoon at Coventry, the poems he read were far less personal and mostly skilfully wrapped political invective, delivered powerfully and dramatically. One poem he always liked to read was prompted by a story he'd read in the *Daily Express* headed 'Britain Builds a Chain of H-Forts'. It was written, he announced disparagingly, 'by a man called *Cha*pman Pin*che*r' (how Michael Garrick, a born mimic, loved to imitate Logue's distinctive voice, with the heavy emphasis he placed on the 'ch' in the name of the famous whistle-blower). It was enjoyable to listen to Logue read and to watch the effect on the audience, though I seem to recall mutterings in the wings from a disapproving Laurie Lee, whose kind of poems these obviously weren't. Still, it takes all sorts, and this kind of mixture made for an interesting programme.

As for Laurie, he had his own way of winning an audience over even before he read a line. Watching him from the wings that afternoon in Coventry, I saw close up the master-charmer at work. As he often did, he recalled the occasion when a young schoolboy accosted him in the street and, fixing him with accusing eyes, asked, 'Did you write a poem called "Apples"?', and when Laurie admitted that he had, back came the aggrieved response: 'Our teacher made us learn it.' Then followed the poem, read very slowly and musically. Another of Laurie's favourite stories was about a stork that wandered into a bodega on a hot day in Jerez and got drunk. His 'Stork in Jerez' always went down well and one felt Laurie was a little envious of that bird. Another poem he read, movingly, sprang from his experiences in Spain during the civil war. It began:

> Less passionate the long war throws
> its burning thorn about all men,
> caught in one grief, we share one wound,
> and cry one dialect of pain...

Arnold Wesker was in the audience at Coventry. I hadn't then realised what a strong association Arnold had with this go-ahead theatre, which had premiered his *Chicken Soup with Barley* before it transferred to the Royal Court Theatre in London, triggering his career and fame. The Belgrade had also premiered the other two plays in his landmark trilogy, *Roots* and *I'm Talking about Jerusalem*. Maybe that accounted for his presence at the theatre that day, but whatever the reason, Arnold approached me afterwards and asked if I'd arrange similar concerts for the series of Centre 42 arts festivals he was planning in conjunction with the trade unions. This followed the adoption of Resolution 42, whereby the unions formally recognised the importance of the arts in the community. Taking this as his springboard, Arnold was planning week-long festivals in Wellingborough, Nottingham, Leicester, Birmingham, Bristol, Hayes and Southall.

It was a hugely ambitious project, but such was his charisma, passion and social zeal that he won people over with apparent ease. He already had a formidable line-up of artists and performers, and naturally we were thrilled to become a part of it. As an artistic director of Centre 42, it would be my responsibility to arrange the poetry programme alongside the other events. It would all kick off in Wellingborough in mid-September.

Before that, though, we had four concerts of our own – at Cheltenham Town Hall in April, Oxford Town Hall in May, Hintlesham Arts

Festival in July, and Birmingham Town Hall in early September. Spike read at Cheltenham and Oxford. Oxford in particular was fun, while Hintlesham Hall was inevitably a more formal setting than we were used to – Shake Keane's high notes rattling a few chandeliers – but it was packed and we were well received. Spike appeared at Oxford with his new bride, Patricia (Paddy) Ridgeway, an opera singer. They had interrupted their honeymoon in Cornwall to join us. Spike was on great form, declaring to the audience, 'You think *I'm* mad. *You* paid to come in!' Then he invited Paddy up onto the stage to sing Gershwin's 'Summertime'. Laurie, too, was in a mischievous mood, telling the audience he was a little drunk, since, having arrived too early, he had waited in the public library, where he'd drunk gin out of an inkwell. Reading a review of that concert in the *Oxford Mail* headed 'The poets came in all shapes and guises', I am amused that their critic was more interested in the poets' dress sense than their poetry. Logue, he said, 'appeared in a cardigan with a will of its own', Laurie was in 'an elderly brown suit with bandy trousers', while Spike was wearing 'a turtleneck sweater on loan from a giant'. It seems that I had 'a talent for unhappy images', but at least my clothes were not remarked upon, and nor were those of Lydia Pasternak Slater, who also read that night, along with Dannie and Adrian Mitchell.

It was at Birmingham that Vernon Scannell took part for the first time. I hadn't met him before, and he struck me as being a rather reserved and shy man, looking a little like a clerk or schoolteacher in his sober sports jacket and grey trousers, but he had a fine deep reading voice, as I knew from hearing him on the radio. How wrong first impressions can be! Rather wary of the jazz at first, Vernon became one of the musicians' favourite poets and a frequent reader. Michael Garrick's setting of his powerful 'Epithets of War' is both inventive and haunting, and Vernon loved to perform it. We became close friends and he stayed with us many times when he was in London. Indeed, Robson Books later published both his poetry and autobiographical books, in which he recalled his colourful life – from his troubled childhood under the strict control of a brutal father, through the war years and his court martial 'for desertion', to his time as a boxer, and beyond. Many of these experiences fuelled his poetry, too, particularly his war poems.

Pianist Michael Garrick responds to the humour in one of Vernon Scannell's poems.
His haunting setting of Scannell's 'Epithets of War' was one of his finest works.

Another who was reading with us in Birmingham for the first time was the handsome, much-admired Indian poet Dom Moraes, whose first wife, Henrietta, was the model in several of Francis Bacon's paintings. Dom was the son of the editor of the *Times of India*, and his first book, written while at Oxford, had won the coveted Hawthornden Prize 'for the best work of imagination'. The first non-English person to win the prize, he was also the youngest. As that master humorist Alan Coren put it in a delightfully sardonic memoir of his Oxford days: 'And then there was poetry, or Dom Moraes as it came to be called. Dom's success having carried beyond the city limits, he was the focus of much ambivalent admiration.' And it was Coren who revealed that on one occasion 'a London actress – having found herself in the Moraes chambers with their tenant unaccountably absent and possibly escorting some other lady – had torn up all his manuscripts'. When Alan's piece was published in a book called *My Oxford*, the name of the *very* famous actress had to be withheld for reasons of libel, much to Alan's chagrin – and mine, as the book's publisher.

Dom was to become a legendary figure, covering wars in Algeria, Israel and Vietnam, returning to India, where he married a celebrated actress and beauty (though it was never clear whether he'd actually divorced Henrietta). For some reason that night in Birmingham, although he was an experienced reader, Dom made little effort to communicate with the audience, spurning the microphone, propping himself up against a table and screening himself behind the smoke from a cigarette he dangled from his left hand while reading. I liked him, and he came to dinner several times with our mutual friend, the Israeli poet Carmi, but I have to say that inviting him to read at a poetry and jazz concert was not one of my wisest decisions. Many years later, when I was deep into publishing, Dom phoned me out of the blue and said he'd like to come and discuss a book on India he was working on. He arrived grey-suited and grey-haired at my office and we talked. The soft-eyed, gentle-voiced, beautiful boy who had charmed his way around Soho had gone and he seemed a shadow of his former drinking self. Though he was very friendly, I found it hard to believe it was Dom I was talking to and I have always been sorry that I wasn't free to take up the dinner date that he proposed. Then, ever the mystery man, he vanished, and I was shocked not long after to read that he'd died in India. Apart from a long battle with the bottle, he had developed cancer, for which he'd refused treatment, dying from a heart attack in Mumbai. He was buried in that city's Sewri Christian Cemetery and according to his wishes earth from his grave was scattered in Odcombe in Somerset.

The charismatic Indian poet Dom Moraes.

I also regretted not asking Dom whether his manuscripts had really been torn up by that famous and enraged actress, or whether it was a figment of Alan Coren's extremely fertile imagination. You never quite knew with Alan.

8

CENTRE 42

As the poetry and jazz concerts gathered momentum, back at the *Tit-Bits* office I had acquired a welcome champion in a newly arrived member of the editorial team. Bruce Robb seemed to my young eyes to be an old hand, though I suppose he was only in his forties. He was certainly more experienced than the others and, more importantly from my point of view, he was both keen on poetry and had worked at a literary agency. For some reason he made it his unlikely mission to find me a publisher, urging me to get a collection of some thirty poems together, which I did, calling it (modestly, as I thought) *First Poems*. He then sent it to Sidgwick & Jackson, following this up with a letter with details of the readings I'd been giving, the magazines I'd had poems in, quotes from various reviews, etc., elevating and exaggerating as agents do. For all that, I didn't have great expectations, especially since as far as I could see Sidgwick had only ever published one poet: Rupert Brooke! Still, it was a highly respected publishing house and Bruce remained hopeful, even when there was no immediate response.

The months went by and, despite the occasional follow-up letter from Bruce, they seemed reluctant to make a decision either way; indeed, reluctant to respond at all to his letters. He urged me to be patient, but in my mind I wrote the whole thing off, continued to review for *Tribune* and give the odd reading. But I began to feel restless, and decided it was time to alter the landscape and move on, perhaps change tack a little, and so I applied for a job in the publicity department of Harrap, a venerable book publishing company with offices off the Strand. To my surprise, they offered me the job, and so I took my first tentative steps into the wonderful world of publishing. A Dickensian outfit, it couldn't have been more different from *Tit-Bits*, with everyone walking around on tiptoe, talking in whispers. I adjusted myself as best I could, writing blurbs for books I hadn't read, drafting rather downbeat press releases (for such was their style) and on one glorious occasion helping the respected publicity manager to set up a window display in Foyles bookshop in Charing Cross Road, something I have never had the chance to do since.

To familiarise myself with the Harrap list, which was very large and seemed to go back over centuries, I would creep into the church-quiet library and sometimes take a book away – after I'd signed for it in triplicate and assured the nervous librarian he'd have it back next day. I'd had the experience of publicising our own poetry events, and that is probably what landed me the job, but I didn't really know anything about book promotion, which seemed to me a very laid-back affair. In later years I would become friendly with an eccentric and lovable showbiz publicist called Theo Cowan. If you ever asked how he was, he invariably replied, 'It's a miracle.' Theo had the impossible task of looking after such stars as Michael Caine and Peter Sellers, and once told me his job was to keep his clients *out* of the press, *off* television, *out of sight* of the media, whereas, of course, we'd always tried to do the very opposite with our celebrity authors! Harrap seemed to adopt Theo's approach, but then I don't suppose they ever published headline-grabbing titles. For A level I'd been given a copy of their French dictionary, but apart from their strong educational department there didn't seem to be much to set the world alight. So I'd sit there writing press releases, looking at my watch, wondering whether an author would ever make an appearance, whether the phone would ever ring, and once more found myself wandering at lunchtime around Covent Garden.

Occasionally a charming, chirpy Ian Harrap, who was ostensibly director of publicity, would bounce into our office to offer a few encouraging words, but I always felt he'd be more at home behind the wheel of a vintage car than running a publishing department. Still, it was all very civilised, though I missed the man in the mac with his weekly dose of nubile girls prancing at the sea's edge, just waiting for me to caption them. Bruce Robb, whom I'd occasionally meet for lunch, had inherited that job, and I gathered that there was still no word from Sidgwick. Anyway, here, for the moment, I'd found a port in what was not exactly a storm, and I would at least be able to say I worked in publishing.

* * *

Outside the office, if not a storm, there was a *coup de foudre* in the shape of a strikingly beautiful young girl called Carole de Botton, whom I met at a party I went to – fortunately – at the last moment, having been let down on a blind date by the friend of a French girl my cousin Teddy Stonehill had arranged to take out. I have many things to thank my friend Anthony Harkavy for, but none more so than for agreeing to sit down at the piano and play 'Sunny Side of the Street' – slowly – while I danced with a cautious Carole. But before continuing, and without wishing to enter into the politics of the situation, I must turn the clock back to 1956, the Suez crisis and the subsequent war in the Middle East. This had ostensibly begun when Israel launched an invasion of the Sinai Peninsula in retaliation for a growing number of fedayeen attacks on its citizens, and also because a bellicose Egypt had closed the Straits of Tiran, thus blocking the Gulf of Aqaba to Israeli shipping. For France and Britain, who subsequently attacked Egypt, the motives and aims were different, their main concern being the nationalisation of the Suez Canal by Egypt's President, Gamal Abdel Nasser, and the challenge to their interests there. For them, it was a political disaster, one from which Prime Minister Anthony Eden never recovered. For me, it ultimately led to Carole's family settling in England after Nasser began, with mounting nationalistic fervour, to bring in harsh measures against foreign nationals that led to a large exodus – including Carole's family, though they were hardly 'foreign nationals'.

As it happened, in the months before meeting Carole, I had been steeped in Lawrence Durrell's *Alexandria Quartet*, his classic novels published in the late 1950s and set in Alexandria before, during and after the Second World War. I'd been attracted to the books by an in-depth interview Durrell had given in the *Paris Review*, and through them I'd become aware of the cosmopolitan nature of Egyptian society in that period, and the fact that many nationalities had lived there for centuries in perfect harmony – in the case of Carole's family, more or less since the time of the Inquisition, when the Jews were expelled from Spain, many ending up in Egypt. (Carole's cousin Gilbert, father of the writer Alain de Botton, actually commissioned a book tracing the family history.) But the Jewish community was just one colourful thread in the complex fabric of Alexandrian society. As Durrell described it in *Justine*, the first book in the *Quartet*: 'Five races, five languages, a dozen creeds: five fleets turning through their greasy reflection behind the harbour mirror…' How he brought that city to life with his poetic prose: the beggars wandering the streets, the sun creeping through the leaves of the lemon trees, the beguiling mixture of scents and seasons, the buzz of the many languages. Simply looking at the distinctive covers of those four fine books brings it all back.

And now here I was at a party in north London, having recently been captivated by Justine, the fictional Alexandrian Jewess, and there was Carole, a real Alexandrian Jewess, different in every way from the capricious Justine, but just as captivating. Carole's background and story fascinated me, though I came to learn it only gradually over a period of months, even years, since she has always been reticent to talk about herself. Strangely, in the Durrell novels, too, the stories of the various characters emerge slowly, piece by piece. But eventually Carole's own very real story, and that of her family, came together under my cautious probing.

Born in Alexandria, she was brought up speaking mainly French, though she quickly tuned into the colourful Egyptian language that was all around – her father, Ben, spoke seven languages. When she was about six, her parents moved to Cairo, where her father, one of eleven children, began to establish a business. He too had been born in Al-exandria, where his parents lived, and went to the city's illustrious Victoria College, and though he'd won a place at Oxford, the family fortunes were such that he'd had to forgo it and set about earning a living. So it was in Cairo that Carole went to school – a French school – walking there in the early morning along the Nile, under the cypress trees, bougainvillea exploding on all sides from the gardens and white balconies of the flats and villas she passed. Later, she would join her parents at the Gezira Sporting Club, where her mother played bridge in the shade and her father, work over for the day, engaged in one or other of the sports at which he excelled. Alexandria, though, was a city Carole continued to visit regularly, staying with her grandmother, who had been widowed at a young age and to whom she was extremely close, and enjoying the wonderful beach there. She would also visit her rather more formal paternal grandparents and play among the exotic fruit trees in their lovely garden.

When the Suez war broke out, Carole and her family were on holiday in Europe and couldn't go back. Her father lost everything – his successful business, which was taken over by his Egyptian partner, his flat, his savings. To make matters worse, because he had a Spanish passport, he and Carole's mother, Jocy, were only allowed to stay in England for short periods and had to go in and out of the country, renewing their permits regularly. Meanwhile, Carole, who was then just fourteen, and her brother Gerard were sent to boarding school while their entrepreneurial father, drawing on his contacts in Europe, endeavoured to secure some kind of future for his family. Fortunately for Carole, she'd switched to an English school in her last two years in Cairo, so she knew some English. Her freezing Eastbourne boarding school gave her a lifelong aversion to porridge and semolina; Gerard, some six years younger, was less resilient, and the years he spent at school in Kidderminster were painful in every respect.

The family's luck took a sudden turn, and all because of her father's sporting prowess. In Egypt, at the sporting club, Ben had been an outstanding cricketer, once even playing for Egypt at Lord's, and I

later saw cuttings that paid tribute to the centuries he'd scored and
the wickets he'd taken with his left-handed spin. His tennis was every
bit as good. When by great good fortune his papers happened to land
on the desk of someone who not only recognised his name but who'd
played cricket with him in Cairo, obstacles to his obtaining a British
passport seemed to vanish and the precious citizenship was granted.
Meanwhile, having passed her O levels, Carole was able to continue
her education in London. That was some three or so years before we
met. At the same time, with the drive and tenacity that characterised
his left-handed forehand, her father gradually re-established himself.
Fortunately, I could at least match him on the tennis court, and before
very long we found ourselves battling across the net at Queen's Club,
no quarter given. I was chuffed to learn later that one boyfriend of
Carole's who'd boasted about his tennis had fared miserably when put
to the test.

Carole seemed to me exotic and sophisticated, though shy and reserved, and since she had other boyfriends it was not all plain sailing.
Soon after our slow dance at the party where we met, she took off
on the back of someone's motorbike for another party we'd all been
invited to, and where I eventually caught up with her. Later, after I left,
I realised that I had neither her phone number nor her surname, so
it took some sleuthing to track her down. An inauspicious start. As I
began to get to know her, I sensed that, having been uprooted from her
home, she felt insecure and I was hardly in a position to provide security, even if I'd wanted to at that stage. Yet I started introducing her to
my close friends, especially the Abses, for who could resist Dannie and
Joan's warmth and charm? Max Geldray was another friend I took her
to meet. Max had just come back from appearing at a Butlin's holiday
camp, which he described in amusing detail, particularly the ladies of
a certain age who flocked into breakfast still in their overnight curlers.
What did Carole make of that, I wondered.

Of course, I also had to introduce her to poetry and jazz – with
the Centre 42 and other concerts looming, there could be no escape.
How strange all this must have seemed, and what a long way from the
pyramids. I tried to further my cause by giving Carole a surprise 21st

LEFT Aged about nine and contemplating the future. How was I to know?

BELOW Our war effort. On a farm in north Wales during the Blitz with my cousins, Colin (the future painter), Farmer Davies, me, Barbara (who married cancer specialist Prof. Julian Bloom) and, in the front, stroking the goat, Nicholas (future director of the Royal Festival Hall, Glyndebourne, the Strasbourg Opera House and much else!).

BOTTOM LEFT With my lifelong friend and tennis partner Anthony Stalbow when we first teamed up.

BOTTOM RIGHT In Paris, aged about twenty, and still contemplating my future.

My wary young brother David joins Spike Milligan in the inflatable pool Spike had in his garden. I'm at the back with my cousin Teddy Stonehill (in dark glasses).

In the garden of Peter Sellers's magnificent house in Hertfordshire, Chipperfield Manor, the day Sophia Loren came to tea. I'm sitting on the left, between my parents, dressed for tennis, Peter standing behind me, and the beautiful Sophia on the right.

LEFT I introduce the Poetry Returns to Hampstead concert, while Jon Silkin and Adrian Mitchell wait to read. 4 February 1961.

LEFT Saxophonist Arnon Ben-Tovim, who directed the music, in full flight.

LEFT Lydia Pasternak Slater reads her moving translations of brother Boris's poems.

'Sorry, sir, house full.' Spike Milligan is refused entry to the Hampstead Town Hall.

Spike Milligan and I watch from the wings while Cecily Ben-Tovim sketches.

An explosive Milligan finally takes the stage.

The large Hampstead audience was as surprised as we were.

Reading at the Royal Festival Hall, 11 June 1961, backed by both the musicians and some of the full-house audience.

The charismatic Laurie Lee joins the cast.

Dannie Abse, who, to his surprise, ended up reading in almost as many concerts as me.

Michael Garrick, composing at the piano. We formed an immediate bond.

Poets' Corner. A regular participant over the years, Vernon Scannell added considerable verve and colour. © KEN COTON

The unpredictable Thomas Blackburn was a magnificent reader, his rich, low voice perfectly suited to poems that were sometimes laced with dark humour. © KEN COTON

Christopher Logue was a welcome addition to the 'cast', with his earthy, distinct voice and poems that had immediate appeal. © JOHN HOPKINS

An electrifying reader and a deeply committed poet of the left, Adrian Mitchell had a wide and loyal following for his biting, satirical poems. © JOHN HOPKINS

The dapper John Smith was always a surprise, combining style and wit. Michael Garrick set a number of his poems, very successfully. © KEN COTON

Bernard Kops's passionate and often lyrical poems had, and continue to have, a particular warmth and appeal. © JOHN HOPKINS

Alan Brownjohn, erudite and witty, with a well-timed deadpan delivery (and snazzy suit!) audiences love. © BRIAN DAVIES

Filming *Young Europe* at the side of the Old Vic for Titinus Films of Rome.

Accompanied by Michael Garrick, piano (left, in coat, standing), Shake Keane (trumpet) and Joe Harriott (alto) outside the Old Vic.

With my future wife, Carole, shortly after we met.

Michael Garrick's quintet for Arnold Wesker's Centre 42 concerts: Dave Green (bass), Trevor Tomkins (drums), Don Rendell (tenor), Ian Carr (trumpet), with himself on piano. © KEN COTON

ABOVE The Centre 42 audiences were gratifyingly large.

LEFT Michael Garrick with the sensational trumpet and flugelhorn player Shake Keane, who always thrilled audiences. © KEN COTON

birthday party, but still, for quite some time, it remained a red/green, stop/go relationship. And understandably so.

*   *   *

The Centre 42 festivals were a triumph for Arnold Wesker, who devoted all his creative energies to making them exciting and full of the unexpected. Who would do such a thing now? His headquarters were in Fitzroy Square and I went to a number of meetings there as he called on all those involved in the various events to pool their ideas. These included a trade union exhibition, using historical documents, paintings, banners, emblems, specially commissioned murals, music etc.; the first production of a commissioned play; a jazz dance featuring a fifteen-piece band with an all-star line-up; musical theatre including Stravinsky's *The Soldier's Tale* and an unperformed work; a folk concert and performances in pubs and working men's clubs; a film festival; poetry readings in factories alongside our concerts; an exhibition of works by local artists and children's paintings; a special presentation of a play for schools – and a great deal more, including backdrops for various events created by the artist Feliks Topolski.

I was the youngest and least experienced of Arnold's inner team, but his personal warmth made me feel welcome and part of it. With him, the conventional was never an option, even when it came to transport to the various venues: for some he would hire a double-decker London bus to convey us. In 1964, when the festivals had proved themselves, he took over the Roundhouse in Chalk Farm as Centre 42's artistic hub. Built in 1847 and originally a Victorian railway turntable, it later became a gin warehouse. At the opening event I remember the Prime Minister, Harold Wilson, being present, though not the slightest whiff of gin. Shortly after, Pete Seeger gave an inspiring concert that moved me to write a poem entitled 'Pete Seeger at the Roundhouse':

> You brought us songs from the Spanish soul,
> pure loud voices of the peasant's labour.
> *Guantanamera: I am a truthful man.*

From Little Rock, Montgomery, Birmingham,
charged songs of the Freedom Fighters.
We shall not, we shall not be moved.

From black German camps, Dachau, Belsen,
you brought hope, the human voice rising in song.
Up and down the guards are pacing.

In Turkish, Yiddish, Bantu, French,
gentle man, you brought us strength,
and on that stark, freezing night, a roof.

Only a few months ago, our friends Tony and Lisette Stalbow took us to hear the legendary Joan Baez at the Albert Hall. Before singing a Pete Seeger song, Baez recalled how, when she was fourteen, she was taken to hear him sing and how moved she was, and I thought back to that night at the Roundhouse all those years ago, and how moved I was then. The threads of history.

With regard to our own contributions to the Centre 42 festivals, it was gratifying to read a long article by Michael Kustow, the festival organiser, in which he frankly discussed the successes and disappointments, writing:

The actors and musicians had full houses or empty ones, bad ones or exciting ones. The folk singers in the pubs either had the freeze or sang until they clicked with the customers and when they did click the pubs burst at the seams. The poets-with-jazz always clicked; the jazz band was a hit.

*   *   *

Having just written the above, I was shocked to pick up the morning paper and see headlined there the news of Arnold Wesker's death. I knew he'd been very ill for some time, but nothing ever prepares one

for such news, particularly when it involves someone who has affected your life in a meaningful way, as Arnold had mine. We were in
touch only spasmodically over the years but nevertheless the memories
flooded back, not only of the Centre 42 years, but other things too –
his presence at our wedding, stopping me on the synagogue steps to
discuss the ceremony, which had appealed to his dramatic instincts.
And on the table in our living room now is the special metal pot for
brewing Turkish coffee (an ibrik) that he gave us. I also still have the
candid letter he wrote me about his memoirs: 'I didn't *want* to write
this autobiography. What could I remember? Did I trust my memory?
Did I *know* the truth? But I was made an offer I couldn't refuse ...
Still, I find myself having ambitions for the work. I've written 190,000
words! Not that quantity means anything.'

I'm glad I was able to make him laugh by recounting an occasion
at what was then the Golders Green Hippodrome (it is now an
El-Shaddai International Christian Centre), where Carole and I had
gone to see Arnold's Love Play, *The Four Seasons*, starring Alan Bates
and Diane Cilento. Rarely have I seen an audience (not a Jewish one,
anyway!) so engrossed as at the moment when Alan Bates began to
make a very large apple strudel on stage. As he started to add the
ingredients (perhaps it was the eggs), a woman in the audience suddenly screamed, 'Too much, that's too much!', almost stopping Bates
in his tracks. Arnold loved that story. I was amused to learn that Diane
Cilento had refused to comply with the script, which called for her
to expose her breasts at one point, instead turning her back on the
audience and facing Bates with her nipples covered by Elastoplast.
Arnold was not amused, writing ruefully that 'it was the first of my
plays which appeared on stage not as I conceived it'.

Despite his knighthood, Arnold felt neglected by the British theatre
establishment and locked in the time warp when his trilogy had created such a sensation and he had been top of the theatrical world. I've
known actors who have felt like that: Ron Moody, often only thought
of as Fagin in *Oliver!* when he did so much else; the brilliantly versatile Maureen Lipman, at one time pigeon-holed as Beattie in the

well-loved BT television commercials; Topol, the eternal Fiddler on the Roof. In the fullness of time, though, I'm sure Arnold Wesker and his work will take their important historical place. His friend Bernard Kops, whose background was similar and whose play *Enter Solly Gold* had been premiered in the 42 Festivals, paid tribute: 'Arnold was a great man, a wonderful man, but he didn't act like a great man. He created change.'

*   *   *

Throughout the Centre 42 period I continued dutifully to turn out publicity for Harrap, who were remarkably understanding, perhaps a little intrigued, about my weekly dashes to this or that town. Even when the festivals were over and 1962 moved to its close, there were several more concerts, including an unusual one in the Wood Green Council Chamber, where two outstanding poets, Alan Brownjohn and Peter Porter, made their first appearances. It was Peter's 40th birthday and we ended up having a dicey curry in Camden Town which laid us all flat for some days. Then out of the blue an Italian film company, Titinus Films of Rome, decided that along with Teddy boys and nuclear disarmament we were at the cutting edge of what was happening in Britain, and that they should include some poetry and jazz in a full-length documentary they were making called *Young Europe*. The director, Franco Giraldi, wanted something original and had the bright idea of filming us (or rather, me) reading with jazz accompaniment outside the Old Vic theatre in Waterloo. An upright piano was found for Michael Garrick and placed against the side of the theatre, and there, one cold Saturday morning, we battled against the weather and the noise of the traffic, Joe Harriott playing in his overcoat, collar up, and me doing my best to be heard – not exactly an Oscar-winning performance. A large crowd gathered, which is just what Giraldi wanted as he pranced around, gesticulating and being every inch the director, and it all caused such a disturbance that the police were called to keep order. I have no idea whether the film ever saw the light of day – perhaps in some arty cinema in the backstreets of Rome. It was certainly the nearest I've ever got to performing at the venerable Old Vic.

Very soon after, an even odder performance took place at home when we learned that Max Geldray had decided to move to America. Although Carole and I had enjoyed many convivial evenings with them, I hadn't quite realised that his five-year liaison with the pretty and much younger Barbara had been disintegrating. Lately, however, with *The Goon Show* over, Max had been travelling more and more – playing in Australia, on the *Queen Elizabeth*, and also in Los Angeles, where he caught the American bug. Barbara, meanwhile, had come to several of our concerts, and gradually she'd started to rebuild her own life. I'd always felt a great affection for them both, so when Max made his announcement we decided to throw a small farewell party, inviting his close circle of friends, including Peter Sellers and his then wife Anne, Graham Stark (who'd appeared in many of Peter's films) and his wife Audrey, Carole, and of course my parents. To add some music to the occasion, I invited Michael Garrick, and he and Max played a few numbers, with Peter Sellers sportingly joining in on my rather makeshift drum set – he'd played drums in army bands. Peter was in such a good mood that in a moment of inspiration I showed him a letter I'd received after the Hampstead Town Hall reading from Tarikul Alam, the Pakistani student I'd become friendly with at the Regent Street Poly. Following his role as the Indian doctor in *The Millionairess*, Peter was famous for his Indian accent, and the letter appealed to him, as I thought it might. Turning to Michael Garrick, he asked him to play a dirge he'd heard him play earlier, and then, picking up the mike from my recorder, he read the letter over the music, starting very slowly with the address and date, timing every word and catching every inflection and change of pace and mood to perfection, as if he'd rehearsed it for days. It was the perfect script, and I hope Tarikul won't mind my including it here, just as he wrote it (the reference at the end is to my friends Tony Stalbow and Anne Hooper – Anne of course was at the Poly with him).

```
                              44. Ridge Road,
                              London  N 8.
                              10. 2.61

Dear Jeremy,

        How happily delighted I was last Saturday
eve to be in your glorious sitting of Poetry and
Jazz. It was indeed remarkable and I enjoyed the
report ih the Observer next day. How I wish I coul
write to every individual poet who took part in
that evening's programme, but you know I am now
very busy in preparing some articles for our
papers on Pakistan. Moreover I was going to Denmark
and Sweden. I had to postpone my plan as I am
going to Hammersmith Hospital to morrow and I do
not know when I am coming back.

        Meanwhile, could you kindly do a favour to
me. In Pakistan both English and Bengali papers
are very much interested to know more about the
new trends and development in English Poetry. I
intend to write an article ( in English & Bengali)
and would it be possible for you to help me with
some of the poems of the Poetry and Jazz evening.
I have already taken some notes and when I got
these poems I could finish my article and send to
the respective papers. The Bengali article, you
possibly will not understand but the English one
you can go through. You can send me the copies
to the Hospital address or to Ridge Road address.

        More when we meet. Love to you and to Bosy
and possibly to Ann.
                              Yours
                              tarikul alam.
```

That is a letter and recording I treasure, and Peter followed it with a couple of my own poems, read in different voices. To end a memorable evening, he then treated us to the Demon Barber of Fleet Street act he used to do in variety early in his career, acting it out with great melo-dramatic exaggeration and panache. And so Max left us with laughter in his ears. We were to meet up again several times, in England and in Palm Springs, where he married and settled. Sad to say, Barbara's story ended tragically. We'd met a few times after her split with Max and she'd seemed happy enough, and she, too, married before very long. But then we lost touch with her, and were shocked to learn in a letter from Max that she had taken her own life.

*　*　*

The new year, 1963, began with a string of concerts – in Cardiff, at the Hampstead Theatre, at the Royal Court (courtesy of a prickly George Devine, the theatre's renowned director), and several other venues. But most exciting for me, a maverick record producer called Denis Preston agreed to record a poetry and jazz EP in his Lansdowne Studios in Holland Park. Denis was something of a legend in the jazz world, having recorded not only most of the leading musicians but many young ones he believed in too, always ready to back his taste and instincts. He was a generous entrepreneur but not, I imagine, a man to cross, especially since he was a self-confessed fan of the mobster Bugsy Siegel! When he died, the *Sunday Times* called him 'probably the most important figure to emerge from the British jazz business'. In fact, it was at his studios, where I'd gone to discuss an earlier venture that never materialised, that I'd first met a rather intimidating Joe Harriott, who was then deeply into the free-form jazz he pioneered and which Denis was recording. I was well aware of Joe's great reputation and it was typical of Preston to have produced the revolutionary but exciting music Joe was presenting. That day, in his intense, aristocratic manner, Joe started to explain his free-form vision to me, pointing to a vase of roses and saying he was trying to express the feeling of the inside of a rose petal, to paint it in sound. I was relieved that for the EP we later made together, on which he was joined by Shake Keane, he appeared rather more down-to-earth and his lyrical playing of Garrick's settings is quite beautiful. However, the burden of the title poem, 'Blues for the Lonely', written to Miles Davis's 'Blue in Green', fell to Shake, whose rendition is also masterly. The EP went out on the Columbia label, and at the same time a small booklet of my jazz poems was published in Leicester by Leslie Weston.

The climax to all this came when a phone call was put through to me at the Harrap office and there was a jubilant Bruce Robb telling me that Sidgwick had finally agreed to publish my book of poems. It wouldn't be until the following year, but who cared? I could hardly contain my excitement. The only problem was that by the next year I might have some better poems to include, but then I remembered Dannie Abse telling me that when his first book of poems was accepted by Hutchinson he'd also had to wait some time, and on learning the book was about to go to the printer he'd slipped into the office, asked to see the manuscript, and quietly changed a few poems when nobody was looking. I could always do the same.

Almost immediately after that, in what was becoming a dream period in my life, Elizabeth Thomas phoned from *Tribune* to say there was an editorial job going at a company called Aldus Books and would I be interested? Well, it seemed I was on a roll, and it didn't take much thought to answer, 'Yes!'

9

TO ALDUS THEN I WENT

Nothing could have prepared me for the explosion that was Aldus Books. A subsidiary of the US publisher Doubleday, it was run (dominated) by a remarkable Austrian Jew called Wolfgang Foges, but more on him in a moment. Before that I had to get past first base, and this meant going for an interview with one of their editors, Douglas Hill, a convivial Canadian with thinning ginger hair, a short beard and a clipped accent, who offered me a seat behind a desk and proceeded to give me an editorial test. I hadn't expected that, naively thinking that after Elizabeth Thomas's recommendation it would be a fait accompli. Not so! I don't remember what I was asked to do – perhaps sub or rewrite some copy – but when I'd finished Douglas looked at it quickly, almost apologetically, smiled and said, 'Well, it's not the neatest thing I've ever seen, but I know your poetry, I write poetry, and it would be great to have someone to talk to… So if you want the job, it's yours.'

But not quite… I still wasn't home and dry, as the administrative editor wanted to vet me, and I found myself facing an alarming lady called Frame-Smith, who peered at me in Dame Edna fashion though oversize lenses, asked me some awkward questions about my experience, paused, as if wondering what I was doing there, called me 'honey' several times, then offered me a salary of £1,000 a year and two weeks' paid holiday, with my agreement to being called in on Saturdays if needs be. I was to start on 16 April 1963 on a three-month trial basis, working with Douglas Hill as an assistant editor. I couldn't have been more terrified, or more excited.

To call Aldus Books just a packaging company, creating illustrated books and marketing international editions, would be to sell it very short. In a way it was that, but it was also the creation of Wolfgang Foges, an Orson Wellesian figure who is generally regarded as the pioneer of book packaging. Indeed, the publisher Anthony Blond called him 'the father of them all'. Everything Foges touched had class and extravagance all over it, and if I dwell on him for a moment it is because so much of what followed in my own career stemmed from those larger-than-life Aldus days.

The son of a Viennese obstetrician and gynaecologist, Foges was born into a family which, though Jewish, was not in the least bit observant (it seems Christmas was the only festival they celebrated). Indeed, he loved to challenge prominent Jews he met with the age-old question 'What is a Jew?', proudly declaring that he'd neither been circumcised nor had a bar mitzvah, and never waiting for an answer. On at least one occasion I heard him gleefully throwing the question at David Ben-Gurion, Israel's legendary first Prime Minister, from whom he'd commissioned a book, though I'm not sure B-G understood what he was talking about (especially as Foges would muddle things by muttering something about there having been a famous rabbi in his family). But back to his story: just after the First World War, when Foges was nine and money was tight, he'd been sent to foster parents in Sweden for a year, returning to find his father had died. Then he was shipped off to a boarding school (quite possibly at the suggestion of Freud, a family friend). Is it any wonder he was to become such a contrary personality? Later he studied for three years in Weimar, sharing a room with the future rocket scientist Wernher von Braun. He set up his first publishing imprint shortly after, taking over a glossy magazine and learning to publish in the contemporary Continental style, with striking illustrations sourced by researchers and a carefully integrated text.

In 1937, when things became too dangerous – even for one who was both uncircumcised and unbarmitzvahed (Hitler clearly having his own criteria as to who was a Jew) – Foges decamped to London, starting a small production company called Adprint, and then another called Rathbone. At that time, British publishers had scant experience of this kind of publishing, so when he arrived in England he found a ready market for his visually orientated books and he quickly made his mark, producing the innovative King Penguin series and books for Collins, Hamlyn, Pitman and the Ministry of Information. It's salutary now, in this austere, computerised age, to look back at the books and series and authors he published. There was, for instance, a fifteen-volume World of Music series, followed by a seven-volume poetry series (all now collector's items) with coloured lithography by such contemporary artists as Michael Ayrton and John Piper. A book on butterflies kicked off a natural history series with over a hundred titles; then there was a bestselling history of mathematics by Lancelot Hogben; *The Story of Music* by Benjamin Britten and Imogen Holst; *British Dramatists* by Graham Greene; *English Women* by Edith Sitwell; *British Birds* by James Fisher; and so on.

In 1960, Foges resigned from his other companies and started Aldus Books, backed by the American publishing giant Doubleday. His editorial board included Jacob Bronowski and Julian Huxley and his authors were generally intellectually distinguished, often famous – Carl Jung, Bertrand Russell, Louis MacNeice, J. B. Priestley and Compton Mackenzie are just a few of the names in the Aldus *Who's Who*. In a way, Foges can be measured by the extraordinary people who worked for him. In earlier times he had employed Walter Neurath (founder of Thames & Hudson), George Rainbird and Max Parrish, all of whom followed where he had led. When I joined Aldus, there was a staff of some seventy people – editors, designers, picture and text researchers – all talented, some eccentric, most with outsize personalities. The researcher on the first book I worked on was the future award-winning biographer and novelist Diana Souhami, and among the researchers and designers, past and present, were the avant-garde composer Cornelius Cardew; Edwin Taylor, who was to revolutionise the typography of the *Sunday Times*; and Germano Facetti, who directed the redesign of Penguin Books. Some of the editors were or became successful writers – Malcolm Ross Macdonald, a bestselling novelist; Douglas Hill, a major science fiction writer; David Lambert, a much-published author – while several others went on to found their own publishing companies.

Where Foges was concerned, everything had to be of the highest quality: writing, production, editorial and pictorial content – and no expense was to be spared. No wonder his companies never made money. I can just imagine how his Doubleday overlords must have raged with frustration when they came on one of their regular visits to the London office. Figures? What had figures to do with it? A powerful man both physically and intellectually, with a large, leonine head, Foges was quite impossible to pin down or control. The fact that he could never quite get his tongue around the English language was in some ways endearing, but in others rather frightening. When he wanted to see someone, his summoning cry 'Come!' would reverberate around the building. It was some time before I came into his orbit, but once I did I scarcely left it.

To my surprise, I discovered that Laurie Lee had crossed swords with Foges in the past, for when I wrote to tell him I was joining Aldus Books, he responded in true Laurie style: 'I used to know Wolfie quite well. Astonish him and confuse him with your intelligence and I think you'll find him an excellent boss. But beware if he gives you a cigar.' I had been warned.

*   *   *

Douglas Hill was a sharply intelligent, sensitive, highly cultivated man and a good poet to boot. He was also generous, and on my first day he took me to lunch at the Etoile in Charlotte Street to welcome me to the fold. It seemed extravagant, but I soon learned that Foges lunched there or at the White Tower most days, puffing at one of his expensive cigars as he launched himself down Charlotte Street. Shortly after, Douglas invited Carole and me to dinner at his flat in Holborn so we could meet his wife Gaila (the writer and broadcaster Gail Robinson) and their baby son Michael. The dinner did not get off to the best of starts when we discovered there was a strictly non-kosher rabbit on the menu: I might have succumbed to that steak in Paris, but rabbit was a hop too far. I thought we'd best come clean straight away, and after embarrassed apologies all round we ended up with a welcome omelette. The dessert too posed a hiccup for Carole since pumpkin pie (a Canadian delicacy) was not something her Middle Eastern taste buds could cope with, though she tried valiantly. The Hills didn't seem to mind, and we survived the occasion to eat together many another day.

Douglas was a great editor; working with him was an apprenticeship like no other. From him I learned that with application you could make almost any text work if the will to do so was there. In the case of the first book I worked on, a history of gambling, it was not so much a question of rewriting a sloppy text but of getting the author to expand it, adding colour and detail and making sure it wasn't too English – for, as I quickly learned, everything had to be not just international, but in the Aldus style, which meant American spelling and punctuation, and, because of the pictures, the text had to be written to an exact length. Later, when I left Aldus, I found it hard to revert to British spelling and usage. Should I use 's' or 'z'? I was never quite sure, and the Webster's dictionary that had become my bible wasn't really much help.

At that time Douglas was working on a book called *Man and His Symbols* by Carl Jung. It was a massive and complex project and one of Foges's great triumphs, for Jung had always resisted having his work popularised. But Foges had seen him talking to John Freeman in one of BBC Television's celebrated *Face to Face* programmes, and somehow he'd managed to persuade Freeman to go to Switzerland on his behalf and propose to Jung that Aldus publish a book about his life's work. 'Jung listened to me in his garden for two hours without interruption,' wrote Freeman afterwards, 'and then said no.' But Foges was too excited by the idea to let it go, and he managed to get Freeman to go back once more, with him, to try again. Remarkably, Jung had had a dream (and dreams were all-important to him) in which he was speaking in the marketplace to a great audience who couldn't comprehend what he was saying, and he had read this as a sign. Foges, it seems, was to be his saviour, and this time he agreed to the proposed book, setting down various complicated conditions, and he completed it ten days before his death – a 500-page monster that Douglas was struggling to put to bed. When, some fifty years later, I was offered a book on John Freeman, I remembered this story and was glad to sign up Hugh Purcell's masterly biography of the mercurial Freeman, a man who had nine remarkable careers, of which his famous television series was but one.

Besides all this, the gambling book I was working on seemed rather humdrum, but it was the perfect book on which to cut my teeth and I'd pass edited chapters to Douglas, who would sometimes suggest areas where I could expand or elaborate further. Once I knew him a little better I'd also show him new poems and be grateful for his insightful comments. After a while it became a two-way trade and I appreciated his confidence in letting me see his poems. It was our secret poetry society, which naturally led to my asking Douglas to read at some poetry and jazz concerts. It was good to be able to add his wry Canadian voice to the mix and to introduce him to Dannie Abse and then to Elizabeth Thomas, for whom he started to review science fiction. Later, when he'd left Aldus and Elizabeth moved from *Tribune* to the *New Statesman*, Douglas took over as *Tribune*'s literary editor.

As editors, we were spoilt rotten at Aldus, since on top of everything else there was a copy-editing department of three to put every word under the microscope (inevitably they came back with umpteen per-nickety queries). I think they were responsible for my first migraine attack! Then there was the marvellous team of researchers, and an art editor to liaise with. I quickly got the hang of it all and came to realise that the art of good editing is not to impose one's own style on an author, but to absorb theirs, so that when you make changes it is in his or her voice, not yours. It means having a good ear together with a large dose of humility. It's the author's book, after all, not the editor's. I remember Alan Sillitoe writing in his autobiography that when his bestselling classic *Saturday Night and Sunday Morning* first did the rounds of publishers, several editors came back more or less telling him how he should rewrite or change it. Alan's response was simple: write your own book if you can, but don't mess with mine.

When I first started work at Aldus it was in Lower Oxford Street, near Tottenham Court Road Station, and I would often meet Carole for lunch in the cellar of a nearby coffee house called Bunjies, one of the original folk cafés of the 1950s and '60s, which was down an adja-cent side street. After a few months, the company moved into large,

Lego-like, American-style offices in Fitzroy Square which had been specially designed and more or less rebuilt for Aldus, going way over budget in true Foges fashion. Douglas and I shared an office on the ground floor, overlooking the square, and the other editors – Kit Coppard (son of the short-story writer A. E. Coppard), Roy Gasson and Nick Russell – were alongside, on the same floor, fine editors all. The flamboyant Kit and I became good friends and we would often play squash at lunchtime at the nearby White House. Among his many interests, Kit enjoyed folk music, and we went to enjoyable parties at the Coppards' Belsize Park flat, singing the evening away.

Upstairs at Aldus was the holy of holies, Foges occupying a suitably enormous office, with his stocky secretary/assistant/guard Joyce always on duty outside, dressed in what looked like battle fatigues. The formidable Frame-Smith (known as Frame) was in a nearby office, and along the corridor was a team of Foges faithfuls – Count Hans Coudenhove, who looked after foreign sales; Mr Hellmore, a calm, soberly dressed, indispensable accountant whose first name I only discovered after I'd left; and Frederic Ullstein, son of the youngest of the four brothers who founded the German publishing dynasty. Ullstein seemed to be a kind of Foges troubleshooter, doing his bidding and putting a rather negative spin on whatever he came across. At any rate that was my impression at the time, which may be a harsh judgement on a man whose Jewish origins (as I found out only recently) forced him to leave Germany, where the family lost their business. Coming to England, he'd worked as a farmer before joining the army and marrying into the Guinness family. He and I locked horns on several occasions, but never unpleasantly. His life can't have been easy, and apart from anything else he had Foges to contend with day and night. Upstairs there was also a large art department, and in the basement a library where the researchers worked and gossiped.

One of the great advantages of Fitzroy Square for me was that we'd ended up bang next door to the Centre 42 office, where Arnold Wesker and his co-director Beba Lavrin were based, and opposite the offices of the Scorpion Press, a small publisher with a first-rate poetry list on whom I'd sometimes call. What's more, the clinic where Dannie

Abse worked (and scribbled poems when no one was looking) was just around the corner, so we would often meet up at lunchtime, sometimes going to a salt beef restaurant called Felds in Wells Street where the powerful-looking, extremely rude Mr Feld would raise huge carving knives in the air like the demon barber himself and eventually do us the great favour of cutting us some beef. Douglas would join us occasionally, enjoying both the salt beef and the show. Other times, Dannie and I would stroll through Soho, playing on the pinball machines or dropping into the Patisserie Valerie in Old Compton Street, or into Bob Chris's colourful second-hand bookshop in Cecil Court. It should really have been called Chris Court, since the white-haired bookseller would sit there like a king, rounding on any unsuspecting customer who had the temerity to walk through his door, and generally entertaining the writers who'd stop by to savour the cabaret. Inevitably he'd ask us to post a letter for him when we left. I always found him somewhat intimidating.

Just as formidable was the uniformed doorman who accosted me whenever I went to pick up Dannie for one of our lunchtime sorties. 'Dr Abse, please,' I'd say distinctly, and without fail he'd respond, 'I'll let Dr *Aspe* know you're here.' One evening Joan Abse called for her husband. Time and again over the years she'd tried to correct the doorman, but to no avail. Always her 'I've come to see Dr Abse' was met with the rejoinder, 'I'll tell Dr *Aspe* you're here.' She knew when she was beaten, so one day, in rather a hurry and to save time, she asked for 'Dr Aspe'. 'There's no Dr Aspe here,' came the sharp response. 'You mean, *Dr Abse*.' I can still hear Joan laughing as she told the story.

A colourful Soho denizen we bumped into on one of our lunchtime walks was the poet and writer Paul Potts. I'd first met him at Douglas and Gaila's flat, for they were great admirers of this passionate, highly volatile wanderer, and perhaps the fact that he'd been brought up in Canada (though English) had something to do with their friendship. He was a large, bald man with a stammer which seemed to be compounded by the excited way he talked and the speed with which the words queued up to be released. He produced pamphlets of his own poetry which he sold in the streets and bars of Soho, and when my

own Penny Pamphlet was produced, there were several references
to his in reviews that appeared at the time, for he was a well-known
figure. Eventually, perhaps because he never paid, or just because he
was 'trouble', Paul was barred from some Soho pubs. Dannie had once
run into him outside a restaurant in Charlotte Street and Paul had
begged him for some money, saying, 'Dannie, Dannie, I haven't eaten
for days,' and of course Dannie, feeling sorry for him, had coughed
up. Then, as Paul disappeared swiftly down the street, the restaurant
manager came rushing out shouting, 'Where did that man go? He's
just eaten here and left without paying his bill!' Paul died in poverty,
leaving behind a touching memoir called *Dante Called You Beatrice*,
which I love for its openness and idealistic fervour.

Dannie Abse, my lifelong friend and Laurie Lee's friendly rival
when it came to selling books, at an early concert.

A rather more sober figure Dannie and I came across one lunchtime
was the poet Edmund Blunden, who impressed me greatly. The longest-
serving of the Great War poets, he'd seen continuous action from 1916
to 1918, and here he was, lively and alert and readily accepting Dannie's
invitation to join us for a drink. I thought of this strange meeting

when, a few years later, I went to Hull to give a reading with Vernon Scannell, one of the finest poets of the Second World War. Some students met us at the station and in the car on the way to the university campus one of them turned to Vernon and (getting his wars and their poets confused) said, 'I'm surprised to see *you* here today, Mr Scannell.' An amused Mr Scannell was delighted to be there.

Edmund Blunden was an historic literary figure for me, joined in my mind with Siegfried Sassoon, Wilfred Owen and Isaac Rosenberg, and so was Louis MacNeice, who surprised me one day when Douglas was out by walking into our office and asking if he could make a phone call. More than a little tongue-tied, I pointed to the phone on Douglas's desk and said, 'Of course.' I was far too taken aback to introduce myself and engage him in conversation; besides, he seemed the kind of shy man who valued his privacy. Although in my mind he was one of the mythical '30s poets along with Auden, Cecil Day-Lewis and Stephen Spender, he can only have been in his mid-fifties (a great deal younger than I am now!), had just finished a book on astrology for Aldus which Douglas had edited, and was continuing to write poems with great style and vigour, as I was shortly to discover. Tragically, he died a few months following that visit to Aldus, after potholing in Yorkshire and catching pneumonia. I always regretted my reticence but was at least able to voice my thoughts about him when, towards the end of that year, I was sent a posthumous book of his poems, *The Burning Perch*, to review. They had, I sensed, a disturbing premonition of death:

> The lines of print are always sidelines
> And all our games funeral games...

Unquestionably, MacNeice was that rare thing, a real poet: his mastery and wit, the accuracy and originality of his imagery, his erudition, verbal acrobatics and versatility were exciting and original. To quote from his poem 'Suicide', 'This man with the shy smile / has left behind something that was intact'. I wish I'd been able to say all that to his face.

* * *

Gradually I began to feel at home at Aldus and even Foges, who still hadn't the faintest idea who I was, would nod in a distracted way as, deep in thought, he paced the corridor or walked slowly down the stairs on his way to lunch. All that was to change quite soon, but meanwhile, outside the effervescent world of Aldus, the poetry and jazz concerts continued apace, with three in the month after I'd joined the company – at the Hampstead Theatre, the Bromsgrove Arts Festival and the Victoria Theatre, Stoke on Trent. At Stoke we had an apocalyptic moment when I started to read a poem with jazz called 'Cascade'. The poem starts with the line, 'Can you hear the thunder' and as I read it the heavens opened, there was lightning and the loudest clap of thunder any of us had ever heard, drowning out the words and music. What timing! The applause went on and on.

A more unusual concert was to follow at the instigation of a re-markable man called Harley Usill who ran Argo records. A subsidiary of Decca, Argo had a superb catalogue of Shakespeare, contemporary poetry, traditional folk music, birdsong, steam locomotives and other specialist subjects. Harley always had a sharp ear for the unusual, and profit was rarely his motivating force. Having heard a tape of one of our concerts, he decided to arrange one of his own – in the famous Abbey Road recording studios before a live audience – and that re-corded concert took place on 10 June 1963. The poets reading were Dannie Abse, Laurie Lee, Adrian Mitchell and me, while Michael Garrick's Quintet included Shake Keane and Joe Harriott; the concert was later issued on two LPs. In his autobiography, Garrick wrote that he'd seen the records on sale for £1,400, even though they'd recently been issued on CD. That may or may not be so, but when you pass the crowds of tourists outside the Abbey Road studios, forget the Beatles and remember that we were there too! Mention of the Beatles reminds me that, his young family being huge fans of theirs, Dannie Abse once persuaded me to phone him at home and say to whichever of his children answered, 'Hello, this is John Lennon. May I speak to Dr Abse, please?' I think that impressed them at the time more than any of their father's poems, though Dannie did come clean after a while. It was his eldest daughter Keren who answered the phone, and she told me recently that because John Lennon had just published a book of poems, it had seemed credible that her dad should know him.

Alongside these concerts of ours, another front was opening up in the form of *Tribune* poetry readings. Poetry had become such a strong feature of the paper, what with my almost weekly reviews and the new poems the paper now published regularly, that it seemed a natural progression. When I put the idea to Elizabeth Thomas, she jumped at it, proposing that we start in the autumn – monthly readings to be held in the Regent's Park Library in Robert Street, which was fairly central and had a useful pub on the corner with Albany Street where we'd gather before and after the event. Meanwhile, she would use the summer months to announce the readings in the paper and build up interest. I greatly looked forward to these, and started to draw up a list of possible poets for her to consider. We wanted them to be as wide-ranging as possible, with a good sprinkling of young poets alongside the more established.

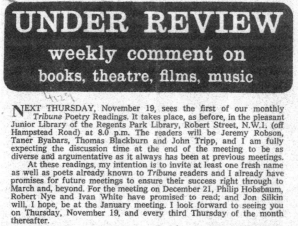

UNDER REVIEW

weekly comment on
books, theatre, films, music

NEXT THURSDAY, November 19, sees the first of our monthly *Tribune* Poetry Readings. It takes place, as before, in the pleasant Junior Library of the Regents Park Library, Robert Street, N.W.1. (off Hampstead Road) at 8.0 p.m. The readers will be Jeremy Robson, Taner Byabars, Thomas Blackburn and John Tripp, and I am fully expecting the discussion time at the end of the meeting to be as diverse and argumentative as it always has been at previous meetings.

At these readings, my intention is to invite at least one fresh name as well as poets already known to *Tribune* readers and I already have promises for future meetings to ensure their success right through to March and, beyond. For the meeting on December 21, Philip Hobsbaum, Robert Nye and Ivan White have promised to read; and Jon Silkin will, I hope, be at the January meeting. I look forward to seeing you on Thursday, November 19, and every third Thursday of the month thereafter.

ELIZABETH THOMAS

Tribune announces the first of the paper's popular monthly poetry readings.

* * *

By this time Carole, if not exactly a groupie, had become a fixture in the poetry and jazz line-up. Since I generally had to get to venues early to check things out, she'd often follow on with Dannie in his car. They never seemed to agree on the route (it became a running joke), but somehow they always arrived in time – just. Selling books was an important part of the concerts for all concerned, especially for Dannie and Laurie, who would appear with competing piles under their arms, and Carole quickly found herself looking after sales during the interval and after the concert.

Laurie Lee exhorts Carole to sell more of his books.

By then the 'ons' in our relationship seemed to have become far more frequent than the 'offs', and Carole's parents were definitely getting edgy, her father even inviting me to Queen's Club, where, walking me round and round the car park instead of facing me on the courts, he aired his concerns. I suppose that even though I was now earning £1,000 a year, I didn't offer the greatest security for his young daughter. He must have known, though, that she was in some ways a chip off the old block, quite capable of making up her own mind – and as far as I knew she hadn't done so yet, and nor, for that matter, had I!

But when Carole's mother Jocy invited me to tea a few days later, I realised things were getting a little too serious. Perhaps she'd never really recovered from the day Carole told her a poet was calling for her and I walked in with my just-under-seven-foot friend Michael

Rivkin. Endearingly, Carole's mother never quite came to terms with English manners, nor for that matter with the English language, so would address anyone in a shop she went to as 'Madame', try to shake hands with all and sundry, and always felt fruit carefully before buying it – which might have been acceptable in the markets of Cairo, but didn't always go down well in Maida Vale. Perhaps at that stage I was just another of those English things she didn't quite fathom, though in time she would, and we'd enjoy many a six o'clock whisky together. She really was the gentlest and loveliest of women, not to mention stylish. Looking back, I can well understand that coming from a Middle Eastern background and having been uprooted, their world turned upside down in the way it had been, Carole's parents would have felt especially protective of their daughter, particularly as the worlds of publishing and poetry must have seemed very alien to them. I'm not sure I was that understanding at the time!

My family could not have been more different. My father has already featured in some of the early chapters of this book, so let me introduce my mother, Charlotte, and her side of the family. Her mother, the gracious Harriette of one of my poems, was the daughter of a remarkable man, Morris Wartski, founder of the antique jeweller's of the same name, in whose house in Llandudno I was born. An immigrant from Turek near Karlisch in Poland (then part of Imperial Russia), Morris had landed with his wife Flora in Liverpool. There, at first he followed the traditional family business as a licensed pedlar, travelling around with his stock of silver watches, jewellery and silks in a bag on his back, for sale to local gentry and farmers.

The story has it that one hot day the young Morris had called at a farm and was crossing the Menai Bridge in Anglesey when a dogcart drew up and the driver offered him a lift, which he gratefully accepted. The two of them fell into a learned conversation about the Bible, and the man was so impressed by Morris's erudition that he gave him his card, urging him to be in touch. It was Morris's lucky day, for the man turned out to be the Earl of Uxbridge, soon to inherit the title of Marquess of Anglesey and a fortune, and in due course he set Morris up in business with a shop in Bangor High Street. Fifteen years later,

in 1910, Morris moved the flourishing business to the more fashionable Llandudno, taking two large premises in Mostyn Street, the main
shopping area. A man of great taste and entrepreneurial flair, he also
rented showcases in the two main hotels.

My grandfather Emanuel Snowman (my mother's father), who
had originally worked as an estate agent and auctioneer in Kilburn,
joined the Wartski business shortly after it opened and a year later
married Morris's daughter Harriette. That was *his* lucky day, for my
future grandmother was a strong, highly intelligent, elegant woman
who was to make her own mark in many areas. In 1911, the young
couple moved to London, where Emanuel opened a branch of the
Wartski business in New Bond Street. Like many Jewish families of
that era, the Snowmans had their colourful roots in Eastern Europe,
Emanuel's father Abraham settling in Spitalfields when he first came
to England, before setting up business as a picture dealer and framer.
He and his wife Rachel had ten children, most of whom I knew. They
were a remarkable tribe. Three brothers were involved with the royal
family – Emanuel, who became a royal jeweller; Isaac (Icky), one of the
foremost portrait painters of his day, who painted a number of royal
portraits, many of which appeared on the popular Raphael Tuck postcards; and Dr Jacob (Jack) Snowman, who circumcised several royals,
including Prince Charles. When Prince George was born, there was
widespread speculation in the press as to whether his parents would
follow royal tradition and have him circumcised. Most of these stories
referred to my great-uncle Jack, calling him a rabbi. He wasn't, although he was fairly Orthodox. He was a medical doctor who became
famous as a *mohel* (circumciser). A highly cultured man, he gave me a
set of leather-bound Dickens novels for my bar mitzvah, and whenever
I visited him he loved to talk about Browning, a poet he greatly admired. Jacob's son, Dr Leonard Snowman, inherited the mantle when
his father died. The family used to say he lived on tips!

Another of the Snowman brothers, Louis, was also a painter, but
far less successful than Icky. I remember Uncle Louis well, often going
to his studio in Kilburn. A small man, always neatly dressed with a
bow tie, he was more bohemian than Icky, possibly even a communist,

and he seemed to rather resent his brother's success. My mother told me how she once took her Uncle Icky, with whom she was close, to Louis's studio and that he wouldn't let them in until he'd turned all the paintings to the wall. She was also with Icky in Jerusalem when he was stabbed by an Arab (fortunately not fatally) near the Wailing Wall, a subject he painted several times. Louis claimed to know the painters Jankel Adler and David Bomberg, and perhaps he did. On one of my visits to his studio, he gave me a book by the Irish writer George Moore in which Moore wrote that every young man's ideal mistress was thirty years old. I went around for quite a while looking for women of thirty! When Louis died, he left his studio to my cousin Colin Snowman, a fine painter with whom I've always felt a strong kinship. Indeed, I helped him find a gallery in Sloane Street for his first major solo exhibition. I thought of this recently when the highly esteemed critic John Berger died, for he had reviewed Colin's work enthusiastically in the *New Statesman*. I looked up to Colin, not just for his artistic abilities or because he was several years older than me, but because he was the bohemian in the family whose way of life chimed with my poetic aspirations. During the later part of the war (I was born two days after it began), when bombs were exploding on London, the female members of our inner family circle were dispatched with their children to the relatively safe haven of a farm in north Wales. It was there that I locked Colin in a barn, returning to the farmhouse feeling not a little anxious and rather guilty – only to find him waiting for me. It had been easy enough for him to climb out of a window, but he didn't reveal that at the time and I remained puzzled by his sudden magical appearance, just as I later marvelled at his ability to model life-like figures out of clay or to paint with striking originality. We must have spent some time in London during the Blitz, for I vividly remember sitting with my mother on the staircase of our house in Edgware, her arms around me, when there was a ferocious explosion and the house shook. She tried to make light of it, pretending it was nothing, but it wasn't – far from it.

Emanuel Snowman was a formidable man. Mayor of Hampstead in the coronation year and seemingly formal, he had a deadpan sense of humour and wasn't above playing practical jokes or hosting a game of poker in his house on Sunday evenings with a bunch of cronies he called '*gunovim*' (thieves). He also liked to play golf on a Sunday, and Carole and I were with him once when he gave his unsuspecting partner a ball made of soap to tee off with, collapsing with laughter when it flew into pieces all over the course. It was Emanuel who established the firm's international reputation as an antique jeweller specialising in the work of Carl Fabergé, goldsmith to the Russian Imperial court, and obtaining the royal warrants Wartski still enjoys. It all came about when, in 1925, he had gone where few dared to go at the time – the Soviet Union, where he searched out those objects that were anathema to the Bolsheviks and was able to acquire many of the Imperial treasures of the seventeenth and eighteenth centuries, including some of Fabergé's most famous Easter eggs. These masterpieces were to be the backbone of the Wartski business. Following in his father's footsteps, Kenneth Snowman, my mother's brother – charming, erudite, eccentric, and also a painter – became head of the Wartski firm after Emanuel's death, building the business further and becoming, through his books, the acknowledged world expert on the work of Fabergé.

I was close to Kenneth and his wife Sallie from my earliest years and I remember fondly the exciting annual Boxing Day outing to Tom Arnold's spectacular circus at Haringey Arena to which they always took me and my young cousins. I always felt rather sorry for the clowns and the lions in their cages, but those high-wire artists would have me on the edge of my seat, peering through half-closed eyes. The clubbable Kenneth was a character. He never learned to drive (his adored, ebullient wife driving him everywhere, in more senses than one), he always took a jar of marmalade and a bottle of Macallan with him when he went to America, and his wide circle of friends ranged from Prince Yusupov, one of Rasputin's murderers, to Bing Crosby and Ian Fleming (he even featured fleetingly in one of Fleming's books). The witty Kenneth was a real ladies' man. On one occasion I was on holiday and about to go in the sea when a woman came out of the water and rushed towards me, her arms extended, only to recoil in embarrassment at the last minute, apologising, 'I'm so sorry, I thought you were someone

else.' 'You must have thought I was Kenneth Snowman,' I responded, for we were said to have a strong family resemblance – and I was
right, much to her amazement. After his beloved Sallie died, Kenneth
was rather a lost soul, although he enjoyed the warm company at the
Garrick Club bar, and lunched there most days with a circle of friends
that included Kingsley Amis. We did, however, manage to lure him to
France, where, dressed like Monet in a crumpled white suit, he arrived
with paint, brushes, palette and easel, and set himself up on a slope
above the house and painted away. A cherished memory.

There were, too, several other Snowman brothers I came to know
quite well – particularly Henry, a solicitor with a sharp tongue and
a mischievous sense of humour who enjoyed poetry and encouraged
mine. Strangely, when looking through the deeds of the house we
moved into some twenty years ago, we discovered that Henry had
handled the conveyancing for an earlier owner. In his later years,
which was when I knew him, he lived with his daughter and son-in-
law (my cousin Teddy Stonehill's parents). I'd often seen him stalking
around the lawn when I went there on Sundays to play tennis with
Ted and some friends, and at the Christmas Eve parties the hospitable
Stonehills gave, at which many well-known performers sang or played
(and where in future years I would read a poem or two). A large man,
Henry appeared a benevolent Victorian elder with his three-piece suit
and walking stick, and our encounters and conversations were always
spirited. Then there was Sam, an insurance broker – and grandfather of
my historian cousin Daniel – who lived opposite us and whom Carole
and I would often see walking arm in arm with his wife Rosie. (In
our teenage years, Daniel and I were fervent autograph hunters, swapping when we had duplicates and racing to be the first to have 1,000
famous signatures in our collections.) Ezra, another brother, was in the
furniture business (which was mighty helpful when Carole and I set
up home!). Joey, who lived in Israel and used to write me long letters
enclosing postcards of his brother Isaac's royal portraits, was the image
of Albert Steptoe. The brothers Snowman always made me think of
Galsworthy's *Forsyte Saga*.

I have a particularly vivid teenage memory of accompanying

my grandfather as he strode down the exclusive Rue du Faubourg Saint-Honoré in Paris, going from antique jeweller to antique jeweller, asking to see what Fabergé pieces they had, carefully examining each in turn, and then declaring them to be substandard, damaged or copies, leaving the startled salesman to recover his objects and his dignity as he moved on to the next shop, relishing every moment. I suspect it wasn't just the game it appeared to be, and that if something special had caught his eye he might well have tried to acquire it for Wartski – at a special price, that is!

My grandfather's death was a traumatic milestone for me. It was the end of an era: the weekly Shabbat (Sabbath) lunches for twenty or more – my grandmother serving at one end of the table, my grandfather next to her – and the all-welcome Passover Seders for fifty or sixty people, soon to be memories. Highly principled, always immaculately dressed with a diamond tie pin given to him by the Queen Mother, he was the head of the family in the old Victorian way, and to my young eyes seemingly indestructible, so his death greatly affected me. As I put it in a poem:

> ...when the clogs dropped
> shattering the day, a bird flew
> and something final snapped.

Finally, to end this family saga, my mother: like Carole's mother, dear Charlotte was sweet-natured, always optimistic, and she looked after my father with unstinting devotion when he had a stroke. She had a fine voice and loved to sing jazzy numbers, my father playing behind her on the piano and sometimes on his accordion. 'Some of These Days', a song made famous by Sophie Tucker, was one of her favourites. The regular musical soirées they held at home were one of the joys of my childhood, and I would lean over the banisters to listen long after I'd been sent upstairs to bed. The actress Miriam Karlin often came, and Theodore Bikel too before he became a star and moved to America. The hugely talented Bikel, who was to be Oscar-nominated and win Tony Awards on Broadway, sang in many languages, accompanying himself on the guitar, which greatly appealed to my parents' multi-cultured friends.

A strong-minded woman, my mother had played hockey for England in the first Maccabiah Games in Tel Aviv, returning soon after to teach English to young children. She loved Israel (though not its Prime Minister at the time, Benjamin Netanyahu, of whom she was fiercely critical), and her many Israeli friends, and worried about that tiny country until her last breath. Many of those she met there joined the British Army during the war as members of the Jewish Brigade, and they would come to my parents' house in Edgware, diving under the Anderson shelter in the front room when the sirens went. She lived until she was almost ninety-nine and even in her nineties managed to create a stir when she went to hear Leonard Cohen at the O2 Centre. Somehow Sky News got wind of it and sent a crew to interview her – 'Leonard Cohen's oldest fan' – in her flat, and she talked to them for hours, being rather disappointed they only used a few minutes on the news that evening!

In his later years Spike Milligan would come to stay with my mother, and they would reminisce and down a few glasses of Italian wine together. Just before Spike died, I drove my mother to see him at his house in Rye. As we left, I took several pictures of him standing at the door waving goodbye, the last goodbye, but when I got home I discovered to my dismay that there was no film in my camera. What would Spike's idiot *Goon Show* character Eccles have made of that?

My mother's spirit was such that she defied death on a number of occasions, amazing the specialists each time after they'd written her off. 'She's done it again' is all her devoted doctor, Lewis Sevitt, could say.

> This, we are told, is a fight she cannot win,
> she's old, her life's been rich.
> We've heard those lines before,
> it's a script we'd like to ditch.
>
> As always, my father's photo watches
> from her bedside table. A doctor, he'd
> be relieved to see her stable.

A kind nurse adds a little brandy to her drink.
She beams a smile again.
'*Le chayim*' we hear her quietly proclaim.
She calls me by my name.

A toast to life.
The mood's completely changed.
There's talk now of her going home.
She's sitting upright in a chair,
no longer seems deranged.

She looks towards the door. Born in
1914 she knows a thing or two about war,
and will defy them all once more.

I raise an imaginary machine gun to
the sky to let triumphant bullets fly.

Somehow she always managed to do it again – or at least until that sad day in March 2013 when she finally smiled goodbye.

10

IN THE HOT SEAT

It was a hot summer's afternoon and Aldus Books was like a ghost town, with most people on holiday. That was the moment a man named Max Nurock, calling himself the Ambassador of Israel, chose to announce himself. Since there was no one else around in the editorial department that day, it fell to me to receive him. A tall, white-haired man with a slight Irish lilt to his voice, he explained that he had been sent by David Ben-Gurion to discuss the book he was writing for Aldus.

In fact, as I discovered, Ben-Gurion was not so much the author but the overall editor of the book in question, *The Jews in Their Land*, a history of the continuous Jewish settlement in the land of Israel from biblical times to the present. He had conceived the book, was writing the important modern section himself, including the years he was Prime Minister, and had assembled a team of eminent scholars to write the earlier chapters. I knew hardly anything about it, being much too new and lowly to be involved in such a major project, but things were to change as a result of that afternoon's meeting. Had he been there, Douglas Hill would have taken charge, but there was only me and only one thing for it, and that was to see whether Foges was available and willing to receive our visitor. So I plucked up my courage and, having answered Mr Nurock's questions as best I could, I left him in my office, climbed the stairs and was relieved to see Joyce in her usual guardian position outside Foges's half-open door. She went in, explained who I was, explained who Nurock was, told me to go in and explain it all myself, and when I'd hesitantly done that, Foges suddenly bellowed, 'Bring him up!' (Foges never spoke, always bellowed.) He added that I should stay – and that is how I became involved in the Ben-Gurion project, which I was eventually to take charge of, alongside the art editor, Felix Gluck, who was designing what was to be a lavishly illustrated book. A refugee from Hungary, Felix was a person of immense charm and flair, another of those remarkable creatives in the Aldus office. He was a highly sensitive man, unsurprisingly considering he'd been interned by the Germans in the Mauthausen concentration camp, where he'd contracted TB, having to spend two years in a sanatorium in Davos before coming to England. He was also a considerable artist, and his linocuts and pastels on leather have won prizes and been exhibited in galleries around the world.

Listening to the high-pitched conversation between Foges and Nurock, I came to realise that the book was a nightmare of a project which was floundering, since none of the editors Foges had sent to Israel to work on the text – which had been originally written in various languages and badly translated – had got very far. These included a bestselling American author Foges had hauled in at God-knows-what cost in desperation. Thus there was still no agreed text, as Nurock kept pointing out, to Foges's obvious irritation. However, he had the latest version with him, which he handed to Foges, who handed it to me, and suddenly I was in the hot seat.

And hot seat it was, for once I'd read through the draft text I realised what a ticking bomb had landed on my desk. This was Aldus's big project and all eyes were on it – and now on me. The complex problems of the Middle East seemed like nothing compared to this. But slowly, paragraph by paragraph, I waded through the chapters, looking up and double-checking everything in the growing mountain of history and reference books piled up on the floor around me. Unlike my great-grandfather Morris, I was no expert on the Bible, but I was slowly becoming one as I worked my way through it all. What a long and enthralling story it was (or at least should have been), and what a fought-over land, from Canaan and the battles with the Philistines through the various bloody occupations and revolts over the centuries to the tragedies and triumphs of the modern era. Fortunately, Felix Gluck was by my side and determined to make the book visually stunning, approaching it like one possessed, rooting out rare pictorial material, commissioning maps and even at one point (to Foges's fury) persuading (paying!) the Israeli Air Force to take aerial photos for him. If Foges could be uncontrollable, so too could the wayward Felix, and it was inspiring to work with him.

Apart from all this, it was to Felix I turned when Sidgwick & Jackson finally sent me the proofs of my new book of poems along with a mock-up of the jacket. It filled me with alarm since, as I mentioned earlier, I'd called the book *First Poems*. Big mistake, since the Sidgwick designer had assumed it was a book of children's poems and had a picture on the jacket of a little girl in a field holding up a book called *First Poems*! How the editor at Sidgwick had let it go through, I couldn't imagine (although having been in publishing this long, I now can!) but he was full of apologies when I phoned him in panic. He agreed I could change the title to *33 Poems*, and took up Felix's offer to design a new cover. As a result, four of Felix's linocuts now featured on the jacket, and they reflected the mood of those early poems of mine perfectly. I was pleased to be able to return the compliment a few years later, when he asked me to write the preface for a book of exquisite linocuts he had made while in the sanatorium, a touching love story without words, published first in Germany and then posthumously in England under the title *When We Are Together Again*.

By now, Felix and I had become firm friends, and he did his best to shield me from Foges's impatient interventions. It was not a job that could be rushed, for apart from making the text read well in English, it had to be accurate. Although I now seemed to be working day and night on the book and at weekends too, the clock had to stop, if only momentarily, as Carole and I had finally decided to tie the knot. My first port of call with the hot news was the Abse home. Their approval was important! 'How wonderful,' said Dannie (what else could he say?), only to be interrupted by their young son David declaring, 'But Daddy, you said Jeremy was too young to get married.' Not even Joan could cover that one up, and many were the times I reminded Dannie (and David!) about it over the years.

Dear Laurie Lee responded in characteristic style:

Congratulations and welcome to the happy band of those already
under contract. I felt strongly that something was in the air and only
just resisted, when I last wrote to you, asking you, wasn't it about time.
Beautiful Carole, we're lucky to have her signed up for us. There's only
one small uncertainty. I've noticed that footballers' girlfriends turn out
in all weathers to watch their heroes playing, but once married they stay
home and dry. If your marrying Carole means we shall lose her at the
readings I shall create a scene at the wedding.

Laurie's letter ends by thanking me for finding a replacement for him
at a concert in the Birmingham Festival as his wife Cathy was due to
give birth 'that very day', as indeed she did, to a daughter named Jessy,
for whom Laurie wrote a beautiful book called *First Born*, in which he
expresses in fine poetic prose his wonder at the birth. (We were lucky
enough to republish this little classic at Laurie's request shortly before
he died.) Meanwhile, he'd made a typically Laurie suggestion for his
replacement: 'T Blackburn is sure to love Birmingham. He even looks
like B/ham.' On another occasion, when he'd had to cancel through
illness, Laurie wrote, 'I'm out of hospital now and happy to get out of
London before anything worse happens. Medical confusion was such
that I nearly sacked my surgeon and called in Dichter Abse. So you
can tell how bad it was!' I loved getting Laurie's notes, with their dry
humour, but was always sorry when he couldn't make a concert. What I
didn't know then was that Laurie suffered occasional epileptic fits. I once
appeared with him on a television programme from Bristol on which we
both read poems, and during a break in the recording he asked me to
accompany him while he went in search of a chemist, clutching my arm
tightly all the while. It was only much later that I realised why.

* * *

In September 1963, the first of the monthly *Tribune* poetry readings
took place at the Robert Street Library, with Elizabeth Thomas in the

chair and five poets reading. The library was packed, and I was thrilled to see Michael Foot standing at the back. Those CND marches, and his electrifying speeches in Trafalgar Square, were not something one could easily forget. The readings drew more and more people as the word spread and were becoming quite a major feature of London literary life. As Elizabeth reminisced in a letter she sent me some thirty years later:

> I remember very well indeed your coming into my office and suggesting that *Tribune* should try to organise poetry readings – something almost unheard of in those days. If you remember, they went on successfully for about three years and had almost every poet with an established reputation – and a number of newcomers, some good, some awful! A number of poets from overseas came to read there too…

There was indeed a great variety of poets, and there were some memorable moments. I recall Brian Patten wanting to read by candlelight (am I imagining that? I think not), and a quite ill-tempered exchange between Dannie Abse, who'd been reading, and the poet Philip Hobsbaum, who was in the audience. 'But Dannie,' Hobsbaum interrupted at one point. '*Dr Abse* to you,' shot back Dannie – so uncharacteristic of him, he must have been really riled by whatever it was Hobsbaum had said. I remember Joan, ever the peacemaker, trying to calm everyone down afterwards. A recently rediscovered correspondence with the poet Robert Nye, who was then living in north Wales and was to become a bestselling novelist, reminds me that we were both reading on that lively occasion, and I must have been more roused by Hobsbaum's intervention than I remember – maybe in those young days I felt more passionately about things – to judge from the letter I wrote to Nye at the time:

> I must say I admired Dannie for stepping so smartly on what was obviously a personal attack by Hobsbaum. It seems to me remarkable that anyone who writes poems as dull as his should have the audacity to talk like that to someone who writes real poetry. However, that is London

literary life for you … they hate to have anyone around who won't jump into the ring where they crack their particular whips.

Robert agreed, and had been kind enough to invite me to Wales, to which I responded, 'I would like to come back to Wales for a lengthy visit some time, and I envy you the peace and time for writing – though I must say that I may well need the pressures of London to produce the kind of poems of solitariness that I write.' Robert's tempting response was, 'I take your point about London being necessary to you in one sense. Still, come and see me some time. It's very quiet and the land-scape has a curious hanging quality which makes for some inwardness of one's feelings, I find.' He concluded with a reference to the *Tribune* reading: 'I liked some of the poems you read … I feel there's a lot of wildness in you that you really ought to open up. There are few enough now with any wildness at all. Ignore my remarks if they seem to you tactless.' They certainly don't seem to me now at all tactless and must have given me pause for thought at the time, though I'm not sure I've ever released that supposed tiger in my tank.

Much more dramatic than the brief *Tribune* spat which prompted that correspondence was the tour for the Welsh Arts Council that took place later that autumn – three nights, starting at the King's Hall, Aberystwyth, on Friday 22 November 1963, with further concerts at the Brangwyn Hall in Swansea and at the New Theatre, Cardiff, all more or less full houses, and four poets reading – Laurie Lee, Dannie Abse, John Smith and me. John, dapperly dressed and immaculately coiffed, always surprised the audience with his deadpan wit and original approach, and although he was a devotee of classical music he'd quickly responded to Garrick's creative brilliance, writing several long poems specially to be read with jazz ('Mr Smith's Apocalypse' was particularly successful).

We arrived in good time at Aberystwyth, testing the mike and going through a few things before withdrawing in the usual way to the local pub as the audience began to arrive. Then someone shattered the laughter and general bonhomie with the words, 'Kennedy's been shot'. Nobody could quite take it in and we all gathered around a radio as the manager of the hall entered to confirm the news.

The concert was due to start in thirty minutes; the hall was packed. What should we do? A decision had to be made, and the manager made it. We would continue with the concert but would begin with a two-minute silence with us all on stage. We agreed and huddled nervously in the wings, still only half-believing, while the manager marched on stage and made his solemn announcement, bizarrely ending it with the words: 'Now, Laurie Lee and his boys will come on stage and lead the silence…' And Laurie Lee and his boys did just that, and when the electric silence ended the audience unexpectedly burst into applause. They were in a theatrical environment, and in a theatre that is the natural reaction, I suppose. So the memorable concert continued, with cheering after the music and applause after every poem as never before, the audience seeming to find hidden meaning and significance in almost every word. Where were you the night the news of Kennedy's assassination broke? I certainly know where we were.

The night that President Kennedy was shot – the programme cover for that memorable concert.

After that the whole weekend tour was more than a little surreal. On the coach from Aberystwyth to Swansea, Laurie got out a recorder from his case and started to play (perhaps that's why I always thought of him as the Pied Piper). Then, arriving early at the large Brangwyn Hall on Saturday afternoon, with the concert not due to start for several hours, Laurie walked on stage with his violin and began to play Stéphane Grappelli-style jazz. Michael Garrick joined in and Shake Keane, too, on a bass that happened to be lying there. As Laurie launched into a piece called 'Dinah' ('Dinah, is there anyone finer, in the State of Carolina…') he directed his violin towards Carole, wooingly and as though playing especially for her. What a man of mystery and surprises he was, as I was to discover.

Then, after the sell-out Swansea concert, on to Cardiff, Dannie's home town. And next morning the home-town boy appeared at breakfast in the hotel we were all staying at to say that he'd found a pair of blue knickers in his bed, demanding to know who'd put them there. ('Explain *them* to Joan' was our response!) It was some time later that the mischievous Laurie confessed that he was the culprit, though we never discovered where *he* had got them from. So much for the innocent lyrical poet! Cardiff always seemed to produce surprises. On a return visit the following year I remember a very intoxicated Vernon Scannell swaying on stage and Dannie's unworldly mother saying afterwards, 'I think your friend Vernon was a little *shikker*.' The way she used the colourful Yiddish word 'shikker' – which means drunk or tipsy – made it sound as if a naughty Vernon had been taking an illicit sip or two from the sherry bottle. A *little* 'shikker' was definitely not what the unsteady Vernon was that night.

The Ben-Gurion book and the year moved on. My handwriting was all over the manuscript as I struggled to produce an accurate text that flowed and made sense, while keeping as close as possible to the content and spirit of the original. As I finished each chapter we had the text copy-edited, retyped and set, with a view to sending it to the great man early the next year. Foges was getting more and more impatient, chewing on more and more cigars, but I was working flat out and I think he realised that. Typically, he'd found out about the poetry and jazz concerts and, intrigued and a little adventurous, he decided we should give a Christmas concert in the Aldus basement. He'd hire a piano for Michael Garrick and pay everyone (except me!). Michael brought Joe Harriott and Shake Keane with him, and Laurie and Dannie agreed to join me in reading (Laurie writing, 'OK for the Foges Festival'). Our neighbours Arnold Wesker and Beba Lavrin turned up, too. The basement was echoey and noisy, and Foges made the great mistake of laying on far too much drink far too early. It was pretty daunting for me, but somehow we slurred our way through it and the year ended with a bang – mainly in all our heads. Fortunately Vernon wasn't reading that day, and Dannie's mother wasn't there to call us to account.

*   *   *

Looking through my diary, I see there were several concerts at the beginning of 1964, including the St Pancras Arts Festival, and then a gap from May until September before they took off again in earnest. The reason was quite simple – our May wedding, though this was preceded by the publication of my book *33 Poems* and the issue of Argo's two *Poetry and Jazz in Concert* LPs recorded at the Decca studios. Both book and records were received more generously than they perhaps deserved to be – or so it seems now, looking back at them (though I have to say that reviewing the LPs the influential Steve Race was kind enough to write that my poems with jazz 'sound better than anyone else experimenting in the medium'. At the time I was happy to believe him!). But for all my feelings now, the book was an important landmark for me – I was a properly published poet.

I was also about to become a bridegroom, and with Foges huffing down my neck I negotiated a deal with him. Carole and I would go to Israel for our honeymoon and I'd try to see Ben-Gurion and get him to approve the text we'd sent him. Aldus would contribute to the cost of the trip. It seemed fair enough.

I suppose most weddings are like a dream to those involved, and ours too seemed to have a magical quality – Carole wearing a beautiful headpiece and veil made of old lace given to her by her grandmother and looking as if she'd walked straight out of the Bible. The fact that Rabbi Dr Isaac Levy was conducting the ceremony added a further emotional tug to the proceedings. A chaplain to the Forces and among the first to enter the Nazi concentration camps, he was a close friend of both my parents and grandparents, and he spoke with immense personal warmth and passion that day, bringing tears to many eyes (including the bride's). Douglas Hill, always the great romantic, was inspired to write a touching poem called 'Jewish Wedding Ceremony' which brings it all back. It starts:

> Magic in the hand that holds the ring
> utters itself – mingling with the light
> that focuses the consecration…

After the service, there was an afternoon tea hosted by Carole's father, and a jazz party in the evening at my sporting grandparents' home, to which a stream of friends and poets and relatives came. Michael Garrick played, and the saxophonist Tony Coe was among the other musicians. Paddy Milligan sang and then, in the middle of it all, came a touch of comedy when the eccentric Thomas Blackburn, who'd been at the service, phoned to ask me what the stamping on a glass by the bridegroom (which always concludes the Jewish wedding ceremony) symbolised ('the breaking of the hymen, eh Jeremy?'). I got off the phone as quickly as I could and returned to the fray! Then Arnold Wesker appeared with his son and, just when we'd given him up, in walked Laurie in his wellingtons. Carole had sent him a telegram saying simply, 'No Laurie, no wedding', and he had responded to her *cri de coeur*. But missing from the celebrations were Dannie and Joan Abse, who were in America, and so Dannie was unable to read his much-anthologised poem 'Epithalamion' as we'd hoped. Still, some forty years later he more than made up for it by reading it under the chupah (wedding canopy) at our daughter Deborah's wedding to Gareth, whom she had met at law school.

Douglas's poem was gift enough, but he and Gaila also gave us an exquisite piece of pottery, accompanied by this note from Douglas, set out in the shape of a poem:

This is a Hans Coper pot. Hans Coper – a Jew from Germany – lost his loved ones many years ago, but not his capacity to love. He makes his pots with love. Lately the Marlborough Gallery asked Hans to make a pot as a birthday present for Henry Moore. Is there a greater tribute than to be the potter who makes pots for an artist to put flowers in? We give you – with all our love – this vessel to put your flowers in.

That fragile pot (which had become very valuable) sat on a shelf in our living room until, very recently, I came down one morning to find it in several large pieces on the floor. I was as shattered as the pot and I'm now looking for someone skilled enough to put the parts I collected together. It will of course have lost its monetary value, but not its emotional worth as a symbol of a special friendship. The fact that, horrifically, Douglas – that brilliant, sensitive, kind man – was later knocked down and killed by a bus adds even more poignancy.

Tom Blackburn might have brought a touch of the bizarre to the proceedings, but in fact the day had started on a farcical note when the photographer we'd engaged to take photos of Carole in her wedding dress turned up without film for his camera. Having rushed out to buy some, he then went on at length about his broken marriage. A great start to the day! But I went many comedic stages further when we eventually left the party that night and drove to the small bungalow we'd managed to buy in Temple Fortune, having pooled our resources and taken out what seemed like a huge mortgage at the time (I seem to remember that the bungalow cost £5,000). There'd been builders finishing off a few last-minute things, and I'd arranged for them to leave the key under a stone by the front door. Carole waited in the car while I went ahead to open up, but there was no stone and no key. I didn't want to spoil the magic of the evening by admitting this so I went around to the side gate, which luckily was open, and made my way to the back of the bungalow, where there was a small window into the bathroom. Fortunately, the top of the window opened upwards and was ajar, and I reckoned that if I climbed up I could just about lower myself head first through it. What I hadn't counted on was the latch on which my trousers caught, leaving me more or less dangling above the toilet – until there was a loud tear and I went shooting down, cutting myself and almost landing in the toilet bowl. Finally, more than a little shaken, I emerged through the front door, clothes in disarray, blood on my arm, to carry my new wife across the threshold. She had the grace to laugh.

Next stop, Tel Aviv.

11

PROPHET IN THE DESERT

The El Al flight from London had been relatively smooth and un-eventful – unlike my first trip to Israel in the summer of 1959, when with two friends, Anthony Stalbow and Jeremy Morris, I had braved the alarmingly aggressive seas of the Bay of Biscay in a small old Turkish ship, sailing from Marseilles to Haifa. On that occasion I had celebrated my 21st birthday there; this time it was my honeymoon, though of course a certain amount of work was on the agenda.

It was to be Carole's first time in Israel, and I was excited at the prospect of introducing her to this enthralling country which I'd trav-elled all over in Egged buses, from the kibbutzim in the north to Eilat (then a shanty town) in the south, where I slept on the beach. I had stayed then in a small room in Tel Aviv, which, as I was soon to discov-er, was just around the corner from Ben-Gurion's residence in the city.

Now here I was with my new bride, going through the security and formalities at Tel Aviv's Ben-Gurion Airport, and as we came out into the forecourt with our luggage I was thrilled to find an old family friend, Professor Moshe Brawer, waiting to greet us. A world-renowned geographer and an authority on political boundaries, Moshe and his delightful wife Rina had held their wedding recep-tion at my parents' house. He'd met them in 1945 when working as a war correspondent in London for various Palestinian papers and completing his studies at King's College and LSE. I was intrigued to learn later that he had shown Arthur Koestler (author of the classic *Darkness at Noon*) around Israel on his first visit there in 1944 and introduced him to various leading Arab figures with whom he had close contacts.

Although he and Carole had not met until then, within minutes they were like old friends, Carole relishing the running commentary we were getting from this most erudite of guides as he drove us to the Validor Hotel in Herzliya, the coastal resort on the outskirts of Tel Aviv where we were staying. If anyone could find the way there, he was the man! As Moshe left us in the hotel reception, he promised to be in touch the next day to discuss plans. Ever generous with his time, he wanted to make sure we – and Carole in particular – saw as much of the country as possible. But for the moment, finally, we were alone, tired but exhilarated. We had been given a spacious room with a view towards the sea, and were admiring the flowers and reading the congratulatory cards kind Israeli friends had sent us, beginning to relax, when the phone rang.

'This is Ben-Gurion,' a voice rasped.

My immediate thought was that it was a prank, and for a few moments I prevaricated, wondering which of our friends it was, trying to place the voice. But slowly it dawned on me that it was no joke and that Ben-Gurion really was on the line. I had expected one of his aides to contact me at some stage to set up a meeting, but not B-G himself, and not so soon nor so urgently. I quickly changed my tone!

'Come to my kibbutz at half past ten tomorrow morning,' the voice continued, and only when the phone went down did I take in that this was the meeting I'd been trying to arrange from London for weeks. Sde Boker, the kibbutz in question, was in the Negev desert in southern Israel, a little over a hundred miles from where we were staying and where we'd planned to spend a few days relaxing on the beach, seeing friends and travelling around before dealing with the book. At that moment Sde Boker could have been on the moon, it seemed so remote and the prospect of going there so unreal.

As things came back into focus, I realised that there was only one way to get there early the following morning, and that was by car. After a few minutes of panic and confusion and a quick look at a map, Carole phoned down and asked the bemused concierge to arrange for a car and driver to collect us at 6 a.m. After all, I was working for a man who never considered expense to be an obstacle to anything, and who had already spent a fortune on the book, including the commissioning of a special cover by the celebrated American artist Ben Shahn. I tried to remember that as we ordered the car. For the moment it seemed our honeymoon was on hold.

Sde Boker had been founded in 1952, and B-G had gone to live there a year later when he resigned from office. Even when he returned to politics in 1955 he continued to keep his home there, and that is where he and his wife Paula are now buried. It was part of his vision of cultivating the desert, and he believed in leading by example. As he wrote, 'It is by mastering nature that man learns to control himself.' He felt the desert was an uninhabited area where new immigrants could settle and flourish.

A young David Ben-Gurion, with his wife Paula, his father and three children.

The drive itself, let alone the thought of the coming encounter, was wondrous enough, taking us directly south into the desert, past the biblical town of Beersheba. What an introduction to Israel this was for Carole, especially as the landscape and the Bedouins we encountered when we stopped at a roadside café for a drink, and the camels that milled around, reminded her of her childhood in Egypt and the small summer house her parents had in the desert, where she used to invite her school friends to stay. As for me, I had been slowly coming to terms with the thought that we were about to meet the great prophet

of modern Israel, the man who had tilled the land when he came from
Russia as an idealistic youngster and who had gone on to lead his
country to independence and then through the desperate war that followed, and on – for being voted statehood by the United Nations was
one thing, securing it when surrounded by hostile forces quite another.

Thus it was with apprehension that I sat clutching my copy of the
revised manuscript as the car slowly entered the gates of the kibbutz
and the driver explained to the guards on duty who we were. We were
obviously expected and they quickly waved us towards the small,
bungalow-like building where B-G lived. There were soldiers with
rifles outside the door, and I realised that they were puzzled by the fact
that I wasn't alone, so I quickly explained that we had just got married
and were in effect on our honeymoon – and naturally I wasn't going
to leave my new wife back at the hotel. One of the guards went inside
and returned a moment later to say that Mr Ben-Gurion wanted both
of us to come in, which of course is what I'd hoped, though Carole was
a little reticent, not wishing to intrude.

David Ben-Gurion was seated behind a large wooden desk but
rose immediately as we entered, walking towards us and pointing in a
friendly way to some comfortable chairs, where he joined us. Smaller
than I had expected, but with the white flaring hair I'd seen in hundreds of photos, his eyes sparkling beneath a broad forehead, he looked
very much the biblical prophet. I thought of all the liberties I'd taken
with the text and waited for the explosion. It didn't come. On the
contrary, B-G put us at our ease, wishing us *Mazal Tov* and offering us
a glass of brandy to toast our wedding, which we happily accepted. He
raised his glass and said, '*Le chaim.*' He didn't seem to be in a hurry to
discuss the text I'd sent him, but instead turned his attention to Carole.
'Where do you come from?' he asked, and when she told him she was
born in Egypt, he responded, 'Ah, the land of Moses.' He then began
to talk to her at length, reminiscing about his own childhood and his
early days in the Land, as he called the country he had done so much
to create – the early hardships, the malarial swamps, the good relationship they had then with their Arab neighbours, the first settlements,
the importance of creating Hebrew as a modern, spoken language so

that all who came, from whatever country, would be bonded by it. As he spoke I remembered reading how impressed the then British Prime Minister, David Lloyd George, had been when B-G told him in London how Hebrew was being revived as a spoken language. Here was history talking, and I had to pinch myself to make sure I wasn't dreaming. After a while, B-G paused and looked down at Carole's glittery sandals, asking if she had bought them in England. 'Yes,' she replied, 'do you like them?' 'Well, not really,' he responded with a gleam in his eye, 'but I'm afraid my daughter would!' Suddenly he seemed like a cuddly grandfather!

With a pause in the conversation, I seized my chance and asked B-G if he'd found time to go through the proofs I'd sent him and to consider my changes and queries. 'Yes,' he said, handing me the proofs. 'I've been through them and made a few corrections, but your English is better than mine. Let's go and have lunch.' And that, as far as the text went, was more or less that, and off we went to the kibbutz dining room, which was soon full and buzzing with conversation as the members came in from their morning labours under the blistering sun. I still have those proofs with his handwritten corrections, and looking at them now I'm reminded that the only thing that seemed to worry him in the earlier biblical chapters was the use of the word 'Palestine', which he had changed either to 'Canaan' or to 'The Land'. Otherwise there was hardly anything. Ben-Gurion was kindness itself, and when I explained that we had tried without success to persuade his country's President to write a foreword, he offered to contact Zalman Shazar himself, which he did, arranging for us to go the following week to the President's office in Jerusalem. There we were warmly received by Shazar, who explained that he received many requests to write forewords, often from friends, and that he always refused because he felt that in his position he should remain neutral; also that if he did it for one, he'd have to do it for all. But Ben-Gurion was Ben-Gurion, he continued, and the book was an important one, so yes, he would do it. A few days later I had a phone call at the hotel to say it was ready and we collected it.

Keen to know our plans, and eagerly making suggestions, B-G had invited us to visit him in his home in Tel Aviv, where he intended to be the following week, and of course we were delighted to take him up on this offer, easily identifying the modest building on what is now Ben-Gurion Boulevard, close to the sea, by the guards outside. Once again we were expected and given a warm reception by B-G in his small, book-lined study, which must have been the setting for many history-making meetings and confrontations.

That I had experienced such an easy passage when others before me had failed was not so much the testament to my editorial skills I'd have liked to imagine, but due to the simple fact that B-G's notoriously difficult and outspoken wife Paula had broken her leg and was out of the way in hospital. She it was who'd sent packing the writers and editors and the bestselling American novelist who had gone before me, so now here was Ben-Gurion on his own, glad of the company and ready to help in any way he could. As it happens, Paula was to resurface in my life in another context some five years later, after I had left Aldus Books and gone to work as an editor at Vallentine, Mitchell. There, I published a collection of the letters Ben-Gurion had sent to his young wife in the years between the two world wars when he was away from home, travelling the globe as the political struggle to establish a Jewish homeland was at its height. Beginning in 1918 when, newly married, he was a soldier in the Jewish Legion attached to the British Army, *Letters to Paula* offers a remarkably human and eye-opening first-hand account of his meetings with world leaders. History indeed, and we had been privileged to spend our honeymoon (or part of it!) with the man who had been so central to it.

*   *   *

The staff at our hotel in Herzliya must have wondered about us, what with phone calls from B-G, the President's office and Professor Moshe Brawer, who would call for us and drive us to different parts of the country, including the Dead Sea, the lowest place on earth, where amidst the lunar landscape we had a memorable dip in the deepest hypersaline lake in the world, in which it is hardly possible to swim and impossible to sink (Moshe added a touch of comedy by hiring a black bathing costume that turned out to be several sizes too big and made him look like Charlie Chaplin). We also received calls from another Moshe – Moshe Sharett, Israel's first Foreign Minister and Ben-Gurion's successor as Prime Minister. Sharett and his wife Zipporah were long-standing friends of my parents and grandparents – in fact, we all felt he had a rather soft spot for my mother Charlotte (and she for him). An intellectual with a lawyer's mind, he too had played a crucial role in the state's creation, and had been deeply involved in all the behind-the-scenes negotiations with the various diplomats whose support was vital. Those talks were often acrimonious in the extreme, particularly with Ernest Bevin, Britain's Foreign Secretary, who was no lover of Jews, and Moshe would arrive for Shabbat lunch at my grandparents' house, where he always came when in London, still white with anger. My father also looked after him medically from time to time, calling to see him at the ambassador's residence where he stayed.

Carole enjoys lunch with Moshe and Zipporah Sharett.

Thus the Sharetts, wanting to celebrate our wedding, invited us to lunch at the Acadia Hotel by the sea, and later to tea at their home, and while I don't have any photos with Ben-Gurion at Sde Boker, I do have a rather grainy one of Carole and the Sharetts at lunch. In later years, Moshe Sharett sent me kind comments about poems of mine he'd read, and often asked us to talks he was giving when in London.

One letter I cherish was written much earlier, in September 1947, when I was about eight and Sharett was flying back from the United Nations. Imagine the importance of the meetings he'd been attending at this key moment in the diplomatic struggle for a Jewish state, and yet he still had time to write an encouraging letter to a young boy. The handwritten note starts:

> I am writing you this letter from over the Atlantic Ocean in the middle of the night. The moon shines very brightly so I can see through the window the vast area of dark water and the little white clouds floating over it and beneath our plane. I am sorry I cannot stop in London. I am flying home for one week only and then will fly back to New York where I still have much work to do.

I remember an occasion some years later at my parents' home when he was asked how things were in Israel and, ever the diplomat, he replied, 'It all depends on whether you want the optimistic or pessimistic answer. The pessimist would say, "They are good, but very, very hard," while the optimist would say, "They are hard, but very, very good."'

Sharett and Ben-Gurion could not have been more opposite in character or approach – B-G the firebrand leader, Sharett more cerebral, more cautious – and it is not surprising that they eventually fell out. Yet in all the key years they were a team, both fighting – along with Chaim Weizmann and others – to create a state out of the ashes of the Holocaust, and in many of the photos of those times they are side by side, as at the United Nations when the vote for statehood was taken, and again at the Tel Aviv Museum on 14 May 1948 when the Declaration of Independence was signed and proclaimed, and the state was born.

The remarkable land of Israel has produced many miracles, but for me, returning home with Ben-Gurion's signed-off proofs and President Shazar's foreword counts as one of them, and the fact that Foges had cabled to say he was impressed was perhaps equally remarkable. It certainly never happened again in my seven-year stay at Aldus!

*   *   *

That was not quite the end of the Ben-Gurion saga, and I was to meet him again – twice in London, and a couple of years later in Israel. The first of these meetings, the year before the book was published, was at the Savoy Hotel in 1965, when B-G came to London with President Shazar to attend Winston Churchill's state funeral on 30 January at St Paul's Cathedral. Since this fell on a Saturday, both men felt that as representatives of their country they should follow Orthodox Jewish observance and refrain from taking transport on the Sabbath, so despite their age they walked from their hotel to St Paul's, determined to pay their respects to a man they had admired and who had proved a true friend of Israel. I recently saw a film of the funeral, and there on the steps of St Paul's was a very lively Ben-Gurion, and behind him the haughty and aloof figure of General de Gaulle – two proud men who, like the man they were honouring, knew what it meant to fight for their country.

Never one to miss an opportunity, Foges arranged to see B-G at the Savoy, and Felix Gluck and I were to go with him. Even more agitated than usual on such occasions, Foges seemed in no hurry to leave his office, bellowing at Felix when he bravely ventured in to remind him of the time: 'Felix, this is not a coffee shop!' followed by words I have long cherished: 'He is only the author.'

Only the author or not, Foges was certainly respectful when we did finally arrive at the Savoy, but he seemed to get nowhere in his attempts to interest B-G in writing a book about the Prophets, even though he excitedly said he planned to get Kokoschka to illustrate it. Perhaps his muddled English muddled B-G's understanding of what he was proposing, or perhaps B-G had not heard of the great Austrian artist who was to illustrate whatever book Foges was trying to persuade him to write. 'I know Marks,' a bewildered Ben-Gurion finally declared, 'but show me Spencer.' And that was the end of that little encounter.

Ben-Gurion did return, however, the following April for the launch of his book at a reception at the Aldus office, arriving with the Israeli ambassador, staying for a couple of hours and talking affably to the various journalists we'd invited. This was followed by lunch in a private room at the White Tower. Although I wasn't privy to the figures, and given the complexity of Foges's international dealings would probably not have made head nor tail of them anyway, it was obvious that he had spent a king's ransom on the book – on one loud occasion he was heard in the Aldus lobby complaining bitterly about it to George Weidenfeld (who in turn responded volubly about *his* Ben-Gurion book). Nevertheless, the book was published by Doubleday in America and in many languages and editions throughout the world, so appeared to be a success.

At the press launch for his epic book, B-G signs my copy... finally.

But whatever the bottom line, it didn't stop Foges sending me to Israel again in August 1968 to try to get the rights to a two-volume history of the Jews he'd heard B-G was working on with the Israeli publisher Am Oved. After being given the run-around for a few days, I finally tracked down a still-friendly B-G to a hotel in Haifa, where he told me he had hidden himself away to write in peace. I had three meetings with him there, trying to get some kind of outline for Foges to take to the Frankfurt Book Fair. Ben-Gurion was not proving as easy to pin down on this occasion (he was, after all, a master politician) and Foges, straining at the leash in London, began bombarding us both with telexes, which didn't really help. The last one ended: 'If no outline exists in English, if you spend an hour with Robson going through the Hebrew text with him he will be able to write the paper for me.'

What a nightmare scenario that would have been, but fortunately for me it never came to that, as I had a sudden breakthrough at our final meeting, which I managed to get his Israeli editor to attend. The upshot was that Ben-Gurion finally said he was willing to let Aldus have all rights for an illustrated edition of the book, subject to the same conditions (whatever they were) as for *The Jews in Their Land*, and he even proposed drawing up a contract there and then with the help of a lawyer so that all the formalities could be completed before I left Israel.

Now it was my turn to prevaricate, since of course I wasn't in a position to agree, let alone sign a contract, and I explained that only Foges could do this and that I really needed a full outline of the book to take back to London. Suddenly seeing the sense of this, B-G asked the Am Oved editor to prepare it for me and I received a copy in Hebrew just a few hours before leaving.

After all that, Aldus never published the book, perhaps because Foges failed to get the international support and underwriting he hoped for at Frankfurt, or because something else had excited his interest – a pity, since B-G liked and had confidence in him, more so than in any of his other British publishers, he told me. That was perhaps a misjudgement, because in 1972, some three years after I'd left Aldus, Foges got in touch in his usual urgent way and said he wanted me to update Ben-Gurion's own final chapter in *The Jews in Their Land*, taking in the Six Day War of 1967. Of course, it wasn't as straightforward as that (with Foges things never were), as became clear when Frame-Smith wrote to me explaining that Doubleday wanted a special, cheaper edition of the book for the American gift market, and that to make the costings work they needed to cut forty pages from the book (after taking in the new material). What made it difficult was that they wanted all the cuts to come from the end of the book so as to avoid as much re-setting and re-designing as possible.

In short, they were looking to me to 'telescope' B-G's 100-page chapter while at the same time adding – and all in his name. Ben-Gurion's ghost! That made me uneasy, and I hesitated, since I felt Foges should get B-G's permission or at least show him the revised text. I was given an undertaking that he would (I had it in writing, along with an assurance that my name would not be mentioned), and on that basis I went ahead with what turned out to be an extremely tricky and time-consuming assignment. One particular section really needed to be cut for reasons of space but I felt B-G might well be unhappy about it. I flagged it and left it to the in-house Aldus editor to decide. Rather amusingly, he wrote in his report, 'So, do we let a conscientious and sensitive editor override an honoured elder statesman, or vice versa?' I'm ashamed to say the editor got the vote.

In the light of this, I was relieved my name was being kept out of it, for I've always wondered whether, despite all his promises and assurances, Foges ever sought Ben-Gurion's approval, or even let him know what was happening. I have my doubts. But then, after all, B-G was only the author.

12

SEPTEMBER COHEN

I knew that Douglas Hill had been thinking of leaving Aldus Books, but waiting for us when we got home from Israel was a letter saying that he'd done the deed – a characteristically wry missive. Aldus would not be the same without Douglas, so I didn't have much of a spring in my step that first Monday morning back as I squeezed onto the crowded Northern Line train to Warren Street, the heat and mystery of the Negev desert and the spectacular beauty of Galilee a fading myth. Stepping out of the station there were

> Two ways to choose
> and today I go left –
> past the confectioners,
> skirting the roadworks,
> quick quick slow past the Tower,
> nodding to the newspaperman
> clutching his dailies.
> Today I take *The Times…*

Returning hero I might have been for a few days, but after putting the final touches to the Ben-Gurion text I was quickly thrown into two new projects. First, though, while the iron was hot, I had my own negotiations to pursue, and these resulted in a raise of £400 per annum and my promotion to a fully fledged editor. Instead of Douglas I would be working with the dry-witted Roy Gasson, who in addition to his editorial skills did a spot-on imitation of Foges.

Towards the end of 1964, the poetry and jazz concerts began again in earnest and so did Foges, with a major project. I was charged with editing, and Felix with the art direction and design. *The World of Marc Chagall* was indeed a huge undertaking and once again money was no object, for it was to show the celebrated Russian artist as never before through a spectacular combination of specially commissioned photographs of him at work, an in-depth analysis of his work by the American author and critic Roy McMullen and, throughout, reproductions of some of Chagall's finest paintings. The chosen photographer, Izis Bidermanas, was considered one of Europe's best and most poetic. A member of the French Resistance, Izis had become Chagall's Boswell ever since he'd met him on an assignment for *Paris Match* in 1950. Some of his stunning photographic sequences for the book showed Chagall in the process of creating the murals for the Metropolitan Opera House in New York, the ceiling of the Paris Opera House, the tapestries for Israel's Parliament and the scenery for the ballet *Daphnis and Chloë*.

Without Chagall's cooperation the project would not have been possible, and his only concern was that the reproduction of his work should be of the highest quality, a challenge Foges responded to by going to the most expensive printer in Switzerland. No problem there. Although Felix and I were in charge of the design and text, the overall editor was the head of the Doubleday office in Paris, Beverly Gordey. A chic, savvy, highly cultured lady, Beverly was married to Michel Gordey, one of France's most distinguished foreign correspondents. Like Chagall, he was born in Russia and there were evidently family ties which had helped bring the book about. Beverly's involvement (and no doubt Doubleday's) was crucial as she seemed to have a hot-line to Chagall. She was one of the few people to whose judgement Foges would generally defer. We became good friends, and her son Serge worked for a few months in the Robson Books office when we first opened our doors.

In all Foges's projects, it always seemed to be the text that proved troublesome. McMullen, who lived in Paris, had written several excellent biographies of major artists, but one of his chapters seemed inadequate – that on Chagall's Hasidism (the Jewish mystical movement dating back to the eighteenth century) – and in one of his high-octave moments Foges turned to me and commanded, 'Jeremy, get me an expert on Hasidism!' Luckily, Carole had recently started work as a secretary in the offices of the Liberal Synagogue, so I phoned her for help, and after making enquiries she came back with the name of Rabbi Dr Albert Friedlander. There could not have been a better recommendation. Friedlander readily agreed to come to the Aldus office next day, where, erudite and articulate, he held the meeting in thrall as he delivered an impromptu lecture on the Hasidic movement, answering Foges's provocative questions with great intellectual panache. Foges was impressed (so much so that he forgot to throw his usual 'What is a Jew?' question at him), and wanted to take him and me to lunch. 'Ask him if it has to be kosher,' he whispered to me loudly, 'or will the White Tower be all right.' It didn't take the good rabbi long to decide, and off we went to the sophisticated White Tower. Friedlander's widow Evelyn laughed when I told her the restaurant story recently – she knew only too well which her husband would have chosen! We'd become friends with them over the years. Albert was not only the highly respected rabbi of a loyal congregation, he was also a scholarly writer with strong literary interests and it was at his house one Friday night that we were privileged to meet the legendary poet Paul Celan, whose percussive poem 'Death Fugue' is one of the great poems of the Holocaust. Celan was a handsome, charismatic man with piercing eyes who, though born in Romania, wrote in German. It was heartbreaking to learn in April 1970, a few years after our meeting him, that having survived the Nazi camps (where both his parents died), Celan had drowned himself in the Seine. One cannot begin to imagine what demons had continued to invade him after he returned to the living. 'There is nothing in the world for which a poet will give up writing,' he once wrote, 'even if the language of his poems is German.' Such haunting and inspiring words.

Eventually, inevitably, Foges began to lose patience with Roy

McMullen, who was running late and failing to deliver the goods. Beverly Gordey too was growing increasingly testy. Just as inevitably, Foges turned to me and commanded, 'Jeremy, go to Paris and don't come back until the text is completed.' Well, there are worse places to be dispatched to, and I arranged for Carole, who was still working full time, to join me at the weekends, and off I went to do battle with the unsuspecting author. Beverly Gordey was welcoming, and the first thing she told me was to check out of the cheap hotel I'd booked on the Left Bank where I'd stayed in my bachelor days. 'Foges spends more on cigars in a day than you're spending in a week, so for goodness' sake find somewhere decent to stay!' The meetings we had with McMullen in Beverly's flat in the Rue de Savoie were often tense. It became clear that when riled she was not a woman to cross. Strangely, it was in Montparnasse, on my way back from one of these meetings, that I bumped into my old schoolmate Michael Kustow, who was with a group of French actors, and I joined them for a drink. At the time he was working with the French playwright and director Roger Planchon. It was a welcome interlude.

But I had work to do and saw the author most days, getting him to pass me the text to edit almost as it came off his typewriter. Eventually I was able to return to London with a complete manuscript, to everyone's relief. Meanwhile, Felix had been working on the photographs with Izis and gathering the pictorial material. As everything started to come together, I began creating extensive captions and to draw in quotes from Chagall to add more of his voice to the book. I had only one real problem – Madame Chagall, the artist's second wife, Vava, who wanted all references to his first wife, Bella, removed from the index. This was preposterous, since it was Bella who hovered with the young Chagall in the dreamy blue skies above their native Vitebsk in some of the artist's best-known early paintings. But Chagall, it seemed, was not inclined to take up arms against a sea of marital troubles, so Bella's name had to be removed. At least Vava had not asked for her to be airbrushed out of those magical images of the two eternally youthful lovers!

* * *

It was now 1965, and I was relieved to have broken the back of the Chagall book as a series of poetry and jazz concerts loomed. The one in September – our second at the Theatre Royal, Stratford East (Joan Littlewood's theatre) – was memorable for the fact that both Ted Hughes and Stevie Smith were reading for the first time, along with Dannie, Douglas Hill and me, with Michael Garrick's Quintet augmented for the occasion by Tony Coe (with Coleridge Goode on bass, and percussionist Colin Barnes). I'm amused to see that in the flyer put out by the theatre, Douglas is called 'a young poet from Canada' and Dannie and me 'old stagers'. I recall that *The Observer*'s influential poetry critic Al Alvarez came with Ted that night. It was an electrifying concert and I managed to capture it on my very basic tape recorder – the recording now a collector's item which I copied for Ted's widow Carol quite recently. Given Ted's passion for classical music, Beethoven especially, she seemed surprised that Ted had readily participated, and indeed I had wondered myself how he would react to the whole scenario, particularly to the jazz. I was relieved to receive a friendly and positive letter from him saying, 'Thanks for the reading the other night, I enjoyed it all very much indeed.' Furthermore, he went on to suggest that I approach the head of the English department at Exeter University, Professor Moelwyn Merchant, who, Ted said, was 'very wide awake and new and determined to get some fresh air into the university'. He also suggested that I write to Clifford Fishwick, the head of the College of Art at Exeter, who 'tries to get all the lectures, readings, etc. that he can for his students'. Following the Theatre Royal reading, it was also gratifying to receive a note from Stevie Smith saying, 'I did enjoy it very much', and being complimentary about the whole 'splendid programme'. She was only sorry she'd been 'unable to go off to the Chinese restaurant as Ted suggested', and concluded by sending her best wishes and thanks to Carole 'for transporting [her] so kindly like'. She had added greatly to the evening's success, singing and chanting her way through her vivid poems, including the famous 'Not Waving but Drowning'.

In another letter written in light-hearted vein shortly after that concert, Ted asked me – referring to the magazine which he founded in 1965 with Daniel Weissbort and co-edited with him – 'Would you be interested in distributing or getting some stunning juvenile beauty to distribute for 2/6 per copy our *Modern Poetry in Translation*? Copy enclosed. The second edition – French – is out on Friday. You could keep 6d per copy. It's easy to sell, at 2/6, and your concerts would be just the place.'

Among the other contacts Ted gave me was Rolle College in Exmouth, where if I had any luck I was to tell him 'and I'll give you two more names in Cornwall', his idea being that we should try to arrange a tour, to make it economical. Naturally I was grateful for his enthusiastic interest and quickly followed up his suggestions, but while I had an encouraging exchange of letters with Moelwyn Merchant, he was never able to get the necessary financial support from the university. However, we struck lucky with Rolle College, where two readings were arranged for a Saturday and Sunday the following March, Ted readily agreeing to read at both. They were to prove memorable in several ways.

Meanwhile, the Belfast Festival was our next port of call, with a concert at Queen's College. Everyone had flown there except Joe Harriott, who'd opted to go by sea, and the next morning we found him sitting disconsolately in the hotel lobby. He'd been to the port, where massive waves were making it impossible for ships to leave the harbour and all sailings had been cancelled. Joe had already suffered the terrors of a storm on the way out, arriving late and shaken as a result. We offered to try to get him on our plane, but he wouldn't fly. Yet the night before, there was no end to his daring as he threw himself into solos that had the audience on the edge of their seats.

For some time I had been involved with an international poetry magazine in Geneva called *Poésie Vivante*, advising the editors on British poets they should look out for. They had invited me to compile an anthology of up-and-coming British poets for their *Cahiers Franco-Anglais* series, which entailed selecting and writing to the various poets, but also corresponding with both Rosemary Marie, who ran the English side of things, and Jean-Jacques Celly, who was doing the translations. The attractive little book, a paperback, featured sixteen poets, and as well as drawing on books and pamphlets I was excited to get some unpublished poems too, especially from Seamus Heaney, who sent me a few he'd written since handing in his forthcoming first book, *Death of a Naturalist*. He asked me to excuse his 'atrocious' typing and said that if they weren't 'up to scratch' he'd send me more. They most certainly were up to scratch. (Earlier, he'd sent me *Eleven Poems*, a pamphlet containing some of the wonderful *Naturalist* poems – now, modestly, he was saying he was glad 'they hadn't put [me] off'.)

As all the poems were to appear in both English and French, most of the poets were concerned about the accuracy of the translation. To some extent I found myself drawn in, discussing meanings and nuances with the translator, all too aware of the famous mistranslation of the opening line of Eliot's 'Journey of the Magi', which begins: 'A cold coming we had of it' and which was interpreted as 'They had a cold coming'. I don't believe we committed any sins as cardinal as that!

*   *   *

Douglas Hill was still in Canada, finishing a book on the supernatural and writing another, *The Opening of the Canadian West*. He was also compiling several science fiction anthologies for Sonny Mehta, who was then working as an adviser on science fiction for Rupert Hart-Davis, and was shortly to start the Paladin imprint for Granada Publishing, before moving to Pan Books a few years later. It was in Douglas and Gaila's flat that I first met the handsome and hugely gifted Sonny, who was to become a major force in American publishing. At that stage, Douglas hadn't yet started to write the series of sci-fi novels that were to make his name, but he had discovered a 'remarkable young Canadian poet called Leonard Cohen'. He asked me to find out whether any of Cohen's books of poems or any of his novels had been published in England, ''cos if not I'm going to try to grab him; he's a wild man, way out, and funny and dangerous. He's also very beautiful in a soulful way that presumably grabs the heartstrings and other anatomical parts of women.' A great many years later, after I'd joined up with another company, I had the opportunity to 'grab' two of Cohen's books myself but was outvoted by people who thought there wasn't sufficient interest in him. I gnashed my teeth as some months later I sat in the O2 Centre amidst a vast cheering audience of Cohen fans.

I too became an instant Leonard Cohen fan (though maybe not as fanatical a one as my mother some forty years later) when Douglas went on to describe a TV programme he'd watched in which Cohen was interviewed by a very prissy woman who kept prodding him about his Jewishness:

'I've often thought of changing my name,' Cohen eventually conceded. The interviewer perked up and said, 'Really, to what?' 'Oh,' said Cohen, looking innocent, 'I think September.' 'September?' she said, incredulous. 'Isn't that pretty unusual?' 'No,' Cohen continued, still innocent. 'It's very common. September, once a year, very familiar.' The interviewer blinked. 'Leonard September?' she said, testing its sound. 'No, no,' he said. 'You've got it wrong. September Cohen.'

Douglas had missed the next ten minutes of the programme through laughing at the expression on the interviewer's face, 'a superb combination of distress (at the assumption that he wanted to lose his Jewish name) and anger at the delicacy with which he'd trapped her and showed her up on her own programme'.

By now Foges and I were on relatively friendly terms and Carole and I were invited to several parties at his Hampstead home, where we met his charming and elegant wife Catherine and their son Peter, who would become a successful film producer in America. Foges was always at his restless worst on such occasions, though welcoming. It seemed I'd earned my spurs, if not yet the salary I felt I now deserved. I think Foges liked parties in a strange kind of way, and occasionally he'd try to let his hair down and even make uncharacteristic attempts to please his staff, which is why, one July day, we all found ourselves invited on a trip down the Thames on a boat that seemed wider than the river, where he joined in a hearty rendering of 'Lili Marlene' (just the song for a summer cruise down the oh-so-English Thames).

Pipe in hand, Wolfgang Foges leads a chorus of 'Lili Marlene' on the Aldus boat outing on the Thames.

With Ben-Gurion published and Chagall more or less completed, I
wondered what Foges's next demanding extravaganza would be, while,
as 1967 unfolded, the poetry and jazz concerts (and the poems and
reviews) continued at an intense pace, with about forty around the
country in sixteen months. In March 1967, the Rolle College concerts
brought Ted back into the fold, and he turned up with a strikingly
beautiful woman, 'tall and slender, sooty-haired with startling eyes', as
Dannie Abse recalled, whom he introduced simply as 'Assia'. (I could
not have imagined then the dramatic role Assia Wevill was to play in
Ted's life – nor, of course, the tragic consequences.) It was a strange
reading, largely because the college authorities were clearly suspicious
of us. On no account could the grand piano in the hall be used; another
had to be brought in. In fact, despite Ted's presence in the line-up
(Dannie and Vernon Scannell were the other readers), official support was withheld until the last minute, when it was realised that both
concerts were virtually sold out. The audience listened intently to the
poems we read and applauded the jazz loudly. Afterwards almost every
book on the table was sold. The principal of the college, who had decided at the last moment to attend, exclaimed of the jazz, 'Why, it's like
chamber music!' She was surprised that it was organised, disciplined
and melodious, and bought two LPs. Later, in the bar, a tipsy young
man tried hard to provoke Vernon – the ex-professional boxer – into a

fight. It was his luck that Vernon managed to brush him off without a punch being thrown.

I imagine the principal came to the concert out of courtesy or duty rather than for the poetry. The students might have come for the jazz or because they were curious, but as the classically inclined John Heath-Stubbs put it when he ventured tentatively into our midst, 'It doesn't really matter why they come as long as they come.'

13

SIX DAYS IN JUNE

1967. A date that for me always means the Six Day War, the beginning of a special friendship with the Israeli novelist Hanoch Bartov (at that time his country's cultural attaché to Britain), and the editing of a book that would eventually lead to a new job. Since the war and the events surrounding it indirectly affected my own story in unexpected ways, I feel I should recall it all as I saw it then, for, like most people who cared about Israel's future existence (and not just Jews), I was alarmed, as it really looked as if that tiny country would be swept away by the combined forces of the Arab armies massing on its various borders. We were frightened, and the spectre of the Holocaust still hovered in many minds.

The fuse that ignited it all was President Nasser's demand that the UN withdraw its peacekeeping forces from Egypt's border with Israel, following this up with the closure of the Straits of Tiran to Israel's shipping. After that, things escalated as King Hussein of Jordan placed his troops under Egyptian control, Nasser declaring, 'Our basic aim is the destruction of Israel.' When troops from Algeria and Kuwait arrived in Egypt, and Saudi Arabia and Iraq joined with Jordan's Foreign Legion, from Israel's point of view the situation could not have been more grave. Suddenly it found itself facing 900 tanks deployed in Sinai, 200 of them poised to attack Eilat and cut off the Southern Negev, and 50,000 troops dug in on the steep Golan Heights overlooking the villages and kibbutzim of Galilee, their positions fortified by concrete and steel. The vultures were circling.

Israel called up its reservists, and Moshe Dayan, the cavalier Israeli general who had lost an eye fighting for the British in Syria during the Second World War, was brought into the government as Minister of Defence. Gas masks were distributed, shelters made ready, everyone was on high alert, and there were chilling reports that in Tel Aviv mass graves were being dug in the night and consecrated by rabbis, which moved me to write a poem called 'The Rabbis' Prayers', which was widely published at the time. It begins:

> They say that in the night
> you stole your way to parks
> and public spaces to consecrate
> ground for the ritual burial
> of your people: that when the
> catches on the guns snapped back
> and eyes, Belsen-red, gazed
> down the unfamiliar barrels, you
> called upon an ancient God
> who some say heard you.

It was a matter of life and death, and in Britain Jewish writers, feeling that they had to do something – anything – came together under the enlightened chairmanship of the director, writer and historian Louis Marks in a group calling itself Writers for Israel. It was at one of these meetings that I met Hanoch Bartov. We all loved him. Warm, vitally intelligent and a fine writer who had fought in Europe under the British (his book *The Brigade* is a classic), he galvanised us and brought us what up-to-date information he could. At that time the press was generally sympathetic to Israel's plight and letters poured into the embassy, mostly from non-Jews, some offering to fight, some offering their services as doctors and nurses and ambulance drivers, or simply expressing their sympathy. It was a terrible time and we all sat glued to the radio, fearing the dreadful news we might hear. But what could we do except write letters, protest, use every means possible to highlight the situation, as many others did?

The Israeli novelist Hanoch Bartov, who was to affect my publishing career in a very real way.

You had to be blind in both eyes not to see the perilous military situation as it was. Fortunately, Moshe Dayan was only blind in one, and he sent the following message to his troops: 'Our aim is not to occupy, but to prevent the Arab armies from occupying our country and to break the vice that is closing in on us. They may outnumber us, but we shall win.' Then, in a brilliantly coordinated, highly skilled and greatly daring attack that stunned the world, Israel's air force, flying low beneath the enemy radar, destroyed ten major air bases simultaneously, followed by a further nine. In less than three hours, Israel's pilots had destroyed the greater part of Egypt's air force and air defences, before turning their attention to Jordan, Syria and Iraq, all of whom had begun shelling Israeli settlements.

While the air battles raged, the ground offensive commenced, Israel's forces (under the command of Yitzhak Rabin) striking first against Egypt, then against Jordan and Syria in ferocious battles that saw many losses on both sides, but which ended with the entire Sinai Peninsula as well as the Gaza Strip and Sharm el-Sheikh in Israeli hands (victories that took just four days). The Old City of Jerusalem, lost to Jordan in the 1948 war, was taken, as well as the entire West Bank, which had been part of the Hashemite Kingdom since 1948, and finally the Syrian positions on the Golan Heights, in the bloodiest battles of all, were overrun. By 10 June, all parties had agreed a ceasefire.

To us, following these remarkable events in peaceful London, it seemed like a miracle. No one was triumphant, just incredibly relieved. The embassy continued to receive hundreds of letters. Written spontaneously by people who had no ties with Israel, they were deeply moving, and when things were a little calmer Hanoch approached me and asked whether I would be willing to edit a book of the letters the embassy had received: it would be a permanent record of this momentous point in Israel's history. Reading the many files he gave me, it didn't take long to realise that with careful selection they would make a moving and very human testimony, and I agreed, working on the book in the evenings and at weekends.

All we needed now was a publisher, and Hanoch arranged a meeting with the proprietor and chairman of the *Jewish Chronicle*, David Kessler, whose book publishing company, Vallentine, Mitchell seemed the perfect outlet. The *JC*, founded in 1841, was the oldest continuously published Jewish newspaper in the world, and when David, a man of wide business experience, took over the chairmanship from his father, who had purchased a majority shareholding in the paper in 1907, he endeavoured to ensure that the paper reached out to all sections of the community and above all retained its editorial integrity. A Cambridge graduate, he had the bearing of a major, a rank he had held in the British Army. He received us with great courtesy and, after listening to Hanoch's proposal, readily agreed to take on the publication. Since I was to edit the book, this was the first of several visits to Kessler's office, and as the months went by we found ourselves having friendly conversations and from time to time he'd invite me to lunch, always keen to talk about publishing and to get my views on how Vallentine, Mitchell should develop.

Time-consuming and involving though all this was for me, poetry remained at the centre of everything, and I was thrilled to have a poem accepted by the *New Statesman*, and then another by the influential magazine *Encounter*, which had been founded by Stephen Spender and Irving Kristol in the 1950s. At the same time, the poetry and jazz concerts continued, one of them – at Malvern Girls' College – being recorded for transmission on Radio 3 by the poet and BBC producer

George MacBeth. Meanwhile, *Letters to Israel* was published and well received. Hanoch and his wife Yehudith had by now become friends, and the parties they gave at their Swiss Cottage flat were always brimming with interesting people and bonhomie. I remember the booming voice of the bearded novelist and political writer Mervyn Jones cutting through the chatter with a lament about his new book, which had been widely reviewed: 'I wish someone would compliment me on the book rather than the reviews!' On another occasion, we took Vernon Scannell with us, but we should have realised that the embassy whisky would take its toll. After we had left the party at a more or less respectable hour, Vernon had stayed on, entertaining the remaining guests with an account of his experiences with the British Army in wartime Egypt, where he'd been put in the slammer for one misdemeanour or another. Next morning we were woken by a phone call from the filmmaker Mira Hamermesh saying she had a rather worse-for-wear Vernon in her flat and would we like to pick him up. I think that giving him a bed for the night had been an act of compassion on her part rather than one of passion. In any case I can't imagine Vernon would have been at his priapic best.

I believe it was at one of the Bartovs' parties that we met the novelist Alan Sillitoe and his wife, the poet Ruth Fainlight, or perhaps it was at one of the Writers for Israel meetings, but we certainly became friendly with them both at around this period. The war had brought its terrors, but it had also cemented a number of valued friendships, as war so often does. Later, we were lucky enough to publish several of Alan's books, including a delightful children's series about a marmalade cat that led a gang of felines in the back streets of London. We also reissued his *Collected Stories* and published a book about his travels in Russia. Alan was such a quiet, unassuming man – always with a pipe, and usually wearing a waistcoat – but also a man of great strength of character with firm views and principles who went his own way with unwavering determination, sure of his own exceptional abilities, and rightly so.

* * *

In 1969, I found myself drawn into another of Foges's ambitious projects, a six-volume history of Western literature which I was to steer and oversee. The general editors of the books were to be David Daiches, the highly respected dean of the School of English and American studies at Sussex University, and Anthony Thorlby, professor of comparative literature at Sussex, and under their direction the many and varied chapters would be written by internationally distinguished scholars to produce what was described as 'a new sociological approach to the whole literature of the Western world from antiquity to the present time'. For me, having never even been to a university, editing this vast enterprise was an alarming prospect, but I attended various meetings with the eminent professors at which Foges shouted and cajoled, finally telling them that I would be writing a report on the detailed outlines and sample texts they had produced. There was really nowhere to hide!

If I felt I was having to punch way above my weight then, an encounter I had in the George, the famous literary watering hole in Mortimer Street, made me feel just as inadequate. I had wandered in one lunchtime to see if anyone I knew was there, and a tall, imposing man with white hair started talking to me at the bar. The name Goronwy Rees didn't mean much to me then, but I soon discovered that he was an eminent political journalist and writer, and that among other things he was an editorial adviser to *Encounter*. After we had chatted for a while, he surprised me by asking if I would like to review for the magazine, saying he would suggest it to the literary editor, Nigel Dennis (he seemed to know I'd recently had a poem published there). Some days later, I received a short letter from Rees, in which he enclosed a note from Dennis saying:

> Wouldn't Robson be just the fellow to do a sizing up of Auden's Longer Poems – how they have worn, how they look to the present-day poet, their influence, etc. We would commission the essay if you agree – or any other that you and he agree on, of course.

Well, if reworking Professor Daiches's scholarly proposal was daunting, this seemed to me even more so. But it was a challenge I felt I had to accept and somehow I wrote and delivered the required 2,000 words, though I was ill-equipped and readily admit that I struggled to come to grips with Auden's often complex poems – and even to understand some of them. I expected an immediate rejection, so was amazed to get a letter from the demanding Dennis saying, 'We were all very pleased with your Auden piece and would, of course, like you to do another.' He said he would leave it to me to suggest to Goronwy Rees what I'd like to do, something of 'special interest' to me. It was some while later, when it made headlines, that I discovered the charming man I'd met at the bar of the George had been befriended by Guy Burgess while at Oxford, having been introduced by him to the Cambridge Five spy ring, though there seemed to be much confusion as to whether Rees had any links to either MI6 or the KGB.

After such exacting involvements it was something of a relief to get a commission from Aldus to write a small book in their Adventure Library called *Destination the Poles*, a promotional book for young adults – probably given away in packets of cornflakes. Extra money towards our mortgage was welcome at the time, and so I found myself writing of an evening about four famous Arctic explorers: Fridtjof Nansen, Roald Amundsen, Robert Scott and Vivian Fuchs. Although there was only a chapter on each, they had to be researched and written in a vivid and dramatic way, so it entailed quite a bit of work, especially as it was not the kind of writing I was used to. I can't pretend it had great literary merit, but with nice line drawings throughout it made for an attractive little package and I was relieved that I'd actually managed to get through it. I also got a very different kind of commission from Marshall Cavendish, who were running a part series on the Bible and wanted me to write two historical essays for inclusion – one on Jerusalem and one on the creation of modern Israel. It seems I'd become an expert! Be that as it may, much research was required, but the money was reasonable and welcome.

The summer of 1969 was to be a significant period as far as both poetry and publishing were concerned. As the 250th poetry and jazz concert approached, I felt we should mark the occasion with a special event, and Harley Usill, the valiant MD of Argo, came up with the exciting idea of arranging and recording an anniversary concert at the Queen Elizabeth Hall with a view to issuing another two-LP boxed set. At the same time, Ernest Hecht, the maverick publisher of the Souvenir Press, agreed to bring out an anthology of *Poems from Poetry and Jazz in Concert* – a collection of ninety-two poems by twenty-four of the poets who'd participated, accompanied by an attractive poster to display at readings. As well as his publishing and his passion for Arsenal, Ernest was involved with a number of theatrical productions over the years, and it was perhaps his interest in the theatre that attracted him to our poetry and jazz venture. Whatever the reason, he made a success of it, with an unusual cover designed by Felix Gluck, and following the Souvenir hardback edition, he arranged for Panther (then the paperback imprint of Granada Publishing) to bring out a mass-market edition of the anthology. Looking at it now, I must say I'm still proud of the quality of the poets and poems represented.

The book was launched at the Queen Elizabeth Hall concert, which took place on 22 June, a rather more disciplined affair than our first, somewhat anarchic, appearance on the South Bank, and it was nice to welcome Spike Milligan back for this special occasion (he hadn't taken part for several years). Laurie Lee replied to my invitation saying he'd been 'quite ill for the past six months' but that 'if I am back in full-throttled health by May–June, you can count on me... I'm glad you are doing this.' He was indeed back to good health and there on the day, along with Dannie Abse, Thomas Blackburn, Douglas Hill, Vernon Scannell, John Smith and me. As always, of course, Michael Garrick directed the music, but there was now a new look to his quintet. Shake Keane had gone to Germany and been replaced by Ian Carr, while Don Rendell had taken the place of Joe Harriott, with whom Michael had finally had a clash. Completing the line-up were Dave Green on bass and Trevor Tomkins on drums, both regulars. To add extra lustre to the occasion, Michael had added the wonderful Art Themen – saxophonist and doctor – to the group. It was always reassuring when Art was playing to know that one had an orthopaedic surgeon at one's back.

Rehearsing with Joe Harriott and Shake Keane.

Don Rendell, a Jehovah's Witness, played tenor saxophone with great attack as well as the flute. Because one of the poems I sometimes read in those days had a biblical context, I sensed Don felt a kind of kinship, and whenever I drove him to a concert he'd bring out his pamphlets and try to draw me in. He must have been disappointed to find himself knocking at the wrong door, but that never affected our warm relationship over a long period. In contrast, Ian Carr was literary and intellectual as well as being a dazzling and assertive trumpet and flugelhorn player, and he wrote several books, including a biography of Miles Davis. He went on to form the ground-breaking jazz-rock group Nucleus, winning first prize at the Montreux Jazz Festival. I should also mention here two other fine bassists who, along with Dave Green, played at a number of concerts: Jeff Clyne (who always seemed to be reading weighty paperbacks as he waited to go on stage) and the veteran Coleridge Goode, who'd played with Django Reinhardt and Stéphane Grappelli and other jazz legends. I recall Vernon Scannell being particularly amused when he heard Garrick announcing, 'And on bass – Coleridge.'

Saxophonist Don Rendell in full flight.

John Smith, who had read that exciting day at the QEH, was also a literary agent with his own company, Christy & Moore, and it was he who had floated my idea for a poetry and jazz anthology to Ernest Hecht. Now John felt it was time I had a new book of my own poems and he approached another lively independent publisher, Allison & Busby. As well as Faber, most of the main companies published poetry in those days, though few do now and it is largely left to small but excellent companies like Carcanet, Bloodaxe and Smokestack to carry the flag – and Faber too, of course. The iconic photo of T. S. Eliot, W. H. Auden, Louis MacNeice and a young Ted Hughes at a Faber party speaks well for the wisdom of those who signed them up: proof enough that quality will out in the end – though who could have anticipated what the musical *Cats* would do for the Faber coffers at a time when, reportedly, the company was struggling. Allison & Busby had been started by Clive Allison and Margaret Busby, both young, and had an attractive poetry list. They sat on the manuscript for quite some time, as publishers invariably do, while making encouraging noises, and whenever John ventured to prod Clive, he'd say he had the manuscript spread out on the floor beside him along with other collections they were considering. Naturally, I wanted it off that floor and between covers. Then one bright day, I received a note from John saying a miracle had happened: he'd actually had a letter of acceptance and a contract from Clive for my book (*In Focus*). I was thrilled to be with a lively publisher committed to poetry and so in tune with the current mood – publishing not only poetry but also classy contemporary fiction and non-fiction, with a string of big-name authors on their list. Eventually – I suppose inevitably – after twenty years, the company was sold. Clive died in 2011 at far too young an age, but I was delighted to run into the wonderful Margaret Busby recently at a launch in Finsbury Park. Margaret had been editorial director of the company throughout its twenty years and was the UK's youngest and first black woman publisher. Now a much-lauded writer herself, she has worked assiduously for more black representation in British publishing and has received many awards, including an OBE. When I recalled my manuscript lying at Clive's feet, she laughed, saying it would have been one of many, given his chaotic way of doing things – she'd had to struggle to keep everything in order. I sensed that without her the company would not have lasted as long as it did, despite Clive's flair. A few days later she emailed me an unexpected photo of the three of us celebrating my book in the George, which was near their office. It was wonderful to meet up with her after all those years, for the publication of that book, which they brought out simultaneously in hardback and paperback and with a signed limited edition, was an important moment for me, and it was good to be able to tell her so. It was also a privilege to attend a celebration at Goldsmiths College in November 2017 to mark her fifty years in publishing.

In the George, celebrating the publication of In Focus *with my publishers, Clive Allison and Margaret Busby.*

Things were about to change, for shortly after the QEH concert David Kessler invited me to lunch and, over steak and chips and a glass of lemonade shandy (his favourite tipple), offered me a job as editor of Vallentine, Mitchell. He wanted to grow the company, he told me, and not just with books of Jewish interest, to which VM had hitherto confined itself. This would be my first chance to acquire books as opposed to editing them, and I nervously accepted. Giving notice at Aldus was not an easy thing – Foges liked to sack people, not have them give him notice – but he and his colleagues realised it was an opportunity for me and accepted with good grace. Indeed, Foges continued to invite us to his parties and, as I have already recounted, persuaded me a few years later to pick up my Ben-Gurion pen again. I had to give three months' notice, and he was anxious to have my report on his Great Western Literature project, for which he now had several more sample chapters and a fuller outline. And so I found myself pontificating about the 'lack of any apparent sense of purpose', calling one chapter (on Latin literature) 'a total failure', and asking, 'Why is the literature of Russia considered more worthy of inclusion than the modern writing of Spain, Germany and Italy, and why, for that matter, is the whole of modern poetry from 1930 overlooked when the novel is covered so fully?'

Amazingly, Professor Daiches and his colleagues seemed to have taken it on the chin, for a week before I left, Foges gave me a revised outline and a number of new chapters to read (my leaving present?), and I was able to report that the editors had reshaped everything very considerably; they had dropped certain authors and brought in others, finally realising that simply allowing a long list of distinguished academics to do their own thing in the abstract didn't make for a strong, unified book.

Thus was Western Literature saved.

14

MOVING TIMES

Vallentine, Mitchell, where I started in September 1969, had its offices in the same building in Furnival Street as the *Jewish Chronicle*, just around the corner from Chancery Lane Station, and far enough from the Law Courts not to give me daily reminders of my unhappy days as an embryonic lawyer. We had just two small rooms, and apart from me there was a secretary, Lesley, and David Kessler's son-in-law, Guy Meyers. Guy was an accountant and he had been looking after the publishing company for several years. He was extremely friendly and seemed to welcome any potential input I might have. He was a great one for phoning people for information, and when faced with the question 'Can I help you?' would invariably reply, 'We live in hope.' I soon discovered that as far as the paper was concerned, David Kessler (*aka* 'K') liked to surround himself with the great and the good, and his board included at least one top lawyer, several historians and distinguished others, as well as the editor William Frankel, a barrister and a man of considerable authority, widely respected in the community.

Vallentine, Mitchell had its own directors, several of whom came fairly regularly to our weekly meetings in K's office. One was John Gross, an eminent man of letters whom *The Spectator* called 'the best-read man in Britain'. John held various important literary posts and was to become editor of the *Times Literary Supplement*, a position he held for seven years. Some while after I'd left VM and had started Robson Books, John, who lived around the corner from us, dropped in for coffee and asked me what books we had coming up. When I told him there was a collection of Vernon Scannell's poems and (coyly) *The Max Miller Blue Book*, he amazed me by reciting two of Vernon's poems, and then singing one of Max's saucy songs: such was the range of his interests and knowledge. He was also reputed to be an expert on the East End. Another frequent attendee at our meetings was Chaim Bermant, novelist and the *JC*'s popular columnist. Chaim, who spoke impossibly quickly with a strong Scottish accent, combined wit and erudition and would often take a provocative position on matters Jewish, which readers loved but sometimes took exception to. In due course, Robson Books published a collection of his columns called *On the Other Hand*, a novel, and the first in a planned five-volume autobiography. Shockingly, Chaim died shortly before the publication of that first volume, a wonderfully evocative account of his Lithuanian childhood which we launched posthumously with his wife Judy's help. Chaim had called it *Genesis*. It was perhaps the emotional strain of returning to Lithuania to research his book that caused his fatal heart attack.

There was thus lively and formidable company on the Kessler couch, and I did my best to come up with ideas and proposals they might find appealing. I soon realised that for all his expressed intentions, K was reluctant to take on anything that wandered too far off his normal path or appeared to him risky. Fair enough, but one thing I did get off the ground was a series of Modern Jewish Classics, reprints of novels and autobiographies in an attractive format with a matching look to the jackets. It was wide-ranging within its obvious limits and included Elie Wiesel's *The Jews of Silence*, Isaac Babel's *Benya Krik the Gangster*, Mordecai Richler's *The Apprenticeship of Duddy Kravitz* and Sholom Aleichem's *Tevye's Daughters*, as well as fine books by Saul Bellow, Bernice Rubens, Bernard Kops, Dannie Abse, Dan Jacobson and Frederic Raphael. It seemed a good way to get some big names on the list quickly and raise our profile.

Another author I was able to bring in early on was Lynne Reid Banks, whose *The L-Shaped Room* had been a huge bestseller and made into a film starring Leslie Caron. Though not Jewish, Lynne had spent eight years on a kibbutz with her sculptor husband Chaim Stephenson. I had read an evocative piece by her in the *JC* describing how she'd taken the children from her kibbutz on an outing to celebrate one of the Jewish festivals and told them stories. It made me think she could write an excellent novel for older children, and I wrote to her suggesting this. She responded quickly with a number of questions as she hadn't written for children before – what length, what level should the writing be pitched at, etc. Since I, for my part, had never published a children's book, I sought advice, and everyone said, 'Tell her not to write down, not to condescend,' so I passed this on to Lynne and she decided to accept the proposal. The book she wrote, *One More River*, the moving story of a developing friendship between a young Israeli girl and an Arab boy, divided by the Jordan river and eventually by the Six Day War, was superb. Simon & Schuster bought the US rights, and Penguin agreed to publish a UK paperback edition. For Lynne, it was the beginning of a successful career as a children's writer.

I'd been at VM for about six months when copies of my new book of poems, *In Focus*, landed on my desk. Like any author, I anxiously awaited the reviews, but I got off relatively unscathed and my publishers seemed satisfied with the reception. There were a few readings lined up to tie in with the publication, and I undertook these gladly. I also had an invitation from Peter Orr, head of the British Council's sound section, to record eleven poems from the book, together with an interview, for a series of poets reading their own work which they had instigated in collaboration with the Poetry Room of Yale University, copies of the tape going to various universities and British Council offices overseas. At about the same time, I was asked by the BBC to read one of my poems for a Radio 4 schools programme, and also to read two for a TV programme about the poetry and jazz scene, which was to include an interview with Robin Ray. Finally, to end a very busy period, Michael Garrick wrote with the good news that he'd been booked for the BBC's *Jazz Workshop* programme and that the producer would like me to read three of the poems I'd written for jazz, to be recorded at the Aeolian Hall in New Bond Street. All this greatly boosted my new book and was an exciting diversion from the day job, though I tried not to let it intrude too obviously.

As thrilling as all this was, it was swiftly overshadowed and swept aside when Carole discovered she was pregnant – and not just pregnant, but pregnant with twins. If I was taken aback, she was even more so, staggering into the office of my cousin Teddy Stonehill, who was working as a doctor in the hospital where she'd just had the scan, and collapsing on his couch. Apparently a little brandy did the trick (you can always rely on Ted for a drink).

Expecting a first baby probably throws most people into something of a tizz, and you tend to forget that women have been having babies for quite some time as the world about you shrinks (I nearly said contracts) and you find yourself focusing on this one wondrous event. Having twins doubles all that. Like any young couple, we looked up books and tried to discover as much as possible. Strangely, there was very little about twins at that time (we were to change that in due course with the publication of our *Twins Handbook*). One thing we read everywhere was that when a baby is on the way, you shouldn't add to the tension and anxiety by moving house. However, with only one bedroom in our little bungalow and the sudden prospect of being four, we ignored the advice, put the house on the market and started looking around for something a little larger, which we'd been saving up to do anyway. Carole went to antenatal classes with an exuberant childbirth guru called Betty Parsons, whose credo was 'Relax for pregnancy and life'. I attended an alarming fathers' evening with this enthusiastic lady – just in time, as it turned out. She didn't quite get all the expectant fathers to 'push', but I felt she might do so any minute.

Meanwhile, the world and the publishing (and the poetry) continued. There were two books I was proud to sign up during this period. *Hannah Senesh: Her Life and Diary*, a story of great heroism and sacrifice, was particularly important. Hannah was among thirty-seven Jews from Palestine who volunteered to be parachuted by the British into Yugoslavia during the Second World War to assist in the rescue of Hungarian Jews. She was caught, but, despite being tortured by the Nazis, refused to reveal details of her mission or the code to her transmitter. Hannah had kept a diary right up to the night she left, and this, together with some of her poems, formed the bulk of the book, but it also included dramatic accounts by two of the men who parachuted with her and were also captured. Thrown into the same prison as Hannah, they were able to recount how she was caught, brutally tortured and executed by firing squad. The book also included a heartbreaking account by Hannah's mother Catherine, who was still in Budapest at the time of her daughter's capture and tried desperately to save her. I worked carefully on the translation and even tinkered with the English translation of a few of her poems, to the evident satisfaction of her mother, who came to London to speak about her daughter and help launch the book. It was a moving occasion. Hannah is a national heroine in Israel, where her poems are widely read. As VM had published the original British hardback edition of *Anne Frank's Diary*, it was fitting that we should bring out this classic too.

The other title I brought in at this time was by the actor David Kossoff. Apart from his distinguished film and theatrical career, Kossoff had written a book of Bible stories for Collins, which, because of his uniquely dramatic style, had become a bestseller. David Frost had labelled him 'Bible storyteller to the nation'. When I was introduced to Kossoff at a reception, I asked him if he would be willing to write a book for us. He seemed reasonably receptive, asking me whether I had any particular ideas in mind, and on the spur of the moment I suggested that a Kossoff-style retelling of the Masada story would make a powerful book. Masada was the mountain stronghold on the eastern edge of the Judean Hills, overlooking the Dead Sea, where at the end of the Jewish revolt against the Romans in around 73AD nearly a thousand Jewish men, women and children committed mass suicide rather than surrender to the Roman legions besieging them. According to the historian Josephus, only two women and five children survived, and David had the imaginative idea of telling the story, both of Masada and of the Jewish revolt, through the eyes and voices of the two women. A trained draughtsman, he also agreed to illustrate and draw maps for the book he called *The Voices of Masada*. It was an outright success and led to his writing other books for us, and to a friendship with him and his wife, Jenny. David was said to be a prickly man, though I never found him anything but friendly and accommodating, and when we were promoting his book I enjoyed listening to him at literary events recounting how his Bible stories book had evolved into a TV series. 'This', he would say, referring to the lunches he was invited to at TV headquarters, 'was no carry-your-own-tray affair.'

By now it was September 1970 and Carole was really large, although only just into her ninth month. My father (who had predicted twins very early on) warned us to be on standby since twins generally arrive early, and he was right, for on the 17th Carole woke me at around 1 a.m. to say she thought things were on the move. They certainly were. Panicking a little, despite Mrs Parsons's explicit instructions, we threw on some clothes, alerted the hospital and fell into the car. There was hardly any traffic as I drove as fast as I dared along the Edgware Road towards St George's Hospital, then near Hyde Park Corner, only to be stopped by the police. I explained the urgency of the situation and they waved us on, wishing us luck and telling me to drive carefully. I think they would have provided an escort had we asked for it! Carole was in labour through the morning and into the early afternoon when, to the delight of the medical students who had asked permission to attend and the immense relief of her husband (who'd been drawing on a small flask of whisky throughout), she finally gave birth to two tiny, beautiful girls, Deborah and Manuela. I couldn't have been more thrilled and more at sea, but in the middle of it all I suddenly remembered that I was due to take part in a poetry and jazz concert that night in Sutton, and I phoned Michael Garrick and explained that I would not be there. It was the only concert I'd missed in all the years we'd been giving them. But what better reason could there be?

As the new house we had managed to buy still had decorators all over it, we decided to accept my grandmother's gracious invitation to stay with her. It was a blessing in a way, since my grandfather had recently died and our company was a great comfort to her; it also made life much easier for us. And so, several days after they were born, we eased our tiny daughters into the back of our car as if they were the most delicate and valuable of breakable items (which to us they were) and I edged away from the hospital a great deal more slowly than when I'd driven Carole there. Our world had changed, and nothing would ever be the same.

*   *   *

At that time, the *Jewish Chronicle* was in many ways the paper of the Jewish community (they used to say that if you didn't have your obituary in the *JC*, you weren't dead). But though it carried considerable authority, David Kessler never really seemed to me to be an establishment figure. Not an Orthodox nor even an observant Jew, he nevertheless cared about community matters and had a lifelong interest in the Falashas, the black Jews of Ethiopia, about whom he wrote a book. But he was also very much the country gentleman, with a lovely home in the pretty village of Stoke Hammond in Buckinghamshire, where he and his wife Matilda were pillars of the local community – in fact, David, who enjoyed walking, was known locally as 'the squire'. Matilda, who was not Jewish, was a magistrate, something I'd forgotten when David invited Carole and me to tea one Sunday. As Vernon Scannell happened to be staying with us that weekend, I asked whether I could bring him with us. David said he'd be welcome. However, what I'd also forgotten was that poor Vernon had only recently spent a short time at Her Majesty's Pleasure for being drunk in charge. It wasn't as bad as it sounds: he had been drinking after a reading (as one does) somewhere in the country and on returning to his car had rightly decided he wasn't in a fit state to drive, so he'd run the car onto a verge and gone to sleep. Unfortunately, in doing so he'd scraped the fence of the adjacent house and the enraged owner had called the police, who woke Vernon up and arrested him. The literary world was up in arms when he was given a jail sentence, but to no avail.

We poets all felt Vernon had acted responsibly in the circumstances, but Mrs Kessler was far from sympathetic when the story came out over tea and scones on the lawn, and I realised I'd committed a faux pas which had embarrassed everyone. David was decent enough to gloss over the incident (even laugh), and our relationship was unaffected by the gaffe. (What I didn't tell the Kesslers was that when the milkman called at the Scannell household one morning, Vernon's little son told him, 'My dad is on holiday in Brixton.')

Around this time, the publisher Chatto & Windus accepted my proposal (via John Smith's literary agency) to edit an anthology of *The Young British Poets*, an expanded and more comprehensive version of the bilingual book I'd edited a few years earlier for *Poésie Vivante*. Although my reviewing for *Tribune* (which still continued) had brought me into contact with many of the young poets then writing, I still had to do a fair amount of fresh reading and also, once I had selected the poems I wanted to include (the poets had to be born after 1935, thus being thirty-five or under), I then needed to contact them or their publishers for permission. In some cases the poets sent me new poems, and it was good to be able to consider these along with, or instead of, those already chosen. I was pleased to have made some discoveries and to have included poets who were then relatively unknown but are now the very opposite. My 'cast' included three outstanding Irish poets – Seamus Heaney, Michael Longley and Derek Mahon – as well as Brian Patten, Tony Harrison, Robert Nye, Kevin Crossley-Holland, Douglas Dunn and Hugo Williams. One of the rewards of editing this anthology was the friendly correspondence I enjoyed with many of the contributors, some inviting me to stay or suggesting meeting up when they were in town. I must have mentioned to Michael Longley that we'd recently had twins, for he wrote me a warm letter revealing that he himself was a twin and that his father's phrase to describe his 'privilege' was 'tuppenny stung for a penny bung'. How colourfully Irish! Interestingly, the Irish poets didn't seem to be worried by the word 'British' in the title of the book, though I suspect they might have been later, especially Seamus.

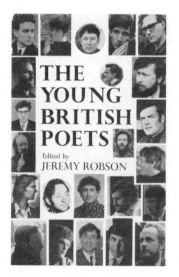

The Young British Poets *anthology, which I edited for Chatto, brought me into contact with poets who are now among our finest.*

There was wide and generally very positive coverage in the press, and I was amazed to wake up on the Sunday of publication to find a lead review in *The Observer* by Kingsley Amis, who seemed to approve of my introduction and selection, writing: 'A look through the text bears out these heartening declarations ... no stock tactics, no word-salads, no obscurity, no trip-taking, very little mere showmanship.' I felt relieved, knowing the sharpness of his pen. *The Guardian* was also kind, saying the book 'should be useful for anyone who wants to find names to watch for', while the respected poet and critic Richard Church, writing in *Country Life*, called it 'a valuable surprise for readers who are sick of so much pretentious nonsense that is offered as the poetry of our day ... Every one of these young poets has something to offer that is distinctly a personal revelation of experience.' I'd happily settle for that, or for the *Irish Press*, which said, 'All the poets are first class.' To counter this, however, there was an interminable review in the *London Magazine* in which the venerable Geoffrey Grigson seemed to devote most of the space to claims he thought I'd made for the book in the blurb, taking issue with the fact that it drew comparisons with the earlier influential anthologies *New Signature* and *New Lines*. What he hadn't realised was that the blurb was written not by me but by the Poet Laureate, Cecil Day-Lewis, who was a director of Chatto! I smiled quietly to myself, leaving Mr Grigson to prattle on and vaunt his wit, and I did so again just now on reading this description of him on Wikipedia: 'Fiercely combative, he made many literary enemies for his dogmatic views.' Not of me, he hadn't. He'd just made me smile, as I remembered the old adage about measuring your reviews, rather than reading them. Despite Mr G, the book did well enough, going into a mass-market paperback edition with Corgi and being published in America.

*   *   *

I'd never been to the Frankfurt Book Fair, though at Aldus Books I'd heard endless talk about it, since this was where Wolfgang Foges always held court in the salons of the exclusive (and very expensive)

Frankfurter Hof. Whether he ever graced the ordinary fair halls with his presence is questionable. Guy Meyers hadn't been to Frankfurt either and we both felt that with our expanding list we should take a small stand. To save money, we drove there and stayed in a hotel outside the town.

I hadn't realised until we approached the German frontier from Belgium just how uneasy I felt at the prospect of stepping onto German soil. It was almost dark when we reached the customs post, which made it seem all the more eerie, and I felt a surge of panic as we were approached by two heavily armed policemen. But Guy calmed me down and we drove through. That first fair was memorable for one thing in particular: a man with a black bag full of books stopping at our stand, pointing to a poster and asking, 'What's *your* David Kossoff book?' That man was Tom McCormack, CEO of St Martin's Press, and he'd just bought Kossoff's book of Bible stories from Collins. I described *The Voices of Masada* as vividly as I could and he said he'd like to publish a US edition of that, too. Not only was it my first sale of American rights, it was my first meeting with a publisher I came to admire greatly: Tom, a man of exceptional business acumen and publishing flair, took the relatively small, academic imprint of St Martin's Press and built it into one of the giants of American publishing. Coming to England regularly with his black bag and doing the rounds of publishers and agents, his sharp eyes always on the lookout for *that* book, special both in content and in style, he would make a number of purchases, some relatively modest, and turn many into bestsellers. James Herriot's semi-autobiographical veterinary books were a prime example – seemingly very English books that Tom had spotted on an agent's shelf and bought. Then, with a change of title, he took them to the top of the US bestseller lists, making a great deal of money for all concerned. *All Creatures Great and Small* was the first of these. He'd shut himself away, hermit-like, in his room at the Connaught Hotel, reading the manuscripts and proofs he'd stuffed into his black bag during his daily forays, working late into the night, his publishing antenna on red alert. When his wife, Sandra – like him, a fine editor – was with him, she would do much the same. And when it came to a deal, he was a master in judging the right offer to make – high or low – for the book he had in his sights. His editorial input could also be considerable. Tom was always generous to us, inviting us to lunch or dinner at the Connaught, or in New York when we visited. We did our best to reciprocate, but he was not an easy man to lure away from his books.

Over the years, apart from our growing family friendship with Tom and Sandra and their daughter Jessie (still a close friend of our daughters), we did many deals together, and even since Tom's retirement and the sad death after a long illness of the warm and effervescent Sandra, we have stayed in touch, dining together only recently in New York. One of our joyous memories of them is the long weekend they spent with us in Normandy. We have also retained a special relationship with St Martin's Press and the exceptional people there – Sally Richardson and Tom Dunne in particular. It is a company like no other I know of in the US, since despite its size it manages to retain a family feeling.

The poetry, the concerts and the reviewing continued. Handsomely produced limited editions seemed to be in vogue at that time, and I was thrilled when the entrepreneurial Bernard Stone, whose Turret Books, a second-hand bookshop in Kensington Church Walk, was a literary oasis, proposed issuing a limited edition of ten of my poems (*Poems Out of Israel*) – 100 copies, numbered and signed by me. It was part of a Turret Booklets series edited by the poet and critic Edward Lucie-Smith, and to have his imprimatur was gratifying. He'd been the chairman of 'The Group', which had been formed in Cambridge in 1952 by Philip Hobsbaum and continued by Lucie-Smith in London. It wasn't a literary movement of any kind but a weekly meeting of various poets who'd circulate their new poems, which would then be discussed frankly – very frankly – by the others present. I'd gone once with Douglas Hill, and we both found it unpleasant and intimidating and beat a hasty retreat, since neither of us fancied offering our necks to that literary guillotine (or perhaps it was more the sight of Edward Lucie-Smith's slippered feet dangling from an armchair and the all-round smugness that did for us).

* * *

For some while, Dannie Abse and I had been working on a series of critical anthologies for Corgi Books, commissioned by their editorial director Mike Legat, for whom this was quite a courageous departure, given that Corgi was the mass-market paperback imprint of Transworld Publishers. Working closely together, Dannie and I edited alternate volumes, each featuring six poets and including introductions to their work by one of us, comments on their own work by the poets themselves, and a selection of their poems. There was a pattern to the volumes, all featuring a modern master, a living poet celebrated on both sides of the Atlantic, a poet's poet who had been somewhat neglected by the reading public, a poet who had recently died but whose work was very much alive, a young poet with a growing reputation, and a poet never before published in book form by a London-based commercial publisher. This was quite a challenge, since as well as choosing and clearing the poems, there were six separate introductory essays to be written for every volume. It also meant liaising and corresponding with various poets to get their cooperation and involvement. My first volume (following the order of the categories just listed) focused on Wilfred Owen, Philip Larkin, Thomas Blackburn, Keith Douglas, Seamus Heaney and the American poet William Meredith; my second featured Thomas Hardy, Dannie Abse, Vernon Scannell, Stevie Smith, Tony Harrison and another leading American poet, Daniel Hoffman.

The first volumes were now ready, and although by mass-paperback standards our sales must have seemed relatively modest to the publishers (initially about 7,000 copies per volume), in modern poetry terms they were substantial, and I hope Mike Legat felt that this and the wide attention the books received justified going out on a limb in the way he did, especially since the books were adopted by various schools and colleges and hopefully would go on selling. Looking back now at the extensive correspondence, I can see that apart from the poems chosen to represent them, what exercised the poets most were the pieces on themselves we asked them to write or provide – Seamus Heaney, for instance, writing, 'Jeremy, what can I say? I'm totally tongue-tied.' In the end he most certainly wasn't, producing a well-thought-out, carefully crafted piece about himself and the nature of poetry which began:

A poet at work is involved in a double process of making a discovery, a process that at the best of times is unique, unselfconscious, and unpredictable. Every real poem that he makes represents a new encounter with what he knows in himself, and it survives as something at once shed and attained ... I began to write poetry in 1963, craft-ridden and compulsively attracted to those guardians of technique like the water diviner and the untutored musicians, men whose wrists and fingers receive and encode energies into meaning...

Precious words. I also found Tony Harrison's contribution enlightening as he confessed:

In our street in Hoggarty Leeds I was the only one who used his literacy to read books, the only 'scholar', and so every kind of throwaway from spring-cleaned attics and the cellars of the deceased found its way to me. I acquired piles of old 78s, George Formby, the Savoy Orpheans, Sophie Tucker, Sandy Powell, Peter Dawson, and sometimes the odd book, an old guide to Matlock, the Heckmondwike Temperance Hymnal stamped 'not to be taken away', and above all Livingstone's *Travels*, so massive I could barely manhandle it. Sometimes it seemed that my two early ambitions to be Dr Livingstone and George Formby, were compromised in the role of the poet, half missionary, half comic...

The responses from Philip Larkin were, not unexpectedly, more formal than those of the other poets, yet helpful enough. He did write to me after the book was published, querying my interpretation of a line in 'Church Going', but not in an intemperate way. I suppose I was lucky he was only taking issue with one line! Apart from that, I recall that he was more concerned with the fee we were paying for his prose contribution than any literary considerations.

My involvement with the American poets William Meredith and Daniel Hoffman was particularly rewarding, each sending me a number of letters with their thoughts and credos, as eager to be published in Britain as I was to introduce these fine poets to a British audience. In

view of my earlier comment about The Group, I was amused to reread
Daniel Hoffman's memories of a trip to London:

> I attended meetings of a group of poets who discussed each other's
> work. On one occasion the poem on the agenda was mine. I recall that a
> passage describing a still blue sky bisected by the trail of a jet occasioned
> comments that surprised me. 'The halves of heaven / Are bluer than
> each other', my poem claimed. In the US such a seminar would most
> likely have considered the technical aspects of the poem – consistency
> of diction, handling of images, the rhythmic assumptions beneath the
> movement of the language. But in that intense circle off Earl's Court
> Square, debate centred instead upon the truth or falsity of the statement.
> It was the moral character of the speaker of the words in the poem
> which engaged the discussants. 'It is not possible', one maintained, 'for
> one half of the heavens to be a different shade of blue from the other
> half.' I was dumbfounded for I knew the proposition to be true; I had
> tried faithfully to record my own experience.

That meeting must have been – it surely was – an evening with The
Group. Two cultures dissected by the same language! But to end this
discussion about the Corgi anthologies on a different note, I should
add that the second of the books I edited included Stevie Smith's last,
intensely moving, short poem, 'Come Death', generously sent to me
by her close friend and literary executor, James MacGibbon, just as we
were about to go to press. It was its first publication.

15

WALKING ON WATER

Wolfgang Lotz was a colourful visitor to our office.

I was in my second year at Vallentine, Mitchell when an Israeli literary agent appeared in my office saying he represented a man called Wolfgang Lotz, whose life story he wanted us to publish. Lotz, it transpired, had been one of Israel's master spies operating in Egypt in the 1960s, and his story was indeed extraordinary. Jewish but German by birth and an expert horseman, Lotz had adopted the cover of a wealthy German horse breeder, opening a riding school and mixing in the upper echelons of Egyptian society. He and his attractive wife Waltraud (who was not Jewish) had thrown extravagant parties, becoming the trusted friend of generals, Cabinet ministers and intelligence officers. Convinced he was an ex-SS officer hiding from his war crimes, Cairo's German colony had also welcomed the Lotzes into their midst – and it was from the German military experts advising the Egyptians that Lotz had discovered vital military secrets, including precise details of the rocket sites Israel was to knock out in the opening hours of the Six Day War.

Then their radio transmitter was discovered and they were suddenly arrested, becoming the centre of a public show trial. Ironically, they were saved by the Six Day War, when the Israelis made the repatriation of Egyptian prisoners (some 5,000, including nine generals) dependent upon the couple's release. Another thing that had saved Lotz from being summarily executed was the fact that he wasn't circumcised, which enabled him to maintain that he wasn't Jewish. (When he died in May 1993, *The Times* obituary phrased it thus: 'The fact that he wasn't circumcised kept his cover intact'!)

It seemed a sensational story, perhaps too sensational, and with his customary caution David Kessler rightly decided to have it checked out through the paper. It all stacked up, and as Lotz himself was due in London the following month, we arranged to meet him. Charming, handsome and full of good humour and engaging stories, not surprisingly he won us over, readily agreeing to work closely with me on whatever editing was necessary. A deal was struck, and over the following months we set to work. Slowly I entered the world of Israeli espionage.

It was on a Sunday afternoon, when Lotz (or 'Rusty', as he was known) was at our house going through some papers, that the phone rang. It was Tom McCormack, who'd just arrived from New York and was calling from the Connaught Hotel, wanting to set up a meeting. When I told him we had Israel's notorious 'Champagne Spy' in our living room, Tom immediately said, 'Then what am I doing here? I'll come right over!' And so St Martin's Press became partners in the deal, acquiring the US rights, with Rusty spending some time with Tom as well as with me, polishing and expanding the text for American consumption.

When we launched Lotz's *The Champagne Spy* in 1972, Frederick Forsyth had just brought out his bestselling Nazi-hunt thriller, *The Odessa File*. Noticing that Lotz appeared in it in a small way, our publicist asked his publishers whether Forsyth would like to meet him. The answer came back that indeed he would, and a meeting was set up for the two of them in the well-known Fleet Street watering hole El Vino. Rusty asked me to accompany him and I was the proverbial fly on the wall as they downed the wine and swapped stories, Rusty providing colourful detail on the Germans he'd been friendly with in Cairo, but – ever the professional – not giving much away about the Israeli Secret Service. He in turn was greatly impressed by the depth and detail of Forsyth's research and his ability to create a nail-biting story within an accurate political and historical framework. I hadn't realised until we got down to working on Lotz's book that he'd not only lived in Israel but had fought with the Haganah, the Jewish paramilitary organisation, being seconded to the British Army during the Second World War because of his perfect German. Later, he'd been sent back to Germany by the Israelis, where he lived lavishly and loudly for several years before going to Cairo in order to ensure that his story could be authenticated if checked, details which fascinated Forsyth. Lotz was an exuberant character, and it was easy to see why people enjoyed his company and were taken in by him.

Another – very different – character was about to come my way, who was inadvertently to affect the course of my life. Frank Cass was a publisher who had started out as a bookseller and now published academic books – generally, expensive reprints of books for which experts had advised there was a demand. Cass was also interested in Jewish affairs and that is how he must have met David Kessler, who was then sixty-five and evidently seeking to retire in the not-too-distant future. K called me in to meet Cass, and it became clear that he was interested in involving him in Vallentine, Mitchell. And, just as K had done when I was at Aldus, Cass started inviting me to lunch, asking me lots of loaded questions, plainly bent on acquiring VM in some way. He also wanted to make sure I would remain on board, for he was a canny man and it was not only Jewish books he was interested in, as I was to discover.

But all this had to be put on hold, since towards the end of 1970 I received an enticing invitation to join four other British poets on a ten-day reading tour of Israel, which was being arranged by the British Council in association with the Israeli Foreign Office and its cultural attaché in London, the novelist Aharon Megged. The poets were D. J. Enright, Ted Hughes, Peter Porter and Dannie Abse. Normally it wouldn't have taken a lot of thinking about, but with our twins barely three months old I was reluctant to leave Carole. However, she was insistent, appreciating what an exciting opportunity this was for me.

It seems that all my visits to Israel were destined to be both memorable and rich in experience, and this was no exception, beginning somewhat inauspiciously when, at London Airport, several policemen swooped to halt our slow progress to the El Al plane. Even in those days, where Israel was concerned, security was especially tight. Finally, after we and our fellow passengers had been vigorously frisked, we were allowed to move forward – all of us except Ted Hughes, that is, who had to spend several loud minutes convincing the police that the five-inch tiger's tooth in his pocket was indeed a tiger's tooth, a present for the Israeli poet Yehuda Amichai, with whom he was friendly, having worked with the Hebrew-speaking Assia Wevill on an English translation of some of Yehuda's poems. Ted also had with him his attractive new young wife Carol, so for them it was a kind of honeymoon. As always on El Al flights to Israel, there was a cluster of bearded, ultra-Orthodox Jews on board, clutching their prayer books and intoning as the engines began to rev up. It seemed that Peter Porter was a nervous passenger, and I heard him whisper tensely to Dannie as the plane soared into the sky, 'I hope their prayers will be heard.' I think he was only half-joking.

I knew Ted a little from the various poetry and jazz concerts he'd taken part in, and Peter Porter too had read with us on several occasions. Born in Australia, Peter was at that time very much at the centre of the London literary scene, and a regular of The Group. Feisty and fast-witted, he was doubtless more than able to fight his corner there. I'd originally come across his poetry when reviewing his superb first book, *Once Bitten, Twice Bitten,* for *Tribune.* Dennis Enright was the only poet I hadn't met before. A highly respected academic and poet, he turned out to be both friendly and funny, reminding me of Danny Kaye in both looks and the droll way he delivered his bons mots. I think the laid-back manner in which he introduced and read his poems, and his general persona, rather surprised the academics who knew his books and had come to pay their respects.

For the tour we were joined by six of Israel's leading poets, reading in rotation, two or three at each event. They were all formidable, with histories I found quite humbling as I pieced them together. Only one poet, Haim Gouri, had actually been born in what was then Palestine, in 1923. The legendary Abba Kovner had been a leader of the Vilna Ghetto uprising; Dan Pagis had spent several years in a Nazi concentration camp; Amir Gilboa had emigrated illegally from Poland to Palestine in 1937 and fought with the British Army before becoming involved in smuggling Jewish refugees out of Germany. Yehuda Amichai had been born in Germany in 1924 and emigrated with his parents to Palestine in 1936; he too had served in the British Army, then in the Palmach, the elite fighting force of the Haganah. What deep and disturbing experiences they all had to draw on.

The sixth poet, T. Carmi, had been born in New York, and emigrated to Palestine in 1947; he and I had met on my first visit to Israel when I was twenty-one, and had been taken to the artists' colony of Ein Hod. And there in the café of this enchanting hillside village, with a beautiful woman and smiling his wide, characteristic smile, had been Carmi. The two of us had fallen into conversation and he'd invited me to his home in Tel Aviv, where, over a glass or two, we had discussed poetry and struck up a friendship. Nearly all the time I knew him, Carmi had been working on *The Penguin Book of Hebrew Poetry*, which finally came out in 1981, a magnum opus if ever there was one. It was Carmi who later introduced me to the Indian poet Dom Moraes, whom he'd met in Israel when Dom was covering the Six Day War for an English paper.

In the course of our tour, we were to give five major readings and shake many hands. But before we even began the readings we had to face the press. I sat shyly behind a long makeshift table in a large hall as I looked to my more experienced and much better-known colleagues to take the lead, but they too sat in an uneasy silence, nobody wanting to break the ice.

Ranged in front of us were the literary and features editors of Israel's various dailies and weeklies, asking polite questions, politely ignoring our evasions. We batted carefully, watched over by the experienced eye of Charles Osborne, literature director of the Arts Council, who had accompanied us. We were unsure of our audience, unsure at that early stage of each other. Were we a school? *No*, we were not. *No*, there was no *one* concern in our work. *Yes*, readings were popular in England – *very* (I had happily answered that one!). Finally, in reply to one question, Peter Porter rose stoically to the rescue, improvising for some five minutes before concluding with words to the effect that in about fifteen years, it (whatever 'it' was) would probably have sorted itself out. 'That may be OK for you,' boomed a loud American voice from the back, 'but Mr Feinstein here has to have his copy in today!' Next morning, the *Jerusalem Post*, Israel's English-language daily, carried an ambiguous headline above a photo of the five of us, 'No school we say British poets'. All the papers featured long articles with photos and profiles and included poems translated into Hebrew. Imagine British newspapers giving such serious coverage to a reading tour by foreign poets! But then, as we were to discover, this was a highly literate and cultured society and for them, despite the language barrier, despite the pressures they were under politically and militarily, poetry mattered. The People of the Book, indeed. (Many years later I was to hear the eminent Oxford historian Diarmaid MacCulloch proclaim that it is not scientific progress that dictators fear, but poetry. An arresting thought.)

The first of our readings was to an audience of some 900 in the large Nahman Hall in Tel Aviv, named after Israel's national poet, Chaim Nahman Bialik, who had lived nearby. The next two were in Jerusalem at the Khan, a one-time stable (not *that* stable!) now converted into an exotic theatre; then one in the Haifa Theatre, and one on a kibbutz, Kfar Menachem, some thirty miles south of Tel Aviv. There were also some less formal readings and discussions. Just as it was fascinating for us to watch the styles of our Israeli counterparts and to come to recognise their individual mannerisms as surely as they must

Waiting to be served at Felds – Dannie Abse, Douglas Hill and me.

ABOVE LEFT At Max Geldray's farewell party, with Peter Sellers on my makeshift drums, Michael Garrick at the piano. Max is at the front.

ABOVE RIGHT By now, Carole was in charge of book sales at the concerts.

LEFT Things were getting serious – Carole meets my grandfather. He never liked her to wear black.

Putting on the style. My grandparents Harriet and Emanuel Snowman on board the *Queen Mary*.

Carole's lovely parents, Ben and Jocy de Botton. I was one of those English things her mother eventually got used to!

A portrait of Queen Alexandra by my great-uncle Isaac Snowman, pictured left.

My mother (nearest camera) in the British hockey team for the first Maccabiah Games, held in Tel Aviv in 1932.

My parents with members of the Jewish Brigade. Moshe (later Professor) Brawer is on the right, next to my father. Some twenty years later he would drive me around Israel.

My uncle Kenneth Snowman relaxes in Normandy with his brushes and easel.

ABOVE My parents, Charlotte and Joe, who gave us so much.

FAR LEFT Felix Gluck, with whom I worked closely at Aldus Books and after.

LEFT The jacket of my first book, *33 Poems*, using Felix Gluck's much-admired linocuts.

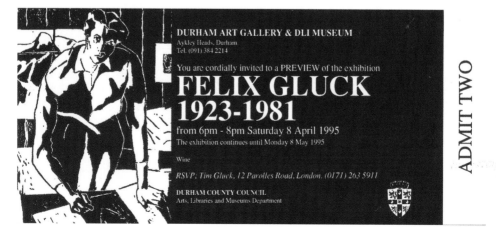

DURHAM ART GALLERY & DLI MUSEUM
Aykley Heads, Durham
Tel. (091) 384 2214

You are cordially invited to a PREVIEW of the exhibition

FELIX GLUCK
1923-1981

from 6pm - 8pm Saturday 8 April 1995
The exhibition continues until Monday 8 May 1995

Wine

RSVP: Tim Gluck, 12 Parolles Road, London. (0171) 263 5911

DURHAM COUNTY COUNCIL
Arts, Libraries and Museums Department

ADMIT TWO

The entrance ticket for the exhibition of Felix's work held at the Durham Art Gallery after his death.

The night after President Kennedy was shot. Before our concert at the Brangwyn Hall in Swansea, the surprising Laurie serenades Carole with his violin.

At the Aldus Books poetry and jazz concert, Joe Harriott demonstrates his evident appreciation of the hospitality provided by my boss, Wolfgang Foges.

ABOVE At a calmer moment of the Aldus Books concert, I chat to our neighbour Arnold Wesker, and to Laurie Lee, who had agreed to read with me and Dannie Abse.

LEFT Here comes the bride. Carole is wearing a specially designed headpiece incorporating some beautiful old lace given to her by her grandmother, to whom she was especially close.

LEFT Talking with Dannie Abse and David Ben-Gurion at the London press launch for B-G's mammoth *The Jews in Their Land*, on which I worked for many months.

BELOW Wolfgang Foges, Aldus MD, can hardly believe Ben-Gurion's book is finally complete as he welcomes him to the Aldus office. Afterwards we celebrated in true Foges style at the White Tower.

The Theatre Royal reading in Stratford East was the first at which Ted Hughes (left) and Stevie Smith (right) appeared. © KEN COTON

Also reading with us at Stratford was Douglas Hill, who added a welcome Canadian twang to the proceedings. © KEN COTON

have done ours, so it was equally compelling to watch the various English reading styles adapting to the warm-blooded, responsive audiences, and to see the reaction to the dry wit of Enright, the learned ironies of Porter, the cutting insights of Abse and the intensity of Hughes reading from his recent book, *Crow*. Ted, especially, made few concessions to his audience, holding his book up high, reading slowly and with great power. The atmosphere was electric when he read. It was sometimes hard not to think back to the reading at Rolle College in Devon where he'd introduced me to Assia Wevill, his then partner, who, like Sylvia Plath before her, had taken her own life. She had also taken the life of the little daughter, Shura, she'd had with Ted. But Ted seemed to have come through the Greek-like tragedy of those years and to be relaxed and happy with Carol, and they were both particularly warm and friendly to me throughout the tour, Ted turning to me one night in the wings as we were about to go on stage and saying, 'You're missing your family, aren't you?', as indeed I was. Ted loved Israel, and at one point, doubtless encouraged by his friendship with Yehuda Amichai and his wife Hannah, was said to be thinking of buying a home in Jerusalem.

Speaking of Jerusalem, I remember how those of my fellow poets who'd not been to Israel before found it hard to believe that the glittering toy façade they looked down on from the Intercontinental Hotel was indeed the walled old city of Jerusalem. And when we were led through the old city by the writer and guide Yehuda Ha'ezrachi to the Temple Mount, to the Mosque of Omar, to the Church of the Holy Sepulchre, to the old Jewish Quarter – even when the city's ghosts and associations had been lovingly recalled for us, even then the spell of unreality remained. Only later, when Ted, Carol, Dannie and I returned to wander the alleys and colourful bazaars and we were treated to a truly oriental display of bargaining by the lively Mrs Hughes, did the place take on some vestige of reality. (Amusingly, in Acre a few days later, Ted tried to match his wife's performance, and when quoted £10 for a set of Turkish coffee cups offered £5. 'Ah, so you want to bargain,' came the fast reply. 'OK, £20.') I couldn't help thinking back to the first time I'd looked down at the old city, in 1960, where Jordanian soldiers manned the walls, their rifles glistening in the sun. It was

enemy territory then that could not be entered, but now we were free
to wander there and when, guided by Yehuda Amichai, we returned for
one last visit, Ted startled us as we came out of the Mosque of Omar
by throwing himself full length on the ground and intoning into a
metal grille beneath him, 'Dark, dark, dark.' He seemed to be trying
to summon some kind of spirit from its depths. Then, rising, he held
up his hands, proudly displaying the marks the grating had made on
them, as if they were some kind of mystical sign.

Just as unreal as Jerusalem was an early morning drive through Galilee to Lake Tiberias (the Sea of Galilee), where several of us decided to
swim, right by the remains of the ancient synagogue at Capernaum. It
was February and the water was cold. 'No wonder Jesus *walked* on the
water,' declared Dannie as he plunged bravely in. In nearby Nazareth,
in the Basilica of the Annunciation, the traditional site of Joseph and
Mary's home, our guide rounded on Ted and Carol for holding hands
(as honeymooners do), shouting, 'This is no place for love!' 'Maybe not,'
whispered the ever-ready Enright, 'but I know a handy cowshed.' After
that, we drove swiftly south through the desert down to the Dead Sea,
where Carol Hughes and I and one or two of the others swam again, or
tried to – not swimming but floating, as Stevie Smith might have put it.
Then, finally, we reached Masada, where we stood in silent awe, trying
to imagine the dramatic events that had unfolded there. I recalled how
vividly David Kossoff had described these in his book, *The Voices of
Masada*. It was a windy day, and I have several photos of us standing on
the summit's edge, as in a school photo, our hair wild in the breeze. On
these journeys, Ted and I discovered that we shared a passion for the
freshly squeezed orange juice that was invariably sold at the roadside
stalls, and we raced to be first out whenever we stopped for a break.
Messrs Porter and Enright, however, seemed to prefer the ice-cold
Goldstar beer. Their thirst and their energy seemed unquenchable, and
long after most of us had fallen into an exhausted silence on the way
back from here or there, they'd continue their sparkling double act at
full blast, whether talking about literature, the Bible, music or whatever. No wonder a pale Dennis Enright came down to breakfast one
morning saying, 'I feel like the Six Day Whore.'

*Peter Porter cautiously leads Dannie Abse, me and Yehuda Amichai
into the freezing waters of Lake Galilee.*

It wasn't just the beer, though. There were so many lunches and parties
– before and after the readings. In Jerusalem, there was a lunch for us
at the spectacularly situated Hebrew University, and in the evening
the city's famous mayor, Teddy Kollek, hosted a cocktail party where
one of the guests was the Irish-born Chaim Herzog, who was later to
become the country's sixth president. Knowing that at one time this
lively and genial man had been head of Israel's military intelligence,
I put on my publisher's hat for a moment and tried to engage him in
a conversation about Wolfgang Lotz, but the shutters went down in a
flash and the subject was swiftly changed! Another evening we were
invited for drinks at the home of the British Council's director in Israel,
who lived in Herzliya, now a rather affluent seaside suburb of Tel Aviv,
where Carole and I had received the summons from Ben-Gurion six
years earlier. After the British Council reception we found ourselves
whisked to a lovely house where an enormous spread awaited us. The
party had been arranged by the owners on spec and in the hope that
they could lure Ted there. This was confirmation, if any were needed,
of Ted's fame and the regard in which he was held. That became yet
clearer later that evening when the doorbell rang and a man, a little the
worse for drink (doubtless he'd been at the earlier party), entered with
his young son. He told us he'd been going from house to house looking
for Ted, whom he greatly admired. It was the novelist Lionel Davidson, the award-winning author of such bestselling books as *The Rose*

of Tibet and *A Long Way to Shiloh*, at whose quaint home in Hampstead Village Carole and I had spent several pleasurable evenings. He seemed to revere Ted, sitting rather embarrassingly at his feet, asking him questions. Ted had no idea who he was until Dannie tactfully explained, and next day I showed him a display of Davidson's books in a shop window. It had been a bizarre visitation.

Generally, we were driven in small, air-conditioned 'executive' coaches, but sometimes we found ourselves in spacious taxis that accommodated us all. That was always an experience, for Israel's taxi drivers must be among their country's most volatile citizens, high-wire artists and clowns rolled into one. The show had started on the way from the airport to our hotel when our driver turned and announced solemnly, 'The last poet I drove around Israel was Mr Priestley.' They drove as though practising for a dash to the Suez Canal, and when a back door flew open on a Jerusalem bend our numbers might well have been reduced had not Ted grabbed hold of Dannie and pulled him back into the car. They all told involved stories, talked sadly about their sons in the army and the tensions of living in a country surrounded by enemies, and sang – and wouldn't you sing if, as one driver claimed to have done, you'd once performed with Gigli at the Scala Milan? 'Mirage,' boomed another proudly as a plane swooped low over our heads. It had seemed real enough to me!

Jerusalem line-up (left to right): D. J. Enright, Dannie Abse, Carmi, Peter Porter, me, Ted Hughes, Charles Osborne and Yehuda Amichai (front).

That whole extraordinary trip might have seemed like a mirage were it not for the photos, posters and programmes I still have, and for the friendships that endured long after some of those mementos began to fade. But for all that, it was marvellous to be home and to share it all with Carole. A month or so later, the Arts Council held an event in London at The Place, at which we were all invited to read and share our experiences of Israel with the audience, and then Ted and Carol came to us for dinner. That was a warm and relaxed evening as we sat in the kitchen looking at photos and reminiscing. My Carole had been at the Theatre Royal when Ted first read at a poetry and jazz concert, so she was prepared for the power of his personality, but not perhaps for his gentleness and the consideration he displayed that night. However, I know she felt and still remembers the hypnotic power of his eyes. A few months later, in June, Carmi and Yehuda Amichai came to London to participate in Poetry International, the festival Ted had founded, and we gave a small party at home. It was gratifying to be able to return just a little of the hospitality we had received.

16

UP AND RUNNING

Back in a fairly grey London, it took me some time to get the excitement and buzz of the reading tour out of my system and buckle down to the daily publishing routine. I kept in touch with the others, with whom a kind of bond seemed to have been formed. Shortly after, Dennis Enright gave up his job at Chatto & Windus, where he'd been working as a literary adviser, to become literary editor of *Encounter* magazine, and I was delighted when he got in touch asking me to write for the magazine and to send him a few new poems. I wasn't sure, when we chatted in Israel, that the intellectual Dennis was really cut out for the commercial world of publishing, but he'd amused me by recalling that on arriving at Chatto, Norah Smallwood, the company's *grande dame*, had told him it was important for him, as a publisher, to attend as many memorial services as possible. I can't imagine that this was part of the original job description, though Dennis had a mournful streak that it might well have appealed to.

David Kessler and Frank Cass now seemed close to some form of marriage, though knowing K's cautious nature and discovering in due course that Cass was one of the world's great procrastinators, it was a show that could have run for some time. Later, Frank boasted to me that at school he'd been able to stay at the wicket all day without scoring, but in truth I never saw any evidence that he'd ever wielded a cricket bat. Eventually, however, a deal was struck, though I never knew its exact nature, and we upped sticks (to use a favourite Kessler phrase) and moved from the *JC* offices to the Frank Cass offices in

Great Russell Street. From time to time, K would join us for the occasional meeting, so he must have retained some interest in the company. The list had really been growing, and the finance had to come from somewhere.

I got on well with Frank, and it was clear that he was thrilled to be entering the world of general publishing and by the prospect of meeting authors, especially if they were personalities. He had a small team of exceptional editors – Elizabeth Rose, Ursula Owen (who amidst much else was to become, with the formidable Carmen Callil, a founder director of Virago – two dazzling stars in the publishing firmament) and Jim Muir, who came with a first-class Cambridge degree in Arabic and eventually moved to Beirut, becoming the BBC's award-winning Middle Eastern correspondent. Frank welcomed me into their editorial meetings, and it took me a while to realise that he'd only go ahead with the specialised academic titles he'd announced once he had sufficient orders on file. Sensible man! I also began to see that he frustrated his highly intelligent editors by prevaricating and using all kinds of diversionary tactics to avoid being pinned down. They, however, were never slow to speak their minds and to force matters when necessary. For all this, the Cass list was an impressive one and included a number of academic journals, each with a distinguished editor. He was an astute man with a real love and knowledge of books acquired from his bookselling days.

Frank's invaluable right-hand man was Michael Zaidner, a top-flight accountant. Frank kept up a jovial front at all times, generally leaving Michael to deal with any unpleasantness that might arise. They were a good double act. I liked Michael and appreciated what a hard job he had containing Frank's flights of fantasy and his Billy Liar approach to life. A disagreeable aspect of my first few months *chez* Cass was that Guy Meyers came to feel there wasn't a place for him, and left. Apart from the fact that he was an accountant and Michael Zaidner controlled the financial side of things, being Kessler's son-in-law must have made things awkward for Guy, and perhaps for the others too, for I sensed that Frank was wary about K knowing too much about his affairs. But maybe that was just my own projection.

Guy was always very decent, and the whole episode made me feel extremely uncomfortable.

What quickly became clear as the list expanded was that I needed an assistant and, thinking back to my Aldus Books days, I approached Carolyn Fearnside, who had worked there as personal assistant to one of the directors, and after some thought she agreed to join us. Carolyn was efficiency itself – organised, painstaking, thorough – all the things I wasn't. She also spoke German and was knowledgeable and passionate about classical music; her skills were later to prove invaluable. Looking back now at the editorial minutes, I realise that I managed to slip through titles K would never have thought right for Vallentine, Mitchell. These included *Great German Short Stories* edited by Stephen Spender, *Great English Short Stories* edited by Christopher Isherwood, and a book of Irish short stories too – part of a series I'd picked up at Frankfurt. The Jewish Classics series had expanded, and there were some quirky titles too, a favourite of mine being *The Life and Crimes of Ikey Solomons*, a Victorian underworld character on whom Dickens was said to have based Fagin. And then there was the dynamic Wolf Mankowitz, a man of so many parts it would require a special kind of superglue to hold them together. Sadly, Wolf is probably unknown to the younger generation, but in those days he was very much at the centre of the film and theatrical world, a wild cannon who fired in many directions – playwright, scriptwriter, director, novelist and the world expert on Wedgwood china. An odd mix. At Cambridge, Wolf had won the respect of the legendary F. R. Leavis, but he could not be academically contained. His most famous books (both made into films starring David Kossoff) were *A Kid for Two Farthings* and *The Bespoke Overcoat*. He also wrote the musical *Expresso Bongo* (the film version starred Cliff Richard and Laurence Harvey), the script for the *The Millionairess*, the West End musical *Pickwick* (in which Harry Secombe 'ruled the world'), and the screenplay for the James Bond film *Casino Royale*. He was one of the original investors in the left-wing Partisan Coffee House and part-owner of the Pickwick Club in Piccadilly, and as if that weren't enough, in 2010 files that came into the public domain revealed that for ten years after the war MI5 had suspected him of being a communist agent and kept him under surveillance. His many famous friends included Orson Welles, Topol, Richard Burton and Elizabeth Taylor. A man for all seasons, indeed.

While at Vallentine, Mitchell, I published Wolf's play *The Samson Riddle*, and to launch it he arranged a rehearsed reading at the prestigious Gate Theatre as part of the 1972 Dublin Theatre Festival (Wolf had gone to live in Ireland, which had tax advantages for writers). What's more, in typical Wolf style, he'd somehow persuaded Miriam Karlin and Susannah York to take part in it. Carole and I flew over for the Sunday performance, and Frank and Michael Zaidner and their wives joined us. As it was our first time in Dublin, we made the most of it, walking the city and loving its Joycean atmosphere. After the play, which was well received, Wolf and his psychologist wife Ann gave a party at their stylish home.

I hadn't really encountered Miriam Karlin since the days of my parents' soirées, when, as a young boy, I'd peered through the banisters, not wanting to leave the party and go up to bed. Since then she'd become extremely well known for her role as the shop steward in the TV series *The Rag Trade* with her 'Everybody out!' catchphrase. She'd also appeared opposite Laurence Olivier in the film adaptation of John Osborne's *The Entertainer*. That night in Dublin she surprised me by revealing that only a year or so earlier my father had come to her rescue when she was offered the part of Catlady in the film *A Clockwork Orange*, for she had a phobia of cats, and in the film they would be crawling all over her. The prospect terrified her, but she was able to go through with it after my father had treated her by hypnosis, and she was for ever grateful. It was a year or so before Carole and I saw that frightening film, along with our friends Andrea and Jeremy Morris, at the Gaumont State Cinema in Kilburn. I'd seen some of the American jazz greats performing there in my younger days, but though their music was thrilling it was a rather different kind of thrill from the one we experienced that night, sitting on the edge of our seats in the circle as the film reached its violent climax. Afterwards, the lights still dim, Carole and Andrea followed the audience to the exit while Jeremy and I walked slowly to the toilets at the back of the circle to relieve ourselves and the tension. As we were winding up (or, more exactly, zipping up), we heard a disturbing noise behind us, and looking round saw a large man by the door, whirling a chain in the air. With the film still filling our minds, we both had the same thought, and raced without a word past the intimidating man and down an emergency staircase – Jeremy running so fast that he stumbled and broke a collarbone. When we sent for the manager we were told the man was just waiting to lock up, and Jeremy's painful complaints fell on unsympathetic ears.

Wolf Mankowitz was always fun to be with, and in due course after we'd started Robson Books, Carole and I returned to Dublin to talk to him about various projects, one of which was a book of original fables, *The Day of the Women and the Night of the Men,* for which he co-opted Charles Raymond as illustrator. I think Wolf liked the idea that in addition to being a protégé of Augustus John and winner of several awards, Raymond had illustrated the mega-selling *The Joy of Sex* (not for us, alas). Some of the drawings in our book turned out to be a great deal sexier – Raymond gave me several, which I must confess are not on display on our walls (I can hear the questions they'd provoke from our grandchildren and am not sure I'd know the answers!).

Another reason for our going to Ireland was to meet the famous Irish actor Micheál MacLiammóir, whom Wolf was encouraging us to publish. Some years earlier I had gone with Spike Milligan to see MacLiammóir's remarkable one-man show about Oscar Wilde, *The Importance of Being Oscar,* at the Apollo Theatre in London, so was well aware of his remarkable talent. One critic called it an 'oral biography', for in writing the show MacLiammóir had not only presented Wilde as a great wit and man of letters but had reached beneath the surface to bring out the real tragedy of his life. As with most great comedy, there were tears amidst the laughter, and when the actor took his bow, Spike was quickly on his feet with the rest of the audience, proclaiming him 'a genius'. The performance was so compelling it could have been Wilde himself on stage.

The thought of meeting this legendary actor and wit was rather daunting, especially since we discovered on arriving in Dublin that he was in hospital. 'We'll go and visit him there,' said Wolf, never one to be swayed from his purpose. MacLiammóir was sitting up in bed when we arrived, his silk pyjamas in striking contrast to the rather drab surroundings. He was like one of those dying monarchs one sees in historical dramas on television, except that he wasn't dying and there wasn't a great circle of courtiers around him, but from the way he talked there might as well have been. Fortunately, Wolf took the lead, telling him that we were just the publishers he needed to reissue his out-of-print books and commission a new one. I nodded, Carole nodded, and I'm sure I muttered something about having seen him in London, and then we left this rather surreal scene, amazed that a man who had been seriously ill could still command the stage – even if that stage were a hospital. We brought ourselves back to reality at Mankowitz's house, where we discussed other books Wolf had in mind (he was about to write a TV series on Dickens's London), and as before he dangled the prospect of a book of poems – not his, but Richard Burton's love poems to Elizabeth Taylor – but although I could see the sensationalist headlines in my mind, as far as that project was concerned, that is all I did ever see, and probably just as well.

All that was still in the future, however, and returning to Vallentine, Mitchell, where I was still employed, it was becoming clear that Frank Cass had become smitten by the general publishing bug and was eager to spread his wings. He suggested to me that I build up a less specialised list to run side by side with Vallentine, Mitchell's Jewish one, offering me a 'consultancy' fee of £500 a year to bring in titles that would appear under his dormant Woburn Press imprint (in which I suspect neither the *Jewish Chronicle* nor anyone else had a stake at the time). I went at it like a wild horse released from a stable, with books ranging from *The Poets of the Second World War* by Vernon Scannell to works by F. Scott Fitzgerald and Arthur Calder-Marshall, a biography of Robert Browning, and a study of the films of Jean Renoir. All rather literary to start with, but then I came up with an idea I thought extremely commercial, and on one of our lunchtime walks around the Woburn Square block I said to Frank, 'How about seeing if we could publish the *Goon Show* scripts?' He liked the idea so much he even offered me one of his apples. More importantly, Spike Milligan, who'd written most of the shows, liked the idea too, though he was doubtful whether it would sell. After all, we were talking about old scripts for a programme that was no longer running, though there had recently been a special *Goon Show* to tie in with BBC's 50th anniversary, to which I was lucky enough to be invited courtesy of my old harmonica-playing friend Max Geldray, who'd flown in from LA to take part. What an exciting night that was, with Peter, Spike and Harry relishing every moment and playing up to the audience, which included Prince Philip, Princess Anne, Princess Margaret, Lord Snowdon and a galaxy of showbiz stars. It was a party nobody wanted to end, but one that the Goons' greatest royal fan, Prince Charles, had to miss, as he was on naval duty with HMS *Norfolk* in the Mediterranean. However, he amused everyone with a telegram which read: 'Last night my hair fell out and my knees dropped off with envy when I thought of my father and sister attending the show.'

Spike agreed to let us go through the files that were carefully locked away in his office, and even to take away some of the valuable scripts – particularly valuable since a number of them had drawings and doodles on them by one or other of the Goons. Although Spike had written the scripts and they were his copyright, I thought it only courtesy to mention it to Harry Secombe, who loved the idea, and to Peter Sellers, whom I arranged to meet for lunch at Cranks, taking Frank with me. Peter, too, gave the project his blessing.

Frank then asked me whether I'd like one of his editors, Elizabeth Rose, to work with me on the book. Editorially, that was a great suggestion, but in the light of what transpired, perhaps not so wise from Frank's point of view. Liz was imaginative and full of original ideas as to how the book should be presented. We realised we needed an exceptional designer and brought in Felix Gluck, who by then had also left Aldus Books, and between us we decided that the text should appear just like the original scripts, with all the sound effects and other directions that were such an integral part of the show left in place. Then Felix came up with an inspired idea for the cover, which was to make the book look like a box file.

Some of the scripts were prefaced by brief scene-setting lead-ins, and where these were missing Liz supplied similar synopses à la Milligan, and, after much chasing, Spike (who never went anywhere in a straight line) eventually provided descriptions and cod biographies of the show's famous characters – Eccles, Bluebottle, Neddie Seagoon, Henry Crun, Minnie Bannister, Major Denis Bloodnok, Hercules Grytpype-Thynne and the rest. To our delight, Peter Sellers sent a foreword under the alias of Major Denis Bloodnok, SFI and Bar, written on specially printed stationery with the heading 'Denis Bloodnok and Partner (Deceased)', while Harry Secombe contributed a 'backword', which appeared on the last page of the book ('Now this is where the story *really* starts'). Finally, all the scripts were splattered with drawings by the three of them. Thanks to Liz's flair and Felix's design, it all looked great fun – and was. Everyone involved was excited, and in my precious signed copy Peter wrote, 'I think you have accomplished the impossible.' Given my long involvement with the Goons, that was an accolade I was proud to receive and one I gladly shared with Liz and Felix.

Now all Frank had to do was sell it. I read recently that the original printing was 25,000 copies, but I question this, given that the company had never published a book of this kind and didn't really have the sales set-up to do so. Also, as I recall, booksellers were sceptical at first – until, that is, we managed to persuade all three Goons to appear on Michael Parkinson's popular TV talk show. It being a BBC programme, it was strictly forbidden to display or over-promote a book on air, but nothing was going to stop the three of them from holding up copies and giving it a mighty plug – and we really didn't know what had hit us as the orders poured in and the book went from reprint to reprint, topping all the bestseller lists. And then Frank, having introduced me to Liz, made another mistake, telling *The Bookseller* magazine in an interview and all and sundry that he'd always been a *Goon Show* fan and how he'd had this fantastic idea, etc. Vanity, perhaps, but it didn't go down well in my household. Nevertheless, with Liz now working closely with me, we brought in more books of the same kind, and scripts of *Till Death Us Do Part*, *Round the Horne* and *Hancock's Half Hour* were to follow, some published after I'd left the company. Once started, it was not a difficult line to follow, but it could be risky. I was also on the point of signing a contract with Harry Secombe for a novel he'd had lying in a drawer for some years. But before that...

Before that, we started to get regular visits (or rather visitations) from a strange man in tattered jeans with wild hair and bulbous eyes who looked as if he hadn't two pennies to rub together – except for the fact that he always arrived in an old Rolls-Royce driven by a similarly dressed chauffeur. It was Marty Feldman, responding to my overtures about writing a book for us. Marty was one of the most way-out comic writers of the era, and a great comedian. With another esteemed writer, Barry Took, he had co-written the classic *Round the Horne* programmes, creating, among others, the outrageously camp characters Julian and Sandy (played respectively but not respectfully by Hugh Paddick and Kenneth Williams). For his part, Marty was to branch out, writing and starring in a number of breakthrough TV comedy shows and going on to appear in two Mel Brooks classics, *Young Frankenstein* and *Silent Movie*, and other films. As far as books went, Marty was fizzing with ideas, none of them remotely practical as I recall, including a suggestion for producing toilet rolls with a joke on each sheet. He never did put anything on paper for us (not even on toilet paper), but several years later, via the more down-to-earth Barry Took, we did publish *The Bona Book of Julian and Sandy*, which they co-wrote.

I was saddened to read about the brilliant Marty's death aged only forty-eight while he was filming in Mexico – so much promise unfulfilled, though he did leave an autobiography which was discovered and published just a few years ago. I wish we'd been the lucky publisher. (I also wish I'd managed to persuade a beautiful young girl called Pamela to go to the school dance with me after we'd met one Sunday at the Queensway ice rink, aged around sixteen – long, friendly telephone conversations, but no dancing. I didn't realise until many years later, long after I'd met him, that Pamela was Marty's younger sister. Well, they certainly didn't look alike!)

Not long after Marty drew up in his improbable Rolls, we arranged a dinner party at home. The guests were David and Jenny Kossoff,

Wolfgang and Catherine Foges, Dannie and Joan Abse and my old, very tall school friend Michael Rivkin and his wife. By then Michael had reached other heights as a property developer with ambitious schemes to develop Docklands, riding around in a chauffeur-driven Rolls (his driver dressed rather more smartly than Marty's!) and with a large house in the country – all this without losing his modesty and charm. At the end of the dinner, when the others had left, Michael turned to me and said, 'Why are you doing all this for other people? How much would it need to start a publishing company?' It was completely unexpected, and before I could get my thoughts together, Michael continued, 'Think about it and if you are interested work out some figures and give me a ring next week.' And that, almost, is how Robson Books started.

Of course, nothing is quite that straightforward, and before phoning Michael to test his resolve, I asked my accountant friend Jeremy Morris to help me put some figures together. He willingly came over and worked with Carole and me on the dining room table to create some kind of cash-flow forecast, giving projected sales and associated costs (printing, warehousing, reps etc.) for notional titles, along with anticipated office and staff overheads, and the rest. We reckoned we'd need £20,000 to get under way, and when I called Michael Rivkin to tell him, he said it was the kind of figure he'd expected (which is probably what he'd have said if I had come in higher!), inviting Jeremy and me to his office, where, having poured whiskies commensurate with his size, he went through the figures with us. Michael liked the idea of Jeremy being involved, knowing how good and reliable he was, and offered him a job with one of his other companies, suggesting he spend two-thirds of his week there, and a third with me, with the two companies paying his salary proportionally. He then arranged for me to go with him to Barclays in Pall Mall, where everyone said, 'Good morning, Mr Rivkin', 'Good morning, Mr Rivkin' as he marched towards the manager's office as if he owned the place, with me following in his wake and thinking that when we were at school *I* was the captain of the team in which he'd played! A facility, guaranteed by Michael's company, was quickly agreed.

Michael Rivkin, our original backer.

Once all this and the legal niceties were settled, I gave notice to Frank and resigned immediately from the Woburn Press consultancy. Meanwhile, Jeremy went office searching and came up with small but more than adequate premises in Poland Street, while I approached Liz and Carolyn, explained in confidence what I was up to and asked them to join me. Luckily for me, they were both brave enough to agree. Thinking then about the production side of things, I spoke to Felix Gluck and he recommended a lady he knew from Hungary he thought would fit the bill, and so Susan Schulz eventually came on board as production manager. As it happened, Felix had recently started a high-quality children's imprint of his own, The Gluck Press, and was looking for a *pied à terre* in town. We therefore came to an arrangement whereby he would oversee our design in return for a small room at the back of our office. It suited us both.

It was now May 1973, and we planned to launch our first list in September of that year. No point hanging around – but who and what would we publish? Who would promote and sell the titles, and where would we warehouse? For selling, we turned to Book Representation, run by Roger Smith, and for warehousing to Seeley, Service & Cooper, whose warehouse, run by the military publisher Leo Cooper (husband

of Jilly), was just off Shaftesbury Avenue. Then, realising how important publicity would be if we were to get off the ground in a meaningful way, I approached Carmen Callil, whom I'd first met when she was
working at Granada Publishing and they'd brought out the paperback
edition of my *Poetry and Jazz in Concert* anthology. And so it was the
great Carmen who helped launch both our company, Robson Books,
and our first list, and certain other titles in due course.

Now all we had to do was find the books to publish.

17

OVERTURE AND BEGINNERS

The mid-1970s were probably as good a time as any to set up publishing shop, given that there seemed to be many more openings and opportunities for a small publisher to make a mark than there would appear to be today. Lively reps and good publicity could make all the difference then – provided you had the right books, that is – with reps able to call regularly on the bookshops in their area and draw on relationships they had built up over the years, and at Christmas deliver car stock galore. Now it's nearly all central and frugal. With the Net Book Agreement still solidly in place, the smaller publishers were less easily outgunned by the big guys pushing their wares and giving crippling discounts. What's more, there were fewer of them, with many of the mergers still way off in the future. Once the NBA was abandoned, everything changed – for the worse, in my opinion. Before, with many more bookshops and a far greater variety of titles, there was room for personality in a publishing list and for a number of vigorous independent publishers to make their mark. To an extent, things were author-led then, as they should be, rather than discount-led, so provided you were fast on your feet the world was full of exciting opportunities – or so it seemed. At Frankfurt and other book fairs there were many small companies exhibiting, some with enticing titles on their shelves to be spotted by alert eyes. Now the conglomerates are so conglomerated, and incorporate so many imprints, it's hard to remember who is where, if indeed they are still anywhere.

All that apart, among the larger companies there are and have been some truly great publishers, naturally. As well as Tom McCormack, I think of Sonny Mehta at Knopf; of the phenomenal Gail Rebuck, now chair of Penguin Random House, to whom I enjoyed selling paperback rights when she ran Hamlyn Paperback in the 1970s; and of Peter Mayer, the brilliant cosmopolitan publisher who ran and revived the Penguin empire for nearly twenty years, and later owned Duckworth and the Overlook Press, which he founded in 1971. Peter could be extremely charming, and occasionally he would flatter me by inviting me to lunch, leaning forward solicitously to ask me to tell him how to publish humour – as if he, of all people, needed lessons from a rookie like me!

When Peter moved to America to take command of the struggling Penguin empire, I saw both the charm and the fire of this great publisher at work. Arriving at his office, I was shown into an unusually large room with a couch at one end, to which I was steered, while at the other end sat Peter at a round table facing a youngish woman. He seemed to be upbraiding her about something, and that something became clear as his voice rose. 'You hired her, and you're responsible. She's upset one of our major authors, and *you* had better mend those fences fast!' I imagine he was talking to one of his senior editors, and it was embarrassing to be sitting there and having to witness it all. A few minutes later, she got up and started to move away, but he called her back, saying he hadn't finished with her, and continued his tirade. Then, walking over to me as if nothing had happened, he greeted me with his usual warmth and charm, without any reference to the scene he obviously knew I had just witnessed. When I left, nearly an hour later, I took with me a handsome offer for the US rights to Peter Heller's forthcoming biography of Mike Tyson, then at the height of his power and fame as heavyweight champion of the world. I really couldn't complain.

*   *   *

When we started, it was by no means as easy as I imply, and there were many traps and pitfalls to avoid, just as there are now – overprinting, when enthusiasm carried you away, and overpaying for that title you just *had* to have. And how did we manage without email and computers? Somehow we did. There was time to think, to reflect, even to read, without everything having to be instant, as a more civilised kind of publishing hung on. It was thrilling, too, to open the post in the morning and see a wodge of orders from reps and also direct from bookshops – branch after Waterstones branch, as I recall, giving one a real sense of when a book was in demand and starting to move. I know one can now read computer printouts, but for me it has never been quite the same thing. That was particularly apparent with titles that weren't run-of-the-mill, or where there wasn't a well-known author to promote it. Our *Twins Handbook* was one such title, published at a time when there wasn't a similar book on the market and in virtually every post there was an order marked 'extremely urgent'. We smiled knowingly and made sure we delivered quickly (sorry!) and kept the book in print. Another surprising title that had been recommended by the manager of a WH Smith branch in Wigan, via our rep (such things happened then), was a book on the legendary Wigan Casino all-nighter club, the hub of Northern Soul music in the 1970s. We took a deep breath and published it, hoping there would be strong local interest if nothing else. We banged on Smith's door for a scale-out to branches nationwide, but it was only when we were able to demonstrate that we had received nearly 1,000 direct orders from branches around the country that they relented and agreed to make the book widely available. People might have moved away from their northern roots for one reason or another, but they still cherished the memory of dancing the nights away to those live bands, and they wanted a copy!

Our first list, launched in September 1973 and put together at great speed, set the pattern for the future: the serious, the literary, the so-called worthy sitting side by side with the more popular. Thus *The Thoughts of Chairman Alf* (Garnett) twinned with a political biography of Henry Kissinger, *Dick Emery in Character* with a book on Edgar Allan Poe, and Harry Secombe's novel *Twice Brightly* with a book of conversations with the American poet Robert Frost, and so on. That is not to denigrate the popular and the humorous, for humour was to become one of our strengths, with such stellar writers as Alan Coren, Miles Kington, Jill Tweedie and Frank Johnson flying our early flag. I have always maintained that if you are passionate about something you can make it work, and that's what we tried to do. When, much later on, we were offered a

book on the mathematics of everyday life by Rob Eastaway, we jumped
at it, and tens of thousands of copies later were pleased we had, and
that we had changed the title at the last minute from *How Fast Should
You Run in the Rain?* to *Why Do Buses Come in Threes?* It made all the
difference. It would have been so easy to say when offered that book (as
I hear time and again these days), 'It's not really us' – not a mantra I've
ever subscribed to. Everything can be 'us' if you want it to be, and sometimes life is full of rewarding surprises. For this reason, our more popular,
commercial titles have often rubbed shoulders with books that took us
in different directions – volumes such as *Calling for Action* by Donald
Soper, the legendary Methodist minister famous for his soapbox ora-
tions at Hyde Park Corner, or *Related Twilights*, an illustrated memoir
by the Polish artist Josef Herman, known for his paintings of the Welsh
miners he lived among for some years, or *A Hundred Years of Railway
Weighells*, a colourful family history by the outspoken former General
Secretary of the National Union of Railwaymen, Sidney Weighell.

*The Directors of Robson Books
by courtesy of Martini & Rossi
have pleasure in inviting you to meet*

DICK EMERY

at a Reception to mark the publication of his book

IN CHARACTER
A Kind of Living Scrapbook

*on Monday, 22nd October 1973
from 12.45 to 2.00 p.m.
at the Martini Terrace,
16th Floor, New Zealand House,
80 Haymarket, London S.W.1.*

R.S.V.P.
The Directors
Robson Books
28 Poland Street   DICK EMERY
London W1V 3DB   IN CHARACTER will be
Tel: 01-734 1052/3   published by Robson Books
                            on October 22nd (£1.99)

Invitation to our first book launch – for the very popular Dick Emery's In Character.

Harry (later Sir Harry) Secombe, our highly commercial early contender, was one of the most open-hearted, genial and talented of men, who lifted everyone's spirits the minute he entered the room, and his wife Myra was just as special – warm, down-to-earth and always welcoming. They had met at a dance in Swansea at the Mumbles Pier Dance Hall, and afterwards Harry escorted her to the station, having arranged to meet her at six o'clock the following night outside the Plaza cinema. Harry wrote:

> The next morning I had quite a hangover, and for the life of me I couldn't remember what my date for the evening looked like. I decided I'd arrive early at the Plaza, get behind one of the pillars outside the cinema and keep a furtive watch. If I didn't fancy what I saw I'd stay where I was and forget the whole thing. It was a quarter past six when, tired of waiting, I stepped out from behind my pillar to go home, just as Myra daintily made an appearance from behind hers. And in this atmosphere of mutual distrust, our courtship began.

Apart from his great comedic gifts and startling tenor voice, Harry loved to write and contributed regularly to various magazines including *Punch*. He went on to produce several more comic novels, a series of children's books and two volumes of autobiography, all of which we were lucky enough to publish. I say lucky, since his *Twice Brightly* was very nearly contracted while I was with Frank Cass, but on hearing I was leaving, Harry's daughter Jenny rescued it and brought it to us. At that time Jenny had her own publicity company, but in due course she joined the publicity department at BBC Television, eventually becoming publicity commissioner for entertainment, managing the team responsible for all the comedy/light entertainment output on television. Jenny was extremely close to her father, and she generally handled his publicity. Who better?

Twice Brightly followed the struggles of a young comedian through his first week in variety and conjured up that vanished world of oddball novelty acts, shabby digs, strict landladies and hard-to-please audiences. 'Audience with me all the way, managed to shake them off at the station,' wrote Harry in a later autobiography, recalling his own first week in variety, when his act consisted of shaving onstage in various comic ways. 'I'll not have you shaving in my time,' bellowed the humourless manager, sending him packing.

The allotted publication date for Harry's book – 9 October – was not the most auspicious, since the Prime Minister, Harold Wilson, had called an election for the following day. Naturally, all the media wanted was discussion about politics, but nevertheless we managed to get the popular Harry on several programmes. As he, Jenny and I arrived at the BBC for one of these radio appearances, the lift doors opened and out marched Wilson with various aides, including his controversial political secretary, Marcia Falkender. Seeing the beaming Harry, Wilson stopped and said, 'Look here, Harry,' pointing to the cufflinks he was wearing, which Harry had apparently given him. They wished each other luck, Wilson perhaps needing it more than Harry, as he scraped home with a majority of just three. *Plus ça change…*

Fortune was certainly smiling on Harry when *Punch* magazine made headlines with their coup in getting the *Goon*-mad Prince Charles to review *Twice Brightly*, and what a rave it was. The papers splashed it as a news story in a big way and the orders rolled in. Harry was already a sought-after speaker at literary lunches, but now there were even more requests – hardly surprising given that he was very witty, and often ended on a high C in a bonus cabaret performance! At one *Yorkshire Post* literary lunch, a man came up to Harry as he was signing books and said, 'You nearly had me laughing.' He certainly had Harry laughing on the drive back to London, as he recalled the northern working men's clubs where he'd cut his teeth and they'd say, 'If you please 'em here, you'll please 'em anywhere.'

'It's fun being a turn,' Harry would quip as people queued up to talk to him or ask him to appear at a charity do somewhere or sign autographs in the pouring rain. He was a joy to be with and I still laugh when I recall how he started one after-dinner speech at a Birmingham hotel: 'I have fond memories of coming here some years ago, and particularly of the head waiter.' Pause. 'When he died, they inscribed on his tomb, "God finally caught his eye".'

Harry's second novel, *Welsh Fargo*, about a man called Dai Fargo who ran a rather ramshackle bus service in South Wales, landed us in a brief legal confrontation when someone in Wales claimed we were mocking the real bus service he ran (called Wells Fargo, as I recall) and, what's more, accused Harry of impugning the sexual morals of the proprietor's wife, since there was a little bit of innocent hanky-panky in the story. I wish I still had the long telegrams we received from the complainant's solicitors, which read like a *Goon Show* script. But the matter had to be taken seriously, and we sought the advice of a leading QC, who told us, 'I've never said this to anyone before, but I give you a 100/1 chance of winning any action.' One robust response from our solicitor, Anthony Harkavy, and the claimant backed down at once.

Harry was naturally always in demand for signing sessions in Wales, and after one in Cardiff, while walking with me back to his car, he stopped in front of an intriguing shop that sold penknives, peering into the window like an excited schoolboy. 'Just what I need,' he said, stepping inside – to the delight of the shop owner, who of course recognised him instantly and quickly laid a whole array of knives on the glass counter. 'That's the one for me,' said Harry, pointing to an expensive Swiss Army knife that had blades galore, plus a bottle opener, a corkscrew, screwdriver and something to take stones out of horses' hooves. 'Would you like one?' he suddenly asked, turning to me in his generous way. I tried to say I didn't need one (which I didn't) but he insisted and I too ended up with one of those all-singing, all-dancing knives in my pocket. And now it lies in the glove compartment of my car as a permanent memento of Harry, just waiting for a horse with a stone in its hoof to limp across the road so I can jump out, penknife in hand, and come to its rescue. Climbing into the front seat of his car next to the driver, Harry turned to me as I settled down in the back and asked if I'd like to hear a track from his new recording, which he'd just received but hadn't had a chance to listen to. And so, with that magnificent voice and an aria from *Turandot* ringing in my ears, we sped down the motorway to London.

Wherever he went, the exuberant Harry was always centre stage, always gave at least 100 per cent of himself. I recall a heady lunch in the basement of a restaurant off St James's, where we found ourselves sitting near a table occupied by the sales directors of William Collins and their Australian agents. Fatal! Within minutes Harry was deep in lively conversation with them, swapping stories, the laughter infectious. I'd hardly staggered back to the office when I received a phone call from Helen Fraser, then head of Fontana, Collins's classy paperback imprint, saying she didn't know what had happened over lunch but all her sales people were telling her she *had* to buy the paperback rights of Harry Secombe's books from us, and she did.

Then there was the evening Harry came to our office to talk to our reps, joining Carole and me and one or two others for a quiet meal afterwards at the small and convivial Trattoria La Torre around the corner. A quiet meal? With Harry there was no such thing, and no sooner had Dino, one of the owners, started to sing Neapolitan songs, accompanying himself on his guitar, than the powerful Secombe voice rang out. As the wine went down so the high notes soared higher and higher, and as the restaurant shook, we and the other lucky diners were treated to a thrilling cabaret that went on into the small hours. How did Harry explain that to Myra, I wondered?

When the Secombes lived in Cheam, Harry would arrange a charity cricket match every summer, and what fun these were. The teams always consisted of well-known cricketers and sportsmen together with a good sprinkling of showbiz personalities. Naturally, the high spot was when the short-sighted Harry went in to bat, the bowling suddenly becoming slow motion to allow him to score a run or two, and great cheers erupting around the ground as Harry raised his bat in triumph. No wonder he was universally loved! Although he was immensely proud of being honoured with a knighthood for his services to entertainment and charity, he was never one to take himself seriously, always referring to himself as 'Sir Cumference', and the motto he took for his coat of arms was 'Go On'. Dear Harry – as Max Miller used to say of himself, 'There'll never be another.'

There was one alarming moment in the long-laughing Secombe saga, when, in 1982, Harry took seriously ill on a flight to Australia. Diagnosed with peritonitis, he underwent a life-saving operation and was warned that if he didn't lose weight, his days would be strictly numbered. As a result, and with his wife Myra reading the riot act,

Harry went on a medically controlled diet and lost almost five of his twenty stone in six months, joking that he'd seen his knees for the first time in years, and that he no longer had to get sail makers to make his shirts! Needless to say, there was a book in it, *The Harry Secombe Diet Book*, and, promoted by its much-loved, slimline author, it shot up the bestseller lists, which was an unexpected tonic for us all.

Fast forward to 1998, and we'd just published Harry's *Arias and Raspberries*, the first of his two volumes of autobiography. At that time, *This Is Your Life* was one of the most widely viewed TV programmes, and the show's producer approached our publicist, Cheryll Roberts, about getting Harry on the show. Michael Aspel was the presenter, following in the footsteps of Eamonn Andrews, and the format of the show was simple: a celebrity or interesting person would be surprised at an appropriate venue by Aspel carrying a large red scrapbook and declaiming, 'This is your life.' The surprised subject would then be whisked away to a studio, where an audience would be waiting and the show proper would begin – with people from the many strands of that person's life being brought on in turn to share a memory or recall an encounter: long-lost friends or family, often flown in from a distant part of the world, and so on. In the case of a showbiz person, there would invariably be stars he or she had worked with. The reunions could be very moving, and it really had to be a total surprise – if the 'victim' got wind of what was afoot, it would all be shelved.

We discussed it with Harry's wife and daughter, as their agreement and involvement in the necessary deception was vital. Myra and Jenny gave us the green light, and arrangements began. It was decided that the easiest and most natural thing was to surprise Harry at a signing session for his book. Since he was doing a number of these, there was no reason for him to suspect anything, and there was one coming up at Bentalls department store in Kingston, which seemed the perfect venue. Preparations were elaborate, with the TV company producing huge posters displaying the book cover as a backdrop for the signing… and at a given moment a hidden panel in one of these would be removed and Michael Aspel would step through, announcing, 'Harry Secombe, this is your life.' The startled Harry would then be led away for the rest of the show.

Sadly, it didn't work out as planned: just a few days before the agreed date, Harry's long-time manager and friend Jimmy Grafton died. It was at Jimmy's pub, the Grafton Arms, that the Goons had first got together, and naturally Harry was very upset, so much so that both Myra and Jenny felt we had to pull the plug on what could be a very emotional programme. But what about the signing that had been arranged and widely advertised? Harry, who knew nothing about the original plan and not wanting to let anyone down, insisted on going ahead. For us, for our rep Keith Humphrey, and also for the directors of the store, it was a huge let-down, though the signing was successful enough. However, all was not lost because a few months later the show's producer came back, proposing to set it up once more, and the family agreed. It seemed only right to give Bentalls first option of staging it again and they quickly consented. This time everything went ahead as planned. There was a good crowd, Harry signed, Michael Aspel surprised him in the middle of it all – and Harry really was surprised. But once he had reached the TV studios and was in front of an audience, he rose to the occasion like the true professional he was, joking and responding as the various people from his life appeared in turn and said their bit about him. One story Harry told was about returning to his school to see his old English master at a time when he was at the height of his fame – topping the bill at the Palladium, a Crombie overcoat, a Rolls, all the trappings of success – and the master simply said to him, 'Harry, what went wrong?'

Harry Secombe shares a joke with Jeremy Morris, our financial director, and editor Elizabeth Rose.

Later, with characteristic modesty, Harry – by then Sir Harry – movingly wrote:

> All the average comic is left with at the end of his career are some yellowing newspaper cuttings, perhaps an LP record or two, and a couple of lines in the *Stage* obituary column. The best memorial he can hope for is that sometime in the future a man in a bar might say to his companion, 'That Harry Whatshisname was a funny bloke, he always made me laugh.'

That was Harry, that was his life.

* * *

Johnny Speight, author of the TV series *Till Death Us Do Part*, and another of our launch authors, was a rather more controversial personality. Johnny's famous creation, the ranting, bigoted, loud-mouthed Alf Garnett, played with gusto and brilliance by Warren Mitchell, had created a storm of protest in some quarters when the show was first aired, Mary Whitehouse famously objecting to Alf's foul-mouthed language and attitudes. 'She's concerned for the bleedin' moral fibre of the nation,' was Alf's response in one episode, where he was depicted as a reactionary admirer of hers. Alf's attitudes and language were dreadful, of course, but the whole point was that they were satirically intended and meant to send up and expose Alf's outrageous opinions. They were not Johnny's views, they were not Warren Mitchell's – but you had to have a sense of humour to appreciate that. Fortunately, some twenty million viewers did.

Johnny, who had written for a whole host of radio and TV greats, had a particular kind of genius, and the book he came up with for us, *The Thoughts of Chairman Alf*, was all Alf-speak. The producer of *Till Death*, Dennis Main Wilson, was also a kind of genius, but an eccentric one who always seemed to me like some kind of absent-minded professor. Dennis was a radio legend, having produced the first *Goon Shows* and the first *Hancock Half Hours* and given breaks to such stars

as Stephen Fry, Hugh Laurie, Emma Thompson and Griff Rhys Jones.
How he got Alf Garnett past the BBC censors I can't imagine, but he
loved and admired Johnny and bubbled over with enthusiasm and wild
ideas. Dennis quickly convinced us that the way to produce the book
was for us to gather round, switch on a tape recorder and simply give
Johnny subjects, on which he would instantly extemporise in the voice
and character of Alf Garnett. It worked, and Johnny's flights of invention would amaze us as he laughingly soliloquised on favourite Garnett
themes – the royal family, the army, his wife ('silly old moo'), foreigners,
West Ham Football Club, the working classes, whatever. Liz, Dennis
and I spent many joyous hours with Johnny, tape recorder at the ready,
in our office and at Johnny's house in Northwood, where we had to
compete with his parrot, which would imitate Johnny's stammer and
interject a stream of unprintable words. Hilarious – unless you were up
against the sort of deadline we were facing. Once Liz had transcribed
and edited it all, Johnny would go over it, rewriting and tailoring, and
the book, with the addition of illustrations by the cartoonist Stanley
Franklin, was done.

The venerable *Bookseller* magazine has long been the organ of the
book trade, but when we started there was another influential magazine, *Smith's Trade News*, whose columnist, Eric Hiscock, seemed to
have an inside track on the publishing world, and both his gossip and
his tips were taken seriously. So when (perhaps prompted by Carmen
Callil) he wrote that *Chairman Alf* 'can't fail to sell 40,000 copies', we
believed him. I've no idea how often his predictions were right, but
I'm sorry to say that on this occasion they weren't. It could and did
fail to sell that number, though fortunately we'd been cautious in our
print run, so we did well enough – enough to follow it up later with
Johnny's more substantial *The Garnett Chronicles*, Alf's 'autobiography',
produced over many hilarious, parrot-interrupted sessions.

We had not planned to publish children's books, but with Felix
Gluck's expertise to hand and an introduction (through Jenny Secombe) to the extraordinary Michael Bentine, we were tempted to dip
our toes into those rather specialised waters. Michael had been one of
the original Goons, writing the first programmes with Spike Milligan

and appearing in them, but he'd pulled out after the first thirty-eight shows for reasons that have always been a little blurred, none of the Goons ever wanting to be drawn about it. A creative clash with Milligan is generally held to have been the cause, as they both had extraordinary imaginations and distinctive personalities. With Bentine, such were his gifts of invention, you never knew what was real and what was fantasy. Harry Secombe once told me of an occasion in their early days when they were appearing together in variety somewhere in the provinces, and a woman was knocked down by a car just as they were about to cross the road. Without a moment's hesitation, Bentine had rushed forward, kept the crowd at bay, issued directions to the police as they arrived, and attended to the woman until the ambulance appeared. Harry had looked on in amazement as Bentine transformed himself into Dr Kildare, believing utterly in himself and convincing everyone around him that he was a doctor. On another occasion, Peter Sellers, doubting Bentine's claims that he was a champion fencer, had set him up with a German who really was a champion and arranged for them to have a friendly duel. Once again Bentine hadn't hesitated, had displayed great skill – and ended up the winner. He was also said to be a crack shot but Peter, wisely, didn't put him to the test. Michael called himself a Peruvian Briton but was actually born in Watford and went to Eton, though he did receive the Order of Merit of Peru for his work in raising money after the Peruvian earthquake of 1970. He worked for RAF Intelligence during the war and for MI9 under Airey Neave, and took part in the liberation of the Belsen concentration camp, about which he wrote most movingly. In the showbiz world he'd won a BAFTA for his off-the-wall TV series *It's a Square World*, just one of his many surreal and highly influential TV shows.

The astonishing Michael was a delight, as we discovered when we went to his home in Esher to discuss a series of books based on his popular children's television series *Michael Bentine's Potty Time*, for which he designed the Potty puppets, wrote the scripts and did all the voices (as he had for his earlier series, *The Bumblies*). But while his ideas flowed like lava as we settled down to lunch in his kitchen, prepared on tiptoe by his enchanting wife Clementina, a former ballet dancer, getting Michael to write to a deadline was another matter, not to mention the illustrations he promised to accompany the text. Liz and Felix, in tune with him from the word go, did their best, Liz even gallantly flying to Guernsey where Michael was in summer season to draw the words out of him. And eventually the first two books appeared: *Michael Bentine's Potty Treasure Island*, and *Michael Bentine's Potty Khyber Pass* – complete with potty Bentine pictures.

*   *   *

An early disappointment was Rosemary Clooney, whose life story we'd taken on. Famous as the blonde who sang 'I'm Dreaming of a White Christmas' with Bing Crosby in the perennial film, Clooney was a fabulous jazz singer, and her tumultuous life was unsparingly chronicled in her book (which was later made into a film). But to make a success of it we needed her support, and when she was in London to star in a live BBC concert at the Royal Festival Hall, we had dinner with her afterwards at a restaurant in Kensington. She was charm itself, agreeing that if we could arrange bookings for her, she would come back for a book tour. Meanwhile, a young man joined us at the table. 'This is Bing's son,' she said casually. Hollywood royalty indeed! I was impressed, and even more so to find, when I went to pay the bill, that she'd already settled it.

A tour was duly arranged – a week at Ronnie Scott's, a week in the north, linked to TV, radio and several nightclub bookings. Carole and I went on holiday, returning the weekend before she was due to find a note through our door which said simply, 'Rosemary Clooney cancelled' – on medical advice, we were later told, but we couldn't help wondering. It was a salutary introduction to the vagaries of the show-biz world, and the fact that George Clooney is her nephew doesn't really redeem it.

Still, our own show had to go on and a story in the *Evening Standard* caught my eye about the actor Robert Morley having just been voted wittiest writer of the year. Morley was a household name in those days, both as an actor and as a raconteur, and was a much sought-after guest on the chat shows of the day. Larger than life in every way, he was the archetypal Englishman in many of the films and plays he appeared in (and indeed in real life), dominating every scene and often improvising as he went along, which must have been alarming for the rest of the cast. Later, he became the unmistakable face of Britain on the ubiquitous British Airways adverts of the time. I had always enjoyed reading and watching him, so wrote to congratulate him on the award and to propose a collection of his entertaining magazine pieces. These were on various subjects – the theatre, food, travel etc. – many of them autobiographical. Almost immediately I was contacted by his son, the theatre critic Sheridan Morley, and we met for lunch. The Morleys were a theatrical family, Robert's mother-in-law being Dame Gladys Cooper, one of the great actresses of her day, while an aunt of Sheridan's had married Robert Hardy, and Joanna Lumley was a cousin. Sheridan had actually been named after the character his father was playing in a long-running production of *The Man Who Came to Dinner* at the Savoy Theatre.

Sheridan was very much in favour of our proposal, introduced us to Robert, and a series of highly successful books followed: *A Musing Morley*, *Morley Matters* and *More Morley*. I remember Liz recounting how, when she'd dropped off some proofs one Sunday lunchtime at Robert's house in Wargrave, she'd felt as if she'd walked onto a stage set, the entire family declaiming in all directions as they assembled for lunch – apart, that is, from Robert's rather quietly refined wife Joan, who must have been reduced to silence long before. As I was to discover once I got to know Robert (and as I should have divined from his girth), food was of great importance to him and the Morley family. Indeed, at one point Robert had placed the following advert in *The Times*: 'Father with horrible memories of his own school days at Wellington is searching for a school for his own son where the food matters as much as the education and the standards are those of a good three-star seaside hotel.' Despite that, Sheridan still managed to get to Merton College, Oxford, and was a highly respected, much-in-demand critic, author and broadcaster, presenting the popular BBC2 programmes *Late Night Line-Up* with Joan Bakewell, *Film Night*, and also the Radio 4 arts programme *Kaleidoscope*.

Given his high profile and his wit as a speaker, Robert was the perfect author. In some ways he was a kind of English version of the cosmopolitan, multilingual Peter Ustinov, and in fact Carole and I were once enjoying tea at the Morley home when Ustinov and his wife made an entrance. Together with the other guests, we sat around in a circle not quite believing our eyes or ears as he and Robert held court – Ustinov perhaps the most famous raconteur in the world, and Robert, on home ground, sardonically holding his own. Sitting there, I knew how Liz had felt that Sunday lunchtime: it was as if we were in the middle of a show and whenever there was a pause in the conversation we felt we should clap. Robert was very much aware of his own image – he was, in truth, his own greatest creation – and he was never above laughing at himself, as in the story he told in one of his books about meeting Rex Harrison in the Burlington Arcade. After congratulating Robert on his appearance as the subject of *This Is Your Life*, the flamboyant, six-times-married Harrison continued, 'You've been so sensible; one house, one wife and, if you'll forgive me saying so, one performance.'

Sheridan was also a great talker, and a walking encyclopaedia of all things theatrical. At the time of our meeting he was *Punch* magazine's theatre critic, and he made a suggestion over lunch that changed everything for us, professionally and personally: 'You should do a book of Al's Idi Amin pieces.' 'Al' was Alan Coren, then deputy editor of *Punch*, and Sheridan was referring to the spoof column Alan wrote each week in the voice and persona of the notorious Ugandan dictator. Amin's many crazy outpourings had made him seem like a buffoon, whereas in reality he was a psychotic monster of the highest order, repressing his people with unimaginable cruelty and murdering opponents at will. It would be impossible to get away with that column today, despite its obvious satirical intent, but somehow Coren made it hilarious despite its gruesome undertones. What a field day he'd have had with Donald Trump!

Years later, Sheridan was the man who came to dinner, to us, turning up early and alone, having been reviewing a matinee in town (or so he told us), his wife, Margaret, arriving a little later. We'd also invited the

Abses as well as Maureen Lipman and Jack Rosenthal, and it was a dinner party that neither we nor they would ever forget. It was as if we were on the stage set of *Who's Afraid of Virginia Woolf?*, with Sheridan and Margaret publicly engaged in a private battle to see who could talk loudest and longest, the pitch becoming more and more strident and the volume increasing with every course. No one, not even the witty Maureen, could get a word in. One story I recall Sheridan telling (in the calmer early part of that evening) was about Marlene Dietrich, and how she would invite people round to listen to recordings of her applause. It takes all kinds…

Not long afterwards, the loquacious Sheridan had a complete breakdown and was virtually unable to speak for quite some time. Benny Green stood in for him on his various radio programmes, telling me later that he never knew there *were* so many arts programmes, as he raced from studio to studio.

I'd met Alan Coren several times socially, but we'd never had a real conversation, and when I put Sheridan's Idi Amin idea to him he was hesitant, but suggested lunch. Alan was dazzling, both as a writer and as a conversationalist, and widely considered to be top of the pack where humorous writers were concerned. Clive James, himself no mean wordsmith, wrote of Alan, 'He has a comic imagination which actually renders your jaded scribe flabbergasted,' while *The Times* simply called him 'a comic genius'. Our lunch went well, and we ended up publishing not only two volumes of *The Collected Bulletins of Idi Amin* but also some twenty-six volumes of humour and ten children's novels (written for his children, Giles and Victoria). Alan remained fiercely loyal over the years as his fame grew both on the page and on air. He became a team captain on the popular TV programme *Call My Bluff* (opposite Sandi Toksvig), and star of Radio 4's *News Quiz*, where his imaginative wit found a wide and appreciative audience.

I suppose you could say the Idi Amin books were a risk, and nobody was more amazed than Alan when he picked up a copy of the *Sunday Times* while on holiday in France and found himself high on the bestseller list. Altogether the two volumes sold over half a million copies, and John Bird recorded them on disc. It was a great way to start an author–publisher relationship and a friendship that lasted up to Alan's death in 2007.

As the books started to roll out and the list of authors grew, Michael Rivkin took a proud but hands-off interest. He'd taken us – Liz and her husband Brian, the Secombes, Carole and me – to a celebration dinner in Soho when *Twice Brightly* came out (Esther Rantzen, then a young reporter covering the general election, was also there, brought by a friend of Michael's), and from time to time he'd invite us to dinner parties at his flat. At one of these I found myself sitting next to Gemma Levine. Gemma, then married to the lawyer Eric Levine, was starting to make her way as a photographer, and as it turned out a fine and imaginative one who would go on to publish a number of successful books of her own, including one with Henry Moore. As it was early days for both of us, I invited her to photograph some of our authors and to cover some of our launches, which she did brilliantly. While Gemma built up her portfolio, she provided us with arresting author photos, quite a few of which ended up as covers. I think especially of a series of books with Frank Muir.

On the first anniversary of Robson Books, Michael, always generous and hospitable, suggested that we invite some authors to lunch and a swim one Sunday at his magnificent country home near Basingstoke. The Corens, the Abses and the Bentines all came. A traditionalist, Rivkin liked to pass the port after a meal while the ladies tactfully withdrew (imagine!), but when it came to that moment (one I was dreading), dear unworldly Dannie, utterly oblivious, got up and left the room with Michael's wife and the other ladies, and the rest of the men were quick to follow suit. Having put paid to Michael's plans, we all went to relax around the pool. It began to cloud over, and Michael Bentine, ever mystically inclined and never deterred, announced that he could disperse the clouds. He set to, staring intently up for a few dramatic minutes before declaring that there was no point going on as we could all see they were breaking up. We gazed up and the clouds gazed down, as threatening as ever, so we filled our glasses, toasted Bentine – still talking animatedly – and dived into the pool before rain could stop play.

*   *   *

Our Poland Street offices, located just around the corner from the BBC, were convenient to drop into, and one welcome early visitor was the publisher Anthony Cheetham, who had just launched Futura Paperbacks from his rather larger premises further down the same street. We sipped coffee together in our office, he buying the paperback rights to several of our early titles and we agreeing to hardback some of his paperbacks. Anthony has always operated on the large scale, and very successfully, whereas we always remained relatively small. He may even have launched more publishing imprints than I have!

John Simpson, now famous as the BBC's world affairs editor, but then fairly recently down from Cambridge, where he'd shared a room with my cousin Nicholas Snowman, was another early Poland Street visitor. We'd given a poetry and jazz concert in Cambridge which John may have come to with Nicholas, but I don't believe I'd met him then. John was writing a political thriller and wanted to know if we would be interested. We were, very, and eventually published two: *Moscow Requiem* and *A Fine and Private Place*, as well as several timely non-fiction books, which got a lot of attention. John has always struck me as Mr Cool, though the situations in which he has found himself over the years have been far from cool. In the early days, when we were publishing him, I remember watching him reporting on the BBC News from Paris one evening amidst smoke and tear gas as the police fought to gain control of what were extremely violent student riots. I was due to meet him early the next morning on Paddington Station to escort him to the calmer waters of a literary lunch in Harrogate, but didn't imagine for a moment he would be there. But there he was, bang on time, ambling towards me, not a hair out of place, and shrugging off my surprise and concern for his well-being as if he'd just come back from reporting on a cricket match. Has he always been like that, I wonder, when facing bombs and rockets in far more dangerous parts of the world? That, at any rate, is how he has always seemed to me, reporting with his usual knowledge, insight and great sangfroid from one hot spot or another.

John Simpson, one of our most distinguished early authors.

It was also through Nicholas Snowman that I came to meet and publish the great pianist Alfred Brendel. Nicholas was at the centre of the
music world. At Cambridge, together with conductor David Atherton, the youngest ever to conduct at Covent Garden, he'd founded the
London Sinfonietta, a highly esteemed chamber orchestra dedicated
to championing contemporary music. Nicholas went on to work with
Pierre Boulez at the Centre Pompidou in Paris before becoming chief
executive of the Southbank Centre, then general manager of the Glyndebourne Festival Opera, and later director of the Opéra National du
Rhin in Strasbourg. Additionally, he is undoubtedly the only member
of my family to have been awarded the Légion d'Honneur.

*My cousin Nicholas Snowman, who was instrumental in developing
our early music list, and his wife, Margo.*

Given my own strong interest in most kinds of music, it wasn't long before I was itching to start a music list, and Nicholas, with his knowledge and wide contacts, was just the person to advise us – on the classical side, at least. As he was still working with Boulez, I asked him whether he might be able to effect an introduction: to have a book by this ground-breaking composer/conductor on our list would be a coup indeed. Nicholas gladly agreed to float the idea to him, and when Boulez next came to London to conduct a Festival Hall concert he agreed to join us for dinner afterwards. At the last minute, he asked via Nicholas whether we would extend the invitation to Alfred Brendel, who was attending the concert as his guest. Naturally we were thrilled to do so – Carole and I had been to the series of enthralling masterclasses he had recently given. Sad to relate, we never managed to tie Boulez down to a book. However, something momentous did result from that RFH dinner: as everyone was leaving, I plucked up courage and asked Alfred Brendel if he would be interested in writing a book based on his masterclasses. If he was surprised, he didn't show it, but, courteous as ever, he thanked me for the suggestion and agreed to come to our office to discuss it.

It transpired that Brendel, famed for his intellect as well as his phenomenal pianistic skills, had written a number of essays on the composers he admired and played, some in English, and after several meetings at our tiny office, in which Carolyn Fearnside joined, he agreed to our collecting these into a book, along with some new essays and extensions of the existing ones. The result was *Musical Thoughts and Afterthoughts*. Carolyn, with her excellent German and knowledge of music, was ideally placed to work with the fastidious Brendel, especially since some of the essays had originally been written in German, his native language. The fact that she admired him greatly and had been to all his concerts was a bonus. The book brought us much kudos – the reviews were fabulous and extensive – and we sold a number of editions to major publishers around the world. We collaborated closely with Philips, who were bringing out a boxed set of Brendel's recordings of Schubert's sonatas, and launched the book at the Austrian Institute, whose director had approached us and had tuned their grand piano in expectation. They were not disappointed – Brendel asking me whether I thought it would be a courtesy for him to play a little after the usual speeches! In due course, Alfred wrote a second, rather larger book for us, *Music Sounded Out*, which won several awards. Both are required reading for anyone seriously interested in the piano. I've used the word 'serious' here, and remarked on Brendel's intellect, but it would be remiss of me not to mention his love of humour – written, musical and otherwise – and the fact that he wore plasters on his fingers when he played. As he liked to joke, 'I can only play when I'm plastered.'

Mark Boxer's Times *caricature of a plastered Alfred Brendel.*

Alfred's sense of humour was certainly put to the test when he came to a housewarming party of ours some years ago. He hadn't answered the invitation, so when he bounded through the door bearing his latest CD as a gift, we were both surprised and delighted. But then I had a moment of panic, since I had unwisely engaged a pianist to play and he was pounding away on our old upright in our very crowded sitting room. From the first notes of the popular songs he was playing I realised it was a mistake, as nobody could hear themselves speak, and Alfred's sudden appearance made me all the more aware of this. As politely as I could, I suggested that the pianist take a break, have a drink and join the party, which to my relief he did. Some of the guests I knew went to Alfred's concerts and I asked several of them (including two very well-known writers) if they would like to meet him, but they recoiled in alarm, suddenly tongue-tied and totally awed. It was now some time since Alfred had arrived, and he asked me if there was a quiet room upstairs he could sit in for a while. I led him up to a room where the shelves were full of Carole's art books, which I thought he'd enjoy. But when Spike Milligan, who'd been swapping stories with Harry Secombe, heard that Alfred was there, he asked to join him, so I took him up and left them to it... and there they remained closeted together for an hour or so. What did they talk about? Did Brendel know who Spike was? Had he even heard of *The Goon Show*? And what did he make of Spike's anarchic, off-the-wall humour? I've always wondered.

Part of the great privilege of publishing Alfred Brendel was attending all his concerts at the Festival Hall, especially the spellbinding cycles of the Beethoven and Schubert sonatas he undertook – a mammoth endeavour, and for us a real musical education. I am for ever grateful to Nicholas Snowman for the introduction. Very few things have moved me as deeply as Brendel's performances and recordings of the Schubert sonatas. The audiences at those concerts were like an intellectual *Who's Who*, the same instantly recognisable people regularly in their places, queuing for drinks in the interval, waiting afterwards at Brendel's dressing room door to congratulate him – among them Isaiah Berlin, A. J. P. Taylor, Al Alvarez, Bernard Levin, Stephen Spender, Antonia Fraser, David Sylvester, Hans Keller, and our neighbours, Sir Ernst and Lady Gombrich, to whom we often gave a lift. It felt like a party, the atmosphere electric, the audience always on their feet calling for yet another encore, Brendel gracefully obliging.

Alfred Brendel at the Austrian Institute for the launch
of his first book, Musical Thoughts and Afterthoughts.

In February 2018, some eight years after his last concert performance, Carole and I attended a fascinating talk Brendel gave at the Dulwich Picture Gallery entitled 'My Life in Music'. His commanding presence, erudition and wit brought it all back in an intensely moving way, especially when the talk ended with the playing of a recording by Brendel of the first movement of Schubert's Impromptu in G Flat major, D899 No. 3, bringing the large audience to its feet, just as he had done at those historic Festival Hall performances.

Other publishers, including George Weidenfeld, as he once more or less intimated to me, have eyed Alfred over the years (just as they did Alan Coren), but he has remained a loyal author and a true friend, from those early Poland Street beginnings right up to the present day.

18

A WRONG NUMBER

As we entered our second year, more and more American-originated titles started to come our way, either via the various US publishers and agents we dealt with or through their British representatives, along with original offerings from those agents too. We didn't have Amazon or the internet to worry about as we do now, with US-published titles on sale here almost as soon as they appear in the States, with any hot stories being picked up instantly and splashed across the British press, often spoiling any serial deals that might be in the offing.

As a small, tightly knit team, we had the advantage of being able to make decisions and move quickly. Our Hungarian production manager, Susan Schulz, had gently won over a number of printers to her exacting ways and they would call on her regularly. Whenever a manuscript was delayed, or when last-minute corrections or additions were holding things up, she would berate us, proclaiming: 'There will not be a book!' At that time, printing in England, especially for colour books, was expensive; Susan was able to draw on her contacts in Hungary to get excellent prices and quality from printers there, which helped immensely with certain titles and put her in a good bargaining position with their British counterparts. That enabled us to handle the definitive, highly illustrated *The Gershwin Years*, and also Isaac Asimov's 1,000-page science fiction anthology of the 1930s, *Before the Golden Age*, both early titles for us. The size of these books seemed to have scared other publishers off, but they were perfect book club titles, and Book Club Associates took goodly quantities of both, underwriting them. Amazon has virtually brought about the demise of book clubs, but in those days they were major outlets.

Fortunately, not all our early books were the size of the Asimov. At the other end of the scale was *An Introduction to English Literature* by the great South American writer Jorge Louis Borges, who in just eighty-eight quirky but captivating pages provided a wealth of minor information on major subjects not found in the grander literary histories, effortlessly distilling the essence of the works he discussed. Also, of particular importance, there were the three short books by Elie Wiesel we were offered. Each had been published individually in various languages but never before in one volume, which is how we published them. *Night, Dawn* and *The Accident* are quite simply masterpieces by an author the *New York Times* called 'one of the great writers of his generation'. A survivor of Auschwitz and Buchenwald, Wiesel had already received a number of awards for his writing and was to win a Nobel Prize. Powerful and painfully moving, these semi-autobiographical works – *Night* especially – bring the Holocaust into terrifyingly close focus. They should be rammed down the throat of any Holocaust denier. I was fortunate enough to meet Wiesel in his flat in New York, and later in London when he came to speak at the Lubavitch Centre. Face to face with him in his living room, I was mesmerised by his haunted, compelling eyes and his soft, urgent voice. When he spoke publicly, as he did in London a year or so later, his voice drew the large audience in so that they felt they were engaged in an intimate conversation with him. He had come through an unimaginable hell but had somehow retained his hope and humanity.

There was an awkward moment for Carole at that London meeting when, on being introduced to the director of the Lubavitch Centre, she held out her hand politely in her Continental way, only to see him pull back. So Orthodox are the members of that extreme Jewish sect that they will not touch a woman unless married to her, even to shake her hand, still less dance with her, lest they be tempted. Coming from a completely different cultural background, Carole was both surprised and shocked. (There's an old Jewish joke about a man who went to his rabbi for some confidential advice. 'Tell me, Rabbi,' he said, 'is it permitted to make love on the floor?' 'Absolutely,' replied the rabbi, 'why not?' 'And in the bath?' the man continued. 'Why, of course, what could be more natural,' replied the rabbi. 'And standing up?' the man persisted. 'No, absolutely not,' declared the rabbi, shocked and wagging his finger. 'Could lead to dancing.')

* * *

When it came to publishing a second volume of *Goon Show* scripts, Spike felt he was too strongly committed to Frank Cass to be able to snatch it away. However, he suggested that Cass publish it jointly with us, promising a third book if he did so, but not surprisingly Frank rejected his proposal. Once the second book was out of the way, Spike offered me what was in effect a third *Goon Show* book. This was quite special, however, for as well as a few more scripts, *The Book of the Goons*, as we called it, contained something unique: the authentic correspondence the three Goons had engaged in over the years, in character and often on specially printed letterheads, sometimes by telegram, and from all over the world. The first cryptic telegram, sent by Harry Secombe to 'Sergeant Milligan', contained just the one word: 'FIRE!', and led to a whole series of hilarious 'military' cables which went back and forth between them. Other communications were more elaborate, especially legal ones from a Mr Henry Crun (Peter Sellers) on the notepaper of his firm, those well-known solicitors 'Whacklow, Futtle & Crun'.

In addition, we were given drawings by the Goons and a rich harvest of photos taken by Lord Snowdon. Liz Rose was the perfect editor to bring it all together creatively, and the book caused a minor sensation. In this we were helped by the Buckingham Palace press office, as, through Nicholas Soames, a friend of Michael Rivkin, Prince Charles had agreed to attend a private dinner for the Goons at the Dorchester. What Soames had actually said when we met in Michael's office to discuss it was, 'Charles will bust his arse to get there.' Well, I don't know about that but he certainly agreed to come, on condition that there were no announcements, no photographers and no press, and this

we readily agreed to, deciding to have a separate cocktail party at the
Dorchester beforehand to launch the book publicly while the Goons
were together. Imagine my consternation when, on the morning of the
dinner, the phone in our office exploded with the press bombarding
us with questions about the supposedly secret dinner. I was alarmed,
thinking I might be sent to the Tower or – worse – the Prince would
pull out, and I anxiously phoned the Palace press office to proclaim
our innocence, only to be told not to worry since they had released
the details by mistake. As a result, unable to keep the press at bay, the
Palace agreed that there should be a brief photocall, designating one
photographer to take pictures for all the papers... and there we were
next morning on the front pages, Milligan playing the fool as always,
seated and wearing a peaked cap in every photo. It made for imaginative captions.

An early morning surprise: our royal Goon Show *dinner makes the* Daily Telegraph *front page.*

Prince Charles, who was accompanied by his private secretary, Squadron Leader Sir David Checketts, had met Peter and Spike on various
occasions and was especially friendly with Harry Secombe. But dear,
dependable Harry, the anchor I'd been relying on to hold the others in
check, was unwell, leaving his daughter Jenny to represent him. HRH
had not met Michael Bentine before, and once he'd been formally received and introduced to the various guests (we were about thirty in
all) and the promised photocall was over, the Prince sat wide-eyed as

the unstoppable Michael took off on one of his fantastic soliloquies, reminiscing about secret wartime aerial missions he'd been involved in (or imagined he'd been involved in – who knows?), from time to time turning to the squadron leader at the end of the table for confirmation, airman to airman. Checketts, as captivated as his boss, nodded sagely.

Spike Milligan has his own special message for our royal guest: 'Dear Prince – Please send Open University knighthoods to c/o Mrs D. Prolls, Mange Buildings, Tower Hamlets, London.'

Seated on one side of Charles and silent at first, but not to be outdone, Milligan waited his moment, and when there was a pause he suddenly entered the fray, reducing us all to fits of laughter as he recounted hilarious stories of his own wartime experiences, creatively embellished. Meanwhile, on the other side of the Prince, Peter Sellers twitched, getting up and pacing the room as if waiting in the wings to make an entrance. He'd been anxious about the evening from the word go, phoning to say he was bringing a lady friend, and then to say he wasn't, then getting his secretary to check that it really wasn't black tie, finally demanding that a car be on standby all evening in case he suddenly wanted to leave. On arriving and seeing there were more people there than he had expected, he asked me who had 'fucked up'. I explained that I hadn't wanted to leave out anybody who'd been closely involved with the book or who had made the dinner possible, and he calmed down – a little. In any case, as I told him, the Palace had approved the guest list.

The menu for the Book of the Goons *dinner with Prince Charles.*

Nevertheless, it was hardly relaxing, but the excellent food and fine wines began to work their magic, and Jenny Secombe came up trumps by producing a humorous poem her absent father had written for the occasion entitled 'Ballad of a Sick Ned'. I asked Peter if he would read it to us all, which he did in great style, and once he was in actor's mode he settled down to join in and savour the evening. Harry's poem, which Jenny, the supreme publicist, had circulated to the press, appeared in next day's papers. At least Harry had been with us in spirit, if not physically. Later, when the Prince had said his goodbyes and departed and the party had broken up, I found Michael Bentine in the lobby of the hotel having an intense conversation with a journalist from a popular daily, the *Mirror* I think, who claimed he'd heard from a waiter that the Prince had been telling racist jokes. Absolute malicious nonsense, and Bentine was telling him so in no uncertain terms. It was an insight into the way some of the press sometimes work – flying a ludicrous kite, or fishing. Charles had behaved impeccably, laughing heartily and joining in the general conversation, plainly enjoying every moment, but there's no story in that. He kindly signed my menu and, looking up at my tie – my BEST tie – he asked whether the patterns on it were ear lobes (after that I saw the tie in a new light, and it was the last time I wore it). Encouraged by his jokey remarks, I was probably only a drink or two away from mentioning that we had my great-uncle Jack the *mohel* in common. That might really have meant the Tower.

A postscript to the evening: when Peter Sellers died, Prince Charles was formally represented by Michael Bentine at the memorial service held at St Martin-in-the-Field. Soberly dressed in black tie and tails, walking slowly to the front of the church and kneeling solemnly, with his trimmed black beard he looked like a character out of a Russian novel – one that Peter might have enjoyed playing. And when Michael himself was critically ill, Prince Charles, described in the press as 'a close friend', visited him in hospital. A touching and unexpected outcome of an evening full of laughter. As for Spike, referring to his promise to give us the third *Goon Show* book, he wrote in my copy, 'You see, I remembered.' He had, and I am grateful. But while I'm on the cheerful subject of memorial services I'm reminded of Spike's quip when Harry died: that he was glad Harry wouldn't now be able to sing at *his* funeral service as he had done at Peter's. However, Harry had the last laugh, as his family unearthed a recording of him singing 'Guide me, O thou great Redeemer', which was played – to the congregation's delight – when the time came to say goodbye to Spike. Goons in life and Goons in death.

I had always hoped to get Peter to write an autobiography. Given his colourful and often anguished life and the many women in it, it would have made a fascinating story. Peter was a descendant of the eighteenth-century prizefighter Daniel Mendoza, the first Jewish boxer to become a champion, and he and I had often talked about republishing Mendoza's memoirs with an introduction by Peter, but we never managed to get even that off the ground, although it would have involved him in relatively little work. The nearest I got was the inscription he wrote in my copy of *The Goon Show Scripts*: 'Fred Mendoza, son of Sid Mendoza, and of course P Sellers Esq'.

As far as an autobiography was concerned, the closest I ever came to *that* was shortly before his death when Carole and I were enjoying a pre-Christmas curry at the Gaylord restaurant in Mortimer Street. Leaning forward, Carole whispered, 'I'm sure that's Peter Sellers over there.' From where I was sitting I could only see that there were two men huddled in conversation, but the voice, the theatrical laugh, were unmistakable. As they left their table and were about to pass ours, Peter saw me and, smiling, stopped to talk, friendlier than he'd ever been, but white as a ghost, as if his face were covered in powder. He introduced us as 'old friends' to the man with him, Lord Rothschild, and since he was in such an approachable mood I brought up the question of the book as gently as I could. 'Phone me in the New Year,' he said, 'and we'll get it going. I think it's time.' I had the feeling that it wouldn't be a question of money, but of working with someone he knew and trusted, but very sadly his frail heart forestalled our intentions, and he died the following February. It was left to others to trawl among the shadows of his life.

*   *   *

In those exciting early days, we advanced in many directions, and we were glad to acquire a series of thrillers featuring Jacob Asch, Private Investigator, an out-of-work crime reporter. Witty, bitter, with his ideals battered but still just about intact, Ash moved in the bizarre underworld of southern California, and the books had received high praise from both the *LA Times* ('they won't be bettered') and the *New York Times*. Very different were the crime novels we took on by W. J. Weatherby, well known in England for his *Guardian* features. Superb though all these books were, they were rather overshadowed on our list by Jack Lynn's *The Turncoat*, an explosive novel of worldwide intrigue, corruption in high places and political assassination that had its roots in actual events and came to us in a large, unpublished manuscript. It was riveting. We made copies and passed them around the office. Everyone agreed, we *had* to buy it, but the asking price was high – seemingly too high for us. One possible solution (and a good way of testing the commercial waters) was to try to pre-sell it to an American publisher, and this we managed to do – to Ross Claiborne at Dell, who paid a six-figure sum for it. We went on to publish several more books by Lynn, including *The Professor*, a Mafia thriller that was optioned several times by various movie companies but was never made into a film, such being the fickle ways of Hollywood. Those books did reasonably well for us, but not as well as I suspect they should have done, and from then on we were cautious as far as fiction was concerned, realising that it needed a special kind of publishing skill and sales force to make it really work.

Gardening was another area into which we plunged our early exploratory fork, commissioning a series of books from Daphne Ledward, then a regular on the BBC's popular *Gardeners' Question Time* (no half-measures at that early stage), and also taking on her offbeat *Idiot Gardener's Handbook*, which became a perennial seller.

Humour, music, fiction, biography, literature, gardening – but so far no cookery, and it was to remain that way, with one notable exception – Evelyn Rose's *Complete International Jewish Cookbook*. At that time the doyenne of Jewish cuisine and the *Jewish Chronicle*'s popular columnist, Evelyn had been working on the book for some years, and it was due to be published by Vallentine, Mitchell. But something had gone wrong, and I was contacted by the *JC*'s editor, William Frankel, who asked whether we would take it over, promising his backing. We were happy to do so, and if the Jewish people really are the People of the Book, this was *the* book, for it sold out instantly, going from edition to edition – some sixteen in all – encouraging the supremely professional Evelyn to write more books for us. However, shortly after we'd published, there was an uncomfortable moment when the phone rang late one Friday afternoon. On the line was a woman, clearly at her wits' end, saying she had people to dinner and the soufflé she'd been preparing from the recipe in Evelyn's book just wouldn't rise. We phoned Evelyn to confer, and on checking she discovered that the eggs had somehow been left out of that recipe! She phoned the distraught lady herself to apologise. The soufflé eventually rose!

Evelyn Rose, the doyenne of Jewish cookery writers, whose books were in most Jewish households.

While we were inserting erratum slips into the few remaining copies of the first printing of Evelyn's book, we were beginning, through Alan Coren, to be drawn closer to *Punch* magazine. Soon, a number of *Punch*-related titles came our way, and we became, in effect, the magazine's unofficial book publisher, with such compilations as *Punch on the Theatre* (edited by Sheridan Morley), *Punch on Scotland* (Miles Kington), *Punch Down Under* (Barry Humphries), *Punch at the Cinema* (Dilys Powell), *The Punch Book of Cartoons* etc. Libby Purves, too, was an early 'catch', with a book called *Britain at Play*, which drew on a column Alan had commissioned. Some of the *Punch* books were paperbacks, others large-format books, amply illustrated and ideal for Christmas, and once again, thanks to our Hungarian printers, we were able to produce them at a reasonable price. From time to time I was invited to the weekly *Punch* lunches in their Tudor Street offices, joining the magazine's writers, cartoonists and various guests at its famous long table engraved with the signatures of some of the royal and famous invitees who'd attended over the years. At the head sat the editor, William Davis, presiding over some thirty uninhibited guests talking non-stop – until the moment when he banged the table with his gavel, demanded silence and threw out a topic for general discussion, calling on people in turn. I'd shrink into myself, praying his eyes wouldn't turn on me, and mercifully he always seemed to pass me by. When Alan became editor, the intellectual and competitive level rose as he led the conversation, and I would enjoy the cut and thrust. I felt safer with Alan in command – he knew me too well to put me on the spot.

Alan and I and our families became close, and he and I would often walk together on a Sunday over nearby Hampstead Heath, the endlessly inventive Alan regaling me with the highly original plot for a novel he had in mind. A week later he'd have forgotten what it was and come up with an even more original storyline. Having the ideas seemed to be what excited him. He wanted to write a novel but never did (other than a teenage novel he regretted once showing me), telling me whenever I pursued him that he was a sprinter, not a long-distance runner. Given the brilliance of his short pieces and his many books for us, all wonderfully titled, I could hardly complain. Nor did he ever write the autobiography we'd contracted – his idea was to write it in different decades through the various cars he and his parents had owned over the years ('Auto-Biography', he wanted to call it). What a shame. But, as I mentioned earlier, he did write a series of highly successful children's stories, the Arthur Books – *Buffalo Arthur*, *The Lone Arthur*, *Arthur the Kid* and so on. Set in the American Wild West, they featured a mysterious young boy called Arthur who would appear from nowhere, help clueless adults get out of the stupid messes they'd found themselves in, then disappear into the sunset. After six Westerns, Alan brought Arthur to England to help Sherlock Holmes (*Arthur and the Great Detective*, *Arthur and the Bellybutton Diamond* etc.). Arthur was roughly the age of Alan's son Giles – no coincidence. The stories were funny, with authentic backgrounds, and more sophisticated than I think Alan realised, and we sold editions all over the world thanks to the help and connections of Felix Gluck, who was still running his company from our office and knew everyone in the world of children's publishing. Felix also introduced us to John Astrop, who illustrated the books with great style.

A Bookseller *advert for Alan Coren's 'Arthur' books, which we sold in many languages.*

There were two memorable 'Arthur' launches – one at the Martini Terrace in Haymarket where Robert Morley made an impromptu speech, saying wittily that he was looking forward to *Le Morte d'Arthur*, and one in France where Gallimard published the books and Alan had everyone in stitches by delivering a speech in his usual dazzling way – but in French (he'd checked several expressions with Carole on the way there). In America, where Little, Brown published the books, ABC Television made an hour's film of one of them, and they were read on the BBC TV children's programme *Jackanory*.

For Alan, everything was possible and everything permitted, as he told me when we shared a family villa in Portugal one summer. He also told me I'd have made a good tennis coach, which I was never sure was meant as a compliment! It was on that holiday that, as Carole and I drove Giles and our daughters to the sea (Alan and Anne preferred the villa's pool), Giles, who was then around eight, begged us to get his father to give up smoking: both his parents were militant smokers. Not a chance. Nobody could get Alan to do anything he didn't want to do, but he was very proud of his children, with good reason.

* * *

A number of *Punch*'s high-profile authors approached us as a result of our involvement with the magazine. George Melly was one. I was rather in awe of George, perhaps because I'd been a fan of his since my teenage days, perhaps because I was conscious of his erudition and colourful past, or maybe it was because his eyes seemed to mock you as he talked – what was he thinking, one wondered? But in truth he was generosity itself, inviting me several times for lunch at the fish restaurant Sheekey, where he was entitled to bring a guest once a month at their expense in return for having advised on and helped procure the paintings that adorned the restaurant's walls. It was there, appropriately, over a long boozy lunch, that he came up with the idea of writing on one of his passions – fishing – and the result was an engaging book called *Hooked!*, which he laced with a goodly number of personal stories and ribald confessions.

Frank Keating, The Guardian's *popular sports writer and a regular contributor to* Punch *magazine. Frank had his own special touch, which endeared him to readers and players alike.*

Frank Keating, *The Guardian*'s fine sports writer who called everyone 'm'dear', was another *Punch* catch and someone I became fond of. Frank's writing had a particularly romantic hue about it – he absolutely loved, with wide-eyed boyish enthusiasm, the sporting events and great sporting figures he wrote about, whether a rugby match or a superb innings, a Botham or a Borg. Frank had a magical way of conjuring up the scene, but he was far more sophisticated than he let on and was greatly admired by the sporting legends he wrote about as well as by those he wrote for. His *Punch* and *Spectator* essays made several winning books for us – *Passing Shots*, *Long Days, Late Nights*, *Gents and Players* – but his original *Classic Moments from a Century of Sport* and his autobiography, *Half-Time Whistle*, were particular highlights.

I saw Frank in action once, when he came to a lunch at Wembley for the great Hungarian footballer Ferenc Puskás, whose autobiography we were launching there, courtesy of Wembley's then chairman, Jarvis Astaire. Puskás had played the key part in destroying a rather arrogant England team 6–3 at a famous Wembley match in 1953, and then 7–1 in Budapest the following year. For the lunch we had assembled as many members of that humiliated English team as we could, including Sir Stanley Matthews. Frank sat down afterwards and, on a borrowed typewriter, wrote a perfect 1,000-word piece about the lunch for *The Guardian* in under half an hour, without hesitation or repetition. But he missed my own great moment when, to my amazement, I found myself walking though the Wembley tunnel onto the pitch with Puskás on one side and Matthews on the other. Not a photo, not a selfie, not even a Keating to record this unbelievable Boy's Own, schoolboy's dream of a moment!

Roy Hattersley was somewhat untypical of *Punch* authors, but he was an award-winning writer as well as being Labour's shadow Home Secretary, and his regular 'Press Gang' column gave an informed insight into the workings and shenanigans of the press and made compelling reading – well worth collecting into a book. Roy had agreed to speak at a Reading literary lunch as part of the promotion for his book, and I drove him to the hotel where it was to take place. As soon as we arrived he was given an urgent message (no mobiles in those days!) saying there was going to be a vote in the House on capital punishment and he needed to be there to respond to the Home Secretary, Leon Brittan. Time was short but, not wanting to let the organisers down, Roy came up with the suggestion that he speak before lunch was served, sign books and then leave. As soon as he'd finished, away we raced, Roy listening to the Test match as I drove. Then, as we approached Westminster, he said, 'You see that No Right Turn sign? If you were to ignore that and turn right, you'd save five vital minutes.' Who was I not to comply with the shadow Home Secretary's obvious wishes? It was, after all, in the national interest, and he arrived with five minutes to spare.

Roy's partner at the time, Maggie Pearlstine, later to become his wife, had been the main buyer at Book Club Associates when we started up, taking several of our early titles, and we'd become friendly. That's probably how we ended up having Christmas drinks with just the two of them at Roy's Westminster flat – and when I say 'we' I mean Carole and me and our young daughters, Deborah and Manuela – not too young, however, to show Roy how to work all the controls on his new TV set and recorder, which he and Maggie had been struggling with. Roy and Maggie always remind us about that when we meet, as we did only recently and unexpectedly at the Oxford Literary Festival.

Simon Hoggart, *The Guardian*'s acerbic political sketchwriter, let little that went on in and behind the scenes in Parliament escape his irreverent 'On the House' columns in *Punch*. These formed the basis for three highly successful books, superbly illustrated by John Jensen, who in one volume depicted the 'cast' as Tudor conspirators. The first of Simon's books twinned nicely with another that we published at the same time by his opposite number on *The Times*, the very classy Frank Johnson, and we gave a joint launch party in our office. Strangely, Frank had been to our house for dinner quite some while before he started writing for *The Times*, along with Nicholas Snowman and Arianna Stassinopoulos, whom Nicholas had brought. That can't have been long after Arianna came down from Cambridge, where she was president of the Union, but long before she became involved with Bernard Levin, and even longer before she moved to America, married and became the Huffington of the Huffington Post. I remember both she and Nicholas telling me that Frank was the coming man, and indeed he was. And Carole remembers how Arianna got up at the end of the meal and began to help with the washing up. Frank's first book was *Out of Order*, and his last, published posthumously with the help of his widow Virginia, was *Best Seat in the House*. His books started a kind of tradition for us, followed as they were by Matthew Parris's *Times* sketches and those of Ann Treneman.

When *Private Eye* did us the honour of featuring us in its 'Greatest Publishers of the World' series, I always suspected, perhaps wrongly, that it was Simon Hoggart who wrote it – he was certainly the first to phone and tell me about it. On the other hand, now that I come to think of it, perhaps it was Alan Coren, for it contained details (one third right, two thirds wrong, in the usual *Eye* manner) that only an insider would have known or indeed cared about. The best thing about it was that it was long.

Then there were Miles Kington's bestselling Franglais books. A jazz bassist and member of the popular group Instant Sunshine, Miles was literary editor of *Punch* at the time. Quieter than Alan Coren, who tended to overshadow everyone at *Punch*, Miles had his own dry, deceptive wit, and his 'Franglais' column in the magazine had built up a cult following. Written as short, self-contained scenes under such titles as 'Dans le Health Food Shop' or 'À la barbecue', Franglais was, as Miles put it, 'plus facile que l'Esperanto, beaucoup plus facile que le Français, more fun que le yoga ou karate, et absolument painless'. There were five Franglais books, Miles signing off with an original tome entitled *Le Franglais Lieutenant's Woman*, a highly inventive compendium in Franglais of some of the world's most famous novels, plays and stories – from 'le book of Genesis' to 'Mlle Marple'. As well as introducing a word into the English language, the books spawned a Franglais TV series – short episodes, each taking a scene from the books and featuring famous stars: the episode I saw being recorded featured Wilfrid Brambell and Ron Moody. Ron was extremely patient with the aged Brambell, who, not surprisingly, kept stumbling over his tricky Franglais lines.

After the Franglais books came another cult book, this time drawn from *The Guardian*, where the influential feminist writer Jill Tweedie, whom we had already published, raised eyebrows with her weekly 'Letters from a Fainthearted Feminist'. These letters, ostensibly from

Martha to her younger, more liberated sister Mary, became a runaway success for us and then a BBC TV series starring Lynn Redgrave. A classic, the book was described by one critic as 'the only published book I know which manages to be howlingly funny about the women's movement without a shred of spite or cruelty'.

It was at about this time that the very popular actress and impersonator Janet Brown came into our lives. Janet was charm itself. She'd been making people laugh with the accuracy and wit of her mimicry since she was a child and now she was particularly famous for her uncanny impersonation of the Prime Minister, Margaret Thatcher. So good was it that the talk show host Johnny Carson invited her to America to take part in an elaborate candid-camera hoax that he planned to spring on the outrageous and very funny Joan Rivers. The 'hit' involved inviting Rivers to a dinner in Las Vegas, putting his private jet at her disposal, and arranging for Janet, in full Thatcher rig-out, to arrive in the VIP lounge of the airport at the same time. Janet marched in smartly, surrounded by 'security guards', and graciously allowed Rivers to be presented to her. Initially charming, Janet abruptly changed tone and began to berate the fawning comedian for the 'absolutely disgusting' things she'd said about the royal family. 'I've spoken to President Reagan – as you must know, we've been friends for years,' she went on, improvising brilliantly, 'I've been told you have great difficulty understanding English people … Can you understand what I'm saying, Miss Rivers?' 'Oh, perfectly, Mrs Thatcher,' Rivers stammered, wriggling beneath the onslaught and condescending tone.

Janet took a letter from her handbag and ordered Rivers to read it out, which, putting on her glasses, she did. The note was from Johnny Carson and read, 'Dear Joanie, this is just a joke. And we hope you take it as such. If you don't, we don't care a ****.' And, after she'd got over the shock, Joan did take it as such, roaring with laughter and requesting a photo of herself with 'Mrs Thatcher'. The film of the hoax was broadcast three times on American TV, the sporting Rivers accepting that 'if you dish it out, you have to be prepared to take it'.

Janet's appearance at the Annual Bookseller's Conference, held that year in her native Scotland, was less dramatic although important for us, as she wowed the main buyers with a sparkling cabaret performance that ensured we had her book, *Prime Mimicker*, everywhere. The perfect author, and great fun.

*   *   *

The 100 Club in Oxford Street was where I'd cut my jiving teeth, and as far as I was concerned Humphrey Lyttelton was a legend. But in addition to his trumpet playing and his key role in British jazz history, he was also a natural writer and, having greatly admired a mock obituary he'd written of himself for *Punch* – in which he spelt his surname differently each time it occurred – I wrote to him. But I made a bad mistake. After an agreeable exchange of letters, I thought I would phone and invite him to lunch, having obtained his number from Alan's unsuspecting secretary. 'Where did you get this number from?' he blazed at me like a not-so-muted trumpet before I could get through a sentence. Taken aback, I told him I thought it was on his letter, but he knew all too well that it wasn't and I owned up. 'Erase it,' he said, 'and never use it again.' I didn't!

Despite the bad start, Humph agreed to have lunch – in fact he invited me, as he was reviewing restaurants at the time for *Harpers & Queen*, and we ended up at a restaurant in Pimlico (I was doing rather well out of my jazz authors). Humph was all for publishing a collection of his witty and often autobiographical pieces, but he also came up with the idea of a series of informal jazz histories. Given the popularity of his long-running *Best of Jazz* programmes on Radio 2, that was an exciting prospect, especially as he wanted to use the title of his programme for the book. His approach was unusual, discussing the great jazz figures through their key recordings, and throwing in personal anecdotes along the way, Humph-style. The first of his *Best of Jazz* books was subtitled *Basin Street to Harlem*; the second, *Enter the Giants*; the third… Well, he never did get around to writing that, but brought us instead a book called *Why No Beethoven?*, based on the amusing diaries he'd kept during a tour of the Middle East with his band. At the end of their concluding concert, a man had come up to him wanting to know why their repertoire didn't include Beethoven's Fifth, hence the enigmatic title.

Humph's last book for us was a free-wheeling memoir, *It Just Occurred to Me…* By that time he'd become the droll chairman of *I'm Sorry I Haven't a Clue* and his fame extended way beyond the jazz world. We launched the book at a Mayfair jazz club and were treated to a couple of numbers from the exciting Elkie Brooks, a present for Humph, who'd done a great deal for her career at a point when she'd been weighed down by personal problems. 'Trouble in Mind' is what Elkie sang that night, and she was to sing it again even more poignantly at Humph's funeral when, aged eighty-six, he failed to come through a major heart operation. The president of the Society for Italic Handwriting, Humph had been working on a book on handwriting for us at the time, and he would come to our house, spreading his books and papers over our dining room table. Even at that advanced age he was still playing with vigour, and every month or so we'd go to hear him and his band at the Bull's Head in Barnes. Sadly, he died before finishing the handwriting book.

Humph's book launches were always a special thrill for me,
taking me back to my teenage years at the 100 Club.

I hadn't at that stage met Humph's son Stephen, but after the funeral he approached me suggesting a book based on the diaries his father had kept, written every day in his beautiful hand – even his tax returns had been completed in his fine script! Stephen and I worked together around the clock, choosing appropriate passages and pages, linking them, turning it all into a 450-page book we hoped Humph would have been proud of, with Susan da Costa, his partner, checking and vetting it before we went to press. We called it *Last Chorus*.

Reading Humph's diaries, I was surprised to see a number of (fortunately polite) references to us, as his publishers, but also stories about various people we'd published. But even though they were essentially private diaries, he was never bitchy, never self-indulgent, always displaying the wit, generosity and sharpness of observation for which he was known. There were things I'd forgotten, which I was glad to be reminded of, like the time I accompanied him to a literary lunch. The other speakers were the irrepressible Michael Bentine, Robin Day, and the ballerina Nadia Nerina. Humph's vivid account brought it all back:

> Drove to Jeremy Robson's house, left the car there, went to St Pancras with him in a mini cab. 8.48 train to Sheffield where I am to be one of the speakers at a Yorkshire Post literary lunch… Petrified to see that it is a huge room with tables stretching way into the distance. Over 500 people there, most of them women in flowered hats. Sat between two businessmen's wives, made conversation between bouts of nerves. Robin Day spoke well… Nadia N chatted amiably about the ballet and Michael B went stark raving mad… Returned on the train with Jeremy Robson and Bentine who talked without drawing breath from Sheffield to St Pancras.

Yes, that's exactly how it was, how the extraordinary Michael Bentine was, and how those lunches were in those heady publishing days. It must have cost us a fortune to take our celebrity authors to these events, just to sell a few books, get a paragraph or two in the local press, but we never seemed to count the pennies.

Perhaps we should have done!

Given the continuing success of *I'm Sorry I Haven't a Clue*, which Humph chaired for some thirty-five years, it was amusing to read his diary entry for 17 July 1975:

Final session of I'm Sorry I Haven't a Clue. I'm not sure that this game hasn't finally run its course… I shan't be sorry if it expires. I'm rather tired of people coming up and saying, 'I enjoyed your programme the other day', and finding out they mean this bit of nonsense!

Since we published a Clue book based on that nonsense, with silly photos of the original team taken in our backyard and round our old upright, I'm glad that on this occasion Chairman Humph was wrong!

Ever since that early faux pas of mine, whenever I wanted to contact Humph, I would have to phone Susan, who would then phone Humph and ask him to phone me. But suddenly, as we worked on the handwriting book he was never to finish, he wrote down his mobile number and said I should use it. It was a touching final gesture of friendship and trust.

19

REVIEWING THE SITUATION

Dannie Abse and I continued our lunchtime strolls, but just as the wise Faber director had warned at the start of this saga, the poetry had indeed begun to dry up as the all-consuming demands and strains of publishing took over. My interest remained strong, but somehow the lines didn't come. There was still the occasional reading to give, but since I was not writing I felt rather a fraud, finding poetry hard to talk about. I recall Dannie once saying that you were only a poet while you were writing a poem. I knew what he meant, and though I was well aware it didn't matter to the world at large, it mattered a great deal to me. I'd never been able to look on poetry as a hobby. It had to be an all-or-nothing commitment, and for the moment it was nothing. Now I always seemed to have my head in the words of others, urging them on, editing their work, sharing their highs and lows. If I'd ever had a style or voice of my own, it was no more.

It was during one of our walks that we came up with the idea of producing a poetry annual. It seemed a worthwhile thing to do and a slightly compensatory activity for me. We published the annuals for seven years, with me editing the first one under the rather meaningless title of *Poetry Dimension 1*, and Dannie the other six under the more obvious title of *The Best of the Poetry Year*. The annuals contained what we thought were the most arresting poems, reviews, interviews and articles about poets or poetry published in the given year on both sides of the Atlantic, and they were well received. At around the same time, we took on a new book of poems by Vernon Scannell, *The Loving*

Game, and were gratified when it was made the Poetry Book Society 'Choice'. Apart from the personal satisfaction it gave me, it also meant the society purchased a decent number of copies for its members. We continued to publish Vernon's poetry over many years, which was balm for the soul even if it did not bring great riches to either of us. That said, he gave a good many readings where books were sold, and his poems were much in demand for school anthologies, the permission fees from these bringing in a steady trickle of income, of which, quite rightly, the lion's share went to him. In modern parlance one could say that his books just about washed their faces, and that was good enough for me. Later, we published Vernon's powerful sequence of autobiographical books.

Vernon would stay with us fairly regularly at around this time when he came down from Leeds for a reading or broadcast from the BBC. He was good enough to include me in a programme he presented about Thomas Hardy's poetry. Nobody did that kind of programme better and his deep voice was perfect for radio, which made him a favourite with producers. It was while Vernon was staying with us that we were burgled. Carole and I were out and our twins were at school. Vernon was sleeping off a heavy night, so he heard nothing, which was the intruder's luck, given Vernon's boxing prowess. In fact, he was doubly lucky, since an American professor, Joseph Cohen, whose biography of the First World War poet Isaac Rosenberg we'd just published, was also staying with us, and he'd left the house early. Cohen's *Journey to the Trenches* was the first biography of that fine poet-painter, so different from the other major poets of that cruel war in that Rosenberg wasn't an officer, having come from a poor East End background. 'Genius' is what F. R. Leavis called him, and we were proud to play our part in bringing his work to the attention of a wider public.

I mentioned Vernon Scannell's sequence of autobiographies, and *Argument of Kings*, which covers his war experiences, is a classic of its genre. When it appeared, we'd arranged for him to be interviewed live on the excellent John Dunn radio show. Vernon was tickled at the idea of being interviewed by someone of that name, even if it was spelt differently from that of the poet. I was at the Frankfurt Book Fair at the time, but Carole was in the office when the interview went out. So powerful was it that, instead of confining it to the normal twenty-minute author spot, the producer let the interview run on for nearly an hour as Vernon talked vividly and movingly to the captivated Dunn about his experiences. A little while later, Vernon phoned the office and asked Carole what time he had to be at the BBC for the interview. Seemingly traumatised by having revisited such deep and troubling experiences, he had no recollection of having done the programme, which was very alarming. Unusually for Vernon, he hadn't touched a drink, and to everyone's relief he wandered into the office a little later, stone-cold sober.

Another writer who came into our orbit at around this time was the Cornish poet Charles Causley, with whom we were to publish three books – one a verse play, *The Gift of a Lamb*, often performed at Christmas; the second a traditional children's story about the lovely daughter of an ancient King of Colchester, *Three Heads Made of Gold*; and the third, *Hands to Dance and Skylark*, a rather more salty book of autobiographical stories which drew on Causley's experiences in the navy. We'd met at the Queen Elizabeth Hall during a reading to launch a strange anthology of 'poems for those who choose to care' titled *Doves for the Seventies*, in which we both had poems. Charles was an extremely popular poet, one of our finest, his deceptively simple style making his poems both accessible and memorable, appealing to young and old, especially his ballads, which are much anthologised. One glorious summer, just after we'd taken on his third book, we rented a house in the picturesque fishing village of Port Isaac in Cornwall, and on discovering that we were going to be there, Charles invited himself to tea. I didn't know him very well then, so Carole and I were both thrilled and apprehensive. But warm, modest, jolly and unassuming, he quickly made himself – and us – feel at home in our rented house, which happened to have a baby grand piano in the living room. His rapport with our young daughters (then about eight) was instant and as he chatted away to them I could see why he was so popular with schools. Then, sitting down at the piano, he led us all in a singsong. The scones may have got burnt, but that didn't in any way spoil what was a memorable afternoon, and one which led him to dedicate *Three Heads Made of Gold* to Deborah and Manuela.

* * *

Knowing that we were keen to expand our music list, Nicholas Snowman suggested that we start a series on contemporary composers. Being at the heart of the contemporary music world, Nicholas was ideally placed to be the general editor of such a series and to draw in the composers whose involvement we felt to be important. Michael Tippett, Peter Maxwell Davies and Harrison Birtwistle were the first to be featured. Later, outside the series, we were to publish a book of Maria Callas's masterclasses, and biographies of a number of major performing artists. I also had several long discussions with the great pianist Claudio Arrau about a possible book, following in Alfred Brendel's considerable footsteps, but while Brendel attached great importance to his writings, I sensed that for Arrau it was an occasional departure, and despite his manager's encouragement the book never materialised. We were to have more luck with the celebrated Amadeus Quartet, enlisting the broadcaster, writer and historian Daniel Snowman to work with these remarkable musicians, three of whom, refugees from Nazi Germany, had met in a British internment camp during the war before linking up with the English cellist Martin Lovett to make a sensational debut in 1948. With his sensitive appreciation of the music and his understanding of the historical background, Daniel was able to get to the heart of the very special dynamics of this great string quartet, while at the same time skilfully drawing out the musicians' own personal stories. Daniel had already edited an intriguing book for us, *If I Had Been...*, in which he'd invited ten distinguished historians to place themselves in the position of a major historical figure of their choice at a pivotal moment, and to suggest how, with hindsight, they might have acted differently, and with what result.

Through Gyles Brandreth, and on a lighter note, we also acquired a book of musical anecdotes, *Musical Bumps*, by the multi-talented Dudley Moore, then at the height of his Hollywood fame, which was an entertaining diversion. Given his classical background (he'd won an organ scholarship to Oxford) and his brilliance as a jazz pianist, it's not surprising that his stories ranged widely. I'd become a Dudley Moore fan from the day I first saw him in the ground-breaking satirical review *Beyond the Fringe*, with Jonathan Miller, Peter Cook and Alan Bennett, and had later spent many late evenings listening to him playing with his trio at the Establishment club in Greek Street. I enjoyed the transatlantic phone calls in which he tested out stories for the book, though he never seemed to be there at the times he asked me to call. Still, my admiration for him was boundless, and the cost of a few extra phone calls seemed a small price to pay.

* * *

Towards the end of 1973, Dannie Abse took up the post of writer in residence at Princeton University, but we kept in close touch and visited him and Joan there the following February. From Princeton, Dannie wrote:

> We arrived eventually at 40 Pine Street only to find it occupied. By fleas and fleas and fleas ... We retreated – that is the correct word – to an hotel, arranged for an exterminator of fleas to call at our future abode and thought of William Blake and John Donne. (Do you know his poems called Fleas?) We also thought of blue murder.

To raise Dannie's spirits, I sent him a copy of the first poetry annual, hot off the press, which cheered him greatly. 'It really is a first-class anthology and will be hard to beat,' he wrote. He began to seek out books on our behalf, putting me in touch with Professor Joseph Frank, who'd just completed the first in a projected five-volume biography of Dostoevsky which Princeton University Press was publishing. It was magnificent, and we jumped at the opportunity of producing a British edition, all commercial considerations swept to one side. We were to be rewarded by lead reviews and a long feature article in *The Times* by Bernard Levin in which he called it 'one of the outstanding biographical achievements of modern times'. Where, he asked, congratulating us, were all the large publishers? We were to publish all the Dostoevsky volumes, but Joseph Frank moved at a slow pace and it took many years – too long for an impatient Bernard Levin, who would write to me from time to time asking how long he'd have to wait for the next volume. I recently found a letter from him dated 6 March 1995 – I'd just sent him the fourth volume. He wrote, 'I'm already devouring it – if anything it is even better. But how long will I have to wait for the fifth and final volume? Anyway, it is a magnificent achievement, for him and for you.' Others concurred with his judgement, the *Observer* critic writing, 'It is difficult to conceive terms of praise too high for this masterly achievement.' Just occasionally, publishing brings rewards quite unrelated to money, and this was one such occasion.

In a convoluted way, it was through Bernard that we met the actor Ron Moody, whose masterly portrayal of Fagin in the musical *Oliver!* we enjoyed watching on TV every Christmas with our young daughters. The meeting came about through a series of books we'd commissioned in which famous graduates from different eras wrote about their university years – *My Oxford* and *My Cambridge* were the first two titles, and *My LSE*, which Joan Abse was editing, was the third. The editors of those first in the series had produced a formidable and varied cast of contributors, and one of the LSE graduates Joan wanted for her book was Bernard Levin.

Ron Moody catches up with his old LSE mate Bernard Levin at the party for Joan Abse's
My LSE. He never really forgave Bernard for stealing his girlfriend!

Bernard and I weren't exactly friends, but we'd exchanged those cordial letters about Dostoevsky and were both devoted regulars at Brendel's concerts, usually exchanging a few words in the interval. So, knowing Joan had drawn a blank with Bernard, when we next met at a concert I tried to press her cause, but he was evasive, suggesting we ask Ron Moody, who had been at LSE with him. That was an idea that excited me, as it did Joan, who wrote to Ron, then spoke to him several times on the phone. Moody seemed willing enough to do it, but he was often away, appearing in various plays and films, and he could never be pinned down. A rather more gentle soul than me, Joan decided to call it a day but was persuaded to have one more go… and Ron came up with the goods, a superbly written, colourful piece in which Bernard Levin featured quite a bit, especially when they appeared in revues there together (Ron was 'discovered' at LSE), and worked together on the college magazine, the multi-talented Ron being its cartoonist. Ron wrote:

> I was quite mad. With nine months to go before Finals I plunged impetuously into all the time-consuming, life-involving, wildly fascinating activities that go into putting on a show … Bernard Levin was to impersonate Harold Laski and compère. I first met Levin one evening as he was walking towards Holborn Station. I caught up with him and said, for no reason whatsoever, 'Did you know that Finsbury Park, spelt backwards, is Y-RUB-SNIF-CRAP?' He pointed out that KRAP-Y-RUB-SNIF might be more accurate, and I had found a fellow lunatic!

Fortunately, Ron was in town when we launched the book at the Arts Club in Dover Street, and turned up at the party. Talking to him, it became clear he was keen to write more, so we had the occasional lunch and he'd come to our house, talking, talking. Then, a year or so later, he surprised us by producing the manuscript of a kind of science fiction thriller, *The Devil You Don't*. Everything with Ron was 'kind of', for he had a quirky and original mind and his approach to everything – on stage, on the page – was unconventional. He could be his own worst enemy, difficult and provocative (as Liz Rose, who edited *The Devil*, can testify), but he had an exceptional talent and wanted everything to be perfect, and once you got to know him you came to realise that his unpredictable behaviour was often a cover for his insecurity. At the time we met him he'd become involved with a blonde lady in Hollywood (fatal!), and when the relationship ended he was bitter and lost and would come to us to let off steam. Out of his Hollywood experiences came a second novel, *Very, Very Slightly Imperfect* (VVSI being a grade of diamond). It was his often very funny take on Hollywood. In one scene the main character takes his fiancée to buy a ring. The nearer they get to the shop, the stiffer his arm becomes, so that by the time he has to write a cheque for the expensive diamond ring his fiancée has chosen, he can't move his hand. Did this happen to Ron? I'd put money on it!

Ron never wanted to play Fagin again, though after his success in the stage and film versions of *Oliver!* he'd had a number of offers. But in 1984 (an ominous year), he was approached to star in a Broadway revival. He kept saying no, but every time he did so they upped the offer, until he eventually relented. We were in New York when the show opened, and Ron's performance was mesmerising. He had the audience cheering from the first number. I thought he'd be there for years, but I was wrong, as these lines from a letter he wrote us in his wry style and signed 'Ronaldo' make all too clear:

> On Monday May 7th I was told I had been nominated for a Tony Award! On Tuesday May 8th, the producer of Oliver rang up to congratulate me with the news that the Notice was going up the next day! On Sunday 13 May, Oliver closed! And you thought VVSI went too far? It was a giant managerial disaster – a real Broadway cock-up.

There was a PS to his letter: 'I won the Theatre World award for the most outstanding debut on Broadway. Wheeeeee!'

Then, back in England, a wonderful thing happened: Ron met a delightful redhead called Therese. A former ballerina and a great deal younger than him, Therese was caring, gentle, saintly – and they married. And had six children. We'd go out with them both for dinner, and as he sipped his vodka Ron would announce with a wicked glint in his eye, 'We have news! Therese has written a novel, and I'm pregnant!'

Carole and I are godparents to their first-born, Catherine, the only girl, conceived while we were all on holiday together in France (so that's why they were late down to the beach!). When, one Christmas, the whole Moody family came to us for tea, it seemed as if the entire cast of *Oliver!* had descended, the youngest boy – a double for the Artful Dodger – setting off the burglar alarm and bringing the police to our door. We bought Ron and Therese a wooden Indian box, and Ron conjured up a fantasy/adventure story around it called *The Amazon Box*, somewhat in the vein of Harry Potter (though written earlier than the Potter books and sadly without their sales). Fully aware that his sales hadn't exactly hit the jackpot, Ron belatedly wrote to thank us for the advance: 'I can't call it an "advance" because it was so far behind, but I very much appreciated it.' He'd just made three films, so he was happy enough, and always appreciative of our support of his writing.

However, as I wrote earlier, Ron could be difficult, very difficult, and touchy, as I discovered when, shortly after his second book was published, I called for him early one morning to drive him to a *Yorkshire Post* literary lunch in Leeds. He got into the car slowly and sat with his Sherlock Holmes hat pulled down over his eyes for most of the journey, ignoring my feeble attempts to start a conversation. What was wrong, I wondered, and only found out when he eventually passed me a flyer for the lunch which listed previous distinguished speakers – but not him, though he had been there the year before. He was deeply offended, and when the editor of the paper called on him to speak to the packed hall, introducing him with the words, 'And now Ron Moody, who needs no introduction,' Ron handed him back the microphone and told him to introduce him properly, as he had the other speakers, and only when he had done so did Ron leap to his feet, stealing the show with a bravura performance that brought the house down… and sold a great many books.

Our Jekyll and Hyde friend could be generous, though. When our daughter Deborah was getting married, I asked Ron if he would give one of the toasts at the dinner afterwards, and he readily agreed, adding,

'I could sing.' 'Sing?' I replied hopefully. 'What would you sing?' 'Well,' said Ron, "Reviewing the Situation" would seem appropriate for a wedding.' And so we got the music for that famous *Oliver!* number, primed the musicians, and didn't say a word to Deborah. Cometh the hour, up sprang Ron and, as I'd hoped, launching into an hilarious speech, deliberately confusing Deborah with her twin sister Manuela and suddenly (realising that they had French- and German-speaking Swiss friends there) speaking in what sounded exactly like French but wasn't, then switching to what sounded like German, but wasn't, working himself up into such a crescendo you felt a Nazi salute was coming any minute. He stopped himself in the nick of time, saying, 'Control yourself, Moody' and breaking into the song. Deborah, who'd been brought up on *Oliver!*, who knew every note, was both amazed and deeply moved. 'He's doing this for me...?' was all she could stammer.

Fast forward to July 2010: *Oliver!* was running at the Theatre Royal, Drury Lane, with Russ Abbot as Fagin, and it was fifty years to the day since Lionel Bart's great musical had first taken London by storm. The producer Cameron Mackintosh wanted to do something special to mark the occasion and he invited Ron, now aged eighty-six, and his family to watch the show from the royal box. Ron asked us to join them. But he was not to be just a spectator, and at the end of the show he was called on stage. He strode on from the back, a glamorous girl on each arm, passing through the assembled cast who'd just taken their final bows. Russ Abbot then came forward and announced simply, 'The legendary Ron Moody!', stepping aside to leave Ron to command the stage. Surprised, the packed audience rose to their feet, applauding as he began to speak.

Now, Ron was not only no ordinary, conventional performer, he was also no ordinary, conventional speaker, and famed as such. He joked with the audience in his tongue-in-cheek way, and when the young actor playing the Artful Dodger came forward and diffidently asked, 'Please, Mr Moody, sing "Pick a pocket",' Ron bellowed back at him teasingly, 'Sing! I'm doing this for nothing, and you want me to sing?' But the young boy (as pre-arranged, of course) persisted and, in the end, pretending to clip his ear, Ron gave in, the orchestra started up, the cast stood back and Ron launched into that famous number, his signature number perhaps, as magnificently as he'd ever performed it, his glorious voice rising to the gods. The applause went on and on. When, at a reception afterwards, I found myself talking to Russ Abbot and commented on how generous his introduction to Ron had been, he modestly told me what a privilege it had been to be on stage with such a great performer, and what a thrill it had been to hear that famous voice close to. Watching Ron bring the audience to its feet, seeing his wide-eyed children applauding their father, was a rare experience. That night a star was reborn.

However, that wasn't the end of *Oliver!* as far as Ron was concerned. Finally, after years of pondering, he began to plan an autobiography (well, *a kind of* autobiography!), in his usual methodical way, mapping it all out in meticulous detail. What an optimist he was: it was to be in seven volumes, the first one ending with the London production of *Oliver!* in which Nancy was played by the powerful, husky-voiced singer-actress Georgia Brown. Ron and method-actress Georgia had been at loggerheads from the word go, and as the show progressed the two of them became like Joe Frazier and Muhammad Ali on stage, stepping on each other's lines, flaring up at each other, competing. Ron had kept detailed diaries all his life, and there, written at white heat at the time, was his impassioned night-by-night account of it all, just waiting to be transposed onto the printed page.

In his opinion, the tension between them made their performances all the more powerful, but it took its toll on them both. As Ron started to write, and as the book grew, it became obvious that the material had to be cut and toned down, and the only editor he trusted was Liz Rose. So once again Liz bravely took up the challenge, and somehow she kept him on the rails. It's a strange book, with a strange title scribbled on a paper napkin in a restaurant and intended to be just a working title: *A Still Untitled (Not Quite) Autobiography*. But it is a powerful and compelling book, and all Ron. He went on the television programme *Loose Women* to promote it, and captivated that lively group with his witty ripostes and humour. He spoke at various literary festivals and what he really gave them was a one-man show, recalling the great stars of the past and performing snatches from their acts (never had Bing Crosby sounded so uncannily like Bing, nor Max Miller like the Cheeky Chappie himself). We both opened the *Daily Mail* one Friday morning with trepidation, knowing there was to be a review... and there it was, a full-page rave from Roger Lewis, himself a maverick and, with his extensive knowledge of showbiz history as well as of literature, just the man to appreciate Ron's unconventional approach. His review was headed 'Consider Yourself a Legend, Mr Moody'.

That was our Ron.

* * *

But publishing life was not all musicals and royal boxes, and back in the real world of the late 1970s, where the Moody saga began, we were facing a crisis. Naturally, moving in so many directions, building a quickly growing list, our financial demands had grown. The strain was considerable, both on Jeremy Morris as financial director and on me, as we fought to keep things going and to retain the bank's support. Michael Rivkin had backed us so far, but with a crash in the property market, in which he was a major player, he was himself under pressure to pull in his horns, sell the country house and reduce his commitments. We had a long, friendly talk, but the bottom line was that he couldn't go on financing our growing business. It was a bleak moment as we contemplated our commitments – the staff, authors, office costs, printers' bills and so on. The situation was compounded by the fact that the long friendship Jeremy and I had enjoyed since our schooldays became fraught as we struggled to cope. Eventually, and perhaps inevitably, we parted company, Jeremy eventually joining an international firm of coffee brokers as financial director. The separation saved our friendship, which thankfully resumed and continues strongly to this day.

That Robson Books was able to continue was due to Carole's father. Alerted to the situation, and after several long meetings with Michael, he heroically stepped in, arranging the necessary facilities with his own bank. Not that it was quite that easy or straightforward, since as a condition of giving that facility the bank insisted that, as well as his guarantee, we pledged our house as a security; and the monthly debenture figures they now demanded were a recurring nightmare. Even now I shudder when I think about them. Nevertheless, we were still there and very much in business.

Considering that he'd once lost everything he had in Egypt, it was both remarkable that Ben was in a position to do this and an unbelievably generous act which enabled us to continue. A modest man who never wanted anything for himself, Ben worked incredibly hard and was highly respected for his integrity and straight dealing. The fact that he spoke many languages had helped him build up a solid export business here, which gave him some leverage with the bank. Above all, he was a family man who helped various relatives around the world, and for him this was a family matter and he wasn't going to let me down. For my part, I was determined not to let *him* down, and didn't, though it was some twenty-five years before we were able to release him from his commitments and pay back everything we owed financially. No one was more pleased than him – not for the money, not for himself, but for the honour involved.

Among other things, Ben's company exported diesels and spare parts for trucks all over the world and had its own warehouse, and he believed we could save a substantial sum of money by doing our own distribution. Accordingly, we took a small modern warehouse in Tottenham and began to do just that. It wasn't a simple matter, however, and it involved setting up a computer programme which linked the stock to sales and royalties, and it needed a special person to set it up, oversee it and run it, someone we could trust. And that is where Carole came in. She'd gained a degree in art history from London University, and had recently qualified as a British Tourist Board Blue Badge Guide, a demanding course. She'd also written a book called *From London for the Day*, which Allen & Unwin had published. But in the circumstances, she felt she had a duty to help, so she set all that aside and took over the running of the warehouse, a tough and unpleasant job, especially given the growing nightmare of returns – the bugbear of the publishing world. And when our sales manager left some months

later, she took over that role too, coming into the office (now in Clipstone Street), dealing with the main accounts, overseeing the reps. It
was a huge sacrifice, but it did wonders for the business.

Outside the office, a rather different kind of drama was unfolding
in the shape of an irrepressible Labrador puppy called Brandy. At the
corner of our road was an off-licence, and the owners' dog had just
given birth. The puppies were adorable and for sale, and every day our
daughters, who must have been about ten at the time, would call in on
their way back from school, imploring us to take one. They would look
after it, it would be no trouble, they'd take it for walks, please, *please*…
In the end we gave way and Brandy entered our family. But, though we
loved dogs, we'd never owned one, and it wasn't a success. The trouble
was that our smallish house was on the edge of the busy (and dangerous) Finchley Road, and our back garden was tiny. Still, we were only a
ten-minute walk away from Hampstead Heath, and day after day we'd
walk Brandy there, trying to get him to do his business. But he never
would, not until he got back to the house, whereupon he'd land it on
our doorstep, or at night on the kitchen floor.

He'd bark and squeal all night long, and the girls would creep downstairs so they could calm him and clear up the mess, since they knew
we were starting to find it too much to cope with. Brandy was obviously unhappy, and we were, too, and something needed to be done.
But what? When I mentioned our predicament to our receptionist at
Robson Books, she said she had friends in Reading who were looking
for a dog. The husband was a chef at the university and they had a
house in the grounds, so we felt he would be well looked after. And so,
finally driven to desperation, like a thief in the night I put Brandy into
the back of my car and drove him to his new home. Never in my life
have I felt so treacherous.

A few weeks later, our receptionist came to tell me that, reluctantly,
her friends couldn't keep Brandy since he was yapping at their new
baby all the time and frightening it. That lunchtime I went for a walk,
thinking about the problem, when I bumped into my friend Jeffrey
Pike. He and his wife Val lived in the country not far from Reading
and had two Labradors and a very large garden. I told him the story,

and he said they'd love to have another Labrador, and offered to drive over that evening and collect him, which to our great relief he did. Two weeks later, the phone rang. It was the forthright Jeffrey. 'I don't know what you've taught him,' he barked, 'but your so-and-so dog will only crap on our doorstep!'

Gallantly, he persisted, and all was well until Brandy broke into their neighbour's duck pond, resulting in the neighbour storming into his garden and shooting at the dog. Miraculously, Brandy wasn't badly wounded and recovered fully. After that, all went well for a while, and whenever we visited the Pikes, Brandy would rush up to us and tears would well up in our daughters' eyes. But (this is a story of buts) several years later Jeffrey's business was taking him to Canada and he was selling the house. After much thought, he had finally given Brandy to a tree-feller he knew who lived in a barn nearby. Brandy evidently relished his new home and accompanied his new master wherever his job took him. Then, one dramatic night, as his owner slept, the barn caught fire. The dog managed to escape through a window and some-how brought help, saving the man's life. The incident made headlines in all the local papers, and Brandy – our Brandy! – was declared a hero. And, as far as we know, they both lived happily ever after.

*   *   *

The advantages of having our own warehouse became excitingly apparent in the autumn of 1984 when, surprisingly for such a small publisher, we found ourselves with two No. 1 bestsellers in the same month. Coping with that was a challenge for all of us, especially for Carole, but it more than made up for the many onerous aspects of the operation – and it certainly relieved pressure from the bank.

It was around June of that year that I had a phone call from Gyles Brandreth. At that time, the multi-faceted and effervescent Gyles was famous for the colourful jumpers he wore for his regular appearances on breakfast television, and for both his fast talking and his fast-working mind. (Those jumpers were quickly shed when he later became an MP.) He also had a publishing business called Victorama, which was really an editorial operation, Gyles using his contacts and charm to bring in celebrity authors to work with his excellent editor, then looking for a publisher such as ourselves to buy the rights and publish the book. Thus it was that Gyles phoned to ask whether we would be interested in a book with Michael Caine called *Not Many People Know That*, which was basically an entertainingly presented trivia book of little-known and unusual facts. All royalties were to go to the National Playing Fields Association.

Without a second's hesitation I said yes, and a deal was struck. The reason I had reacted so decisively (even though it was late in the year to take on an autumn book) was that I had seen Peter Sellers on the *Parkinson* show imitating Caine saying, 'Not many people know that' and talking about Caine's penchant for collecting eclectic information, so I knew exactly what Gyles was offering. Even so, at first it looked as though I had made a mistake, as we got a negative reaction from Smith's and the other major outlets, and our reps found themselves struggling. The only positive was that the on-the-ball Ian Chapman, now MD of Simon & Schuster, but then in charge of Pan Books, bought the paperback rights for Pan, albeit for an extremely modest sum. However, our publicist, Cheryll Roberts, did a smart thing. She sent copies of the book to local radio stations around the country and suddenly snippets from it were being quoted by their presenters whenever there was a gap to fill in their programmes – and, best of all, that *Not Many People Know That* title was mentioned again and again, becoming a popular catchphrase. Suddenly we were flooded with orders.

At more or less the same time, we launched another book, by the popular northern singer/writer/comedian Mike Harding. We had already published several of Mike's books, and they had all done reasonably well, backed by the very popular one-man show he'd tour nationwide every autumn. Mike was fast-footed, very funny and had a strong and loyal following. With his new book, *When the Martians Land in Huddersfield*, something happened – and that something was an appearance on one of the main chat shows of the day, hosted by Russell Harty. Harty loved the book and led Mike into quoting more and more from it and showing on screen some of the funny drawings

A windy day atop the ancient fortress of Masada during the Arts Council reading tour of Israel, February 1971. Back row (l to r): Peter Porter, Charles Osborne, Arts Council representative, Carol and Ted Hughes. D. J. Enright is at the front (left), with me and Dannie Abse.

With Ted and Carol Hughes at the beautiful Kibbutz Ain Harod, a particularly memorable day. Founded in 1921, the kibbutz is situated in the Jezreel Valley, in northern Israel.

The line-up for our first, large reading in Tel-Aviv's Nachmani Hall. Left to right: Ted Hughes, Dannie Abse, Peter Porter, Amir Gilboa, Carmi, me and D. J. Enright.

Robson Books' first book launch, at New Zealand House in September 1973, for Dick Emery, here seen signing our copy of his book, *In Character*.

Outside the Grafton Arms in Westminster (where the Goons originally met up), celebrating the publication of *The Goon Show Companion* by Jimmy Grafton, the pub's benevolent proprietor, and Roger Wilmot, both on the left of the photo next to Harry Secombe, Peter Sellers, Michael Bentine and yours truly. © GEMMA LEVINE

A book signing with a difference – at Bentall in Kingston, Harry Secombe is surprised by Michael Aspel for the TV programme *This Is Your Life*.

Robert Morley and family at a Henley signing for Margaret Morley's biography of her then father-in-law, Robert. His wife Joan is on the left, next to Carole, me, Margaret Morley, Sheridan Morley, Robert and editor Liz Rose. The Morley grandchildren are in the front.

Alfred Brendel in amused conversation with Dannie Abse and Alan Coren at the Austrian Institute's reception for his book *Musical Thoughts and After-Thoughts*. I was the lucky eavesdropper. © GEMMA LEVINE

Alfred Brendel signs my copy of his book before playing for the assembled guests. © GEMMA LEVINE

LEFT *The Book of the Goons* book launch at Grosvenor House. Joan Abse (far left) and Carole converse, while Peter Sellers chats to Liz Rose (left), who edited the book, and me.

Carole eyes her Prince as he arrives for the *Book of the Goons* dinner.

Wake up, Milligan, the Prince has arrived! Peter Sellers and Michael Bentine share in the joke as I try to introduce Prince Charles. Harry Secombe was ill and had to miss the dinner.

Prince Charles prepares to cut the special Goons cake.

At the Martini Terrace launch for Alan Coren's Arthur books,
I prepare to present him with a framed carving of the books' hero.
© GEMMA LEVINE

Alan Coren reading *Buffalo Arthur*,
one of the first titles in his successful
Arthur series. © GEMMA LEVINE

RIGHT The success of our *Twins Handbook* was no doubt due to the
pin-up girls on the cover – our daughters, Manuela and Deborah.

BELOW Here they are again some eighteen years later, in a photo taken
by actor Graham Stark. Deborah is on the left this time.

Marcia Falkender joins me and the witty political writers Frank Johnson (left) and Simon Hoggart (right) at a joint party in our office for their new books.

Nicholas Snowman, general editor of the Contemporary Composers series, speaks at the launch of the first titles, while two of the featured composers, Michael Tippett and Peter Maxwell Davies, listen intently, glasses at the ready.

At a Cambridge literary dinner for his book *The Amadeus Quartet*, historian Daniel Snowman is flanked by the quartet's distinguished members – Norbert Brainin, Martin Lovett, Peter Schidlof and Siegmund Nissel. © GEMMA LEVINE

The outlandish George Melly, a stylish guest at Robson Books' 10th anniversary party at Leighton House.

Operation bestseller. With our reps Adrian Parker and Keith Humphrey unloading much-needed reprints of our No. 1 and No. 2 bestsellers, by Michael Caine and Mike Harding.

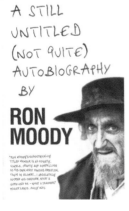

The cover of Ron Moody's enigmatically titled autobiography.

The irrepressible Moody didn't always hide beneath the guise of his alter ego Fagin… though often under a hat.

Michael Winner was less circumspect.

At the party for Maureen Lipman's *You Can Read Me Like a Book*, Carole gives Jack Rosenthal a 'book tie' to match his wife Maureen's jacket.

Jack and Maureen, complete with tie and jacket, joined by our daughter Manuela, Carole and me.

Robson Books are delighted to invite you to celebrate with Maureen Lipman and family the launch of Jack Rosenthal's

*By
Jack Rosenthal*

An autobiography in six acts

At the Fine Art Society
148 New Bond St
London W1

On Thursday 21 April from 6.30 – 8.30pm

RSVP to Sharon Benjamin on 020 7314 1604
or sbenjamin@chrysalisbooks.co.uk

The invitation for the launch of Jack Rosenthal's highly original posthumous autobiography.

he'd done to accompany the text. As with Michael Caine's book, we didn't know what had hit us.

The multi-talented Mike Harding, whose When the Martians Land in Huddersfield *shot to No. 1.*

The orders piled up in their thousands for both books, which went quickly out of print. We put large reprints in hand, beseeching our printers to work wonders, and waited anxiously for more books to arrive. But even before they did, it became clear that still more copies were needed, and so, taking a deep breath, we placed further large print orders. We knew that the publishing tide can turn very quickly and that there wasn't a moment to lose, so Carole and I piled the orders up on our dining room table, got out our calculators and started to allocate the reprints, arranging for direct deliveries to WH Smith (who'd now woken up to what was happening) and other main outlets and wholesalers. We'd also arranged for a goodly number of books to be delivered to our Clipstone Street office, and we were there with other members of staff when the boxes arrived at 8 p.m. Some of our reps were on hand too, helping us unload and filling their cars. We packed up books for the London shops, and arranged for them to be delivered by bike or car early the next morning. The other orders were dealt with at great speed by the warehouse, where Carole had laid on extra help.

THE SUNDAY TIMES
BESTSELLERS

PAPERBACKS

1	Bachelor Boys: The Young Ones Book	Elton, Mayall & Mayer	Sphere	£2.95
2	Chinese Cookery	Ken Hom	BBC	£5.25
3	Man's Best Friend	Jolliffe & Mayle	Pan	£2.95
4	Secret Diary of Adrian Mole, Aged 13¾	Sue Townsend	Methuen	£1.75
5	The Name of the Rose	Umberto Eco	Picador	£2.95
6	Giles Cartoons		Express Books	£1.75
7	A Host of Voices	Doris Stokes	Futura	£1.95
8	Berlin Game	Len Deighton	Granada	£1.95
9	Hamilton	Catherine Cookson	Corgi	£1.95
10	Shame	Salman Rushdie	Picador	£2.95

FICTION

1	The Growing Pains of Adrian Mole	Sue Townsend	Methuen	£4.95
2	Hotel Du Lac	Anita Brookner	Cape	£7.95
3	The Fourth Protocol	Frederick Forsyth	Hutchinson	£9.95
4	Proof	Dick Francis	M.Joseph	£8.95
5	Empire of the Sun	J.G. Ballard	Gollancz	£8.95
6	The Complete Yes Minister	Lynn & Jay	BBC	£8.75
7	So Long And Thanks For All The Fish	Douglas Adams	Pan	£6.95
8	God Knows	Joseph Heller	Cape	£8.95
9	Mexico Set	Len Deighton	Hutchinson	£8.95
10	First Among Equals	Jeffrey Archer	Hodder	£8.95

GENERAL

1	Not Many People Know That	Michael Caine	Robson	£6.95
2	When the Martians Land in Huddersfield	Mike Harding	Robson	£5.95
3	The Royal Shopping Guide	Nina Grunfield	Pan	£5.95
4	Harpers and Queen Official Foodie Handbook	Ann Barr & Paul Levy	Pan	£5.95
5	And Finally ...	Martyn Lewis	Century	£3.95
6	Rolls-Royce: The Complete Works	Mike Fox & Steve Smith	Faber	£3.95
7	What They Don't Teach You at Harvard Bussiness School	Mark McCormack	Collins	£7.95
8	Lives of the Indian Princes	Charles Allen	Century	£12.95
9	Fellwalking with Wainwright	Wainwright & Brabbs	M.Joseph	£12.95
10	In Stitches	Una Stubbs	Ward Lock	£6.95

December 9 – 15

You're always welcome where you see this sign   BOOKSHOP

These lists have been compiled by The Sunday Times from sales figures supplied by a nation-wide panel of retailers

An amazing autumn – our books at No. 1 and No. 2 on the Sunday Times *bestseller list.*

It was Operation Bestseller, and the result was that Mike Harding's book went to No. 1 on the *Sunday Times* and other main bestseller lists, and Michael Caine's book to No. 2 – and then they swapped places, staying there right through until Christmas. The speed of delivery and the fact that we were on top of the orders and in constant touch with our customers had made all the difference. Michael Caine was astonished, Mike Harding rejoiced with the Martians, and we went on to publish further books with them both. What's more, whenever I got a call late in the summer from someone saying they had something really special to offer that needed to be brought out quickly, I've always taken the call. In the strange world of publishing, you just never know.

20

YOU'VE GOT A WHAT...!

Alan Coren, for so many years our star author, had a live-wire cousin called Linda Agran. In fact Linda, whom we'd met socially on various occasions, was not just a live wire, but a creative one, and as a top TV producer had worked on such popular dramas as *Minder*, *Poirot*, *London's Burning* and Jack Rosenthal's *The Knowledge*. Linda had joined Euston Films in 1976 as a script executive working with Verity Lambert, and whenever we met she'd treat us to hilarious behind-the-scenes stories and I'd tell her she really ought to write them down. Eventually, to fob me off, she said I should meet her friend Maureen Lipman. Now that sounded like a very good idea, and the three of us met for lunch at a Greek restaurant opposite the Post Office Tower and just around the corner from our office. The two of them talked... and talked... and talked, while I sat in the middle of it all, pouring the wine and trying to order the next course, relishing what seemed like a comedy cabaret act. As I recall, Linda talked about how she used to get out of games at school, and Maureen about how a naked man had run past her car as she slowed down at a crossroads on a country lane. But maybe I'm adding my own surreal, wine-fuelled touch to the conversation.

At that time, Maureen was writing entertaining articles for the popular women's magazine *Options*, mostly drawn from the everyday adventures of an actress mum, and she thought these might form the basis for a book. Her suggested title was *Every Night That Dawns* – something that her mother Zelma used to say. She sent me a large

batch of articles, and Liz and I went through them carefully, Liz mark-
ing where she thought they could be expanded or linked and cutting
things that were dated or made them sound like topical articles. Maureen rose to the challenge, adding a great deal of new material (she's
a born writer and thinks at great speed), and so in the end we had an
enticing book. It looked fresh and new and not a bit like a collection
of articles, and it was very funny. But that title didn't excite anyone, so
Maureen suggested *How Was It for You?* – which did – and in typical
Mo fashion she posed for a photograph sitting (apparently unclothed)
in a Victorian bathtub with a chamber pot on her head... as any
author would.

We asked her to the office to meet and talk to our reps – about a
dozen of them – which she did, keeping them all in fits of laughter
for nearly an hour with anecdotes from the book – all, that is, except
for one veteran rep, Harry Richley, who tended to doze off at a certain
time in the afternoon, whoever was talking. In fact, I later discovered
that the reps would take bets as to what time Harry would nod off.
One thing one learns is that there is no fooling Maureen, and she
noticed it at once, but being used to matinee audiences she focused
on him and not only woke him up but had him laughing. A triumph
– or so I thought, but that evening she phoned and said, 'Never do
that to me again.' 'What do you mean?' I responded. 'You were wonderful. The reps – even Harry – were bowled over and think we have
a winner.'

She made it quite clear she'd found having to talk about her book
like that a daunting experience, but it was probably just first-night
nerves (it was her first book), and once she'd gone on radio and TV
up and down the country answering the same questions, telling the
same stories, she never looked back. At that time, the TV programme
that publishers vied to get their authors on was Terry Wogan's talk
show, which always did wonders for sales. So we were naturally exult-
ant when they invited Maureen to appear, and our publicist Cheryll
and I eagerly accompanied her to the studios. Well, she certainly gave
them their talk's worth that night, sharp and funny and captivating
both Wogan and his live audience as she rose to the occasion. The only

trouble was, there was no mention of the book Maureen had gone on the show to promote, as she realised as soon as she came off, annoyed both with herself and with Wogan for not bringing it up. But he too was aware of it, and immediately invited her to come back the following week to talk about it – much to the producer's consternation, since to have the same guest two weeks running was unusual, to say the least. But the die was cast, Maureen agreed to return, Terry kept his part of the bargain, and we all felt a lot better when, as she was doing a signing session in Leeds, there was a call from Carole in the office to say we'd just got an order for 10,000 copies from an enthusiastic Chris Rushby at Smith's (those were the days!), and that the book was going to be on the *Sunday Times* bestseller list at the weekend. It was on that tour, at a *Yorkshire Post* literary lunch, that they put their fork in it by serving Maureen pork, which certainly added spice and crackling to Maureen's speech. It was a mistake they never repeated! While driving back from that lunch, Maureen played me a tape of the very Jewish American comedian Jackie Mason, whose low, gravelly voice sounded, she said, just like Hugo Gryn, a rabbi we both knew and loved who was to become widely known through his regular appearances on the radio programme *The Moral Maze*.

Jackie Mason was a revelation to me, as he was to the audience at the Royal Variety Show he appeared on (quite what the Queen made of his irreverent Jewish humour one can only imagine). He took London by storm, incidentally offending quite a few oversensitive Jewish souls with his routines, while delighting a great many others. Consequently, when I was offered a book by him through an American publisher, I grabbed it, and we timed publication to coincide with Mason's next London visit. By that time, we'd been in contact, and I arranged to take him and his manager to lunch at the Garrick Club, which I'd recently joined (having been proposed by Robert Morley, who assured me it would do my career the world of good, 'dear boy'). Anyway, in bounced Mason in a blue blazer, looking around him at the pictures and asking me where the originals were, fortunately in not too loud a voice. Then a tall, elegant, Savile Row-suited man walked in carrying a silver tray bearing glasses of champagne. 'And what do you do?' Mason asked jovially, going up to him. 'Bugger all, really,' came the reply. 'I'm a member of the House of Lords.' 'Well, keep in touch, keep in touch,' responded Mason, unfazed, and in we went to lunch.

I was never comfortable at the Garrick, too shy to turn up by myself and sit at the long members' table and talk to whoever happened to be next to me, and I always recoiled at having to take women guests into a different room for lunch (things have changed now, but at that time women were only allowed into the main dining room in the evening). Even the almost daily sight of Kingsley Amis, deep into his cups at the head of the table, surrounded by his cronies, was not compensation enough as far as I was concerned. You weren't really supposed to talk business there, and when I once took John Simpson for lunch and he brought some maps to show me the area he planned to write about, we were politely leapt on. However, the atmosphere was very different the night Carole and I took Les Dawson and his young wife, Tracy, to dinner there. Les loved it, and everyone in the crowded dining room fell under his spell as he drank glass after glass of Beaumes de Venise and chatted to all and sundry, virtually performing a cabaret act. After they left, all the members there came over to tell me to be sure to put Les up for membership and they would support his candidacy – and I did, but sadly it wasn't to be, as Les had a heart attack shortly afterwards which carried him away.

Like Harry Secombe, Les loved to write and produced comic novels at great speed. Endlessly inventive, he had a flow of comic repartee that could throw even the great Michael Parkinson, who loved him. It took several books before we really got to know Les, but after that we always had lengthy dinners *à quatre* when he came to London, and he would work closely with our gifted editor Louise Dixon. And, of course, nobody played the piano like Les (and if you think it's easy to play all those wrong notes on purpose the way he did, just try it!). Fittingly enough, his last book for us was an autobiography, *No Tears for the Clown*, and he and Tracy would bring their new-born daughter Charlotte to signing sessions. She was always an additional attraction.

Roger Dixon's cover photo for the incomparable Les Dawson's autobiography,
No Tears for the Clown.

Les's funeral, to which I went with Carole and Louise, was extraordinary, the whole of Lytham St Annes lining the streets as if a beloved monarch had died. But then I suppose he was a king of comedy. I resigned from the Garrick shortly afterwards, not because of Les, but because I just didn't fit in. For all that, I do enjoy going there for lunch from time to time when a kind member invites me, and I know that for many it's a convivial haven of friendship and bonhomie. It certainly was the night Les reigned there.

* * *

Maureen by now was not only an Olivier Award-winning actress, but a bestselling author too, and a second book, *Something to Fall Back On*, was swiftly on its way. The words had flowed easily and wittily enough, but the photo for the jacket was another matter, until Maureen decided that the 'simple' solution was to wear a floral dress, hat and shoes specially made out of the same material as her sitting room curtains, and then to drape herself on a matching chaise longue in front of those same curtains. Barry Cryer, never short of a bon mot, pronounced the last word on that: 'A woman who dresses in her own curtains should pull herself together.'

After you… Speaking, or trying to, with Maureen Lipman at the launch of her bestselling Something to Fall Back On.

By now Carole and I had been drawn into the Lipman/Rosenthal family circle and had met her amazing mother Zelma (as much a star in her own way as Maureen, and a major character in Mo's writing). We'd also met Adam and Amy, her super-talented children, and Jack, her husband. Everybody loved Jack – even, I imagine, Barbra Streisand, with whom he was working at the time. Co-writing the film *Yentl* with her was not an easy gig, and many were the stories he and Maureen told about her (see *How Was It for You?* for the hilarious description of one encounter which she was prompted to tell over and over again as she promoted the book). Jack was very much his own man, deceptively quiet and with a self-deprecating sense of humour that was underpinned by a sharp-eyed observation of the world around him, his northern and Jewish roots very much in evidence. Jack's writing career had begun in the early days of *Coronation Street*, for which he wrote over a hundred episodes, and encompassed a number of TV comedy and drama series including *London's Burning*. But it's such classics as *Bar Mitzvah Boy*, *The Evacuees*, *The Knowledge*, *Ready When You Are, Mr McGill*, *The Chain* and *Eskimo Day* that place him in a class of his own.

Maureen and Jack shared a warm and very special kind of humour which seemed to bind them in a unique way. Maureen's stories of their courtship were both hilarious and endearing. I still laugh when I recall her account of the night she took Jack home to Hull to meet her parents. After dinner, Jack had gone up to the room he'd been allocated, leaving Maureen to gossip and catch up with her parents, until her tired father decided to leave the ladies to it, saying he'd sleep in Maureen's room and she could move in with her mother for the night. All of which was fine until Jack crept into Maureen's room in the middle of the night only to find himself climbing into bed with his future father-in-law!

Maureen and Jack were great party-givers and generally there was a theme or a twist to them (one invitation enjoined guests to 'Come as you were'; for this, Maureen dressed as a waitress in a short black dress and pinny, and Jack as a sailor, complete with nautical hat). They had a close circle of friends we always met there, and often we'd end up singing round the upright piano in their living room while the versatile pianist-composer Denis King (one of the popular King Brothers vocal trio) did the honours. Occasionally, once the party had got going, Jack would appear in a side room with his violin, music stand and music and start to play old favourites such as 'Goodnight, Irene' and 'I'll Be Seeing You' (somehow this always made me think of Sherlock Holmes). At one party, the writer, broadcaster and tenor saxophonist Benny Green and his wife Toni were among the guests. It was Benny's first outing since undergoing treatment for cancer and, knowing that he was coming, Julia McKenzie's husband Jerry, who collected old instruments, had brought along a tenor sax. Benny started playing, whereupon Jack produced his violin and attempted to accompany him – reducing the assembled company to tears of laughter. The Lipman/Rosenthal parties were a show of their own.

I was always prodding Jack to write an autobiography and whenever we were out together he would say he'd started – well, had written the first paragraph, anyway – and there it stayed over the years. It was an arresting enough paragraph, but he well knew that one paragraph does not a book make, and he was content for it to stay that way. It became

a running joke until one evening, many years later, which I will return
to. What wasn't such a joke was the occasion when, after the four of us
had enjoyed an Indian meal together in Soho, the car door slammed
on Jack's finger, prompting Carole to rush back into the restaurant
to get a tomato – her patent cure – to squeeze on the wound, while
Jack tried stoically not to show the pain he was in. 'It worked,' wrote
Maureen, 'and Jack could too!' We laughed about that, but not until
much later!

While Jack worked silently at his plays from home, frequently interrupted by Zelma whenever she was staying with them, Maureen
was on everybody's screen as Beattie in the brilliant British Telecom
commercials created by the larger-than-life advertising guru Richard
Phillips. The mini-scenes of those memorable commercials were tailor-
made for Maureen; they won every award going and the catchphrase
'You got an Ology?' was on everybody's lips. Needless to say we made a
book of them. In due course, Maureen decided to call time on the adverts, as there were plays to appear in, books to write, and fancy-dress
parties to arrange, and no actor likes to be typecast. Talking of parties,
one book, *Thank You for Having Me*, nearly caused a domestic bust-up
when, for the cover photo, Maureen decided not merely to festoon her
front door with party balloons and streamers, but to have it 'marblei-
sed' with blue acrylic paint to match her dress. It took the door – and
Jack – some time to regain their normal colour.

Maureen Lipman at a Selfridges book signing with her watchful son Adam.

Our publicity manager at the time, Cheryll Roberts, specialised in getting authors on to more programmes than they knew existed, and for this book she arranged a trip to Manchester which included a literary lunch, a television appearance and umpteen local radio interviews. The only problem was that on the day before, Cheryll had gone hang-gliding, crashed and hurt herself badly. Thus her panicky Sunday night phone call resulted in my being on the station platform to greet and escort our author when she arrived with just a few seconds to spare, since, as always seemed to happen, the minicab hadn't turned up. Maureen had saved the day by rushing to the Underground station and coming by Tube. Well, we didn't do too badly. I clung to my piece of paper listing all the interviews, and to Maureen, who knew her way around Manchester. We only missed one programme, which was pretty good in the circumstances, and there was no pork at the lunch where Maureen spoke with her usual panache and signed lots of books.

However, we were exhausted and peckish by the time we'd done the rounds, and Maureen was up in arms when, just as the train was pulling out of Manchester Piccadilly Station, a disembodied voice smugly announced that there was food available on the train only for first-class passengers; everything else was closed. Now, Maureen would never allow us to book first-class tickets for her, but that didn't mean she considered herself a second-class passenger. Double-checking that there wasn't even a sandwich to be had, she was on her feet in a flash, marching the length of the train, drumming up support and leading a revolt that finally resulted in the first-class restaurant being open to all. Only a couple of thespians on the train refused to support her. (Doubtless they had first-class tickets.) Having won the day but lost her appetite, Maureen hopped off the train as it waited at a station and bought us both a couple of sandwiches. It always pays to travel with a star!

Food seemed to play a recurring part in our relationship with Maureen – whether discussing which Lebanese restaurant we should all go to for dinner, or how to cater for her various book launches (or where to hold them that was unusual and didn't break the bank). I said earlier that there was no fooling her, and we thought we had handled the situation tactfully when, after she'd very reluctantly agreed to go on Des O'Connor's then popular (but by no means high-brow) television chat show, they cancelled at the last minute, on the very eve of our launch. Our publicist made some excuse about it never having been a firm booking, and Maureen seemed to think nothing of it, relieved at not having to do the show, but at the launch, mid-speech, she announced that she'd actually been dropped from *The Des O'Connor Show*. It was, she said, 'like being refused entry to Bejam' (a then popular low-price store selling frozen food), a quip the press quoted with delight.

When it came to speeches, Maureen was every publisher's dream, and I recall our being amazed at the apparent ease with which she walked into a packed Royal Exchange Theatre in Manchester one lunchtime and talked for an hour, moving from anecdote to anecdote with seemingly effortless ease, something I've now seen her do again and again. She is a born raconteur and hones her many stories to perfection. It seems she has only to go out in the street, drive her car, have her nails done, go on holiday, have a sauna, for incidents to seek her out – or is it rather that she seeks them out? Wit and humour pour out of her, and when it comes to charity or a good cause, she is, as she says, the girl who can't say no. It's no wonder people will bid decent money at charity events to have dinner with her.

Every book of Maureen's had a clever title, an inventive cover and an unusual launch. On the jacket of *You Can Read Me Like a Book* she is pictured wearing an outfit hand-painted to look like the spines and fronts of old leather books. Stupidly, we had a printed sticker on the cover saying 'Free jacket with every copy' – a joke that some punters took seriously, writing in for a jacket to be sent! For the cover photo of *Lip Reading*, Maureen lay on a Dalí-esque red sofa shaped like a pair of lips, glancing up from a copy of her own book. And for *Past-It Notes* – well, naturally, she had Post-it note reminders stuck here and there on her dress, telling herself things like: 'Glasses are on nose, phone is in hand', or 'Learn new language… you may even be able to say No in it'.

Just as witty as her book titles were Maureen's quirky lists of acknowledgements: among those she thanked were Clint Eastwood 'for leaving me alone for long enough to write this book'; Margaret

Thatcher and Edwina Currie 'for teaching me that some women's place is in a home'; her fax 'for my fiction'; her homoeopath, analyst, radionics practitioner, osteopath, gynaecologist, Alexander teacher, regular doctor, allergy specialist, optician, iridologist, reflexologist, acupuncturist and shiatsu masseur 'for my natural good health'; her children 'for saying "How's the book coming on?" when they meant "Is there a chance of a meal?"'; and, in *How Was It for You?*, her mother 'for saying "How was *what* for you?"'

For her most recent book, *It's a Jungle Out There*, a collection of her ingenious iPad images of famous people as animals with punning titles such as Mick Jaguar, Spaniel Craig, Harry Otter etc., Maureen turned up at the launch as... a moorhen (of course). The show goes on.

To return now in a more sombre mood to Jack and his autobiography. The year was 2003. He was clearly unwell and in pain but nevertheless felt up to coming with Maureen to join us at our local couscous restaurant. In fact, he was in good spirits, bringing up the question of the autobiography and to my surprise saying he was considering it seriously but hadn't yet worked out quite how to approach it. Obviously it wasn't going to be a conventional 'I-was-born-in' memoir. Both Carole and I expressed our delight, and then Maureen came up with an inspired suggestion: 'Write it as you do your plays,' she said. 'Write your life as a screenplay.' The idea galvanised him, and he started to do just that, Act One being his childhood, and so on. Following Shakespeare's lead, there were to be seven acts – seven ages of Jack. He wrote compulsively, biking each act to me as soon as it was finished. I would read it immediately and go over to discuss it with him. (What was there to discuss? It was dazzling, and totally original – funny, moving, compelling and a powerful evocation of time and place. Only Jack Rosenthal could have written it.) But he was increasingly unwell and growing weaker, and sadly never got beyond Act Six. It was a devastating time for his family, and it was a long while before Maureen had the strength to open the pages of Jack's not-quite-finished book.

Once she had, she decided that it must be published and that she would try to finish it, continuing in the same playscript vein, and their daughter Amy (by then an award-winning playwright herself) volunteered to edit the book and introduce it. At first Maureen did try to write in the form Jack had chosen but gave up after a while in despair. Nobody, not even Maureen, could write like Jack. It was a hard moment for her, but, summoning all her strength, she went on to complete the book, most movingly, in her own voice. It was a dreadfully hard and emotional thing for her to do, and for Amy too, who contributed a poignant foreword.

Jack had wanted the book to be called *By Jack Rosenthal*, since that was how his name always appeared on the screen at the end of his plays, and under that title – with extreme pride – we published it. Maureen, Amy, Adam and some actor friends arranged to give various dramatic readings from the book (it was after all written as a kind of play), including a platform reading at the National Theatre. Since then, Maureen has continued to spearhead various events to raise money for research into the myeloma Jack finally succumbed to. The book sold extremely well, the hardback being quickly followed by a paperback, and the reviews were everything Jack could have wished for when we sat down for that couscous dinner.

21

RUMBLE IN THE CITY

Harry Richley, the rep Maureen Lipman woke from his slumbers when she presented her first book to our sales force, had a number of special accounts and one of them was Lonsdale Sports. Lonsdale, a big name in the world of boxing, had been planning a boxing manual and Harry approached us on their behalf to see whether we would be interested in taking it on. Since we already had a number of boxing titles on our list, it seemed a natural fit and we went ahead, and thus I became friendly with the man who *was* Lonsdale and very much at the centre of the boxing world: Bernard Hart. In addition to running a successful sports business, Bernard is the most generous of men, forever arranging charity dinners to raise money for various causes, often related to boxing, but also for RAF ex-servicemen and others who have fallen on hard times.

As a result, I soon found myself invited to black-tie charity dinners, often sitting at a table with one ex-champion or another – Henry Cooper, John Conteh and Lennox Lewis were three whose lively company I was lucky to find myself sharing – and the leading sports writers and boxing promoters were often there too, Mickey Duff and Jarvis Astaire in particular. There was always an auction, for which we'd gladly contribute signed books by our authors, and I was staggered by the generosity of those present, some of whom didn't look as if they could afford to fork out the large sums that would win them a holiday for two, or a round of golf with a star player. Sometimes Bernard's wife, the singer Stella Starr, would head the cabaret.

I had actually met Henry Cooper once before in embarrassing circumstances that he luckily didn't seem to remember, when he agreed to write a preface to a biography of Joe Frazier called *Come Out Smokin'*, published while I was still at the Woburn Press. He had in fact suggested that we find someone to interview him about Frazier and then work that up into the preface. Vernon Scannell had agreed to do this and he and I duly went to Cooper's house with a tape recorder. But for some reason the machine just wouldn't work, so Henry sportingly hunted around and eventually found an old one under the stairs, which saved the day. Ever the gentleman, there wasn't a word of criticism or complaint. It certainly wasn't the most professional of our operations, and how ironic, in view of what follows, that it should have been a book about Frazier.

Years later, after we'd published his nemesis Muhammad Ali, we published Frazier's autobiography *Smokin' Joe*, and I met the once fearsome Joe in New York, at a Lonsdale dinner to honour the artist LeRoy Neiman, held at Madison Square Garden. I found him friendly and charming, and did my best to persuade him to come to London to promote his book, but he told me he was afraid of flying. Imagine!

Other than Cooper, although we had published books on most of the great champions, until those charity dinners of Bernard's the only one I had met face to face was Jack 'Kid' Berg, and that was because *he* took strong exception to a claim in one of our books that he was a dirty fighter. Berg was a colourful figure: Jewish, born in the East End, he was known as the Whitechapel Windmill, and also for his love of women (he was said to have dated Mae West and, when fighting in America, he had to be locked in his hotel room the night before a fight). He was also friendly with the East End Jewish gangster Jack Spot, who, incidentally, was sometimes present at those charity dinners. Berg had been the world welterweight champion, so when he phoned the office angrily and said he was coming round to talk to the editor, we awaited his visit with some trepidation. Fortunately, we managed to calm him down, and ended up publishing his tumultuous life story. I'd call that a win on points.

Jack 'Kid' Berg, the Whitechapel Whirlwind and former lightweight champion of the world,
flanked by Lonsdale CEO Bernard Hart, and his wary publisher.

When, in the spring of 1991, we took on a remarkable book, *Muhammad Ali: His Life and Times*, written by Thomas Hauser with Ali's full cooperation, I naturally turned to Bernard for support and advice, since we had paid a great deal of money for the UK rights. I should add that Hauser was a writer of real class, the author of *Missing* (on which the film starring Jack Lemmon was based), and an acclaimed writer on boxing, whose *The Black Lights* we'd published several years earlier. We went on to publish several other outstanding books by Tom, including one about Mark Twain.

Hauser was in close touch with Ali and his wife Lonnie, and through Hauser we started to make plans to bring him and Ali to London. We didn't begin to have the resources to do that, but working with Bernard we found a way. I approached American Airlines, waved the magic name of Muhammad Ali, and they agreed to fly him, Hauser, and several of Ali's associates, including a close friend, the *Time Life* photographer Howard Bingham, to London. Through his contacts, Bernard managed to get us complimentary accommodation at a London hotel. The Entertainment Artistes' Benevolent Fund also came on board with a view to bringing Ali back as a special guest on the Royal Variety Show, Peter Stringfellow generously offered to host a launch at his club in Covent Garden, and Bernard arranged a big charity dinner at Grosvenor House, to be hosted by Henry Cooper. As no boxing fan will need reminding, Cooper had a famous fight with Ali in which he'd caught him with his trademark left hook (known as "'Enry's 'ammer') at the end of the fourth round and knocked him down. Ali's swift-thinking cornerman and trainer Angelo Dundee gained his man time to recover by convincing the referee that Ali's glove was split and needed changing. (Whether or not Dundee's agile fingers had anything to do with that large split has long been a matter for debate.) There were, in fact, no substitute gloves to be had, but enough time had been gained for Ali to recover his senses and come back with a vengeance.

A September date was set, the dinner – to which we'd invited the buyers from the main stores – was sold out, and signings were arranged around the country. There was one problem: we were warned that because of the affliction from which he suffered (Parkinson's disease) and the fact that his speech was impaired, the once-loquacious Ali couldn't appear on television or give live interviews or make speeches. How then, we wondered, could we get publicity? The answer came back: 'Just take him to places and you'll see.' We were also advised by Ali's wife Lonnie to produce bookplates and to send them well in advance for her husband to sign, since this would save time and effort at signing sessions when the queues were long. That seemed like good advice, and we looked forward to the queues.

Ali and his retinue were due to fly in on Sunday 22 September, and the night before I went round to my friend Anthony Stalbow's house to watch a world championship fight between two British boxers, Chris Eubank and Michael Watson – a dramatic fight no one who saw it will ever forget, when a virtually beaten Eubank somehow pulled himself off the floor at the end of the penultimate round to land one punch, an upper cut, that sent Watson flying and was to cause him near fatal brain damage. It was horrendous, and one of the great tragedies of modern boxing. We realised at once that we would need to shield Ali from the press, since he would doubtless be bombarded with questions about the dangers of boxing and his own problems with Parkinson's. But we needn't have worried – not on that score, anyway – for while everyone else (and even Ali's dinner suit!) arrived the next morning at London Airport, there was no Muhammad Ali, which threw us all into a real panic. As a small publisher with so much at stake, it was a heart-stopping time, especially when we learned that Ali was in Abu Dhabi, where he'd been taken by his former manager, Herbert Muhammad, to help raise money for a mosque in Chicago. And although the promise was that he'd get Ali to London in good time for the book tour, that promise was not kept. According to Hauser, the reason was that Herbert had taken exception to the way he was portrayed in the book, which may well have been the case.

Next day, I received a message from Lonnie Ali in Chicago saying Ali was on his way, which is what she had been led to believe, and that happened again the following day. She herself was at her wits' end and worried for her husband, since, as Tom Hauser later revealed, he had only a limited supply of the medication he took to control the symptoms of Parkinson's. Howard Bingham had more of the medication in London, but there was no way of getting it to Ali as he'd been cut off from the world in Abu Dhabi – even his own wife was unable to speak to him. Howard was extremely upset that not even he, Muhammad's closest friend, could get through to him, and very concerned for us, realising we had been let down by someone he cared for deeply. I'd never met Howard or Tom before, but they rallied round and within a few days we were all firm friends, Tom doing a number of radio and press interviews and both of them covering for the missing Ali as best they could.

Ali doesn't turn up for the launch party for his book at Stringfellows... but others do!

Muhammad Ali: His Life and Times *wins the William Hill Sports Book of the Year award, and I stand in for the champion. Hugh McIlvanney, doyen of sports writers, makes the presentation.*

At first, believing Ali would eventually arrive, we postponed things day by day, but we were chasing rainbows. The night of the dinner came and we went ahead without our guest of honour, Henry Cooper doing his best to fill in and explain to the hundreds of guests. I was reminded only recently (in the aisles of the London Book Fair) by Chris Rushby, who was the supportive Smith's buyer and our guest at the dinner, that Cooper ended his announcement by saying that if anybody wanted their money back or had a problem, they should 'see me'. Nobody moved. At the Stringfellows launch it fell to me to explain the situation to the disappointed throng, and I even invited the many journalists present to help track Ali down. At the crowded London signings Tom Hauser was left to sign alone, battling on valiantly while the press had a field day. 'Ali held in Abu Dhabi' screamed one headline, above the claim 'Advisers have poisoned his mind'. The *Daily Express* ran a picture of Ali sitting with four men in Abu Dhabi under the legend 'Revealed: The mystery men behind Absent Ali', while the *Manchester Evening News* was even more sensational: 'Ali mystery as wife pleads for safe return'. The *Guardian*, *The Times*, the *Evening Standard* and *The Observer* all ran stories. Even more damaging was a statement from a so-called Ali spokesman announcing, 'Muhammad Ali will not come to London. He does not support the book anymore,' which Lonnie assured us was not the case.

It was a nightmare, and although the book appeared in the bestseller list for a week, had fabulous reviews and won the William Hill Sports Book of the Year award, it quickly vanished. The only fortunate thing was that we had sold the paperback rights to Pan for a goodly sum, which at least helped to underwrite the advance we had paid.

However, Muhammad Ali was a man of surprises, as many an opponent in the ring had quickly discovered, and he still had an ace or two up his sleeve, as *I* was to discover the following spring when Lonnie Ali contacted me. She'd phoned to say he'd be in England to open a restaurant in Manchester, and if we wanted him to stay on and promote the book, he would do so. I conferred with Thomas Hauser and Howard Bingham, and both said the same thing: 'This is Muhammad's way of apologising.' We held a council of war, took a deep breath, went back to the drawing board and arranged the whole thing again – a charity dinner, signings around the country, everything, giving the shops we'd let down last round the first option on signings. Only Selfridges declined. All this, of course, was a massive undertaking for a small publisher, and it was absolutely a matter of all hands on deck. Our editor Louise Dixon put aside her editorial load to help with the signings and publicity, and her photographer husband Roger covered the tour extensively, getting many excellent and exclusive pictures. Our accountant, David Pickin, also valiantly pitched in.

The tour would start in Manchester, since that was where Ali would be for the restaurant opening, but before that the people who were backing it invited us to a small buffet dinner for him in their home, on the edge of London. And there, in an armchair in their sitting room, was the fabled Muhammad Ali. He might have had trouble speaking, but I was the tongue-tied one as Carole and I went over to introduce ourselves. I'd heard all his outbursts and perorations, laughed at his 'poems', watched all his legendary fights – the Thrilla in Manila, the Rumble in the Jungle, even going with my doctor cousin Ted Stonehill to watch the first great fight with Joe Frazier live at the Dominion cinema in Tottenham Court Road – a fight so electric with drama, tension and excitement that Ted actually took his own pulse at one stage of the proceedings. (I later told Ali that and he looked at me in amusement. 'Took his own pulse!' he repeated, wide-eyed, flashing that famous Ali smile.) Surely this couldn't be Muhammad Ali sitting here now? But it was, and talking away to us at great speed. Who said he couldn't talk? He could, but the problem was that his speech was slurred so it was very hard to make out what he was saying, which was embarrassing. Gradually, though, we started to tune in and I mumbled back the kind of platitudes he must have heard a thousand times.

We drove home in a daze and prepared ourselves for the first signing and the rest of the tour. I couldn't have imagined the roller-coaster ride we were in for as we arrived at the Manchester hotel where Ali was staying. Everything was very calm. He was resting and Tom and Howard were waiting for us in the lounge, together with Max Clifford, who was publicising the restaurant launch. Clifford and I had a long conversation and discussed ways he could help to augment our own publicity for Ali. Later, I came very close to signing Clifford for an autobiography – in fact, the contract was agreed, the book announced in the trade press and initial work begun when he threw a tantrum about something or other and withdrew. It was our good fortune, as it transpired. He seemed to have forgotten this when he phoned in the summer of 2002, asking if we would take on Cheryl Barrymore's frank story of life with her former husband, Michael, whose career she had masterminded. We agreed to do so after several meetings with her and Clifford in his Bond Street office. The book, *Catch a Falling Star*, was finished and more or less ready to go, and Clifford offered to handle the serial rights, selling them virtually sight unseen for a very large sum. In those days it seemed he had only to pick up the phone for the coins to start rolling in. The last time I heard from him was when we were about to publish a spoof diary of Simon Cowell, written by his brother Tony. Clifford was looking after Simon's publicity at the time and wanted to make sure his client was happy with the content – I think the rather upbeat blurb he saw in our catalogue had alarmed him. It was as well we did since Simon hadn't seen the final text and when he did was rightly concerned that it focused too much on *The X Factor* and the people involved with him on the show. As he said to me, 'I have to go on working with them!' We had several discussions on the phone, as a result of which Tony adjusted the text so it became the tongue-in-cheek 'secret' diary of Simon's childhood years, still good fun, though much safer and far less commercial.

As we waited in Ali's hotel for him to appear, we got an inkling of what was to come, as a long queue of taxis had formed outside, their drivers loitering in the lobby, vying for the privilege of driving Ali to St Ann's Square for the signing at Waterstones. When Ali came down, hugging us as if we were old friends, we were told, 'There'll be a large crowd outside the shop, so get him inside as quickly as possible.' But had anyone ever been able to control the great Ali (except perhaps Herbert Muhammad)?

There certainly was a crowd in the square, a very, very large crowd chanting, 'Ali, Ali' as he stepped slowly out of the taxi that had won the honour of transporting him… but instead of going into the shop, he turned and walked straight into the middle of the throng, raising his arms to silence them. Now, Ali loved magic tricks, and one of his own was to 'levitate', and this he did as the crowd applauded, believing he actually was defying gravity. It was something I was to see him do on several occasions, and you had to watch those feet very closely – those famous flashing feet that had once moved at the speed of light – to see how he did it. Then, suddenly rounding on a large man at the front he snarled, 'Did you call me a nigger?', raising his fists as the man backed away. Just as suddenly, now smiling, he turned his attention to a middle-aged black man, saying, 'You look like Joe Frazier,' raising his fists again. And with that, doing the famous Ali shuffle with remarkable agility, he smiled, waved and finally went into the bookshop as the crowd cheered. It had been 'showtime', one of his favourite words. He was in that shop for several hours, everyone wanting a photo with him, and those pre-signed bookplates came in very handy. We sold some 600 books that Sunday afternoon, a pattern that was to continue. Now we knew why we'd been told to 'just take him to places', as the cameras flashed and there were stories all over the Manchester papers and on the local news stations.

For the repeat dinner Bernard had organised, to be chaired again by Henry Cooper, Ali's wife Lonnie and their ever-smiling, ever-polite, beautiful twin daughters came over, which created a marvellous family atmosphere. Far from not being able to speak, Ali suddenly got up and related a long and unusual folk story, then turned towards Henry Cooper and said, 'He hit me so hard he jarred my ancestors back in Africa,' shook his hand and sat back to enjoy the other speakers – Cooper, Thomas Hauser and that doyen of sports writers, Hugh McIlvanney. Then it was back on the road – Austicks bookshop in Leeds first, where the crowds matched those in Manchester and we nearly lost Ali when someone invited him to pray at a mosque and he disappeared with a group of people. I jumped into my car to follow, but only succeeded in crashing into the bookshop while trying to turn too quickly in the cramped parking area at the back!

We were supposed to be going on to Nottingham but nobody knew where Ali had been taken, and I began to fear that we had another Abu Dhabi scenario on our hands. We went from mosque to mosque, but Leeds seemed to be a city of mosques and we eventually gave up, driving off to Nottingham and praying that someone with him had details of where he was supposed to be. There were no mobiles in those days. We'd only been at the shop for a few minutes when a smart Mercedes drew up and out stepped a smiling Ali, cool as anything. Nothing would surprise me from then on. The signing went on so long and the crowds were so dense that we had to have a police escort to get us out of town.

The ride from Bentalls department store in Kingston to Harrods a few days later was equally memorable, as I drove him through Balham and Brixton, which have large black communities, and Ali put his head out of the window, waving to passers-by, who waved back, startled. Surely Ali was the most recognisable man on earth, and of course a great black hero. It was on that short drive that Ali, the man who was supposed to be so brain-damaged that he couldn't communicate, began to talk about racial segregation and the problems he had had as a youth in Louisville, Kentucky, where he was born. 'You can't ever have known prejudice,' he said to me, and I told him that as a Jew, I had, at school, and his response was, 'Ah, but that's not the same as being black, when your very colour identifies you at once, and people refuse to let you into a hotel or restaurant and turn violent if you dare to try – until, that is, you become heavyweight champion of the world,' he added, smiling. No wonder people loved him.

Waiting for us at Harrods was the store's owner, Mohamed Al Fayed, and kilt-wearing Scottish pipers who piped us through the store. Once the photos had been taken, Fayed seemed to disappear very quickly as Ali and Hauser got down to the business of signing books. There were over 1,200 people at the signing, and one smartly dressed, wealthy-looking woman was so overcome as she approached Ali to get her book signed that she fainted. At the previous book signings, Muhammad and Tom had been given a gift as a 'thank you' for coming, generally a book or a pen. At Harrods, after the very long signing, the representative took everyone to a back room where some sandwiches and bottles of mineral water were set out on a long table, and then asked, 'Is there anything else I can get you?' 'Well,' said Tom, 'the other day I was in your food hall and you had the best lemon bars I've ever tasted.' The representative asked him if he'd like some to take back to his hotel, and when Tom said he would, someone was dispatched to get a box. Ten minutes later the Harrods representative placed a nicely wrapped box of lemon bars on the table in front of him. 'That will be nine pounds twenty pence,' she said. And that was it, not even a flower for Lonnie, who had been there all afternoon with the twins, talking to people in the long queue as they waited patiently.

As well as being full of surprises, Ali was both generous and caring, as became clear when we set off for a lunchtime signing at Blackwell's bookshop in Oxford, which was to be followed by an evening signing in Birmingham, with me driving and Ali sitting next to me. After a while, he carefully opened his briefcase and produced several Bibles, turning to the back and handing one to Carole, who was sitting between Tom and Howard Bingham, and asking her to read a passage about King David and his archers. He then asked her to read the same passage from another Bible, pointing out a large discrepancy in the number of archers given in the two editions! Following this, he asked me if I could arrange for him to have a discussion about the Bible with someone at Oxford. By this time we were approaching the city and I told him that it was a little late to organise anything. But then I hit on an idea and said I was friendly with a rabbi who knew all about his religion, having been a rabbi in India, and if he would like me to I could try to arrange for them to meet when we got back to London. He asked me to go ahead. The man I had in mind was Rabbi Hugo Gryn. Only the Sunday before we'd been together at a mutual friend's house, and we had been talking about Ali and the forthcoming tour, Hugo telling me he'd watch all his fights and was a great fan. He too was a remarkable man. Born in Czechoslovakia, he had survived Auschwitz, which perhaps explained his warmth and humanity and his renowned ability to empathise with people. He was also a leading voice in inter-faith dialogue.

While Tom and Muhammad dealt with the long queues at the front of the bookshop, I went round the back and phoned the surprised Hugo. 'You'll think I'm crazy,' I said, 'but I'm with Muhammad Ali in Oxford and he'd like to meet you and discuss the Bible.' As it happened, Ali and his entourage were staying at the Cumberland Hotel, which was very close to Rabbi Gryn's synagogue in Upper Berkeley Street, and we arranged to meet at the hotel the next day, Friday, at 5 p.m., before the evening Sabbath service. When I returned to the front of the shop, Ali handed me a note from a man who ran his fan club in England, apologising for not being at the signing and explaining that his mother had just died. 'Where is this?' asked Ali, pointing to the address at the top of the note, and after checking I told him it was about eight miles from Oxford. 'We'll go there when we've finished here,' responded Ali. I pointed out that we were expected in Birmingham. 'We'll go there and *then* we go to Birmingham,' he said firmly.

The address in question was near Abingdon, and when we arrived at the estate where Ali's friend lived we were greeted like royalty: people were hanging out of their windows, and one felt that if they'd had warning there would have been flags and balloons. We stopped outside a modest house and, following Ali inside, offered our condolences and then left the two men alone to talk. After about twenty minutes or so, Ali emerged. 'Thank you,' he said. 'Now we go to Birmingham.' 'That was a very kind thing to do,' I told him. 'You've made someone feel a lot better.' 'No,' said Ali, pointing to his heart, 'I feel better,' and off we drove.

What a drive it was. Once we got onto the motorway to Birmingham, Ali, sitting next to me again in the front of the car, fell into a deep sleep. Then suddenly his fists began to pound the dashboard as he started to cry, 'Joe Frazier, Joe Frazier', louder and louder, his punches landing with increasing ferocity. I tensed, and someone in the back said, 'Hold the wheel tightly, it could get worse' – and it did. Slowing down and moving to the inside lane, I clasped the wheel as tightly as I could as the punches and cries of 'Joe Frazier, Joe Frazier' continued. Carole was sitting forward now, anxiously joining in the 'Hold tight' chorus. Slowing still more, I took a deep breath and snatched a glance at Ali – and he looked back at me and winked! He'd been wide awake and having me on all the time. All I could do was laugh with relief and resolve to get someone else to do the driving next time. I couldn't imagine what it must have been like to be in the ring with him when those large fists were landing real blows!

Birmingham, never a successful town for signings in my experience, came and went with several hundred books sold, and the next day, when he was to meet Hugo Gryn, we went at lunchtime to Leadenhall Market in the City, where the narrow streets leading to the bookshop were packed with people trying to reach it. The signing went on and on, and by the time we got back to the hotel it was 5.30 p.m. and Rabbi Gryn had given up on us and left. I felt terrible, and literally ran to the synagogue to apologise. 'Well,' said Hugo, 'the service doesn't start until seven, so let's go back to the hotel.' We went up to Ali's room and he welcomed Hugo warmly and thanked him for coming. Then he brought out his Bibles and pointed out the discrepancies in the text. Hugo tried to explain that it was the work of different scribes, so figures could easily have been varied. 'Are you saying it is not the word of God?' responded Ali with alarming force. 'No,' responded Hugo, 'I'm not saying that, but humans, fallible humans, were the intermediaries, recording it all at a later date.' The discussion went on amidst a warmth and feeling of mutual respect I found moving. Indeed, when Hugo left to take the Friday evening Sabbath service, I wondered whether Ali would have

liked to join him, but we had a dinner date with Bernard Hart, I reminded him, as he got up to embrace Hugo. An appearance by Muhammad
Ali in West London Synagogue would have turned a head or two!

Towards the end of the tour we went to Scotland for two signings,
taking the early morning flight to Edinburgh for a lunchtime event at
Waterstones, and then on by train to Glasgow, returning to London on
the last flight back. It was far too ambitious, and we had totally under-
estimated the length of time everything would take, as the queues in
Edinburgh stretched around the streets of that lovely city. Fortunately,
Ali had spent his time on the flight signing bookplates, but even so
the mountain-high piles of Tom's 700-page books went down slowly
as they both signed, everyone wanting a photo with the champ. We
had to be on the train to Glasgow at 3 p.m., and I looked anxiously
at my watch as the queue hardly seemed to shorten. A car was standing by but we knew we'd never make it as it raced us to the station
fifteen minutes late… Miraculously, there was the train, kept waiting
by the stationmaster, who'd been alerted to his famous passenger. No
one seemed to mind – on the contrary, there was a great cheer as the
car roared in and Ali stepped out, waving. Where this apparently sick
man got his stamina from I can't imagine, for we were all collapsing
around him. And on the train, more bookplates came out and he willingly signed away, as he did for people on the train who came asking
for an autograph. Glasgow, of course, is a boxing city, and the crowds
matched those of Edinburgh. We were there for several hours, and I
know some people were disappointed, since we couldn't expect the
plane to wait for us, but we took addresses and made sure that signed
copies were sent to all those who had ordered them.

The last signing of all was at WH Smith, in the Brent Cross shopping centre. There was a short gap in the schedule and Ali suddenly
asked if our office was near and whether I thought people would like
it if he came by so he could thank them for all the work they'd put in.
'Thrilled' would have been more accurate, as the owner of the general
store below our office was, too, when Ali ambled in to buy something
to drink. After that we still had a little time, and Ali suggested we
called in at our house, which he had heard was on the way. Now it

was the turn of our neighbours to stare in wonder. Ali, immediately at home, drank some tea and fell asleep on the sofa in our living room. When he stood up, our house suddenly seemed very small.

The tour was over, but two years later we did it again, on a slightly reduced scale, when we published Howard Bingham's photographic book, *Muhammad Ali: A Thirty-Year Journey*. Howard had been with Ali through all his dramas and adventures and had recorded them with great style. He was Ali's loyal friend and Ali wanted to repay him by supporting his book. There was a play about the boxer opening in London at the Mermaid Theatre for which he was coming over, so we tied everything in with that and the cost to us was relatively modest. On that occasion we went to Oxford again, but this time in real style. I'd planned to drive everyone there as usual, but at the last minute a fabulous-looking limo appeared outside the hotel where Ali was staying, the driver offering to take us to Oxford for a nominal sum to cover the petrol: it seemed the experience of driving Ali was recompense enough. So there I was, back in dreamland again, with Ali, Howard Bingham and two of their companions stretched out in the back of the car with me in the middle – four large, powerful black men who suddenly turned on me laughingly and said, 'We've got you, whitey!' as they sang Whitney Houston songs at the top of their high voices, Ali smiling that big grin of his, with no fists flying this time, and no Bibles.

We were all to meet up again in unusual circumstances, and not in England, but that is for another chapter. Meanwhile, as a tailpiece and as a tribute to Muhammad Ali's fine spirit, let me recount a story told to me in New York by the TV boxing commentator Reg Gutteridge. Reg had been rushed into hospital for a major operation, and Ali, arriving in London, had noticed that he wasn't among the circle of friends who normally greeted him. 'Where's Reg?' he asked, and when told he was in hospital Ali immediately took off in a taxi to see him. 'There I was,' Reg told me, 'just coming round from the anaesthetic, and I open my eyes and see the big man sitting on the end of my bed. I really did think I'd gone to heaven!'

And that, apart from his boxing prowess, is why Muhammad Ali really was the greatest.

22

FRANKFURT CALLS

I never really graduated from the noisy, grotty hotels near the Frankfurt Bahnhof, their rooms awash with the flickering, migraine-inducing lights from the neighbouring strip joints. For some reason, even when others were footing the bill, it went against the grain to shell out the exorbitant sums demanded by the better hotels: even the cheaper ones were costly enough. One, where I stayed a couple of years ago, was by far the worst, its tiny doorway squashed between the entrance of two sleazy nightclubs. Embarrassingly, it was in the so-called lobby of that hotel that I'd arranged to meet the American agent Scott Mendel, with whom I was having dinner. It was the night before the fair and I'd only just checked in so it was too late to change the venue. As it was, within seconds of stepping out of the hotel doorway we both had heavily lipsticked young ladies on our arms, and it took us the whole length of the street to shake them off. We cooled down in the Gaylord Indian restaurant opposite the station.

Frankfurt could bring winners and losers, and I certainly made my share of mistakes (though not of the kind the above might have led to). I do, however, vividly recall walking back to my hotel one night and spotting a certain well-respected British publisher slinking out of Dr Müller's Sex Shop – and reading a few days later that he'd suffered a fatal heart attack on the train back to England. A heavy price to pay for what I imagine was just a peep! On a lighter level, and while still on that theme, shortly after I got back from one of my first Frankfurts, when we were all still rather on top of each other in a small office, there was a call from my irrepressible friend Jeffrey Pike, who announced deadpan to the young girl who answered the phone, 'This is the sex shop at Frankfurt Airport. Please tell Mr Robson his goods have arrived' – a message she took seriously and conveyed to me loudly across the room, to everyone's amusement.

However, once you get away from the Moselstrasse there is a more seemly side to Frankfurt, and in the early days when we stayed right through to the bitter end (the fair has always stretched on far too long), I'd take time off and stroll down to the river, on one occasion exploring with Carole the city's splendid art gallery. I've also spent several memorable evenings at the Frankfurt Opera. Generally, I'd try to avoid being alone at night in Frankfurt, there being too many ghosts around, so it was always good to link up with American colleagues like Hillel Black or Herman Graf (who sounds like, and is every bit as entertaining as, Jackie Mason). One indelible evening, however, I found myself wandering alone past a large church and, peering in, saw a woman kneeling in deep prayer. I could sense her tears and realised that grief has no nationality. What her loss was, if loss it was, I could only imagine, but her obvious distress affected me, and I could easily have slipped in beside her and recited Kaddish, the Jewish prayer for the dead.

As I recounted earlier, when I first went to Frankfurt, I was uneasy at setting foot in Germany, and that uneasiness remained. Visiting the fair again just a couple of years ago, I wrote a poem called 'Vigil', which ends:

> And yet, and yet…
> It's over seventy years since
> that war began, but if
> I, a Jew, scion
> of that haunted race,
> forget, who will remember,
> and if none remembers, the
> dead are truly dead.
> I don't accuse,
> am on my guard,
> that's all.

The poem, set on Frankfurt's large railway station, expresses my ambivalent feelings and has been read at various Holocaust events. These days, it must be said, when the fair is on, Frankfurt couldn't be more international and as one mixes with all the American and foreign publishers it could almost be any city. Even the strip clubs don't seem to blaze and twinkle as brightly as they did when first I went there, but then again, perhaps I don't twinkle quite so brightly either, these many years on.

One year, quite early in the days of Robson Books, the dates for Frankfurt clashed with Yom Kippur, a fast day and the most sacred in the Jewish calendar, which even non-observant Jews tend to observe. It was not the day for a Jewish publisher to be offering his wares behind a stand in Frankfurt, and the fact that it was Germany added an extra dimension. Despite the apologies of the organisers, there were many protests, and some publishers decided to boycott the fair that year. However, many did not, and a special service was arranged for the day in question (the US publishers even flying in a rabbi to officiate). I hesitated, but finally decided to attend, a decision I regretted. On the eve of Yom Kippur, I went to the specially arranged Kol Nidre service, and on the day itself to a service at a large Frankfurt synagogue. I should have rejoiced at the fact that there were now synagogues in the city, but for some reason I can't quite grasp I felt uneasy from the moment I went in. Perhaps it was the lack of decorum (non-stop chatter and children racing, uncontrolled, everywhere); perhaps it was because the essential dimension of spirituality seemed to me to be missing. Shameful that I, hardly an observant Jew, should have felt this way when some of those talking, talking were perhaps survivors or the family of survivors. I left after an hour or so, and as night fell and the festival concluded, I joined a table of publishers for a special meal to end the fast – among them Peter Mayer, Erwin Glikes, Roger Straus (of Farrar Straus & Giroux) and Beverly Gordey from Doubleday (my old Chagall colleague).

Yom Kippur has a haunting presence and, after the dinner, as I walked those Frankfurt streets in the dark, I found myself thinking of a great-uncle of mine with whom I'd become friendly, my paternal grandmother's younger brother, Dr Kurt Selmar Rosenberg. Born in Heilsberg in 1886, my uncle Selmar was a physicist and a man of wide cultural interests – an intellectual of the old school. He'd fought for his native Germany in World War I, being awarded the Iron Cross first class, and later, in the pre-war Hitler years, was active in the underground, which led to his arrest in 1938 and internment in the notorious Sachsenhausen concentration camp. He was perhaps too interested in history and fired by politics for his own good. A year later, by then in poor health, he'd somehow managed to escape, travelling through Holland to England. In Paris after the war, descending the Eiffel Tower in a lift, he'd found himself face to face with the brutal commandant of the camp he'd been in. Too startled to confront him, he followed the man into the crowd until he disappeared. My uncle was old and frail then, and couldn't have done otherwise, yet it haunted him, and as he recounted the story to me in his excitable way, he found it difficult to explain how he felt. He didn't need to.

*   *   *

The bar of the luxurious Frankfurter Hof hotel was, and to some extent still is, *the* after-dinner place to go and be seen, but at one time there was also a lavish party given by the German publisher Bertelsmann, who owned Leisure Circle, a long-defunct British book club to whom we sold titles. And while we never actually received an invitation to this wonderland event, we would join the long queue at the door and when people we knew from the book club saw us, they would nod us in past the security guards. That was as much a badge of honour as downing the overpriced drinks at the Frankfurter Hof bar, which could be a lively place. On one occasion, an American publishing couple I was with provided a violent cabaret when the bruiser of a husband thought someone had jostled his pretty, petite wife and he rounded on the man, throwing a glass of brandy in his eyes and smashing the glass on his forehead. That stopped the chatter for a moment or two, while the husband was bundled out and the pieces of glass (and the blood) were cleared up, before normal, expensive service was resumed.

A couple of years ago, I was invited by an American publisher to join him and a group of friends for dinner at an old restaurant by the river. We waited some time for the husband of one of the party to join us. Eventually, he turned up with cuts on his forehead and his eyes blackened with bruises, explaining to his wife in a slurred voice that after a few (!) drinks in the Frankfurter Hof bar he'd stumbled down the hotel steps, hitting his head as he fell. I imagine it was an everyday event for the hotel's poker-faced doormen (perhaps also for the man's poker-faced wife).

Many Frankfurt stories are apocryphal, but an amusing one related by Patrick Kidd in the *Times* diary after last year's fair rings all too true. An American publisher had been drinking heavily in the Frankfurter Hof bar and eventually decided it was time for bed. Staggering down the steps, he hailed a taxi and asked the driver to take him to his hotel – the Frankfurter Hof. 'You're already there,' the surprised driver told him. 'Thank you,' mumbled the publisher. 'Next time don't drive so fast.'

Ironically, it was at Frankfurt, in 1975, that I was made to remove a book from our stand because it displayed a swastika on the cover. It wasn't a book on Nazi Germany, but a humorous book by Alan Coren, who always liked to have arresting titles and jackets for his books. When we were discussing the cover for this one he'd come up with a typically off-the-wall idea: 'Books on cats, golf and the Third Reich always sell, so let's call it *Golfing for Cats* and slap a swastika in the middle.' It didn't exactly spark an international incident, but we got some press coverage and Alan took mischievous pleasure in having created a stir.

Although, as at any book fair, we were there to buy and sell book rights, and that was important, the people we met over the years were a vital part of the mix – intelligent, cultured publishers with whom lasting friendships were often struck, leading to further meetings and dealings in London, New York, Paris or wherever. Many have now vanished from the scene, and Frankfurt is the poorer for their absence, as the rather anonymous conglomerates spread and dominate. I think of George Braziller, whose literary list I always admired and with whom I'd wander out of the halls to share a sandwich at lunchtime;

Larry Ashmead, the courteous éminence grise at Harper & Row, who always welcomed me to his empire, and whose end-of-year 'funnies' I would look forward to – a compendium of odd and amusing gaffes and stories from the publishing year; William (Bill) Targ, the editorial head of Putnam's, who invited me to join him for lunch at his regular table at the Algonquin when I first went to New York. As I now watch the books of the poet/singer Patti Smith climbing the bestseller lists, I remember that it was over that lunch that Bill offered me a volume by the young Patti, of whom I'd scarcely heard at the time, immediately withdrawing his offer when he saw me hesitate. I'd had my chance! Another American publisher who received me warmly in those early days was Sally Richardson's late husband, Sandy, the big white chief at Doubleday. Tall, elegant and handsome, Sandy Richardson seemed to have all the time in the world for the fledgling publisher I then was, just as Sally has always had when I've ventured into the St Martin's Press offices. Erwin Glikes, the erudite publisher of the Free Press, invited me to lunch in the Macmillan private dining room – a privilege – and it was through him that I met the then CEO of Macmillan, Jeremiah Kaplan, who came to our stand at Frankfurt having heard we had a photographic book entitled *Leningrad's Ballet*. But he was disappointed, thumbing through the arty pages and demanding, 'Where are the stars? I see no fucking stars.' Not a man to mince his words. And finally, it was through our dear friend Tom McCormack, about whom I wrote earlier, that I was always invited to breakfast at the Ritz by those other two fine St Martin's stalwarts, Tom Dunne and Charlie Spicer. Tom Dunne has bought quite a few of our titles for his own prestigious imprint over the years, and we have generally lunched together at Frankfurt, too – importantly, we share a passion for the ice creams always on sale near the fair entrance. Colourful times, colourful people, and real publishers all.

Probably our biggest early Frankfurt buy was Uri Geller's autobiography, from Arnold Dolin at Praeger. Uri was then at the height of his spoon-bending fame, and if we had paid half the price it would have been fine, but that's the way things go in publishing. Sell 10,000 copies of a hardback and all's well – but not if you printed 20,000! Shortly after the fair, Carole and I were in New York and the publishers took us for a celebration lunch (no wonder!). Uri was living in New York at the time, and we met up with him to discuss launching the book in London. As always, he was full of enthusiasm and charm, and drove us back to our hotel in his larger-than-life car. Whether or not his psychic powers are just highly skilful deception, I never fathomed. I watched him closely over a dramatic week in England and never saw any signs of trickery, though he was a superb showman. Our own Geller show started at the Martini Terrace in the Haymarket, where somehow Uri identified the famous TV astronomer Patrick Moore, who discovered that all the keys in his pocket had bent, which caused a sensation. The press, of course, loved it, as Uri well knew they would. (Less sensationally, an aunt of mine was unable to drive home when she found her car keys bent.) Uri always knew who to pick on, how to get the maximum attention. At Alan Coren's suggestion, I took him to a *Punch* lunch. Sceptics have claimed that Uri's brother-in-law Shipi always goes ahead to venues to 'fix' things, but Shipi wasn't there on that occasion, and in any case couldn't have known the layout of the *Punch* offices. There were the usual people at the lunch – the *Punch* staff writers and regular contributors, cartoonists and several guests – about thirty in all, with the then editor William Davis at the head of the table.

Uri began in his usual dramatic fashion: to everyone's delight, the editor's spoon not only bent but seemed to turn to rubber as he drank his soup. Then Uri asked one of the cartoonists to go to the end of the table and draw, while he sat at the other end and also drew. When they had both finished and revealed their separate drawings, Uri's matched the cartoonist's almost exactly. After that, he had those brilliant, sophisticated, cynical writers and artists in the palm of his hand.

Then he received an approach from the Marquess of Bath, challenging him to bend the large, solid silver centrepiece on display in the dining room at Longleat. Uri readily accepted, and we all went down the afternoon before the event, spending the night there as guests of the Marquess – or 'Henry', as Uri immediately called him – and joining him for an informal supper at which Uri did his impressive spoon-bending. If the Marquess was impressed, so was his librarian when he discovered that several old books that hadn't been moved for years had 'jumped' off the shelves in the night and were lying on the floor, along with a framed oil painting. Someone claimed to have heard the noise. The only person who wasn't surprised was Uri. Keen to publicise the visit (which suited us nicely), 'Henry' had invited the Queen's jewellers to witness the event, together with special guests and the national press and TV. Before that, however, his son, Viscount Weymouth, took us on a tour of his quarters, the walls of which were decorated with his erotic paintings – the Kama Sutra suite, I believe he called it. Back in the sober of light of day, everyone assembled around the large table as Uri moved in on the centrepiece, rubbing its solid silver arms gently, until they flopped. This was done not only under the close scrutiny of those present, but of the BBC's cameras too, so millions of viewers saw everything in close-up on the main evening news.

Over the years we published several books with Uri. By now, he had come to live in England and had bought a nine-bedroom, Palladian-style mansion in Sonning. He continued to be the ultimate showman, never more so than when he and his wife decided to go through the religious wedding ceremony they'd never had. Conveniently, this coincided with a book we were publishing by Uri and the prominent American rabbi Shmuley Boteach, who'd served for eleven years as rabbi at Oxford University and been voted *The Times* Preacher of the Year. He and Uri had corresponded over the years and their book, *Confessions of a Rabbi and a Psychic*, drew on their letters. Who, then, better than Shmuley to conduct the ceremony under a chupah on the extensive Geller lawn… and who better to be the witness than Michael Jackson, a friend of them both? The only trouble was that the witness was very, very late, but eventually a helicopter appeared, hovered above us and finally landed on the lawn, and out stepped an apparently shy Michael Jackson. The rabbi broke off from talking about his and Uri's book to the assembled guests, and the ceremony took place. A few days later, Jackson appeared again – at a small-scale event for our book being hosted by a Jewish cultural organisation at the Royal Institute of British Architects in Portland Place, which was to feature a serious discussion between the two authors. But as word spread that Jackson was coming, huge crowds gathered outside and the organisers nearly had a fit, as did the police, who had not been alerted. Fortunately, Jackson, who'd come in good faith to support his two friends, didn't stay long, smiling for the cameras, shaking a few hands and disappearing into the limousine that had brought him, leaving Uri and Shmuley to smooth feathers and get on with the main event. It was one of our most bizarre launches, and I wasn't readily forgiven by the philanthropic people who'd arranged it. For all the publicity Jackson's appearances had generated, the book was only a modest success, though I did manage to sell the American rights at Frankfurt to Hillel Black, then working for Sourcebooks, a remarkable company founded and run by the dynamic Dominique Raccah. However, when the whole Michael Jackson scandal blew up and Geller and Boteach at first supported him publicly, it did not help the book in the US, and Dom was understandably displeased with the situation. Happily, it didn't prevent us from continuing to have our regular dinners together in Frankfurt and London.

Michael Jackson gatecrashes the launch of Uri Geller and Shmuley Boteach's book
Confessions of a Rabbi and a Psychic.

I must have been much more adventurous in my early Frankfurt days, as I think back to the year we travelled to the fair via Cologne to talk to the composer Karlheinz Stockhausen, whom I was trying to sign up for our evolving music list. We spent an uneasy night there in a kind of annexe attached to the large main building, surrounded by trees, where he lived and worked. The following morning, he showed us around his studio, pointing out the various electronic devices he used in his compositions while I did my best to understand and conceal my ignorance of the works he talked about so animatedly. The book we ended up publishing with him was a collection of conversations between the composer and Jonathan Cott, a contributing editor to *Rolling Stone* magazine.

You don't expect to meet poets at Frankfurt, but it was there, in 1994, that I met the celebrated Russian poet Yevgeny Yevtushenko, who'd written an epic novel of modern Russia, *Don't Die Before You're Dead*. The book came with strong endorsements from Mikhail Gorbachev, Arthur Miller and William Styron, and I was discussing it with the Canadian publisher Anna Porter, whose company, Key Porter Books, controlled the UK rights, when Yevtushenko himself appeared on her stand. I knew his brave and powerful poem 'Babi Yar', recalling the massacre of over 30,000 Jews in a ravine just outside Kiev, and though we published little fiction, meeting him sealed my fate, and I bought the UK rights – making it a condition that he came to England to promote the book, which he willingly did. Among various other events, we arranged for him to read at the Cheltenham Festival, to which I drove him (in those days, I seemed always to be chauffeuring authors to one event or another). Yevtushenko was a dramatic and demonstrative reader of his own poetry and used to reading to large crowds at home in Russia, where audiences for poetry readings could number in thousands. There weren't thousands in Cheltenham, but there were several hundred, and the hall was full. He read mainly in English, but occasionally in Russian too, to give the real flavour of his poems, and then answered questions. The audience, used to more sedate British poets, was riveted. As it happened, Laurie Lee, with his quiet Gloucestershire burr, had preceded him, and Yevtushenko, who came in to listen for a few minutes, told me I should advise my 'friend' to project more, completely missing Laurie's captivating style and charm (though he couldn't help noticing the long queue for Laurie's books after his reading).

The Russian poet Yevgeny Yevtushenko, who saved my life... and his.

My new Russian friend liked to enjoy himself, and while I was ready to drive back to London after his reading, he was more interested in attending a party that was being given in a large manor house on the outskirts of Cheltenham, where he was the life and soul, enjoying the drink and the company of the good-looking young women who circled around him, and insisting on staying till the bitter end. It wasn't until about two in the morning that I managed to drag him away. I was quite exhausted, even if he was still firing on all cylinders. We discussed poetry for a while as I drove, and then, as we went through a tunnel, I must have dozed off, for I suddenly heard him screaming my name, which brought me round with a start just as we were swerving towards the tunnel wall. I managed to straighten up in the nick of time – but for him, it would have been a catastrophe, and certainly not the kind of publicity we needed for his book. Yevtushenko had saved both our lives. He later signed my copy of his book 'Yevgeny Yevtushenko, your protective angel'.

Cheltenham is a fabulous festival and I was to return there several times with authors, notably with the French actress Leslie Caron. The gamine star of such classics as *An American In Paris, Gigi, Daddy Long Legs* and *Lili*, Leslie was sophistication itself. A former prima ballerina with Roland Petit's ballet company in Paris, she was at one time married to Peter Hall, had a love affair with Warren Beatty, and can claim to be the only woman to have danced with Nureyev, Baryshnikov, Gene Kelly and Fred Astaire. She had also won a BAFTA for her starring role in *The L-Shaped Room*. Not surprisingly, she packed them in at Cheltenham, as she had the week before at the very classy Blenheim Festival, beneath the chandeliers of the palace's enormous dining room, and again at the National Film Theatre. Though Leslie's English is perfect, she remains a true Frenchwoman, as became clear to me when I visited her in Paris to sift through the hundreds of photos she had laid out on the floor of her apartment. I'd only been there a few minutes when she declared, 'I'm hungry. I can't work unless we eat,' and so we left the photos and wandered over to the bistro opposite her flat to recharge her batteries with *steak frites*… and then we went back to work.

* * *

One of my strangest book fair encounters was in 2001. I had noticed a smartly dressed man who looked as though he came from the Middle East standing opposite our stand, observing me closely. When he saw I was free, he came up and introduced himself as a representative of Mrs Mubarak, wife of the then President of Egypt, explaining that she was writing her life story and that we had been recommended as a possible publisher. He had with him a letter of authority on official government notepaper. In response to his courteous questioning, I told him about our small company, and even that my wife had been born in Egypt, not really believing this was for real. I gave him some catalogues and several books he wanted to look at, we shook hands warmly and he went on his way. Shortly after, he returned to ask if I would be prepared to fly to Cairo to meet Mrs Mubarak. I told him that in principle I'd be pleased to, indicating that I would want to bring my wife, and wondering what on earth Carole would make of it. After all, she hadn't been back to Egypt since leaving as a young girl in 1956. Quite why, given that we were Jewish and had published books on Israel, he had come to us, I couldn't imagine, and thought no more about it. There were, after all, a great many larger publishers at the fair much better equipped than us to handle a book with the international potential this seemed to have.

However, a month or so later I received an email from this same man which, among other things, said:

> I briefed Mrs Mubarak about all the meetings I had at the fair and made it clear that you at Robson Books are highly recommended as the publisher for such a prestigious book. The reason I believe so, is your strong personal feeling about it, and also being familiar with the Egyptian culture is very important...

He explained that Mrs Mubarak was currently travelling in the US but that 'as soon as I hear a positive response we will arrange a meeting... I hope our next meeting will be in Cairo.' Several dates were indeed tentatively proposed in the ensuing months, but they clashed with previous commitments, and the dates I counter-proposed didn't seem to work, so it all fizzled out, and if I hadn't come across his email while writing this chapter, I would have thought I'd dreamt it all. Was that book ever published? I don't think so, though Mrs Mubarak would have quite a story to tell now, if she were able to, and given that she is a highly educated woman who has been widely honoured for her work for deprived children and women's rights, it would be interesting to be approached again. But that, I'm sure, *is* a dream.

What wasn't a dream, though in retrospect it seems like one, was the appearance at the 2003 Frankfurt Book Fair of Muhammad Ali. He'd been brought by the German publisher Taschen to promote a book oddly called *GOAT (Greatest of All Time)*. I say a book, but it was actually an 800-page colossus containing 600,000 words of text and over 3,000 images, reproduced on the finest art paper, measuring fifty by fifty centimetres and weighing in at seventy pounds. There were two special editions, one of 1,000 copies each signed and priced at $75,000, and one of 9,000 copies priced at $3,000 each. The publisher had brought not only Muhammad to Frankfurt, but also his wife Lonnie, his legendary trainer, Angelo Dundee, Howard Bingham and several other boxing luminaries. There were huge posters for the book all over the fair, but I hadn't quite taken in that Ali himself would be there until the journalist Roger Tagholm, who was covering the fair for *Publishing News*, asked me if I was going to the press conference. I hadn't realised there was one, so Roger gave me the details and said he'd pick me up and somehow smuggle me in.

Taschen had spent a fortune flying everyone in from America, and had also built a full-size boxing ring in Hall 4, in which Ali appeared, doing his famous shuffle for the huge cheering crowd that had gathered around. That was before the press conference to which Roger now led me, somehow sweet-talking the officials on the door into letting me in. Ali, Angelo Dundee and the others were seated behind a long table facing a packed room, cameras everywhere. Almost immediately I ran into Howard Bingham, who embraced me and told me they were all staying at the hotel by the fair entrance, and that I should join them there afterwards. They were booked in under a different name, which he gave me, and with this magic password I was later directed to their suite.

Diffidently, I knocked on the door, and Lonnie Ali opened it, greeting me like a long-lost friend before introducing me to the others in the room, including Mr Taschen. I didn't tell him that I'd had some correspondence with his company after they'd made the mistake of quoting extensively from Thomas Hauser's book and going to press without obtaining our permission. That didn't put them in a strong position, and as well as extracting a decent fee for Tom, I managed to get them to agree to send me a copy of the book. I didn't know what I was getting until I saw it at the fair, and when it eventually arrived in a wooden case the weight was such that I had to get help carrying it in! It was one of my better deals.

Understandably exhausted by the flight and his appearances that afternoon, Ali was asleep when I arrived. I sat and talked to the others in the sitting room until Lonnie eventually got up and said, 'Go into the bedroom, he'll be glad to see you,' which I hesitantly did, not wanting to disturb him and not knowing quite what to say. Lonnie and Howard followed me in and, as I approached the bed in the dimly lit room, Ali looked up, smiled and pointed to his cheek. 'He wants you to kiss him,' said Lonnie, and kiss him I did.

That night I phoned Carole in London and told her I'd just kissed the man she thought had the most beautiful profile of any man she'd ever met. 'Don't tell me Muhammad Ali is in Frankfurt,' she said. He certainly was, and I was glad to share the story with Roger Tagholm, who'd made it all happen. Yes, Frankfurt brings strange and unexpected encounters, but none, for me, was as memorable as those touching few minutes in that hotel room with The Greatest of All Time.

23

TED HUGHES:
A FAMILY AFFAIR

In the years since we were in Israel together, Ted Hughes had of course written and published many fine poems and books, and been appointed Poet Laureate, but although we communicated from time to time and met up at the occasional reading, I had seen very little of him. Whenever his daughter Frieda had an exhibition of her paintings in London, he would send us a note urging us to come to the opening. We'd had several invitations to visit Ted and Carol at Court Green, and while we always tried to go to Frieda's exhibitions, for some reason we never managed to get to Devon. At one stage, his visits to London had been limited by the cost of coming by train from Exeter, which he bemoaned in an amusing letter to me: 'As for other expenses, I never get away from London these days for under £100. If I stay two nights, I daren't count.' And that was in 1988! In the same letter, he writes of a conversation he'd recently had with a poet who had just returned from a group reading tour of Israel and was describing her experiences. When Ted mentioned that he had been on a similar trip, 'Oh yes,' she said (obviously groping to remember something very faint), 'somebody did say something about some English poets once having read somewhere.' 'So much for rocks impregnable and gates of steel,' Ted concluded wryly.

The fact that my own poetry had dried up had led me to shy away from poetry circles, though my friendship with Dannie Abse was as strong as ever, and I continued to publish Vernon Scannell, who would

stay with us from time to time. The publishing involvement and commitments, and the resulting demands on our time and finances, had
become all-consuming, and when, sometime in 1997, I was taking a
lunchtime stroll along Clipstone Street, where our office was situated,
I was deep in thought and didn't notice the man who walked past me
in the opposite direction until we were some twenty yards apart. Something made me look back at the tall, powerful, sports-jacketed figure
I'd just passed, and I thought, 'Surely that's Ted Hughes.' I turned and
walked back after him, not wanting to call his name until I was quite
sure, but he went into the restaurant beneath our office and joined some
people at a table near the back. It *was* Ted, I could see that now, but I felt
it would be an intrusion to follow him in and I left it, thinking I'd write
to him. Ted had always been warm and welcoming, and if I'd had the
presence of mind to send through a note, he might well have had time
to come up to the office for a chat. He had, after all, suggested in several
letters that we meet up for a meal. But life is full of missed chances.

Not long after, in January 1998, Ted's bombshell book *Birthday
Letters* was published. Written over a period of twenty-five years and
directed almost entirely to Sylvia Plath, these personal and urgent
poems are Ted's account of their turbulent relationship. In October of
that same year came the shocking news of his death. In due course, it
was announced that there was to be a service of thanksgiving for his
life at Westminster Abbey on 13 May 1998, and Carol Hughes kindly
sent me a note asking whether we would like to attend and telling
me how to obtain tickets. She also asked me to pass the details on to
Dannie and Joan Abse. Come the day, I arranged to meet Carole and
the Abses outside the abbey, but there was a huge crowd and, unable to
see them anywhere and realising the service would be starting shortly, I
wandered in alone, somehow bypassing the ushers who were showing
people to their places. Since I still couldn't spot the others, I parked
myself unthinkingly on an empty seat near the front.

Directly opposite me, in the wide area between the high altar and
the quire, there was a grand piano, and looking at the order of service I
saw that Alfred Brendel would be playing the Adagio from Beethoven's
Sonata No. 17, Op. 31, No. 2. I hadn't expected that, nor had I expected

to see the people who slowly made their way to the seats in front of me
and whom I recognised with a start as members of the royal family –
the Queen Mother, Prince Charles, Princess Margaret, Princess Anne,
followed by representatives of the Queen and Prince Philip, and other
dignitaries. Of course! Ted had been the Poet Laureate and commanded royal respect, and in his case considerable affection. And of course I
wasn't sitting where I was supposed to be, though fortunately I hadn't
sat one row further forward! Nearby, too, were the close members of
Ted's family – Carol, his sister Olwyn, daughter Frieda, son Nicholas
and brother Gerald.

That day the abbey was filled with fine poetry, mostly Ted's, and
wonderful music. It was an awe-inspiring occasion. The Nobel Laureate Seamus Heaney delivered a powerful and moving eulogy in which
he called Ted 'a guardian spirit of the land and language'. And then,
as the concluding reading before the Tallis Scholars sang Thomas Tallis's 'Spem In Alium', a recording was played of Ted himself reading
Shakespeare's song from *Cymbeline*:

> Fear no more the heat o' the sun,
> Nor the furious winter's rages;
> Thou thy worldly task hast done,
> Home art gone, and ta'en thy wages.
> Golden lads and girls all must,
> As chimney-sweepers, come to dust.

That powerful, unmistakable, mesmerising voice filled the abbey, sending a shiver down everyone's spine. It was an imaginative and noble
way to end the readings. How wonderful, I reflected, that a poet could
command such reverence and attention. But then it was not any poet.
It was Ted Hughes.

* * *

It's no secret that Ted had lived a dramatic life, full of turmoil and
tragedy, though by the time we met up again in Israel in 1971 he had

married Carol, who brought stability and order into his life. Nor is it surprising that interest in his life, and in Sylvia Plath's, continued, amidst controversy, suppositions, inaccuracies and invective. So when, at the Frankfurt Book Fair in 2005, I noticed the single line 'Biography of Assia Wevill' on the list of forthcoming titles of the American agent Scott Mendel, I approached with a cautious enquiry. 'But how do you know who she is?' asked Scott, since there was no descriptive blurb, and I could truthfully answer, 'Because I met her once at a reading in Devon with Ted Hughes.' It had been only a brief encounter, but it had stayed in my mind.

The book, *A Lover of Unreason*, was by two Israeli writers, Eilat Negev and Yehuda Koren, and a month or two later Scott sent me their meticulously researched and powerful text. The authors had been working on the book for several years, and since Assia's story really started in Mandate Palestine, they were well placed to undertake her biography. Assia's parents – her father a Jewish physician, her mother a Lutheran – had come to Palestine from Germany in 1934 to escape the Nazis. There, she went to school; later, she met a British soldier and came to England, where she married him. They emigrated to Canada but the marriage didn't last long, and Assia, who had enrolled at the University of Columbia in Vancouver, met there a Canadian economist, Roger Lipsey, who became her second husband. Returning to England in 1956, she met on the boat a 21-year-old Canadian poet, David Wevill, with whom she started an affair, marrying him in 1960.

She was with Wevill when, responding to an advertisement, they went to see a flat in Primrose Hill, discovering it was being sublet by Hughes and Plath, who had decided to move to Devon. The Wevills took the flat and met up and ate with Ted and Sylvia several times. 'We got on like a house on fire,' recalled David. It was shortly after the Wevills went to stay with Ted and Sylvia at their home in Devon that Assia, who was then working in an advertising agency and writing poems herself, began an affair with Ted. The subsequent tragedies – Sylvia Plath's suicide, followed a few years later by Assia's (hers made even more horrific by the fact that she also killed Shura, the daughter she'd had with Ted) – are heartbreaking.

In addition to their own exhaustive research, the authors had the full cooperation of Assia's sister, and were thus privy to many letters from both Assia and Ted as well as other personal documents and photos. This gave their book authority and depth. I passed the manuscript to Dannie Abse to read, and he felt, as I did, that it was a powerful story containing much new material, not only about Assia herself, but about Ted and Sylvia too, and that we should publish it. The fact that there were others in the story – poets, critics – we both knew who had contributed their own memories and opinions naturally augmented our interest.

We announced the title at the London Book Fair in 2006, where it aroused huge media attention, which in turn started a bidding war among the main national papers for the serial rights. Finally, Corinna Honan at the *Daily Telegraph* went out on a limb and outbid her rivals. As well as publishing extracts, the *Telegraph* also ran a front-page news story, which was picked up by other papers. The book sold extremely well in both hardback and paperback editions, and incidentally provided a rich source for subsequent biographers of both Hughes and Plath to draw on. Another pleasing outcome was my continuing friendship with the lively authors and a successful collaboration on other highly original books, including *The First Lady of Fleet Street*, the story of Rachel Beer, who was the first woman to edit a national paper in Britain – in fact, two at the same time: *The Observer* and the *Sunday Times*.

* * *

Although we'd been to several of her exhibitions and greatly admired her strong and striking canvases, I'd never had a proper conversation with Frieda Hughes. A considerable poet as well as a painter, she had been writing a weekly column on poetry for *The Times* for some while, choosing a poem and discussing it and the author's work in a highly perceptive and readable way. We had often thought it could make an excellent book, and when I mentioned this to a mutual friend, Annie Quigley, who runs Bibliophile Books, and whom we always met at Frieda's exhibitions, she urged me to contact Frieda. However, by the time I did, Sandra Parsons, who had initiated the column, had moved from *The Times* to the *Daily Mail*, and with her departure the paper dropped it. Without its continuing presence and the paper's support, it was no longer a feasible publishing proposition, bearing in mind also that permissions for all the poems would have to be sought and paid for.

Nevertheless, Frieda and I arranged to have lunch, and it was a long and convivial one during which I gave her some photos of her father she'd never seen and a programme from the Israel tour. Warm and vivacious, Frieda didn't seem at all concerned that I'd published the book on Assia, which was a relief, and the conversation ranged easily in many directions. A few days later, I received a signed copy of her own latest book of poems in the post, followed by an email in which she asked whether I'd be interested in publishing a memoir by her uncle Gerald, Ted's elder brother. This, as I understood it, would focus mainly on his and Ted's childhood in Mytholmroyd, where Ted was born on 17 August 1930. I was indeed interested – what publisher committed to poetry would not be? – and we readily agreed to take the book on.

Ten years older than Ted, and well versed in country ways, Gerald had a great influence on his little brother during his formative years. However, while the book was charming and contained valuable material, it was very short, and much of it covered later parts of Gerald's own life, particularly his time in the RAF, and his life in Australia, where he settled and married. Yet it was easy to see where it could be expanded, and Frieda arranged for me to phone her uncle in Australia and ask him questions in an attempt to flesh out the stories. Gerald was reserved and wary at first, especially when I touched on Sylvia Plath and Assia Wevill (he'd met Assia but not Sylvia, though she wrote him touching letters from Court Green about Ted and the children). That first phone call lasted two hours, and at the end of it, despite Gerald's initial and understandable reticence, I had pages of notes, which I carefully worked into the manuscript. Then, via his son Ashley, who lived near him, I emailed questions and incorporated Gerald's answers, sending him the revised text as I went along. All this had set him thinking, and he started to contribute further details that amplified the stories of their childhood adventures together – the magical years when they fished for pike in the pond Ted made famous, hunted rabbits, pigeons and stoats, flew kites, made model aeroplanes and boats, camped, and swam in the local stream. All these activities, inspired by Gerald's passion for the countryside, had awakened Ted's own love of and feeling for nature. So many of his poems were to have their roots in those early experiences. Gerald's reminiscences were golden, and the book began to grow as he gave fuller descriptions of other members of the family – their mother and father, various aunts and their sister Olwyn, who was two years older than Ted and who also played an important part in his life.

Ted Hughes and his elder brother Gerald at Hardcastle Cragg in 1946 – the cover photo of Ted and I, *Gerald's evocative memoir of their childhood together.*

Ted was at school when Gerald joined the Royal Air Force as an engineer, and was to follow in his brother's footsteps when he did his National Service. When, after working for a while as a gamekeeper, Gerald went to live in Australia, Ted planned to join him there after he'd finished university – but that went by the board when Sylvia Plath came into his life. However, the brothers kept in close touch: Gerald and his new wife Edith visited Ted at Cambridge, touring and spending time with him, and they wrote to each other regularly. Eventually, Gerald sent me copies of letters from Ted he thought relevant and some of these were included in the book. Then Frieda suggested I contact her aunt Olwyn, a formidable and notoriously difficult lady who lived in Kentish Town, not far from us. I knew that she was a highly educated woman who'd studied English literature at Queen Mary College before going to work at the British Embassy in Paris, and then for a publisher as a secretary and translator. Later, she'd become a literary agent and managed Sylvia's literary estate as well as Ted's work.

We spoke on the phone and Olwyn suggested I visit her. Gathering my courage, I took the bus to the corner of her street as directed, and a few minutes later knocked on the front door of her narrow house. Eventually, she answered, looking rather like Maggie Smith's Dowager Countess of Grantham from *Downton Abbey*, but with a fag dangling from her mouth. Eyeing me carefully, she paused, as if thinking she'd made a big mistake, finally ushering me into the tiny kitchen where, amidst piles of books, papers and cigarette ends, I somehow found a place to sit. She made no bones about it: the text she'd seen was inadequate, her brother had missed out or failed to describe properly many vital things. Grumbling and cursing, she finally agreed to help, and in the next few weeks started bombarding me with handwritten letters and pages of notes and long passages in which she elaborated on the text, adding invaluable detail. In fairness to her, she knew her younger brother as well as Gerald did, and was still at home after Gerald had flown the nest, so her memories of that slightly later period brought a further perspective to the book. She patently had no love of either Sylvia or Assia, and I came away from our further meetings with the distinct impression that any woman who came between her and her beloved brother was going to have a rough ride. Since I was not there to become involved in Hughes family politics, I tried my best to keep her focused on the matter in hand, although she continued to press me to include a story about how Sylvia had discovered his affair with Assia, which seemed both far-fetched and way off-message. However, rereading the material she sent me, I realise that even in her old age, amidst the cigarette smoke, she still had a formidable mind and a lively literary style. She later described our cooperation as 'heroic', and perhaps – at any rate from my point of view – it was. At least I had survived!

There was even more to come when I received a letter from Carol Hughes telling me she'd heard about the book and would like to read it. I sent her an early version, for which she thanked me while asking if she could see it again when it was finally edited. Once I'd added all the new material, I sent it to her, hoping it would pass muster. She rang me at home the next morning saying, 'I can see what you've been doing, and I think I can help you.' She said she'd be in London the following week and suggested coming to our office to go through it all. She brought with her a number of photos of Ted and Gerald together which she generously said we could use, and indicated the areas of the text which she could expand. She was wonderfully helpful, annotating the manuscript in precise detail, adding stories about the time Gerald and his wife visited Ted and her in Devon, describing the fishing expedition Ted had arranged for them all in Scotland, and much else. Everything she wrote was vivid and invaluable. She even suggested including several of Ted's poems where they related to the text, which was marvellous. Throughout our meetings I noticed how careful she was not to be thought intrusive, concerned above all that everyone was happy with the final result – especially Gerald, to whom she spoke regularly.

Frieda was equally generous, describing the time she had spent with Gerald in Australia, giving us permission to use some of her mother's evocative letters to Gerald, and writing a sensitive and touching fore-word – and of course it was she who had thought to bring the book to me, which was my good fortune. All three women (even Olwyn, however grudgingly) were aware of Ted's love for his brother, and for both their sakes they wanted Gerald's book to be as good as they could make it. As Frieda put it, 'My Uncle Gerald has always been an impor-tant figure in my life because he was a hugely important figure in the life of my father.' Gerald was thrilled when he finally received a copy. It's a charming and gentle book, and anyone studying Ted's poems should find it illuminating – moving, too, especially Gerald's account of his last telephone conversation with his brother from Australia, when Ted was dying.

Ted and I: A Brother's Memoir, published in October 2012, received wide attention, perhaps even more than the Assia biography, though of a less sensational nature. The *Sunday Times* published a long extract; *The Times* made it a major news story spread over nearly a page, headed: 'Big brother tells evocative story of life with boy who would be Poet Laureate'; and when *The Observer*, in a full-page review, said 'Life in Hebden Bridge blooms from the pages', and referred to 'a sepia-tinted world of tram rides and Sunday hats', I felt we'd got it right. The book appeared in America, published by Thomas Dunne, but perhaps even more exciting for Gerald was the approach we had from an independent filmmaker, David Cohen, who loved the book and felt it would form the basis of a valuable film. David flew to Australia with a cameraman and filmed long interviews with Gerald, and then, on returning to England, spent days filming the areas where the brothers had roamed. He interviewed Frieda and others (but not the prickly Olwyn, who refused to cooperate), and with Carol's considerable help produced a fascinating text, which was voiced by Juliet Stevenson. The film included recordings of Ted reading the poems quoted in the book, the words descending on a blank background, following his voice, as Carol said he would have wished. The film had a special showing at the Blenheim Literary Festival in October 2016, to a large and visibly moved audience, and again at the Oxford Literary Festival a year later. Gerald, who sadly had died earlier in 2016, would have been very proud, and I believe Ted would have been, too.

It had been a family affair.

24

PUBLISHING MATTERS

Looking at the list of the many authors we published over the years, it might seem to have been an easy ride, but it wasn't. Running a small set-up with modest financial resources was always going to be challenging, and many were the nights I lay awake, figures racing around my tired mind as I wondered how we'd meet our end-of-month commitments, let alone how I would handle my next lunch with our bank manager – at my expense, of course, and tax-wise considered a perk! So often it proved to be the low-profile books for which we'd advanced almost nothing that unexpectedly took off and saved the day, covering the salaries, rent, printing bills and royalties, and putting a relieved smile on the face of our valiant accountant, David Pickin, as he struggled to prepare an acceptable cash-flow forecast. I suspect many small publishers will have had the same experience.

Fortunately, we enjoyed relationships with all the major mass-market paperback companies and were often able to 'lay off' the money we'd had to pay upfront to get certain big books by sub-licensing the paperback rights (something that doesn't really happen these days as hardback publishers issue their own paperbacks). We have also always tended to have the kind of books attractive to newspapers, and the income we've received from serial rights over the years has been sub-stantial – often a lifesaver.

One surprise was a small paperback called *Condomania* by Peter Maddocks, just a cheap cartoon book subtitled *101 Uses for a Condom*. This was in 1987 and the book reprinted six times in the first year, and

I have a copy of the sixteenth impression in front of me as I write. I don't know what it was about condoms that year, but the timing was obviously right. Gift shops were the key outlets for books of that kind in those days, and the wholesalers who supplied them reordered in large quantities. We even did a deal with Durex and ended up with boxes of contraceptives all over the office.

Condomania certainly underwrote some of the more prestigious titles on our list, as did *The Blue Day Book*, a small, square hardback of captivating animal photos with witty or poignant captions, its theme being that everyone has a blue day. It must have been the pictures the *Daily Mail* published that set it racing away, for race it certainly did, ending up as No. 1 on the *Times* and other bestseller lists. The book was so appealing that all our sales people had to do was show it and it ended up everywhere – on shelves, on counters, by tills. The man who'd conceived it and put it together was Australian, and he was so thrilled to be on the *Times* bestseller list that he brought a box of Havana cigars to me at Frankfurt. That was certainly a first.

A particular favourite of mine was André Bernard's *Rotten Rejections*, a collection of actual rejection letters and readers' reports publishers may well have regretted, a book that should surely be mandatory reading for all publishers. Thus to Flaubert on *Madame Bovary*, 'You have buried your novel underneath a heap of details which are utterly superfluous…' or to George Orwell about *Animal Farm*, 'It is impossible to sell animal stories…' or on *The Spy Who Came in From the Cold*, 'You are welcome to le Carré, he hasn't got any future…' or on Anne Frank's *Diary of a Young Girl*, 'The girl doesn't, it seems to me, have a special perception which would lift that book above the "curiosity" level…' or to Marcel Proust on *Swann's Way* (Volume 1 of *Remembrance of Things Past*), 'My dear fellow, I may be dead from the neck up, but rack my brains as I may, I can't see why a chap should need thirty pages to describe how he turns over in bed before going to sleep.' However, the last word must go to George Bernard Shaw:

I finished my first book thirty years ago. I offered it to every publisher on the English-speaking earth I had ever heard of. Their refusals were unanimous and it did not get into print until, fifty years later, publishers would publish anything that had my name on it ... I object to publishers: the one service they have done me is to teach me to do without them. They combine commercial rascality with artistic touchiness and pettishness, without either being good business men or fine judges of literature. All that is necessary in the production of a book is an author and a bookseller, without the intermediate parasite.

Despite the constant cash-flow strain, there were moments of hilarity in the office. On one occasion, a very attractive Italian girl with a degree in philosophy came to be interviewed for a job as our receptionist (those were the days!). She had vanished to the loo when I came out to meet her, returning a minute or two later and explaining that she'd gone there to take off her sneakers. Unfortunately her pronunciation wasn't perfect and instead of 'sneakers' she said loudly that she'd taken off her 'snickers', which sounded very much like something else. After the interview, everyone rushed in to ask how it had gone!

The arrival of Derek Nimmo to sign copies of *Oh, Come on All Ye Faithful!*, his book of church humour, was also entertaining. It wasn't just the Rolls-Royce he drew up in, which seemed to float rather than roll on its wheels, but also his wizened old chauffeur, who was as much a character as his employer. Always dressed to the nines in spats, white bow tie and velvet jacket with gold buttons bearing a coat of arms, he looked like something from a previous century, and he was in a way, being of noble stock and now finding himself in a very different kind of driving seat. It was *his* coat of arms, not Derek's. I always felt he was the one we should have signed up, but we did use him to great effect on the cover of Derek's humorous book about class, *Not in Front of the Servants*. The two of them would have made Jacob Rees-Mogg look like a hippie. An ardent member of the Garrick Club, Derek chided me gently for the fact that, as a newish and somewhat reticent member, I only went there occasionally for lunch or dinner. 'I do object to people who just use the club as a cafeteria,' he said. He would not have approved my giving up my membership, as I did later.

It was at another club, the Savile, that I had a narrow escape, having been taken for what turned out to be a very liquid lunch by comedian Jimmy Edwards, former air force pilot, schoolmaster and star of the very popular TV series *Whack-O*, whose book *Six of the Best* we'd just published. I'd survived the meal, but later found myself alone with him at the club's snooker table, feeling that I was being stalked, his trademark handlebar moustache coming ever closer as we potted away. Although his book was mainly about his war experiences, in the TV series (written by Frank Muir and Denis Norden) he played the part of a drunken, gambling, cane-swishing headmaster. Now, as he downed yet more wine, he seemed to be transforming into the character he'd made famous, and when he raised his snooker cue I sensed he might bring it into play any moment – but not on the table. I thanked him for a memorable lunch as warmly as I could and beat a hasty retreat down Brook Street and back to the safety of my office.

Jimmy Edwards, with whom I had a dangerous game of snooker at his club.

* * *

Given the high-profile nature of many of our books, we inevitably ran into legal problems from time to time. I've already mentioned the bother over Harry Secombe's *Welsh Fargo*, but far more worrying was a complaint from Mothercare, the childrenswear retailer, over a book we'd bought from St Martin's Press called *Mother Care*. They accused us of 'passing off', and the case went to the High Court, our counsel arguing that the fact that the words were separate made all the difference, and that you couldn't, in any case, simply remove words from the English language and appropriate them. As Anthony Harkavy articulated it in correspondence with Mothercare's solicitors, 'It hardly lies in the mouth of your clients to complain about our client's use of the words "mother" and "care" in juxtaposition, when our client's publication is concerned about the care of mothers and your client's business is concerned with the care of children and not of mothers' – a proposition which Robert Alexander QC, acting for the plaintiffs, by some magical forensic sleight of hand, managed to entice the judge into rejecting.

Alexander had been retained only the night before, as the previously retained counsel had had to withdraw at the last moment, and he'd evidently been up all night reading the papers. It was our bad luck since, as a result of his brilliant advocacy, Mothercare succeeded in obtaining an interim injunction to restrain publication, and our insurers declined to cover us for the costs that would be incurred in an appeal. Without that cover, we couldn't go on. Some years later, Anthony, who'd been convinced from the moment we consulted him that our case was strong, phoned and told me to look at that day's *Times* law report. Penguin had published a book with the same title as ours, been sued by Mothercare, had presented the same arguments in defence as we had, and won the day! That hurt.

In retrospect, I realise I should have left well alone, and been satisfied with our much better (and safer) book *Blooming Pregnant*, by Kay Burley and Cathy Hopkins. But hindsight is a wonderful thing!

Next in the ring was Barry McGuigan, 'The Clones Cyclone', whose charisma extended far beyond the boxing ring, his career having been brilliantly managed by the millionaire Irish boxing promoter Barney Eastwood. They were an unstoppable combination as McGuigan fought his way to the world title, and those emotional nights in Belfast when Barry's father Pat entered the ring and sang 'Danny Boy' before the action started thrilled fans on both sides of the troubled border. I, for one, never missed a bout. And then, in a nightmare fight in Las Vegas, boxing in extreme heat, Barry lost his world title, and everything fell apart. He had a compelling story to tell, and when we were approached by an Irish agent representing him and two highly respected writers who were working with him – Harry Mullan, editor of *Boxing News*, and Gerry Callan, Ireland's Sports Writer of the Year – I couldn't resist. I wish I had.

The book was explosive in its claims of what went on both inside and outside the ring, and we had several meetings with the agent and the authors (and Barry) in Anthony Harkavy's office, where Anthony challenged and cross-examined them on what he rightly saw were the legal flashpoints. What none of them revealed (and we would have pulled out of the book if they had) was that McGuigan was being sued in the Irish courts by Barney Eastwood over accusations he'd made against him on air. The first I knew about it was when I turned on the TV news one night to hear that Eastwood had won a libel action against the boxer and been awarded substantial damages. It was alarming, since the authors seemed to have covered much the same ground in the book, and it wasn't long before we received a complaint, by fax, from Eastwood's lawyers. I was leaving at that very moment on holiday, and I quickly passed what seemed to me a very alarming and trenchantly worded complaint to Anthony to consider, knowing just how trenchant he too could be. I phoned him from Italy and was worried when he told us our insurers wouldn't let him act and were instructing their own lawyers, Rubinstein, Callingham, Polden and Gale.

On my return, I had a meeting with John Rubinstein, and counsel was instructed, but once we learned that McGuigan had lost the appeal he'd launched against the previous judgment, we were advised that the cost of contesting the case in Ireland would be substantial and the chances of success slim. We settled on the best terms we could and withdrew the book. One thing I learned from that very damaging outing was never to get in the middle of someone else's fight, because you're the one who is likely to end up getting hit.

Then there was Leo Abse, elder brother of Dannie, Labour MP for

Pontypool from 1958 to 1983 and then MP for Torfaen, a distinguished lawyer and a man who had put on the statute books more legislation than any other backbencher of his time, radically reforming many laws that impinged on human relationships – including those relating to children, divorce, family planning and homosexuality. The firebrand Leo couldn't have been more different from his poet brother. A flamboyant dresser whose outfit on Budget Day was always striking, he was a man who could mesmerise you with the power and passion of his oratory and his intellectual agility. Dannie always maintained that Leo hadn't become Home Secretary because he was a constant thorn in the side of the Prime Minister, and that may well have been so. On the other hand, Leo was a rebel and I suspect he never particularly wanted high office, happier to be free to snipe and canvass from the back benches.

The dynamic Leo Abse loved to be controversial and would stand his ground like the brilliant lawyer and crusading MP that he was.

Nothing could muzzle or silence Leo, and where his books were concerned he never held back in his psychoanalytical examination of his subjects. Margaret Thatcher was his first victim, in a book called *Margaret, Daughter of Beatrice*. Tony Blair, yet to become Prime Minister, was his second, in a scorching book we published called *The Man Behind the Smile*. Coming from the pen of a long-serving Labour MP, it caused a sensation, Leo having used all his contacts and his publicity savvy to make sure it did. I watched in wonder. As with all his books, he exaggerated, but at the same time he hit many nails right on the head in his no-holds-barred polemic, and how prescient his book proved to be:

> As an actor or performer [Blair] doubtless brought pleasure; his small step from stage to political platform in search of identity may have assisted him in his personal resolution, but it left my Labour Party shorn; he has taken away the identity of Labour and reshaped it to suit his own psychological measurements. This operation is described by his supporters as 'reform': I call it theft.

Reviewing the book in *The Times*, Matthew Parris called it 'fine raillery … touched by genius' and that sums it up perfectly.

Whenever Leo had a book out, Dannie would jokingly say that he was leaving the country – easy to see why. He would also joke that his dandy brother wore his cast-offs. Dannie, as anyone who knew him will attest, seemed to wear the same sports jacket for years, just as he always appeared to be driving the same small car. It wasn't actually so, it was just that he always bought the same model – of both jacket and car. Leo, by contrast, at one time owned a white Rolls-Royce, and was evidently offended when Dannie used the phrase 'as ostentatious as a white Rolls-Royce' in something he wrote. What an extraordinary family the Abses were!

Another of Leo's books for us was about the Germans, *Wotan, My Enemy*, which opens with the arresting short sentence, 'Despite the Germans, I was born.' Another uncompromising polemic, it won awards, was serialised and widely discussed, and was often over the top. Whenever there was something I thought legally questionable in Leo's books and drew it to his attention, he would laugh at my caution and say reassuringly, 'Leave the law to me.' In the case of *Wotan*, I wish I hadn't. We had recently acquired our house in Normandy and were enjoying an after-dinner Calvados or two with Jan and Anthony Harkavy when Leo phoned to say we'd received a complaint from the law firm Carter-Ruck on behalf of one of their clients, an historian, who'd seen an early review copy of the book and maintained that Leo had misrepresented his attitude towards the Germans in a way that damaged his reputation. (This was shortly to be followed by a similar complaint from a second historian, instructing the same lawyers.) Since our own lawyer was by my side and still sober enough to converse, I put him on the phone, and after Leo had read their complaining letter to him they discussed tactics.

Carter-Ruck's letter was aggressive and challenging, but Leo (who volunteered to respond in our absence) rose to the challenge and retaliated with a series of equally forceful letters – a master class, Anthony Harkavy thought, in legal know-how and expression. In fact, Leo fired two salvoes, one firmly rebutting the allegations, and with it a second 'without prejudice letter' opening the way to a quick compromise and settlement, time being of the essence as we were on the point of publishing. In the end, Anthony and Leo felt it was expedient to moderate the offending paragraphs. However, when a reviewer in the *Telegraph* went too far in remarks about Leo, Anthony moved into action on his behalf and Leo received both an apology and a sum in settlement. This offset the costs we'd incurred in revising the book, and we all celebrated over a lively dinner at Leo's club, the Savile.

Anthony Harkavy takes times off from advising us legally (and from his piano)
to play clarinet with singer Stella Starr at our 25th wedding anniversary party,
held at the historic Samuel Pepys pub in the City.

The launches of Leo's books were always memorable: one at Politico's bookstore near Westminster (then owned and run by Iain Dale) where Tam Dalyell spoke; another at the Freud Museum where Michael Foot, introducing the book, treated us to a demonstration of his own remarkable oratory. But the press conferences Leo would call were the main event, where his eloquence was riveting. The more he was attacked, the more he relished it, his lawyer's mind fashioning a powerful response as he rose to his feet. He could be a difficult man, but he was also a warm and entertaining one, and doubtless only came my way, relatively late in his life, because, as he always told everyone, I was a friend of his brother Dannie. I wouldn't have missed the experience for the world.

*Our daughters Deborah and Manuela take time off from their studies
to give a joint speech at our 25th wedding anniversary party.*

*   *   *

We'd bought our bolt-hole in France when the pound was high against the franc (no euros then!). Our twin daughters were studying French as their main language at university (strangely for two such independent-minded girls, they had both opted for Birmingham, attracted by the strength of its language departments and its large, airy campus). Both had friends in Paris, where Carole also had relations, and so we had the feeling they'd settle in France eventually. That had led us to look around in the Normandy area, not too far from Paris. Manuela had been studying German as a second language, her year abroad being divided between Lyons and Freiberg Universities. When her time at Lyons was up, we offered to drive her to Freiberg, and it was on that trip that we stayed for a couple of nights at the charming French port of Honfleur, looked in the windows of various estate agents, saw how relatively low the prices were, and were hooked.

Deborah, on the other hand, had taken Russian as her second language, and spent some months at Moscow University, sharing a flat with some Russian girls also studying there. We visited her for a week, but despite perestroika and Mikhail Gorbachev's valiant attempts at glasnost and reform, we felt it to be a depressing and threatening city. Perhaps I had been reading too much John le Carré, but we seemed to be under constant surveillance as we entered and left our sprawling hotel and wandered the city, visiting Lenin's mausoleum in the eerie Red Square and the usual tourist landmarks, while dodging the rattling old cars that raced down the wide roads, their spinning wheels clinging on for dear life. There were queues for food, and very little to be found on the market stalls, though if you had dollars you would find a warm enough welcome and a reasonable menu in restaurants that were generally tucked away down several flights of stairs. It was in a dusty market near one of these that we saw several paintings that looked like Cézannes lying on the ground, unframed, the edges of the canvas curled. Students' copies though they were, they were excellent and we happily paid the modest asking price, and also bought a balalaika that lay beside them.

In stark contrast were the palatial Underground stations, and the magnificent city of St Petersburg, to which we travelled with Deborah and a friend on a packed overnight train before exploring the palaces and museums of that magical city together. On our return to Moscow, and deeply conscious of the oppression and persecution Russian Jewry had suffered, we felt impelled to visit a synagogue, finding ourselves walking cautiously down a narrow street until we came to a small doorway. We knocked several times and eventually a nervous guard let us in, leaving us alone to stand hand in hand, in silence, in the small old sanctuary, as tears overwhelmed the three of us simultaneously:

> ... the echoes, the shadows, the Babi Yar memories,
> the wary eyes everywhere as we approached.
> So often the Prayer for the Dead to be said...

We weren't sorry to leave Moscow and as the plane rose from the runway we both felt a sense of relief, and I believe Deborah felt the same when she joined us a month or two later, though she had made good friends there. Ironically, neither she nor Manuela ended up living or working in Paris, but we always spend the summer together in Normandy.

Later the following year, their foreign adventures well and truly over, Carole and I found ourselves at their degree ceremony in Birmingham, sitting expectantly in a grand, crowded hall with other parents and graduates awaiting their proud moment, cameras at the ready, joining the polite applause. Twins arrive together, but they also depart together, and as we waited I couldn't help but think back to that Sunday morning four years earlier when, steeling ourselves, Carole and I had driven them to Birmingham, our car bulging with the usual clobber – and how, returning home that evening as darkness fell, we'd sat together on the sofa, listening to the resounding silence of an empty house, feeling bereft, thinking our daughters were gone for ever. But they weren't, far from it, and now, my mind back in the hall, we waited for their names to be called – but then when Deborah's name was read out we did a double-take, for up went Manuela to shake the Chancellor's hand and receive her sister's degree, and when Manuela's name was called, up went Deborah. Fortunately, nobody noticed except their anxious parents and their friends, who thought it was a hoot. After all the adventures we had shared over the years, and knowing they had occasionally swapped places at school to mischievously fool an unsuspecting new teacher, we shouldn't have been surprised; and they continue to surprise us as they pursue their separate lives and careers, remaining touchingly close to each other and to us. Double fun and double blessing in every respect.

*   *   *

Carole's Egyptian childhood, from which she was so traumatically torn, was something she often dreamt about, occasionally talking about it in her sleep in French.

> Waking, you said you saw your house,
> the Nile snaking into mist,
> Mohammed the one-eyed cook.
> Somehow, you said there were children,
> Running...

From time to time, we would contemplate visiting Egypt, but it was many years before Carole felt ready to face the emotional impact she feared a return would have. But eventually, when our daughters were in their final year of university, we made that pilgrimage together, though instead of flying directly to Cairo we decided to take a more gradual approach, flying first to Israel and then travelling from the southern port of Eilat to Egypt by coach, which one could do in those calmer days before the Arab Spring. Very early one morning, before the sun and heat rose, we set off, hardly believing the breathtaking journey across the Sinai Peninsula, past the Suez Canal, past the burnt-out tanks that remain a poignant reminder of the bitter battles that have been fought there over the years, finally reaching Cairo in the late afternoon. It was a journey full of wonder and expectancy. What *did* I expect?

> ... Crocodiles leaping from the Nile?
> The enigmatic Sphinx resolving its own riddles?
> Cleopatra plying her seductive trade in the market square?

No, there were more earthly wonders... Carole walking me along the Nile to her parents' flat, past her school – how well she remembered the way – and on to the famous Gezira Sporting Club, where her cricket-mad father hit a vaunted century, where she learned to swim... and, later, the Pyramids, where her English husband got the hump from a camel falling to its knees, making her laugh... Then the historic ice cream parlour, Groppi; the cinema where she saw *Gone with the Wind*; the mummies in the museums... Could this be real? If anyone was dreaming now, it was me.

All this is recalled in detail in a poem I wrote years later, but what isn't is the trip we made to Alexandria, where Carole's grandmother had lived. Carole had been born there and spent her early years in that flat before her parents moved to Cairo, and she would return to stay with her grandmother often, enjoying the sea and the beach. Those memories were especially poignant, and she was naturally eager to see the flat again if at all possible, so a few days after we'd arrived in Egypt, keyed up and a little nervous, we boarded the train for Alexandria at Cairo's run-down station. The 120-mile journey seemed to take an eternity, and since there was only one train a day it was packed, Arab music blazing from the loudspeakers above our heads all the way. Opposite, my eyes were drawn to a handsome young man in a long, white silk cloak, who looked like a character out of the Arabian Nights. Who was he, I wondered.

At last we emerged into the city that was for me Lawrence Durrell, and for Carole the scene of a treasured, almost mythical childhood. There was a queue of horse-drawn cabs, and we took one along the seafront towards the famous lighthouse, when Carole suddenly asked the driver to stop, for she had recognised the area and realised her grandmother's flat was down a nearby side street. She made straight for it, and I followed quietly as she approached the entrance. An old doorkeeper was half asleep on the floor near the lift, and as he rose Carole tried to explain what we wanted but he was understandably suspicious and, shaking a stick, ushered us away from the lift into the street. Suddenly, as if by magic, a middle-aged lady, alerted no doubt by the raised voices, appeared on the balcony of a first-floor flat and called down to the man in Arabic, asking who we were, what we wanted, and then repeating the same questions to us in French.

As Carole began to answer, the lady signalled us to come up, and we entered her small apartment. Carole began again to explain, mentioning her family name, whereupon the woman, overcome by emotion, exclaimed, 'Carole!' and flung her arms around her. 'I knew your lovely grandmother,' she said, 'She would come down every afternoon to play bridge with my mother, and you too would come racing down the steps to our flat… and I knew your mother and father and uncles, the whole family.' It was overwhelming. Carole was in tears; we all were. 'Come, let us try to visit that flat,' the lady decided, and up we went in the shaky lift – or was it we who were shaking?

She knocked several times on the apartment door, and after a few minutes a youngish Arab woman, dressed in a dark red robe, answered, naturally wary. Eventually reassured, she let us in, and Carole walked round and round in a daze, her eyes full of tears, remembering which room had once been hers, and which bedrooms had belonged to her grandmother, her parents, and her uncle Emile, who had also lived there; recognising the sitting room, recalling the furniture as it had been all those years before, the kitchen where she helped her grandmother bake. Looking out of the window at the back, she saw the wild garden where dozens of cats would seek sanctuary. Nothing seemed to have changed, yet everything had.

Thanking the Arab lady for her graciousness, we returned to the first-floor flat, where, over tea, more memories were exchanged before we took the slow train back to Cairo. We still talk of going back with our daughters, and indeed with our grandchildren, though given the eruptions in the Arab world we may never be able to do that. But one dream came true, and perhaps one day another will too, and there will be peace. *Inshallah.*

* * *

It was while he and his wife Val were staying with us in France that Jeffrey Pike and I began having a conversation about the business, and he set out to convince us (as if we needed convincing) that the way we were financing it was high-risk, and that we needed to find someone to share that risk. A forthright, highly successful businessman, Jeffrey promised to make it his mission to help us. It was not as though we hadn't had approaches and discussions in the past – we had, with several companies, most seriously with the Spear's games group. The latter had come about via Gyles Brandreth, who was involved with the company through his Scrabble prowess, that game being one of their main products. His idea was to row his own company in, too, as well as André Deutsch, which had been acquired by Tom Rosenthal and was struggling. In the end, nothing came of it.

Another unexpected – and dangerously flattering – approach came, improbable as it may sound, as I was driving Lady Falkender (formerly Marcia Williams) to watch the tennis at Wimbledon. I have mentioned earlier how Harry Secombe and I had bumped into Harold Wilson and Marcia, his political secretary, at the BBC. It so happened that Marcia was a friend of the photographer Gemma Levine and her then husband, and I'd met her again at one of their family occasions, not long after Harold Wilson had resigned suddenly and mysteriously, sending shock waves through the political world. That meeting had led to our signing up a top-secret book with Marcia, to be called *The Resignation*, on which her collaborator was journalist Peter Dacre (father of the current editor of the *Daily Mail*). It was to be a *roman-à-clef*, a thrilling 'factional' account of what had caused Wilson to resign, a story laced with blackmail, break-ins, espionage, sex and skulduggery in high places. Was the Prime Minister in the story Wilson? Did what she described really happen? That was the game she wanted to play and those were the questions she wanted readers to ask. There was, underneath it all, a layer of truth and authenticity, for if anyone knew the reasons for Wilson's resignation, it was Marcia.

Thus it was that, knowing my passion for tennis, she invited me to Wimbledon, where she was a guest of the *Mail*. But perhaps there were other reasons too, for when we were nearly there she turned to me and said, 'George [Weidenfeld] would like you on board and has asked me to speak to you. Would you be interested?' Gratifying though this was, since I admired Weidenfeld greatly, I shied away, realising that those waters were far too deep for me. He was a wonderful publisher and certainly did not need me, nor our company. We drove on without referring to the subject again, enjoyed the *Mail*'s hospitality tent, and watched the tennis. I remember I wore a badge I'd picked up somewhere which proclaimed 'In tennis, love means nothing'. Strangely enough, I had an approach from George Weidenfeld several years later through another source, but I didn't pursue that either.

Marcia Falkender was a highly controversial figure at that time, partly because of the influence she was deemed to have had over the Prime Minister, partly because of his resignation honours list, which she was rumoured to have drafted for him on lavender-coloured paper – the notorious 'lavender list' – something that sounds to me very much like a Max Clifford invention and which she has always vigorously denied. I liked and admired her. A remarkable woman with a rapier wit and pen, Marcia also has a strong sense of humour and fun which her rivals (and some of those who worked with her) gave her little credit for. However, she didn't suffer fools gladly, and that was clearly part of the problem. She might have been a successful barrister, or even a politician, but perhaps she was too honest for that.

I spent a number of evenings with Marcia and Peter Dacre trying to get the book right. Her method was to reel out scenes to him, which she could do without hesitation, and Peter would then transpose them and work them into the story, but she was never satisfied with the result and would rewrite furiously. They were, I felt, on different wavelengths, and the book was never finished. I have a draft manuscript a foot high in our garage, but Peter is gone and Marcia an invalid these days, so there, I imagine, it will remain, the blockbuster that never was, parked behind our car.

Still, we had fun. Marcia and her jovial sister Peggy liked to have small, merry parties in their flat, and Carole and I were often invited. Many of the guests were regulars, loyal friends from over the years, and Mary Wilson was usually among them. Marcia shared a birthday with Harold Wilson, and on one memorable occasion George Weidenfeld (who'd been ennobled by Wilson) gave a joint lunch party for them in his sumptuous Cheyne Walk residence to which Marcia had invited us. As we were led into the formally laid-out dining room, she indicated a tall, elegant lady and whispered to me, 'That's the woman,' and I recalled how in one scene in her book, set in Russia, her fictional Prime Minister had a dalliance with a certain female. Fact or fiction, I wondered?

I'd been to the Weidenfeld residence once before on a less formal occasion, when the American poet Robert Lowell was in London and George had held a party for him to which a number of poets had been invited. Lowell had collapsed on his host's bed at the end of the evening and Dannie Abse, reluctantly donning his doctor's coat, had checked him over, noticing as he did so that on the bedside table there was a photograph of Harold Wilson. I'm not sure what Dannie read into that but he mentioned it several times afterwards. Later, Dannie invited Lowell and his wife, Caroline Blackwood, to his home, where some of the guests seemed to sit at the feet of the famous white-haired poet as he pontificated like some self-appointed prophet about the poor state of British poetry. When, not one to be cowed, even by some-one who was a guest in his house, Dannie drew Lowell's attention to a particular poem by Ted Hughes that he admired, the American dismissed it quite sharply, clearly not used to being challenged.

The last time I saw Marcia was a few years ago when she invited me to lunch at the House of Lords. Having suffered a stroke, she was now in a motorised wheelchair, though her mind was still as agile as the wheelchair she drove. Arriving late, she raced along the corridors at an alarming speed towards the dining room while I tried to keep up and their lordships scattered in all directions before her charge.

* * *

Jeffrey Pike was persisting with his valiant mission to help bail us out and we had meetings with several publishers, one of whom was Colin Webb, whose Pavilion Books, originally backed by Michael Parkinson and Tim Rice, seemed a good match for us. Though I liked and ad-mired the go-ahead Colin, who'd been my successor at the Woburn Press, and despite the goodwill involved, in the end it just didn't stack up (Pavilion eventually being acquired by Chrysalis, and Colin leaving to start Palazzo, which specialises in high-quality illustrated books and where he is the publisher). During the fairly protracted negotiations with Pavilion, I recall that Colin and I used to phone each other covertly using the pseudonyms 'Eccles' and 'Neddie', both of us being *Goon Show* fans. Nothing that light-hearted occurred in our subsequent discussions with Batsford, a venerable firm that had recently been acquired by an American, Gerry Mizrahi, who courted us ardently, eventually coming up with an offer Anthony Harkavy wouldn't allow me to consider, having had previous dealings with him. Jeffrey concurred. He had been somewhat aggressive with Mizrahi when we first met and had stormed out of his office when Mizrahi was late for a meeting with us.

Then Jeffrey told us that John Needleman, one of the partners in the firm of accountants he used, had bought a publishing company and left the firm. Coincidentally, Needleman had been in my office only the week before: what he'd bought was not in fact a publishing house but a book remainder business, Ramboro, with which we had occasional dealings, and he had come with his very experienced buyer, Tim Finch, looking to buy some of our overstocks. I appreciated Jeffrey's suggestion, but an association with a remainder company was not exactly what we were after.

Nevertheless, prodded by Jeffrey, John and I met up several times and eventually he confided to me that he was in the process of selling his company to Chrysalis, who at that time were not only leaders in the music business but also owned radio and television outlets. John told me they were keen, through him, to expand into the publishing world and were interested in us. That was an altogether different proposition and seemed like a perfect marriage. After a long courtship and a protracted negotiation, during which Anthony Harkavy played his usual blinder, protecting our interests (particularly during the final long, tense meeting in the offices of Chrysalis' solicitors, Harbottle & Lewis), a deal was finally signed. It was, in a way, one of the saddest days of my life, giving up our independence, but also an incredibly important one, for, as a result of our agreement, we were able to pay off the bank and remove all the guarantees (ours and that of Carole's father, which was still in place). It was a massive relief.

* * *

John Needleman was in charge of the expanding Chrysalis publishing group, and working with him was relatively easy, since he seemed content to leave the actual publishing to me, which, after all, is what I was there for. Meanwhile, he concentrated on what he was expert at: buying companies, six of which he acquired in quick succession. Several of these were companies that had approached us over the years and which had now hit hard times. As part of the arrangement, we gave up our office in Clipstone Street and moved to north London, where Ramboro was based, and in due course those other companies joined us there. As a condition of the deal, we'd managed to keep nearly all our staff, but after a year or so, two key members (the 'A team', as I called them) left. Kate Mills, our brilliant editor, went to Book Club Associates, then to Orion as publishing director of fiction, and is now publishing director of Harper Collins' HQ imprint, while the dynamic Charlotte Bush is now the high-flying director of publicity and media relations at Penguin Random House. Both stars.

After three years, John Needleman left and was replaced by Marcus Leaver, with whom I was increasingly uncomfortable for several reasons, especially after he brought in an associate publisher for my imprint without discussing it with me. I played it cool, biding my time, and in due course Leaver left for America and the editor he'd brought in also departed. We were back to square one, except that Chrysalis decided that the illustrated imprints they had acquired through Needleman were swallowing money and they wanted to withdraw from the publishing business.

Eventually, there was a management buyout and Anova was born, with Robin Wood and Polly Powell in charge, both experienced publishers. It was shortly after this that Laurence Orbach, with whom I was at school, suggested that I start my own imprint within his huge international publishing group, Quarto, which, in 2006, I did, having negotiated an exit deal with Anova (now called Pavilion) that gave me a continued interest in certain Robson Books titles. When we announced this move, and the new imprint, JR Books, I had two interesting emails. One came from the editor Marcus Leaver had brought in, generously congratulating me and saying I'd seen off 'a number of young guns, myself included'. The other was from Leaver saying, 'You are one of a kind and someone should bottle your publishing instincts,' and he went on to say that he'd 'learned so much' from me and was 'pleased to call [me] a friend'. I quote that not through vanity, since I took it with a large pinch of bottled salt, but because of what I know preceded it.

Laurence Orbach had bought Aurum Books, which was run by the experienced and extremely able Bill McCreadie, but apart from that Quarto was basically a high-quality packager running a totally international business. Our association lasted for five years, but as Quarto people who were not versed in general publishing started to try to impose themselves, it became impossible given the restraints – the more so once Bill McCreadie, who had become an ally, decided to leave Aurum. In some ways, I feel I let Laurence down, but we'd both acted in good faith and we parted as friends. I was saddened to read, a few years after we parted, that some of those same people who had been shackling me had ousted him as CEO of his own company, and how ironic it is that Leaver is now in charge of the whole caboodle, including Aurum. There, but for the grace of God...

Dannie Abse was fond of quoting Louis Pasteur's assertion that 'chance favours the prepared mind', and as things with Quarto were unravelling, it seemed to favour mine. I had known Iain Dale for many years, and indeed had published him at Robson Books, and we'd had several successful launches at his superb Politico's bookstore. Very much at the centre of the political world, Iain had recently started Biteback, a mainly political publishing imprint backed by Lord Ashcroft. He told me he was looking to expand into a more general area alongside the political, perhaps to acquire another publisher, but as we talked it became clear he didn't need to – I could start that imprint for him, and once the idea was floated, we were almost up and running. We just had to think of a name for the new imprint.

In 2011, the Robson Press was born.

25

SOME YOU WIN...

As I mentioned earlier, I always welcomed late summer offerings, but the one Harry Secombe brought to us in around June 1994 when he was 'ruling the world' on tour in *Mr Pickwick* was a heart-breaker: the autobiography of Roy Castle, one of the best-loved and most versatile performers in show business. When Harry steered him to us, Roy was already very ill and much in the news, having gone public in an exceptionally courageous way about the lung cancer that finally took his life. He had never smoked and maintained that it was the result of passive smoking during his many appearances in smoke-filled clubs over the years. The way he faced his illness, launching a £12 million appeal to build a centre for lung cancer research in Liverpool and embarking on a 1,200-mile Tour of Hope to raise money for it, not only made him a national hero but eventually led to the banning of smoking in public places.

I arrived at the Castles' home apprehensive and expecting a difficult conversation, but it wasn't at all, Roy and his wife Fiona putting me at ease at once. Roy was still bravely performing (he continued to host the TV show *Record Breakers* until two months before his death), and putting the finishing touches to his autobiography, about which he was positive and enthusiastic. It was hard to believe he was so ill. I took the manuscript away and read it overnight. Beautifully written in longhand, with great style and hardly a comma needing to be changed, it conjured up the highs and lows of his career since first treading the boards as a child performer, a career that took him to Hollywood

before he starred in his own TV shows back home in England. He
didn't shy away from talking about his illness. It was a truly inspiring
book, funny and moving by turn – without doubt, as well as being able
to sing, dance, play a multitude of instruments and make people laugh,
Roy was a natural writer.

Sadly, although we moved quickly, Roy did not live to see publication. He died in September, just a month or so after handing me
the completed manuscript, but he saw the jacket and proofs, and we
were in close touch all the time, giving him constant feedback, so as
he travelled the country on his Tour of Hope he was aware of the
excitement the prospect of his book was generating in both the trade
and the media. Indeed, our rep Keith Humphrey reported that when
he told booksellers in his area that we had that autumn's bestseller, the
reaction he repeatedly got was, 'Don't tell me Robson Books have Roy
Castle's autobiography.' We had, and with Fiona's help it became the
bestseller it richly deserved to be. And nobody was more delighted
than Harry Secombe.

*   *   *

Of course, many late-season offerings weren't right for us and not all of
those we did take on hit the jackpot – far from it. We learned to proceed with caution. Over the years, many of our most successful books
came through our own initiative rather than the approaches of others
– books such as *The Glums*, tied to the hilarious TV series of the same
name, which had been adapted from the extremely popular radio series
of the '50s *Take It from Here*, written by the legendary comedy writing
team of Frank Muir and Denis Norden. The Glums were a 'truly awful
family' – the son Ron, as thick as a post, seemingly engaged for ever
to the very plain Eth. ('Engagement in those days', wrote Muir and
Norden in the preface to their book, was 'like being given a present for
Christmas and not being allowed to open it until Easter'.) The scenes
featuring the Glums had entertained a whole generation on radio and
did so again twenty years later when they surfaced on television. For
us, *The Glums* was a natural follow-on from our bestselling *Goon Show*

book, and so too were *The Best of Steptoe and Son* and the two *Hancock's Half Hour* books we published with their creators, Ray Galton and Alan Simpson. The second Hancock book contained ten scripts the BBC were reported to have 'lost' and which their authors were willing to reconstruct for a book. A bonus was the fact that the *Little Britain* stars Matt Lucas and David Walliams agreed to contribute a foreword. Such was their admiration for Galton and Simpson that they even offered to interview them for a paper if we lined one up, and so on a Saturday morning the four of them gathered in the upstairs room of a Soho club, with a *Times* writer present to record the interview and me as the proverbial fly on the wall, their conversation ranging widely as they recalled writers, programmes, shows and artists that had meant a great deal to them (and to me!), and doubtless to many *Times* readers. A real treat.

Frank Muir and Denis Norden, the legendary scriptwriting team and TV panellists.

Other books, such as Matthew Parris's witty and insightful parliamentary sketches, originated as quality newspaper columns, leading to more books from the same authors – in Matthew's case, to three, including his highly successful *Great Parliamentary Scandals* and *The Great Unfrocked*, a book of church scandals. The only problem with his very successful parliamentary book was keeping it up to date, since there seemed to be a splurge of scandals whenever we were about to reprint. Nothing changes. We had a packed launch for that title in the Churchill War Rooms, and quite a few of the book's subjects were sporting enough to come. I well remember Jeffrey Archer saying to me as I was about to attempt a few introductory words, 'Don't be nervous. You are only about to address some of the finest speakers in the country.' When the compelling TV dramatisation of the Jeremy Thorpe affair, *A Very English Scandal*, was showing, I was intrigued to see Matthew referring back in his *Times* column to his *Scandals* book and his chapter on Thorpe – and rather frankly, too. Good books, it seems, live on! We had fun too with his *Read My Lips*, a collection of the things politicians wish they hadn't said, an idea inspired by a book I picked up in a New York bookstore. It was a privilege to publish him.

After Matthew came another sparky *Times* writer, Ann Treneman, whose two collections of brilliant parliamentary sketches were followed by a very different but very successful, quirky book for which she travelled widely: *Finding the Plot: 100 Graves to Visit Before You Die*, which we sold to a TV company. At one stage, it seemed as though we had a monopoly on *Times* writers, given that we also published Derwent May's *Times Nature Diary* and *Feather Report*, his weekly bird column... and why not, since nobody else seemed to be mining this rich source of fine writing – until recently, that is, when we lost out on *The Times Diary at 50*, an anthology compiled by the excellent Patrick Kidd, whom I would love to have published.

Another book that got away was *Longitude*, the story of the search for a reliable method of locating a ship's position at sea. I found it enthralling though I can't honestly say I thought it had great sales potential; nevertheless, we offered for it, one of only two British publishers to do so. Our rival offered just a few hundred pounds more and scooped the pot: it became the bestseller of the year. I don't believe that anyone actually foresaw that.

I was also disappointed that, after a promising start, I was never able to tie down the sprightly Ken Dodd – but who could? I had gone to a special lunch in Liverpool at the invitation of broadcaster John Keith, who had written a couple of successful Liverpool-related football books for us and knew 'Doddy' well. This was an annual lunch for elderly artistes which Dodd always chaired, calling on the old-timers to perform bits of their acts and throwing in the odd snatch of his own. It was warm, nostalgic, touching and great fun – rather like an improvised Old Time Music Hall. Some of those present had been stars in their day and still knew how to work an audience, relishing those few minutes in Doddy's generous spotlight. Halfway through the lunch, the great man, who'd been told by John that I was there, signalled for me to come and sit next to him so we could talk. We spoke often after that Liverpool meeting, swapping ideas, and he would phone me from time to time and talk away at great length. If only I'd attached a tape recorder to the phone, I'd have had half the book, but regretfully I never managed to get even that.

It was a similar scenario with Warren Mitchell, star of *Till Death Us Do Part* and Alf Garnett's alter ego. Having published several Garnett books with the show's creator, Johnny Speight, and followed Warren's career from his early days on radio, I felt we were the perfect publishers for him, especially since I understood his Jewish background. The only trouble was that he didn't want to write a book… but when he came to the launch of Jack Rosenthal's posthumous autobiography he seemed sympathetic to the idea, suggesting we meet for lunch. He'd had a stroke and walked with great difficulty, so I called for him and drove him to a restaurant he liked in Highgate, dropping him off afterwards at his GP's surgery. We got on well and I visited him several times after that, listening as he sat back in his armchair and talked entertainingly about his childhood, his parents and their fish and chip shop, his early career. I kept urging him to write it down and he'd promise to start next week, but those next weeks came and went and eventually I gave him a pocket tape recorder, telling him that if he'd just talk into it (and I would prompt him with questions if it would help), then we could get it transcribed and he could rewrite it at will.

All went quiet, then Warren phoned to invite me to lunch at Langhams to thank me for what he called my 'loyalty'. But just as I thought we were getting somewhere at last, I realised we weren't. Yet I still persisted, since although he wasn't at all well physically, mentally he was as sharp as ever. When I began visiting him again, I'd hear what sounded like a record of Louis Armstrong singing from somewhere upstairs, only to find it was Warren imitating him, keeping his voice 'in trim' as he put it. And away he'd go again, giving me a private one-man show, telling the stories, doing the voices, remembering the heyday of Alf Garnett and all the controversy surrounding the character. Alas, the book never materialised, Warren dying before we could get his engrossing story on paper.

Susan George, co-star with Dustin Hoffman of the psychological thriller *Straw Dogs*, which included a controversial rape scene, was another would-be author I was never able to pin down, despite long phone calls and friendly lunches, and the fact that she was keen to write – indeed, had approached me through an agent. The dynamic Susan, a star in Hollywood at an early age, who was associated over the years with a number of famous men (among them Prince Charles, George Best, Jimmy Connors and Jack Jones), had written several enticing draft chapters for her proposed book, including a frank discussion of that famous rape scene, but somehow she could never afford the time to continue, and because she wrote so well herself, getting someone to work with her never seemed to me to be a necessary option. At one of our last meetings, for tea at the Wolseley, she was joined by her hand-some and very charming husband of some twenty-eight years, Simon MacCorkindale, then still starring as a doctor in the popular TV series *Casualty* while battling cancer. Simon too was writing a book about his life and illness, and he gave me some chapters to read in confidence. Sadly, he died soon after, leaving a bereft Susan to continue running the world-class Arabian horse stud farm they had developed together, which remains her passion. When we next met, Susan had the classy Caroline Michel, CEO of Peters Fraser + Dunlop as her agent, and although I enjoyed a lively lunch with the glamorous duo, we were never able to get the book off the ground. However, Susan, more than ever involved with her prize-winning horses, still calls from time to time, so maybe one day we will. She still has an intriguing story to tell, and if anyone can get her to write it, it's Caroline.

Barbara Windsor did get *her* story on paper, but sadly not for us. We had originally met at a recording of Terry Wogan's TV talk show to which I'd accompanied Maureen Lipman, also a guest on the programme that night. Barbara was friendly after that and we kept in touch, with vague thoughts of a book always in the air. One day, her accountant contacted me to ask if I could advise on how to get the rights back on an early ghosted autobiography of hers – she obviously had a new one in mind. I was pleased to be able to help, and the rights were reverted.

Barbara was now starring in *EastEnders* and a new book by her would be highly commercial, as she knew. Getting together with an experienced writer, she produced an outline for a full-scale autobiography which went out to several publishers and for which I made a substantial offer – six figures, as I recall, with higher than usual royalties. Not surprisingly, we were outbid by a large publisher and Barbara, understandably and full of apologies, went with them (though she later regretted it). When the book appeared, she sent me an early copy and her inscription was some compensation: 'Thank you for all your kind advice, even though I didn't do it with you (pardon the expression).' The following Christmas, we received a card with a lovely photo of Barbara, perfectly coiffed and in a long white skirt, apparently taken in front of Niagara Falls. Inside, she had written, 'Happy Christmas' and, above her signature, 'Viagra Falls'. Irrepressible as ever.

* * *

Sometimes, however, the dice rolled the right way. I'd seen a headline in the *Mail on Sunday* announcing 'JOAN LEAVES PUBLISHER'. It could only be Joan Collins, and reading on I learned that the publisher who was about to release her new book was in financial difficulties and she was claiming the rights back. Since Joan had been part of our family circle for a considerable time – that is to say, we never missed an episode of *Dynasty*, recording them all when we went on holiday and binging on them *en famille* when we got back – I thought how exciting it would be to publish her. A little research led me to her agent, Jonathan Lloyd at Curtis Brown, with whom I'd often dealt, and, while explaining that there were still legal entanglements to unravel, he allowed me in confidence to see the book, which was just about ready to go to press. Inevitably, once again it was late in the year.

Titled *Star Quality*, the book was a novel on an epic scale, a theatrical family saga about three generations of alluring women who all become stars – and who better to write it than Joan, not only a glamorous star herself, but coming from a theatrical background, her father having been a leading showbiz agent. Joan's book had a strong storyline with all the ingredients – sex, jealousy, violence – to make it a page-turner as it moved from London to New York to Hollywood. As well as drawing on her own experience, Joan had done a considerable amount of background research on the various periods she covered in the story, from Victorian times on, which she brought vividly to life.

Jonathan was still sorting out the legal side of things and we couldn't progress until he had, but finally he phoned to say things were unravelling and he'd arranged for us to see Joan at her Belgravia apartment. He made it clear that she had to be happy with whichever publisher he recommended, irrespective of the terms. Aware that she had been involved in a major lawsuit with Random House in America (which she'd won), and given the trouble she was now having, I could well understand her concern. I looked forward to our meeting with some trepidation. Was she really real? I was about to find out.

Jonathan and I arrived a little early, having arranged to meet up outside her flat, and he wisely suggested that we wait a few minutes before ringing (later, Joan told me she thought arriving early was ruder than being late). We were led into a dim sitting room, the light obscured by half-closed curtains, and I peered at the various photos that surrounded us as Jonathan and I chatted. Then, like a gust of wind, Joan Collins swept in, her first words to us being 'Look at my legs!' Surprised but quick to obey, we at once realised it was not a flirtatious invitation as she pointed to the bruises she had sustained the night before at the theatre she was appearing in, having stumbled down the narrow flight of stairs that led to her dressing room.

Wondering why the curtains were still drawn, she went and opened them before sitting down and, fixing me with her large green eyes, saying almost accusingly, 'Jonathan tells me you've read my book. Do you like it?'

'Yes, I have read it, Miss Collins, and as I told Jonathan, I do like it, very much, but...' The word 'but' hung in the air as her eyes zeroed in on me even more intently.

'But what?' she challenged. 'But I wonder whether you would be open to a little editing. I've noticed a few things.' 'What kind of things?' I'd started so I had to continue. 'On page 95, Miss Collins, you talk about the Cotton Club in New York and mention a hot young trumpeter called Duke Ellington. Duke Ellington played the piano, Miss Collins. Perhaps you meant Louis Armstrong?' There was a pause, then she thanked me for pointing out what was an obvious slip, cursed the publisher who'd let it through, smiled graciously and said, 'Yes, I'd be glad to consider any points you may have. I want the book to be as good as possible.'

We talked on in general about the book, and that was that. I seemed to have passed my audition, and we struck a deal. We worked closely together, Joan making quite a few changes and welcoming suggestions as we went along, though rewriting in her own words. Thus it was a creative, two-way process and it quickly became apparent that Joan was a perfectionist and that she loved to write, rising early to work and taking as much trouble with the words she put on the page as she did with the clothes she wore. She certainly has 'star quality' as she herself defined it in a note she sent me to add to the text of her book in the voice of one of her characters: 'When you're on the screen, honey, no matter who you're with or what you're doing, the audience can only look at you – that's star quality.'

By then it was late August, and we all decided that rather than rush the book out in our usual headlong way, we should wait until the spring, especially as it had been subscribed and advertised to the trade by another publisher and with a different jacket. Another reason was that Joan was getting married the following February and would be very much in the news then. Born in Peru, her charming husband (her fifth) Percy Gibson is a theatre producer and thirty-two years her junior. When asked how she felt about marrying a man so much younger, she laughingly quipped, 'If he dies, he dies!'

'Would you and your wife like to come to the wedding?' Joan asked as we finalised the text. Well, we weren't going to say no to that invitation! Held at Claridge's, the wedding seemed to us like a scene from *Dynasty*: there were silver chairs for the guests in the candle-lit room where the ceremony took place; enormous vases of lilac and lilies everywhere; the tables in the dining room were given the names of flowers instead of numbers, and stylishly draped with purple velvet and set with white napkins tied with lavender ribbons – everything in harmony with the lilac colour scheme.

As we waited expectantly for the bride to appear, I looked around at the other guests – so many famous faces among them, including Shirley Bassey (who later sang for Joan, unaccompanied), Roger Moore, Ruby Wax, Terry O'Neill, and Cilla Black (in a long black dress slit to the thigh, as I couldn't help noticing when the dancing started!). Then the oh-so-glamorous bride entered, and what an entrance she made, wearing a close-fitting, off-the-shoulder lilac silk dress, and carrying a bouquet of lily of the valley and freesias. Percy wore a tartan of the Monaghan clan (his mother, Bridget Monaghan, was the daughter of a Glasgow railway worker). At the drinks reception after the ceremony, we all drank far too much champagne while waiting for the photos to be taken. It was one of the few occasions Carole and I have had our pictures in *OK!* magazine, which was covering the wedding exclusively.

Tireless Joan might have danced all night, yet in the following weeks she still had plenty of energy left to promote *Star Quality*, and we were happy to ride the wave of the wedding publicity. We launched the book with a champagne reception at the Players' Theatre, where I remember Miriam Margolyes shouting out to Joan as she entered, 'You look fucking marvellous!', Joan responding to the compliment good-humouredly if not in kind. Coincidentally, I had faxed Miriam not long before to ask if she would like to write a book. 'No, I would not,' she had scribbled fiercely at the top of my missive, returning it almost before it had reached her. At the launch of Joan's book, she relented a little, saying that if I introduced her to Alan Coren, whom she greatly admired, we might have lunch and talk about it. As part of our promotion I took Joan and Alan as our guests to the British Book Awards ('The Nibbies'), where they both made speeches and presented awards. Later, Miriam came up to Joan, and I introduced her to Alan, but I never claimed my lunch nor did we ever do a book together.

As well as all the signings, literary lunches and media appearances we arranged for Joan, there was a Foyles lunch at Grosvenor House in her honour, shared with Denis Healey. When told that his co-honouree was Joan Collins, Healey jokingly asked whether a bedroom had been reserved for them. He really should have been Prime Minister!

Always classy and stylish, Joan Collins was exciting to publish.
Her launch parties were always memorable.

After *Star Quality* came *Joan's Way*, her tips on looking and feeling good: a lavish, full-colour, large-format book, with many of the photos specially taken at her request by Brian Aris, some at Grayshott Hall, the lovely health farm near Guildford then owned by my friend Tony Stalbow's company. (Maureen Lipman had once opened a new wing there and talked in her speech about the shag on the floor, referring – naturally! – to the thick carpet rather than any activity that might have taken place on it.) There was no *OK!* magazine to help underwrite the cost, but fortunately the *Daily Mail* came up with a life-saving offer backed by TV advertising, and then an American publisher came on board, so we were home and dry. The only other book of that kind we had done was with Twiggy some years earlier, and that too had been a costly exercise, though watching her smile and pose for the camera so naturally was an experience, and every photo turned out a beauty. For her shoot we'd had to call in on loan whole outfits – dresses, coats, shoes and accessories. I hadn't known you could do this, but I was learning fast.

Now I think about it, there were two other full-colour books on our list – sex manuals by Anne Hooper and Phillip Hodson – but for those no clothes were required. Joan, I hasten to add, brought her own clothes to her shoots, every bit as stylish as any we might have borrowed… or bought.

Robson Books published one more book with Joan, a racy novel called *Misfortune's Daughter*, but then I became involved with the Quarto Group and we moved even further away from fiction. Not surprisingly, Joan has gone on writing and I was amused to see that, lively as ever, she still knows how to command a headline: responding on the television show *Loose Women* to the question 'Name three things that have kept your marriage with Percy strong,' her reply was, 'Sex, sex, sex.' Messrs Hooper and Hodson would have approved.

As a tailpiece, I should add that my *Dynasty* obsession led me to publish two other stars of that infectious saga – Diahann Carroll, who was at the time engaged to David Frost, and Kate O'Mara, the feisty Kate once changing for a 'do' in my office while I averted my eyes (won't I ever learn?). I remember the *Daily Mail* paying a goodly sum for her frank and powerful story.

*   *   *

It was Jonathan Lloyd, too, who brought us one of the jewels in our crown. I had gone to see him in his office in the summer of 2011 when he asked me whether I'd like to publish Peter Brookes. Since the first thing I looked at when I opened *The Times* every morning was Peter's political cartoon, and like a great many other people I considered him a genius, Jonathan got an immediate 'Yes', a deal was done, and a close publishing relationship – and friendship – was born. We've now published four collections of Peter's dazzling cartoons and plan more. Generous in many respects, after his book launches held at the prestigious Chris Beetles Gallery, in tandem with an exhibition of his originals, Peter generally invites us to join him for dinner with his delightful wife Angela (a highly skilled printmaker and herself a considerable artist) and a small circle of friends or family. On one occasion I forgot my glasses and Peter lent me his so I could read the menu. Later, perhaps spurred by the excellent wine, I found myself trying to imagine what the world looked like as seen through Peter's creative lenses, and wrote a short poem. It certainly surprised him and when he said he was chuffed, so was I! Those were the days before Trump's hair and Theresa May's shoes and necklace took centre stage, when David Cameron, flanked by his old Etonian cronies, was Prime Minister. Here's how 'The Cartoonist's Glasses' begins:

> Borrowing his glasses to read the menu
> I thought I'd get my own Private View,
> that they'd reveal a flashlight world
> of bloody tyrants and feckless politicians
> where a pop-eyed prime minister and his
> fellow schoolboy toffs held comic sway...
> but all I saw was the dish of the day.

So, as well as his books and his friendship, Peter gave me a poem... and a fabulous cartoon, included in the plate section to show the colour.

* * *

As I have recounted, Harry Secombe sent us a remarkable bestselling author, but when, a couple of years later, he mentioned that the actress Alexandra Bastedo, who was touring with him in *Mr Pickwick*, was looking for a publisher, I was puzzled. I'd seen her at a *Telegraph* drinks party only a couple of months earlier, where she was telling a circle of admiring men about the animal rescue farm she had started and the book she'd written about it. She had a publisher already (I asked!) and I thought, 'Lucky them', the combination of animals and a beautiful actress seeming to me to be a heady one, as visions of Brigitte Bardot swam before my eyes. Unlike that iconic actress, Alexandra's looks had held up wonderfully since she'd starred at the age of twenty in the cult

TV series *The Champions*. That was before she had become romantically linked with Omar Sharif. From what Harry told me, something had gone wrong with her book deal and she now had a manuscript ready to publish and no publisher. He'd suggested that she should contact me.

Her book was good and Alexandra lively and full of ideas about promoting it. She was married to the writer and theatre director Patrick Garland, who seemed extremely indulgent of the animals that took up more and more room in their seventeenth-century farmhouse near Chichester, an ever-expanding menagerie of rescued donkeys, cats, dogs, hens, ferrets, turkeys, chipmunks and fish. She brought her ferrets to the office to meet our reps, and released them, laughing, much to the consternation of the males among them. She certainly knew how to keep men on their toes!

There was always a gratifying turnout for the launches she gave at the farm, while Patrick looked on wryly from the side. In her book, *Beware Dobermans, Donkeys and Ducks*, she recounted her early film and television career, but one story she didn't tell, which she confided to me, concerned a weekend she'd spent in Paris with Omar Sharif, Peter Sellers and Peter's girlfriend. Waking late and finding no Sharif, Alexandra had dressed and gone down to breakfast, where she bumped into Sellers, alone and looking for his girlfriend. It transpired that she had gone off with Sharif, so the two of them were left to go for a stroll together along the Seine… at least, that's what Alexandra told me they did. I wonder whether Peter would have included that story in the book he never wrote, and what *his* ending would have been!

Another beautiful star of a cult TV series who was very involved with animals was Stefanie Powers, co-star with Robert Wagner of *Hart to Hart*, though the animals she favoured were the more dangerous, endangered species of east Africa. She had become passionate about them through the great love of her life, the actor William Holden, after whose death she established the William Holden Wildlife Foundation. Her career in film and theatre and on television has been a rich and varied one, with appearances alongside many of Hollywood's most illustrious stars and roles that have included that of the sexy

secret agent April Dancer in the TV series *The Girl from U.N.C.L.E.*
In between promoting her book, *One from the Hart*, we enjoyed hearing her sing in cabaret and listening to the talks she gave about her business and philanthropic ventures. An enterprising and versatile woman, Stefanie was also great fun, and although I generally try to keep authors separate so that each gets maximum attention, I invited her to one of our most unusual book launches. This was an awayday with champagne and fine food on the *Orient Express* at the invitation of James Sherwood, who had written an account of how he'd bought the old rolling stock and revived the train. His collaborator was the financial journalist Ivan Fallon, and the book had come to me through Vivienne Schuster at Curtis Brown, every bit as special an agent as *The Girl from U.N.C.L.E.* Naturally, both Viv and Ivan were on the train that day. The lavish party stretched the full length of the train, with guests eating and drinking at tables set on either side of the carriages. We were lucky enough to share a table with Christopher Foyle and his charming wife, and Stefanie, sharing with Tom Conti and his wife Kara, seemed to greatly enjoy being in such an Agatha Christie-esque setting. Not many of us got off the train standing upright that day.

It's odd that Stefanie should find herself on our list alongside the Man from U.N.C.L.E, the elegant, intellectual Robert Vaughn, and while we entertained them both it wasn't at the same time – though that would have been interesting, given their involvement with both *U.N.C.L.E.* and politics. Stefanie had campaigned for Robert Kennedy, and Vaughn, a long-time Democrat activist, was the first actor to take a public stand against the Vietnam War, and went on to write on political subjects. What I discovered from publishing them was the extraordinary cult following they and their respective TV series inspired. I should have been prepared, given that at the height of his series, Vaughn had been forced to put up an electric fence around his home to keep out the hordes of young girls who gathered there. And I should have remembered, too, the personal story told to me by Marilyn Warnick, then books editor of the *Mail on Sunday*, who jumped the queue to buy serial rights in Robert's book. At the age of eighteen, she told me, she'd been in a children's hospital in Pennsylvania for spinal surgery, which required a long period of recuperation. Because she was older than the other patients, she'd been given a private room behind the nurses' station, with a television set. Her favourite nurse – who was in her thirties – would do the ward round then come and sit with her and watch *The Man from U.N.C.L.E.* Said Marilyn, 'I've never forgotten her saying about Vaughn: "That man can put his slippers under my bed any time."'

However, I hadn't realised the strength of Robert's following, so when we took him for a signing at Waterstones in Piccadilly, I was amazed (though he certainly wasn't) to see coachloads of fans waiting for him, all wearing *Man from U.N.C.L.E.* T-shirts, and a queue stretching along Piccadilly. The last time I saw Robert was as I was crossing Lambeth Bridge, and there, to my astonishment, he was, filming a scene for the British TV series *Hustle*, in which he played a suave conman.

The mention of Piccadilly brings back embarrassing memories of another American film star, Ernest Borgnine – or, at least, of Tova, his much younger wife (his fifth). We had signed his succinctly titled autobiography (*I Don't Want to Set the World on Fire, I Just Want to Keep My Nuts Warm*) and several months before we were due to launch it, she contacted me to say she would be in London the following week, staying at the Ritz, and suggesting we meet there to discuss promotion. It was a Saturday and I'd been out earlier driving my granddaughter around, and without giving my appearance much thought had thrown on a polo-neck sweater under a blazer, going straight on to the Ritz once I'd dropped her off.

When I strolled into the hotel, an elegant, attractive woman slipped past me, dressed to the nines and bedecked with jewellery. I asked at the desk for Mrs Borgnine and was told she had just gone into the bar and was expecting me. That vision had evidently been her. 'But, sir,' the concierge continued as I moved to follow her, 'I'm afraid you need a shirt and tie to go into the bar. We can lend you both, and you can change in there.' He pointed to the gentlemen's toilet. I hesitated, trying to decide whether to do a bunk or swallow my pride, but in the end crept into the gents with the shirt and rather drab tie under my arm. Mrs B had clearly been informed, and when I finally joined her, feeling like a schoolboy, I didn't exactly knock her off her feet – or even the bar stool. Near to, her diamonds were dazzling – perhaps not quite as big as the Ritz, but close. I apologised and explained why I was late, she smiled, and we both pretended it hadn't happened, but I could feel her disapproval in the air. Still, she had excellent contacts and was there to help, which she did, pointing out that her husband, to whom she had been married for thirty-five years, was ninety-two and should not be overburdened with too many engagements. Mrs Borgnine herself appeared frequently on the QVC shopping channel, where she sold her own cosmetics and perfumes, and was a regular at the Ritz whenever she was in London. Consequently, she managed to get us a 'very special rate' at the hotel for her husband, and arranged for him to go on QVC with her and sell his book, which was quite a coup. She also arranged for the Ritz to host an exclusive dinner with Mr Borgnine as guest of honour, to which the hotel would invite their special clients.

Borgnine himself was a delight, chatting easily to fans, many of whom arrived with film posters, photos and other memorabilia for him to sign along with the book. There was a full house at the British Film Institute screening of *Marty*, the film for which he'd won an Oscar, and he was interviewed on stage. But somehow, although Mrs Borgnine smiled and was friendly, and though I was always careful to wear a shirt and tie, I don't think I ever redeemed myself from that first encounter. And we never did receive an invitation to the Ritz dinner.

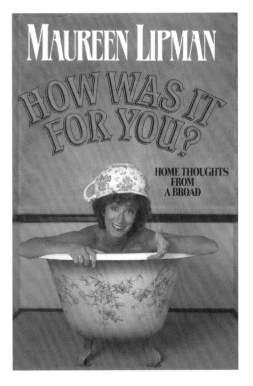

Two of Maureen Lipman's typically original (and costly!) jackets for her bestselling books.

I share a joke with a (relatively) soberly dressed Maureen Lipman.

The JR Books stand at the Frankfurt Book Fair features Maureen and the French actress and dancer Leslie Caron.

The night we met the great Muhammad Ali. Carole and I couldn't have imagined the rollercoaster week that was to follow.

Author Thomas Hauser speaks at the dinner for Ali, here seated between Henry Cooper and wife Lonni.
© ROGER DIXON

LEFT Ali calls for silence as he decides to speak at the dinner. We'd been told he wouldn't… but he most certainly did!
© ROGER DIXON

LEFT Ali meets two young fans at a packed Waterstones signing. Carole is behind him with our editor Louise Dixon. © ROGER DIXON

Manuela watches while Ali signs at Blackwell's in Oxford.
© ROGER DIXON

Enjoying an exchange with Ali at yet another signing. © ROGER DIXON

The crowds in Nottingham were so large we were given a police escort out of town. © ROGER DIXON

Muhammad Ali comes to our house for tea, dwarfing Carole, Deborah and me.

All the way from New York – Tom and Sandra McCormack at our 25th wedding anniversary party at the Samuel Pepys. © MIKE FINBERG

LEFT Matthew Parris, at the Politico's launch for his book of political sketches.

BELOW The cartoon Peter Brookes gave me to go with my poem 'The Cartoonist's Glasses' (page 363).

BUT WE'RE ALL FROM COMPLETELY DIFFERENT BACKGROUNDS... THE CITY, LAW, DIPLOMATIC SERVICE, HEDGE FUNDS, YOU NAME IT!

ABOVE LEFT A happy family occasion. Carole, Manuela, and I join Deborah and Gareth (Amdor) at Burgh House in Hampstead to register their marriage.

RIGHT In the evening, at the Kensington Roof Gardens, Ron Moody delights guests by speaking and singing at the wedding celebrations, following an equally witty and entertaining speech from Manuela, here seen in full flow.

BELOW Deborah and Gareth enjoy the proceedings.

After the launch of Joan Collins's *Star Quality*, a wag in our art department surprised me with this card. Miriam Margolyes is in the background.

And *Publishing News* surprised us with this colourful picture.

RIGHT Rula Lenska and Stefanie Powers – two of our other colourful authors.

BELOW Ernest and Mrs Borgnine signing away, despite my faux pas.

In Normandy with Dannie Abse, celebrating the Booker longlisting of his novel.

A memorable dinner in Honfleur with Dannie and Joan Abse. Happy days.

At the Hungerford Festival with Maureen Lipman and singer Jacqui Dankworth. © BRIAN DAVIES

Sally Dunsmore, the inspiring director of the Oxford and Blenheim Palace Literary Festivals. © KT BRUCE

With Michael and Maureen Joseph at the packed closing party for Joseph's Bookshop.

With Margaret Busby, publisher of my early book *In Focus*, and Andy Croft, publisher of Smokestack Books and my two most recent poetry collections.

With the novelist and poet Ben Okri at Worcester College, Oxford, where we read together in the lodgings of the Provost, Sir Jonathan Bate, and his wife, Paula Byrne. © KT BRUCE

ABOVE At Blenheim Palace concert, with Charlie Wood (left), Ben Davies, Jacqui Dankworth and Maureen Lipman. © MARK LEWISOHN

LEFT The future: our grandchildren, Lauren (the golfer), Sam (the runner) and Caitlin (the tennis player).

26

IN THE PINK

One of the strangest people to come our publishing way was an unusually tall, waxwork-like man with thinning dyed hair called John M. East. A figure from an earlier era, he claimed to have been brought up by Max Miller, the Cheeky Chappie himself, and probably was. In fact, he wrote Miller's biography for us, drawing on a lot of personal material. As well as having been a broadcaster, East was involved in public relations in some mysterious way and appeared to have contacts with various influential and often wealthy people, one of whom was David Sullivan, at that time owner of the *Daily Sport* and *Sunday Sport*, and currently joint chairman with David Gold of West Ham Football Club. East was, in a way, a Mr Fixit, always saying he must interest Sullivan in our company, but I couldn't imagine anything more unlikely. However, he did introduce us to Ralph Gold, David's brother and partner (who had written a rags-to-riches account of their early days in business), and as a result we did get to sell our football titles through Birmingham FC, the club both brothers were then involved with.

Just as improbably, East came into the office one day to say Barbara Cartland would like us to publish her. He then reached for the phone, dialled, and a few seconds later passed me the receiver and said, 'Here's Dame Barbara now, speak to her.' For such moments you have to be prepared, and I certainly wasn't. What on earth does one say to a woman like that, so removed from one's own world, an almost fictional character? Somehow, as on so many other strange occasions in my life,

I stammered my way through, and the next thing I knew Carole and I were driving John East to Camfield Place, the Cartland mansion near Hatfield, to join the family for Sunday lunch.

An apparition in pink – pinker than any of the photos I'd ever seen of her – Dame Barbara was waiting in the sitting room, full of the memoir she wanted to write for us. I felt that any moment she would lie back on her chaise longue and start dictating it, as she had so many romantic novels over the years, but we were called in for lunch before she could get under way. Luckily we weren't placed next to her, nor was I called on to make a speech as some others were, including her son Ian McCorquodale – apparently it was a Cartland family custom. John East, too, was quickly on his feet, eloquently thanking his hostess for her hospitality. As the coffee was served, Carole made a discreet exit and went in search of the loo. At the top of the wide, plush-carpeted staircase she took a wrong turn and found herself in a lavish dressing room with half-open cupboards on either side. Naturally, she couldn't resist peeping into them, to be faced with dozens of full-length dresses, most of them pink. Fearing that someone might catch her, she beat a hasty retreat, finding the bathroom she'd been looking for on the way down and returning to the table mightily relieved in several respects.

Dame Barbara's book, *I Reach for the Stars*, wasn't the greatest book we'd ever published, or that she'd ever written, but it was her 600th, which gave us enough of a publicity handle to get away with it. Far better, and I think a classic of a kind, was her early memoir of the glittering '20s, *We Danced All Night*, which we reissued at the suggestion of her son, who looked after her affairs. It was, I'm sure, written rather than dictated, and captures perfectly the social whirl of that post-war era.

As for John East, who died a year or so after that visit, his exit was even stranger than his entrance, and very sad, as he left strict instructions that no one was to attend his funeral and that he was to be buried in an unmarked grave. Not even a final curtain call for this most theatrical of men.

*   *   *

As must be evident by now, it seems to have been my (generally!) good fortune to publish a number of women of strong character. Another, who phoned persistently and persuasively every six months or so, blowing hot and cold, was the novelist and literary *grande dame* Emma Tennant, and we did end up publishing a satirical 'royal' novel with her, *Balmoral*, in which the ghost of Princess Diana haunts the royal family as they dine, picnic on the lawn, hunt and frolic. A sort of modern Banquo's ghost, it was fun and drew on a lot of royal detail, for Emma was of aristocratic lineage (her father was the 2nd Baron Glenconner). The only problem was that she was writing it with a co-author with whom she fell out, and then decided to hide behind a pseudonym, which wasn't much help when it came to publicity. In her last call to me in 2016, about a year before she died, she proposed writing a 'family memoir', but since she seemed to have written several, as well as an account of the affair she'd had with Ted Hughes, we never got very far.

More down-to-earth and supportive was the striking actress Rula Lenska, a star of the TV musical drama *Rock Follies*, whose fabulous red hair could put even Ms Cartland's pink into the shade. Rula's aristocratic Polish background (her family lost everything when the Nazis came to power) perhaps seasoned her for her battles with her second husband, Dennis Waterman, and added spice to an already colourful story – one that was brought to us by Tony Mulliken, whose company, Midas PR, provides publicity services across the publishing industry. Those summer afternoons spent on the terrace of Rula's house in Putney, drinking vodka with her and David Robson, who worked closely with her, skilfully editing and guiding her book for us, were a reminder that although she had been brought up in England, her Polish roots went deep.

Coincidentally, it was straight after Rula's book that Andrew Sachs's autobiography came our way via our good friend Diana Hoddinott (the on-screen wife of Jim Hacker, the minister in *Yes Minister*, but real wife of actor Harry Towb). Andrew's life, too, had been scarred by the Nazis. Born in Germany to a Jewish father and Catholic mother, he'd come to England at the age of nine without a word of English. His account of those traumatic early years, when one by one his friends

turned away from him, and his highly qualified father wasn't permitted
to work, was both vivid and affecting – a world away from his brilliant
comic creation, the Spanish waiter Manuel in *Fawlty Towers*, who en-
livened the later pages of Andy's book.

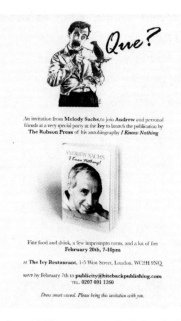

Andrew Sachs, aka Manuel, provided his own waiters for the launch of his colourful autobiography.

There was, though, in his later years the shadow cast by the horrendous
Russell Brand/Jonathan Ross saga that became known as 'Sachsgate',
which had a devastating effect on Andy and his wife Melody. The episode naturally had to be covered in the book, and it could have been
tempting for Andy to use it as an opportunity to hit back, but, the
sweetest of men, he was determined to remain dignified and not sink
to the level of his tormentors. In writing about this painful episode, as
well as the later parts of his book, he was greatly helped by the sensitive
and patient involvement of the writer and film maker David Cohen,
for Andy's memory and concentration were beginning to fail him as
dementia set in. He must have been relieved to get a break from it all
when Dustin Hoffman cast him in *Quartet*, a film he was directing
about a group of ageing musicians and singers living in a retirement

home. Andy played the orchestra conductor of the home's annual Christmas concert. It turned out to be the most moving of films, with magnificent performances from the cream of Britain's senior actors.

With the account of Sachsgate completed and the addition of a little about the film, there remained just one problem: conflicting versions of a scene in *Fawlty Towers* in which Andy, as Manuel, was hit so hard on the head with a frying pan by Basil (John Cleese) that he couldn't get up. According to Andy, they had rehearsed the scene several times using a padded frying pan, but somehow when it came to the recording the pan left for Basil to pick up was not the prop but a real one that came down full force on his head. I suspected that John Cleese would have a very different version, and when he phoned to discuss the foreword he'd agreed to write for the book, I brought the subject up. He was emphatic that Andy had got it wrong, that they had discussed the scene carefully but would never have rehearsed it, and that it was supposed to be only a glancing blow from a real frying pan as Andy turned away, but Andy had got the timing wrong. There was only one thing for it – we included both versions, so honours were even.

There was one real-life comedic moment when chicken was the order of the day – or rather, the eccentric and volatile Melody Sachs's order of the day, for when one Sunday I phoned to say I was coming over with the proofs, she asked me to get my wife to go out and buy her a chicken and other bits and pieces for me to bring too. I duly turned up with proofs in one hand and a bag for life in the other containing the chicken and various vegetables Melody had requested. Now all she had to do was get Manuel to serve it! We'd always prided ourselves on looking after our authors, but this, I must say, was a first.

* * *

One of the major distractions of my early youth, when we still lived in Colindale, had been the girl next door, Diana, who was about two years older than me. Not only Diana, but the group of attractive young girls who were always in her garden. I was then in my *Just William* phase and must have been about eleven, but she was hardly a Violet

Elizabeth. I'd watch them discreetly from the roof of my father's dispensary, which overlooked the garden, eavesdropping on their laughter and far too shy to try to get close. Still, we must have got on well enough, and our parents too, since they fixed a rustic gate in the fence between our gardens so I could retrieve the tennis balls I regularly hit over as I practised for Wimbledon against our kitchen wall.

It was to lead to good things, for some thirty or so years later, out of the blue, I received a phone call from a woman with a slight American accent asking if I was the Jeremy Robson who used to live in Holmstall Avenue and whose father was a doctor. It was Diana. Now married to an American academic, and bearing the surname McLellan, she and her husband lived in Washington, where she had become a witty and feared political journalist whose revelatory book, *Ear on Washington*, had created a considerable stir. Friends, she told me, were giving her and her husband a party in Hampstead, and Carole and I gladly accepted her invitation to join them. It was a happy reunion which eventually resulted in our publishing the sparky Diana's *The Girls*, a compelling book about the Hollywood stars who enjoyed Sapphic relationships. But although we would all meet up for a meal whenever she came to London, and we corresponded from time to time, I never let on about those clandestine peeps over the fence! However, I don't think she could have really objected to my innocent snooping, for when she died in 2014 (and I was shocked to see she had), the *New York Times* called her the 'grande dame of Washington gossip, who perforated the pretentious, skewered the powerful'. But, to me, she remains the girl next door.

*   *   *

I'd met Esther Rantzen at a dinner given by our original backer, Michael Rivkin, for Harry Secombe's *Twice Brightly* back in 1974. At that time, she was a BBC reporter covering the general election. When we met up again in 2011, it was to discuss a book to mark twenty-five years of ChildLine, the national helpline for children she had founded. Esther (now Dame Esther) didn't have long to write the book, but, as

I quickly learned, when she turns her determined mind to something, there's no stopping her. *Running Out of Tears* was delivered on time and written with deep feeling for those who had suffered abuse and turned to ChildLine for help, and with deep anger for those perpetrators she went after, naming and shaming them. When Esther talked to booksellers or gave interviews or spoke publicly about ChildLine (as she did at a reception given in his lodgings by the Speaker of the House), she spoke eloquently and movingly, without notes, communicating her passionate commitment.

The equally feisty Bel Mooney had been an early author of ours, whose *Differences of Opinion* was a collection of her perceptive articles for various papers. Although we'd bumped into each other at the opening of one of Frieda Hughes's exhibitions, we'd never had a real conversation until we met up again at a *Daily Mail* Christmas party in 2014. By then I was greatly in her debt for an extremely generous review she had given my recent book of poems.

Bel is one of the *Mail*'s star journalists, and it seemed to me that an anthology of the popular weekly advice columns she writes, in which she often draws on her own experiences, would be valuable. What she didn't want was just a rag-bag collection of articles, but as she thought about it she realised that by extracting, shaping and adding to some of her most piquant and timeless pieces, she could make a largely original book, punctuated by her favourite quotations – *Words to Help You Through*, as she subtitled her book *Lifelines*.

Not long afterwards, Bel's Maltese dog Bonnie died, which affected her profoundly, to the extent that she wrote a piece about her feelings for the *Mail*. The response was overwhelming: so many people identified with her thoughts and words. By then we were already talking about another book, and here was one staring us in the face. At first Bel was reluctant, but gradually she came to feel that she could tackle the subject at greater length and in a way that would bring comfort to other animal lovers, and so her inspirational book *Goodbye, Pet & See You in Heaven* came into being.

Bel is a woman of many intellectual interests, widely read and with a deep love and knowledge of poetry, and she enjoyed the friendship of Seamus Heaney, as she does of another fine Irish poet, Michael Longley, who, with Seamus, I'd included in my *Young British Poets* anthology many years earlier, when we were indeed all young. Consequently, when Bel and I meet for lunch, our conversation ranges wide, and I hope that before too long another book will emerge from all the ideas we've thrown around.

*   *   *

It was in June 1997 that Christine Hamilton's husband Neil phoned me, at Gyles Brandreth's suggestion, to ask if they could come and see me. That was just after Neil had lost his Tatton seat to Martin Bell, 'the man in the white suit', following the cash-for-questions affair, and Christine had supported him like… well, like a battleaxe, as she had been dubbed in the press. She had worked in Parliament since leaving university in 1971, first as parliamentary secretary to the flamboyant Gerald Nabarro, then, for fourteen years, to Neil. Now, with them both out of Parliament and out of a job, she had had an idea for a book, and as she made tea for everyone in the office, she explained her idea: she'd been called a battleaxe, so why not come out fighting with a book of British battleaxes? She had a list of around thirty formidable women she wanted to write about. I thought it a gutsy idea, but, as we all agreed, it had to be done quickly, so away Christine went, not only writing the book while Neil helped with the research, but, as she neared the finish line, booking the Mothers' Union headquarters for a launch party.

All was arranged – caterers booked, wine bought, invitations printed and sent out, and the required deposit paid – when suddenly, without any explanation, the MU cancelled our booking. Why? In true battleaxe style, Christine marched into their offices and asked to see the director, intent on posing that very question. Nobody would talk to her directly, but it seemed that a tongue-in-cheek diary piece in the *Telegraph* had upset them – all very petty. We changed venue to the much nicer St James's Court Hotel around the corner, got what publicity we could out of it, and pressed the MU to compensate us for the expenses we'd incurred, which they eventually did. It was a pity they cancelled, because they might have enjoyed the party, especially seeing Lord Longford, the campaigner against pornography, in deep conversation on a sofa with Cynthia Payne (*aka* Madam Cyn), who had made headlines when she was accused of running her Streatham home as a brothel where men paid with luncheon vouchers to wear lingerie and be spanked by young women. When the police had raided her house they'd found fifty-three men – including several vicars, solicitors and business directors, an MP and a peer of the realm – in various stages of undress. They were there for a tea party, claimed Cynthia. A cartoon of the time showed a vicar, in bed with a young lady, saying to a policeman who'd burst into the room, 'I demand to see my solicitor – he's in the next room!'

The unsuccessful cash-for-questions libel action, which Neil Hamilton brought against Mohamed Al Fayed and which we attended, proved to be not only highly dramatic, but also entertaining at times, both the Hamiltons responding spiritedly to the sharp questioning of Fayed's legendary counsel, George Carman. At one point there was laughter in court when a seemingly exasperated Carman asked, 'Mr Hamilton, do you have difficulty in paying close attention to anything you find disagreeable?', with Neil responding sharply, 'I'm paying very close attention to you, Mr Carman.' Then there was the question of the sausages Harrods had apparently delivered to Christine, whose response to Carman's question about them prompted a vulgar headline in *The Sun*: 'I never had your sausage, Mr Fayed', which Christine showed us with glee when we arrived in court the next morning.

The loss of this action was both costly and damaging for the Hamiltons, but it wasn't the end of their public ordeal, for six years later, in 2003, they were arrested after an allegation of rape was made against them both. The press had been tipped off by the police and were waiting for them when they arrived at the station. The allegation was shown to be a pack of lies, Neil and Christine were completely exonerated, and the woman who made the claim was sentenced to three years in prison for attempting to pervert the course of justice. She was, surprise, surprise, a client of Max Clifford's, who had sold her story to the *News of the World* (their tasteful headline proclaiming 'CHRIS-TINE'S LESBIAN LUST'), and, following remarks he had made, the Hamiltons sued Clifford, receiving a healthy sum in settlement and a retraction of his defamatory comments in open court.

Characteristically, Christine opted to put some of that money to-wards a champagne party to launch her autobiography, *For Better, for Worse*, and on the invitation she put, 'Champagne courtesy of Max Clifford'. The spirited Hamiltons even sent him an invitation, but for once he must have decided that all publicity was not necessarily good publicity and gone elsewhere.

27

CALL MICHAEL WINNER!

It was around this time that I received a call from the über literary agent Ed Victor, who put to me the idea of publishing a book of Michael Winner's controversial *Sunday Times* restaurant columns. I always enjoyed dealing with the stylish Ed, for all his hyperbole, and we did a number of books together, deals that worked well for us both – the best kind. Not long before he died in June 2017, the papers were full of stories about him getting (or expecting to get!) a million pounds for a book he was selling – David Cameron's memoirs, I believe. In an exchange of emails shortly after that, I told him to remember us if he had anything going for under a million. His response was that he would, 'in the unlikely event of that happening'! I'm content to let him have the witty last word.

Publishing Winner was something I'd often considered, so I welcomed the suggestion (though there were times on my stormy ride with him when I wished I hadn't taken that call!). I came to know three Michael Winners: one rude, one very rude and one impossible. The first of these I met shortly after we had agreed a deal. Ed phoned to say Winner didn't want to be published by someone he hadn't met and would I call him. It was another Barbara Cartland moment, but I picked up the phone and did as commanded. 'Come to my house at 12.30 on Wednesday,' barked Winner. 'I'll take you to lunch.' Down went the phone.

Now, at that time I had just joined up with John Needleman and Chrysalis, and our so-called offices were in a kind of warehouse in north

London, just down the road from Pentonville Prison, a delightful area where you looked carefully over your shoulder wherever you walked. John had a driver called Chris, and I arranged for him to drive me to Winner's house. Chris was late picking me up, so I asked someone to phone Winner's office and say I might be a few minutes late, which I thought was the polite thing to do. It seemed that Winner didn't, and we'd only been driving for a quarter of an hour when Chris received a message on his pager for me to phone the office urgently (those were still pre-mobile days). He pulled up at a phone box, and I scrambled out in the pouring rain, fumbled in my pocket for some coins, which I promptly dropped, finally getting through to learn that Winner had exploded at the poor girl who'd made the call, yelling, 'Tell Mr Robson that if he is going to be late, he needn't bother coming!' Punctuality was an obsession of Winner's, as I quickly learned.

Well, we were on our way, so continued, arriving only about ten minutes late (having lost more time than that making the call). I pressed the buzzer next to the tall iron gates, and after a minute someone opened them and ushered me along the flower-lined path leading to the front door, and once inside I was invited to take a seat in the hall. A few minutes later I was given the all-clear to go up a winding staircase to Winner's study, where he was waiting for me. 'I've just written you this note, and was giving you a couple more minutes,' he said, handing me a sheet of paper. Glancing at it, I saw the unambiguous message: 'Fuck the contract, forget the book, have gone to lunch.'

That might have bothered me once, but I'd weathered enough crises of that kind by then not to be cowed, and I well knew you have to stand up to bullies (and Winner was the arch-bully), so I shrugged my shoulders and told him he could tear up the contract or the note, as he preferred, adding, 'By the way, when you were young you spent a good deal of time in my grandfather's house.' That stopped him in his tracks, and he asked what I meant. I knew he'd been a close friend of my artist cousin, Colin Snowman, who had been brought up in my grandfather's house after his parents were divorced, and I knew Winner was round there all the time, and though they couldn't be more different, he and the gentle Colin kept in touch.

That changed everything, and a suddenly affable Winner said, 'Let me show you round the house' – and what a magnificent house it was, on several floors, with a massive master bedroom overlooking the garden, palatial dining and sitting rooms tastefully furnished with fine paintings on every inch of the walls, then, at basement level, his cinema, with photos of the stars he'd worked with all around, and, finally, the large indoor swimming pool with an electric cover he proudly demonstrated for me.

We then went off to lunch like old friends, and over that lunch I reminded him of an incident involving Colin and him. Every summer there was an open-air exhibition of paintings by local artists along Heath Street in Hampstead Village, and one year, at Winner's prompting, Colin had exhibited a large, dramatic painting of a Black Mass with a naked woman being sacrificed. It had caused an uproar, and Colin had been forced to remove it, the story making headlines in the local press. Since our grandfather was the Mayor of Hampstead at the time, it didn't go down too well at home, to put it mildly. The anti-establishment Winner had loved every minute of the furore at the time, and enjoyed it all over again as he poured me another glass of exceptionally fine wine. He even had his chauffeur drive me back to the office in his stately old Rolls-Royce.

* * *

That was the prelude to a long saga as far as my ensuing relationship and publishing involvement with Michael was concerned, which lasted until his death in 2013. He wrote an entertaining and reasonably frank autobiography, and Dinah May, his personal assistant for some thirty years, has written her own revealing story of life with Winner, so I will confine myself to my own experiences of him, which perhaps add a little to the overall picture. Right from the start, nothing was easy. *Winner's Dinners* did not turn out to be a straight reprint of his weekly column. Restaurants change ownership and collapse with unseemly regularity; chefs leave and are replaced. All these details had to be checked, along with opening hours, phone numbers and so on;

also, there was far too much material, so pieces had to be edited down, revised, arranged into geographical areas, and carefully indexed – a big job which meant bringing in an experienced (and thick-skinned) editor to work with Michael. As well as all this, Michael added his own cartoons and quite a bit of fun to the book, so in the end it wasn't just a stuffy reference book and read as entertainingly and provocatively as his Sunday column.

On top of this, Michael created the Winner Awards, which he got the *Sunday Times* to list and which he announced at the book launch – not just dull ones, like Best Restaurant, Best Hotel, Best Hotel Manager, Best Service etc. (though these were among them), but also more Winner-like ones such as Worst Hotel Service, Worst Ambience, Most Wobbly Table I Ever Saw, Phoniest Restaurant Line ('Your main course will be with you in a minute, sir'), Best Egyptian Manager of a Japanese restaurant – and these are just tasters. When we came to those book launches, of which there were quite a few, we had a deal: he would arrange the venue and the canapés (that is to say, he would bully someone into providing them for free), and we would supply the champagne. Carole and I went to France fairly regularly so it was a reasonable enough deal, since we could then get a decent champagne for as little as £7 a bottle. The fact that we spent £9 for Michael greatly appealed to his *amour propre*, and he wrote a special piece about it and our French odyssey in the *Sunday Times*.

As for the launches, they were packed with celebrities galore, and Michael would get his famous friends (Michael Caine always first among equals) to present the awards, which he announced. Each winner received a certificate of some kind that he must have knocked out on his computer. Shakira Caine eventually told him he couldn't go on handing out tacky bits of paper and that he should splash out on something a little more special. For us, as for those who lived and worked with him, the parties were a nightmare (ask Geraldine, his partner then and later his wife; ask Dinah May), for once his celebrity friends appeared he was impossible to talk to, charging around like a bull, making sure the paparazzi got the photos *he* wanted them to get. Although we spent quite a bit bringing in sound equipment and, at his insistence, a large rostrum, he rarely made any mention of the book, and if by the end of the evening we'd managed to get him to sign a few copies, we were doing well. The focus was entirely on the awards – and Michael Winner. For all this, Michael could be generous, but he could also be vengeful: at the time of the first book launch he was having a public spat with Cliveden House Hotel – not because they hadn't provided him with a swimming pool and Christine Keeler waiting for him in the deep end, but because he claimed to have been served orange juice in dirty glasses (the head waiter claimed it was orange juice residue, which didn't wash with Michael). So, for our launch at the Café Royal we were commanded to lay a special table with dirty glasses and a placard proclaiming 'Cliveden'. Our author thought this was an hilarious jape. He'd also invited representatives from Cliveden to come and receive their award, without revealing that it was for the Worst Service. At first they accepted, then twigged and stayed away – and who could blame them?

Generally, those Winner book launches took place at the Belvedere in Holland Park, then owned by his mate Marco Pierre White, and I remember Michael being quite put out on one occasion there when I presented Geraldine with some flowers, which I thought she well deserved. Clearly, he didn't – or perhaps he was irritated because he hadn't thought of it himself. I enjoyed watching the famous chefs he'd invited quaffing the cheap champagne we'd brought and remarking how good it was. Little did they know, though Geraldine, who had lived in France, did, and winked at me. Towards the end of his life, Michael fell out with Marco for some reason (at one time or another, he fell out with most people, though never to my knowledge with the Caines, with whom he seemed to walk warily). So close had he been to Marco that he gave him and his fiancée their honeymoon as a wedding present – and went with them, which only goes to show there's no such thing as a free honeymoon. When Michael came to write his autobiography, I pointed out that he hadn't mentioned any of the famous chefs he knew or had known. His response was, 'They're all far too boring to write about.' He always said he couldn't stand boring people, and when invited as a special guest to a prestigious

Foyles literary lunch, he demanded to know who he'd be sitting next to before accepting – and when told this wasn't possible, he turned the invitation down.

Michael never sent ordinary emails: they came shrieking through the computer in capital letters like battle orders, and when he left phone messages they were a three-word-long command: 'Call Michael Winner', like a summons to the headmaster's study. Realising quickly that our tiny publicity department would not be able to take the strain, we outsourced the promotion for the first book to Midas, Tony Mulliken's PR company. I took Tony to meet Michael, and all was sweetness and light, Tony being his usual charming, professional self. But the peace didn't last long: whatever Midas did, ever more aggressive emails began to assail Tony, whose name Michael never seemed to get right, calling him 'Terry Pelican' (a story Tony loves to tell). Unruffled, Mr Pelican responded calmly and politely to every email, thanking Winner for pointing out what he should be doing. Michael had met his match, and Tony's refusal to rise to the bait must have made him see red as he set about composing his next email onslaught. It didn't take much to infuriate or upset Mr Winner, but I suspect he was far more sensitive than he cared to admit, even shy. He was obviously annoyed by the fact that we were invited to Joan Collins's wedding and he wasn't (and that, Joan told me, was because he had offended her by failing to go to see a play she was in). They must have mended their fences, though, since she and Percy were in the glamorous party of friends he invited to Venice to celebrate his 70th birthday (*we* weren't!). Then there was his refusal of an OBE for his work in setting up the Police Memorial Trust, saying it was the kind of award given to those who cleaned the toilets well at King's Cross Station. After that, in his correspondence he typed in capitals under his signature, 'MICHAEL WINNER MA (CANTAB), OBE OFFERED AND REJECTED'. In fairness to him I should add that, following the uproar caused by his remark, he invited a Jamaican cleaner who worked at King's Cross Station to tea at his house with her daughter, and when, in the course of conversation, he discovered that the daughter had never been to Jamaica, he paid for them both to go there on a two-week holiday. There were several sides to the Winner coin.

For his autobiography, *Winner Takes All*, published in 2004, I invited Michael to our autumn sales conference in the Chrysalis building in Holland Park, a mile or two from his home. We had a full agenda, starting in the morning, and Michael asked what time we'd finish. When I told him it would be around 5.30 p.m., he said, 'Bring all the reps here and we'll give them a glass of champagne and talk about the book,' adding that we should get someone to take photos. But nothing ever went smoothly with Michael. It was an extremely hot day, and the air conditioning was fully on in the impressive home cinema in the basement of his house, which is where he received us, greeting everyone affably and handing round glasses of champagne. The only problem was that, to save money, our publicist had brought a young photographer with her, an Italian, who was wearing an open-necked, short-sleeved shirt and no jacket... and he was cold. Stopping Michael in mid-flow, he asked him to turn the air conditioning down – and at that, Michael flew into a rage. 'He comes here dressed for the beach and asks me to turn the air conditioning down – what a fucking cheek! When it's his house, he can turn it down, but it is my house and I'll have it as I want it.' Then Michael switched the charm back on, poured more champagne and regaled the reps with stories from his forthcoming blockbuster. But by then the temperature in the room had fallen several more degrees.

The selling of serial rights for that book also produced a little drama, since Michael had a high figure in mind and we had been offered a relatively modest sum by the paper he wanted. 'Tell them you've had a higher offer and to get real,' Michael barked at me down the phone, but I warned him that since we didn't actually have a higher offer that could be a risky business, as they might walk away and leave us stranded. 'If I actually had a higher offer, or one that came close, that might be different,' I told him.

'Then go to your fax machine,' Michael commanded, and five minutes later, on his headed notepaper, came a formal, substantially higher offer from... Michael Winner. 'Now you can tell them you have a higher offer,' he said, laughing.

Fortunately, shortly afterwards another paper put me out of my moral dilemma by entering the ring, and I was able to get a legitimate auction going, ending up with the kind of figure Michael had wanted in the first place – and with my honour intact.

When it came to promoting his book outside London, Michael always chartered a private jet – even to Birmingham and Manchester – which he paid for himself, charging us the equivalent of a first-class rail ticket. Fair enough in theory, but when he went to Ireland for a TV chat show and they not only stumped up for the air fare but also paid him a large fee, I didn't take kindly to receiving a bill from Michael of around £6,000 for the overnight stay in a hotel, and I refused to pay it. Michael said he would sue, but I pointed out (having checked) that you could get a suite in the hotel he'd stayed at for £1,000, and that's what I would pay. Eventually, he accepted that, provided the cheque was delivered by messenger the same day – but he would never deal with us again. However, some months later he was on the phone as if nothing had happened, asking, 'What are we going to publish for Christmas?'

'But Michael,' I responded, 'I thought we weren't talking to each other, let alone doing another book together!'

'Life's too short, Jeremy,' he replied. And away we went again.

As I have said, Michael could be generous, and on the various occasions we had lunch together he always ordered the best wine, and it was impossible to pay. He simply wouldn't allow it – except on one occasion, when he gave a talk at Waterstones in Hampstead and accepted our invitation to dinner afterwards at a popular restaurant near our house. I warned the proprietor that we were bringing Michael and Geraldine, and he was thrilled, but things didn't go well from the start, since instead of taking the order himself he had unwisely given the task to a young waitress who had only worked there for a few weeks and couldn't answer Michael's questions about the menu. Not clever. Still, Michael held back, perhaps because he was our guest. Then he leant over to me, recorder in hand, and asked, 'What's your wife's name, dear?', whereupon Carole, who was sitting next to him and whom he'd already met several times, said, 'Don't you talk to women?' The atmosphere suddenly froze. 'Carole,' I interjected quickly, 'with an "e",' wanting to slide under the table. Somehow the conversation and meal continued, Geraldine and I trying to get things back on an even keel. However, when it came to the mandatory photo at the end of the meal, the chef took ages to appear and when he did the increasingly irritated Michael excluded Carole and Geraldine, handing his camera to Geraldine and telling her to take the picture. I dreaded the piece he would write, but when it appeared a few Sundays later he recalled the incident just as it happened, making the point that Carole had an 'e' at the end of her name and adding, 'She was quite right, I could have asked her.' As a result, Carole received quite a few congratulatory phone calls. Sometime later, in March 2010, the volatile Winner phoned to invite us to dinner at his house and to watch the preview of a new TV series he'd made, *Michael Winner's Dining Stars*. A number of his usual cronies were there, including Andrew Neil, Terry O'Neill (whom Winner had cajoled into taking the cover photos for several of our books), Steven Berkoff (whose graphic memoir of his East End childhood we published) and lyricist Don Black, so it was a lively occasion, if not exactly an intimate one (and the Thai dinner was 'historic'!). He followed this up by sending us a signed photo of himself with Carole, Geraldine and me, so it seemed all was forgiven.

After that episode, Michael went to speak at a *Yorkshire Post* literary lunch in Harrogate, calling from the plane to say he'd forgotten his pocket tape recorder and asking for someone to go out and buy him one, which he promptly paid for when he arrived. I was going to fly with him and Geraldine, but fortunately he decided it was too complicated ('You're bound to be late, and I wouldn't wait' is what he actually said), and so I went alone – and calmly – by train. He spoke entertainingly at the lunch, although he was on edge – perhaps because Geraldine had been placed next to the witty Simon Hoggart, who was also a guest speaker, and whose conversation she seemed to be very much enjoying.

After the lunch, we'd arranged a signing for Michael in a shopping mall, and he became irritable when our driver stopped the car at the entrance to the mall, telling Michael he couldn't drive right up to the bookshop. Perhaps it wouldn't have mattered if it hadn't been pouring with rain. One thing was certain: Michael wasn't going to get wet, and he grumpily ordered the driver to escort him to the bookshop under the large umbrella he kept in the car, striding off and leaving Geraldine and me to fend for ourselves. Luckily, I had a small pocket umbrella, so Geraldine clutched my arm stoically and we followed carefully in Michael's wake. I thought back to the previous year when, at Michael's invitation, the Queen had unveiled the National Police Memorial in the Mall, a triumphant day for him and the result of over ten years' planning. It was raining that day, too, and next morning pictures in all the papers appeared to show Michael safe and dry under the Queen's umbrella while she stood unsheltered in the rain. This caused much mirth in the Winner household, if not in the Palace! If Michael wasn't bothered about the Queen getting wet, he certainly wasn't going to bother about Geraldine and me.

After that rather damp signing, I slipped away, leaving the Winners and taking a local train to visit my old friend Vernon Scannell, who lived on the outskirts of Leeds and had been battling lung cancer for some time. We sat in the cosy, book-lined kitchen of the small grey-brick house Vernon shared with his caring partner Jo, drank beer and talked about old times – the poetry and jazz concerts, the occasions he'd stayed with us just after our twins were born. I made him laugh by reminding him of the time an actress was reading some of his poems and, intro-ducing the one she was about to read, unwittingly proclaimed, 'Taken in Adultery by Vernon Scannell'! I also reminded Vernon of the time we read together one Sunday in Wales in what was then a dry county, and he persuaded me to take a local train with him to the neighbouring county so he could have a drink or two before returning just in time for what was a very spirited evening reading. We had many shared memories, which Vernon seemed to enjoy recalling, among them the weekend we'd come with my cousin Ted and his future wife Gill to stay with the Scannells at Folly Cottage, their aptly named house in Nether Compton, Dorset, strolling across the tall fields to the Griffin's Head, where we drank far too much of the deceptively strong local cider before staggering back for some much-needed food, as the sun sank behind the surrounding hills.

Vernon showed me some photos of himself in the ring, and took down an early collection of my own poems which he said he had been rereading and asked me to sign it. I was deeply touched. Despite how ill he was, he looked remarkably strong and was as articulate as ever, though his voice was a little hoarse and he was struggling to hide the discomfort, even pain, he was suffering – but he was still able to down a pint of brown ale. He seemed genuinely pleased I had come, and I found it hard to contain my emotion. Somehow it brought life (and death) into real focus and was a sharp reminder of where life's true values lay. I went away with two inscribed volumes of Vernon's more recent poems, and we corresponded regularly until he finally succumbed. His last, generous letter to me – a declaration of friendship, really – contained a copy of his last poem, 'Missing Things'; its poignant lines, a few of which I quote below, take me back to the meal we'd enjoyed in that kitchen, and the books on its shelves.

> Already I begin to miss the things
> I'll leave behind, like this calm evening sun
> which seems to smile at how the blackbird sings.
> There's something valedictory in the way
> my books gaze down on me from where they stand
> in disciplined disorder and display
> the same goodwill that well-wishers on land
> convey to troops who sail away to where
> great danger waits. Those books will miss the hand
> that turned the pages with great care…

Fortunately, Vernon's voice still speaks to us through the lines of many memorable poems, particularly those relating to his experiences in the Second World War, which haunted him all his life.

* * *

Back in the world of Michael Winner, all was as surreal as ever. His Christmas cards continued to be sent out early, more like adverts for his latest book than seasonal messages of goodwill – the cover of his book on one side, quotes from reviews on the other. One year, to vary things, he put a photo of himself with the Queen on the front, but the book cover still appeared inside. For his last-but-one book, I took him as a guest speaker to the *Daily Mail*'s annual Christmas lunch at the

Lancaster London Hotel in Hyde Park, where there were hundreds of guests and two other speakers, the journalist and television personality Rachel Johnson, and the BBC's war correspondent Kate Adie. Winner was to speak last. I have always had a good relationship with the *Mail* and have sold many serial rights to them over the years, so I was particularly anxious for Michael to be pleasant to people, but he wasn't. True, he was quite shaky by then, having been taken perilously ill in Barbados after eating raw oysters and been rushed back to the London Clinic in an air ambulance arranged by Philip Green, which had probably saved his life. He'd remained in hospital for a worryingly long time with a horrific wasting disease of his left leg which specialists struggled to identify. He had undergone numerous life-saving operations and been pronounced clinically dead on several occasions. Miraculously, his leg was saved and he survived against all the odds to shout again, though he walked with difficulty, using a stick. Geraldine and Dinah, ministering angels, had been with him around the clock, and again during his all-too-frequent follow-up visits to the clinic. Amazingly, through it all, he'd still managed, with Geraldine's help, to produce his *Sunday Times* column, and even to criticise the hospital food. Leopards don't change their spots.

*When it came to his annual Christmas card, Michael Winner
certainly knew how to plug his latest book.*

At that *Mail* lunch he was at his most restless and tetchy, and Ed Victor, Geraldine and I did our best to keep him under control, but it wasn't easy, especially as the meal was running late and the service was unusually slow. He kept threatening to leave and told his fellow speakers that they were not to go on for more than ten minutes or he would 'walk'. Rachel Johnson, who was sitting next to him, later told me he'd got her so flustered she could hardly speak, which is saying something for a member of the Johnson clan. Wittily introduced by Gyles Brandreth, and helped onto the stage by Geraldine, Michael launched into his usual star-studded speech, attacking Esther Rantzen, with whom he'd had a run-in on her TV show, and sprinkling his overlong speech with four-letter words, which some of the audience – out for a jolly Christmas lunch – didn't appreciate. He was far from his best, and even his entertaining Hollywood stories about Marlon Brando, Burt Lancaster, Charles Bronson, Sophia Loren and others seemed to fall flat. The following week, Sandra Parsons, the paper's literary editor, phoned to say the editor had received letters of complaint and wasn't pleased. Sandra is not only a superb editor but also the most delightful of people, and I was sorry to have been inadvertently responsible for those unfortunate repercussions.

By the time Michael came to his last two books, I had to ask him not to phone other people in the office because he was so rude and aggressive. I told him he could be as offensive to me as he liked, but not to staff who couldn't answer back. He laughed, and almost apologised, and peace reigned for a while, but then he was off again on some tirade or other. At this stage in my journey I had my own imprint within Iain Dale's politically orientated company, Biteback, and after a while Iain, who can himself be intemperate, felt, understandably, that our staff should not be subjected to Winner's outbursts, and wrote him a full-blooded letter saying his behaviour wouldn't be tolerated and more or less telling him not to cross our threshold again. I waited for the explosion, but when Michael finally responded – from Switzerland, where he was spending Christmas – it wasn't in the way we expected. Here's how his email (in caps, of course) started:

DEAR IAIN

I WISH YOU ALL A HAPPY NEW YEAR.

I GREATLY ENJOYED YOUR ROBUST CORRESPOND-
ENCE. I WAS ONLY DISAPPOINTED YOU FAILED TO
SAY I'D KICKED YOUR DOG AND EMPTIED THE WATER
FROM YOUR GOLDFISH BOWL.

He then went on to ask a few polite questions about his royalty statement. And that was that. (At least Iain hadn't wrestled him to the
ground as he did an anti-nuclear protestor who'd got his placard in
the way of the cameras as an author of Iain's, Damian McBride, was
giving a live TV interview on the Brighton seafront for his whistle-
blowing new book.)

After announcing his engagement to Geraldine, who'd been a girlfriend of his when he was a very young film director and she an actress
and ballet dancer, Michael added, 'I've told Geraldine that it took me
seventy-two years to get engaged, so she's not to hold her breath for
the marriage.' Nevertheless, four years later, in September 2011, they
tied the knot at Chelsea Town Hall, with Michael and Shakira Caine
as witnesses. Michael had seemed lonely before Geraldine came back
into his life, though in the time I knew him there had been several
girlfriends. He didn't like to be without a lady at his side, especially as he regularly went off on luxurious holidays and enjoyed trying
out country hotels and restaurants at the weekend. His house, too,
was very large, and although he had staff and Dinah remained a good
friend and confidante, and would sometimes accompany him, she had
a husband and family to look after.

In the same year as his marriage, we published our seventh book
with Michael, *Tales I Never Told* – though you can bet that he had! He
was still making periodic visits to the London Clinic, some requiring
him to stay in, and was clearly struggling. He was especially friendly
during that late period of his life, and we would have long phone conversations in which he told me he was dying and going to be bankrupt.
I suggested he cut down on the private jets and get a bus pass. I also
told him that if he'd kept to his Jewish roots and not eaten oysters

(strictly non-kosher), he would be in better health. He'd laugh and stick to his old ways. He was, though, trying to sell his house, or so he said, and when it was sold after his death to Robbie Williams, I read that the singer had called in an American healer to exorcise Michael's spirit, as his wife was spooked by what she believed was his presence watching her and silently criticising her as she changed the decor of his Victorian mansion. I couldn't help thinking that if Michael had really been there she'd have heard him all right!

We planned two more books, one being *The Hymie Joke Book*, which drew on the often very funny Jewish jokes he'd been appending to his *Sunday Times* column. There's chutzpah for you. Here's a typical Hymie joke: Hymie's friend goes to confession. 'I'm ninety-two years old, got a wife of seventy, children and grandchildren. Yesterday I picked up two college girls hitchhiking and had sex with each of them three times.' The priest asks: 'Are you sorry for your sins?' Abe: 'What sins?' Priest: 'What kind of Catholic are you?' Abe: 'I'm Jewish.' Priest: 'Then why are you telling me all this?' Abe: 'I'm ninety-two years old. I'm telling everybody.' The Hymie jokes inspired quite a cult following, and the book appeared just before Michael died, but he was too frail to promote it.

The second book we'd contracted never came to fruition, but the following email from Michael gives a taste of what might have been:

TRAWL THROUGH MY DIARIES WOULD SHOW WHO I'D SEEN AND WHEN FOR EXAMPLE 1962 I INTERVIEWED GLENDA JACKSON TO PLAY A HAMBURGER DUMP WAITRESS, CHOSE SOMEONE ELSE THAT WOULD LEAD TO GLENDA STORIES. I HAVE WELL OVER 50 YEARS OF DIARIES, REJECTED SPICE GIRL FOR WICKED LADY, MY COMMENTS ON HER WHEN WE MET, ALL A REASON FOR TELLING MORE SHOWBIZ TALES. ACTUALLY MY DIARIES GO BACK TO CAMBRIDGE AND BEFORE WHEN I TRAVELLED THRU USA ON STUDENT TOUR, LOTSA VERY FUNNY STUFF AS I HAVE ALWAYS PROVIDED. RE-GARDS MW

Curiously, when I asked to see his diaries after his death, I was told there weren't any. Could he really have been inventing it?

Michael died in January 2013. I phoned the house to express my condolences and find out when the funeral would be, and was informed it would be the next day, 'since in the Jewish religion burial occurs very soon after death'. I was surprised, because he'd religiously avoided being associated publicly with anything Jewish and never wanted to be interviewed by Jewish papers, although he occasionally allowed me to persuade him. After his death, I also discovered that he had quietly given donations to a synagogue and a school in Israel for troubled children that his parents had been involved with, once taking time to visit it when he was filming there with Jenny Seagrove, who became a long-time partner. Evidently, a grave in the Orthodox Jewish cemetery in Willesden had been paid for and kept for his mother, who for some reason was buried in France, so that was where Michael was to be buried – ironic really, since he was born in Willesden and it was hardly his beat in more recent years. It was even more ironic in that his grave turned out to be just a few yards from that of my great-uncle and -aunt, Sam and Rosie Snowman, the delightful old couple we used to see walking arm in arm along Finchley Road. I suspect they are not the permanent bedfellows Michael would have chosen... nor they him!

Dinah later told me that when it looked as if Michael was approaching the end, a rabbi was called to the house. It was felt that if he was going to officiate at Michael's funeral, it would be helpful to have met him. I gather the rabbi's initial response was, 'In the Jewish religion we don't do last rites,' but he came, and when Michael (who had rallied slightly) became aware of what was happening, he was furious, saying, 'Get that man out of my house.' True to form to the last.

When Carole and I arrived for Michael's funeral, I was approached by Bob Tyrer, executive editor of the *Sunday Times*, with whom I'd dealt and become friendly over the years, and various reporters from that paper, hoping I could explain what the ceremony would entail, and I did my best to fill them in. As we moved from the prayer hall, where the ceremony starts, following the coffin to the grave, Carole and I found ourselves walking beside Michael Parkinson and fell into an easy conversation about Winner. As we passed my father's grave, I pointed it out to him, and he in turn started telling me about his own parents and family background. It was an intimate and affecting moment.

Later, I told Michael that when we had first suggested to Winner that he should try to appear on his talk show, he'd said, 'Parkinson won't have me' (though in the end he did). Michael smiled at this, and answered intriguingly, 'One day I'll tell you why.' I await the day.

28

THE WORST OF TIMES

Dannie Abse was always a reluctant traveller, though happy to go to Cardiff when the Bluebirds were playing at home (frustrating as that experience usually was) and to spend time with Joan in the house they'd bought in Ogmore-by-Sea. We had stayed there several times, and although we tried to persuade Dannie to visit us in France, he always found some excuse, smiling and dodging our invitation – until, that is, the summer of 2002. We had just published an unusual novel of his, *The Strange Case of Dr Simmonds & Dr Glas*, inspired by an old Swedish classic. Set in 1950s London, it was a luminous story of love, infatuation and deceit, and had received marvellous reviews. I think Joan – always Dannie's guiding light and the mistress of his conscience – felt we should all celebrate together in France, and he finally agreed.

We set off for the airport, just the three of us since Carole had gone ahead and would be meeting us with the car at Caen. We arrived early at Stansted and, as we had a little time to kill, I took Dannie and Joan into the large Past Times shop to show them the range of our titles stocked there. Now defunct, it was then a popular chain and a major customer of ours, particularly for titles in the 'Strangest' series (*Cricket's Strangest Matches*, *Law's Strangest Cases* and so on), which they ordered and reordered in very large numbers. Seeing the gift-book style of their stock, Dannie had the idea of compiling an anthology of love poems; when we came back I put his proposal to the Past Times buyer, Susanna Geoghegan, and she went for it. Already a profitable trip for us all!

Having met up with Carole, we suggested that since we were so close they might like to visit the Normandy landing beaches, but Joan recoiled at the idea. The look of alarm – almost panic – in her eyes was a reminder of just how deep her feelings were about war, just how abhorrent she found it. We drove in the other direction, to our more tranquil house.

That week together was a wonderful time. I remember Dannie reading to Joan in the garden poems by Sidney Keyes, whose work he admired. Considered one of the outstanding poets of the Second World War, Keyes was killed in 1943, a month before his 21st birthday, while covering his platoon's retreat in Tunisia. Hearing this very young man's poems read by Dannie in the stillness of a Normandy evening was an uplifting experience. It seemed as if Bloomsbury had come to Normandy.

Late one afternoon, I returned to the house to find Carole and the Abses in high spirits, Dannie saying, 'You know, I've a feeling there's some good news about my book.' After a few minutes he came clean and told me that *Dr Simmonds* had been longlisted for the Booker Prize. It was a Saturday, and Dannie had phoned his daughter Keren, herself a keen Cardiff City supporter, to see whether their team had won that afternoon. She had been highly relieved to hear from him, breaking the news and shouting, 'Dad, everyone's trying to talk to you and the trade press want to speak to Jeremy.' Stupidly, we'd forgotten to leave our number. Now there was a real cause for celebration, and we sat on the hammock in our garden drinking champagne as the sun set. Unfortunately, Dannie didn't win the Booker, but the very fact of being on the longlist boosted our sales significantly and we had an immediate scale-out from Waterstones and repeat orders all round. We also managed to sell the US rights on the back of it. When the book was shortlisted for the Wingate Prize, the sales got a further boost. Since we weren't really publishers of fiction, that was an exciting and rewarding time.

There was one minor let-down in that very special weekend with the Abses. Invariably, when Carole and I went to eat in nearby Honfleur, a striking-looking man with a black cloak and long white hair would appear, moving from table to table and introducing himself as 'the poet of Honfleur'. He had a charming manner and would easily seduce lady diners into buying a volume of his poems – usually love poems illustrated in full colour – especially after he had looked into their eyes and recited to them. They never struck me as being very good, but he claimed to have known Prévert and Aznavour and we generally exchanged a friendly word or two, Carole sometimes feeling obliged to buy a book despite my protestations. I was so looking forward to stopping him mid-flow and introducing him to Dannie and Dannie to him as 'the poet of Golders Green', but for some reason he didn't appear that evening. How disappointing!

*   *   *

We only went twice to BookExpo, the American Booksellers Association's annual book fair. The first time was in 1981 to Anaheim on the outskirts of Los Angeles, when we made a family holiday of it and also took the opportunity to stay with our old *Goon Show* friend, Max Geldray, who'd settled and married there and was working at the Betty Ford Center. He was still in close touch with Peter Sellers and saw him when he came to film in LA. There was a lot of catching up to do, during which I convinced Max to write a memoir of his years in Paris performing with Django and other jazz greats, and of his *Goon Show* days and friendship with Peter. We called it *Goon with the Wind*.

Our second BookExpo was in 2005 in New York, which was far more productive from a business point of view. In some ways, unlike Frankfurt, it had a party air about it – partly because booksellers seemed to hold the high ground, with publishers presenting their upcoming wares to them rather than to other publishers, though not exclusively so, and there were many launches, presentations and celebrations. For me, it was valuable to meet a number of smaller US publishers who never came to Frankfurt, such as the Santa Monica Press, from whom I bought an appealing book, *French for Le Snob*, which fitted nicely into our list alongside *Sixty Million Frenchmen Can't be Wrong!*, which had been a surprising hit for us. Amidst the razzmatazz there were characters galore, including one swashbuckling publisher who tried to sell us several 'hot' Hollywood biographies that would have had us in the libel courts for years, and who also tried to cajole Carole and me into nightclubbing with him. I did my best to keep my feet on the ground, especially since I was in the middle of considering a switch from Anova to Laurence Orbach's Quarto Group, and Laurence, who had an apartment in New York, was in town and wanting to meet up and talk.

When the fair ended, I visited various publishers and rights directors, and then we went to stay with our close friends Jan and Lloyd Constantine, both high-flying lawyers. Carole and I had first met Jan when she was sweet eighteen and had come to London with her grandmother (a friend of my grandmother). It's strange that she should have ended up in the publishing world too, as an expert in intellectual property and employment law, working at one time as the in-house lawyer for first Macmillan (Robert Maxwell) and then News Corporation (Rupert Murdoch), before being appointed general counsel to the US Authors Guild. When we first met Lloyd, he was representing impoverished clients in civil rights and liberties cases, but subsequently became one of America's foremost antitrust litigators, with his own highly successful law firm. As the lead counsel in a class action against Visa/MasterCard, he won the largest antitrust settlement in US legal history, later writing a book about this and about his dramatic experiences as senior adviser to the Governor of New York. They are both the kind of lawyers you would always want on your side, as I discovered when we published an anthology of that most anthologised poet in the English language, 'Anon'. It seemed harmless enough, except that the author of one of the poems turned out to be not so anon, but an American writer with an aggressive lawyer who came out all guns blazing. Fortunately, Jan was there to return the fire on our behalf.

After the exciting hustle of New York, and a few days in the country with the Constantines, where Lloyd and I had our usual battle on the tennis court, we returned to London. Three urgent messages were waiting for us: one from Robert Kirby, Dannie's agent, and two from Keren Abse, all of them almost a week old. With a sense of foreboding,

I dialled Keren's number, to hear her forlorn voice stumbling the words, 'Mum's been killed.' Surely not – it wasn't possible! We listened aghast as Keren explained that Dannie and Joan had been coming back from a poetry reading in Wales and that as Dannie, who was driving, cautiously joined the M4 from the slip road, a car going at reckless speed had crashed into them. Joan had been killed instantly, Dannie had survived, though he had several fractured ribs and was badly cut and bruised. I learned that the funeral had not yet taken place, that there was to be an autopsy, and that the other driver, a young woman, was being charged with dangerous driving. Dannie, Keren told me, was out of hospital and at home with the close family around him.

Carole and I stared at each other, shaking in disbelief. I asked Keren if we could see Dannie, and after consulting him she said we should come round. Dannie well knew that there was nothing one can say in such circumstances, and he stopped us as we tried to express some comforting words. Even in his distressed state, he was aware of how much we loved them both, and our presence there was sufficient. He looked like a ghost and was covered in bruises and cuts, but his real agony was not physical. He could hardly talk, and when he did he kept muttering, 'It should have been me.'

The funeral took place a week or so later, and with Dannie's permission we attended, for apart from us only the family was present. As the coffin was carried into the prayer hall, Dannie said to us enigmatically, 'Joan's not there, you know,' and I could never bring myself to ask him exactly what he meant.

In the period that followed, Dannie was a virtual hermit, not wanting to go anywhere and not able to write, for he had lost his muse. Gradually, we managed to get him to come to us on Friday evenings for an informal meal of fish and chips, and I'd collect him in the car, driving very slowly at his nervous request. Little by little, he started to enter the world again. Carole encouraged him to talk about Joan, realising how important it was that he did. The following November, the Abse family arranged a 'Remembering Joan Abse' evening at Pavlova House in Highgate. Dannie felt unable to speak, and I was touched when he asked me to do so, which I did, drawing on some of the memories Carole and I cherished, and trying to inject a little humour too, since besides all her other qualities as a woman and as a scholar, Joan loved to laugh.

Dannie never really recovered – how could he? – but slowly, over time, he began to write again, movingly and powerfully, though it was about a year before he brought himself to read again in public, and that was for the launch of a book of his poems, *Running Late*, which had been in the pipeline before Joan's death. The launch was at Joseph's Bookshop in Temple Fortune, an oasis of culture which sadly closed its doors in March 2018 following the retirement of its inspiring proprietor, Michael Joseph. The small restaurant that led into the bookshop, which Michael had run successfully for twenty-five years, was an intimate venue for stimulating talks and book events, and he and his warm and lively wife Maureen were welcoming hosts. It was the ideal place for Dannie to start reading again, and the fact that Michael had lined up the actress Eleanor Bron to accompany him, reading some of his often very funny autobiographical writing, must have helped Dannie enormously.

After months of inactivity, Dannie started to write a book that he called *The Presence*, a kind of diary of the year following Joan's death, but also a memoir in which he skilfully reached back into memories, stories, anecdotes of their life together from the earliest days – the Then and the Now. Despite the painful subject, there was a good deal of humour mixed with the tears. It had been therapeutic for Dannie to work on the book, but it proved to be a great deal more than that, and among the finest things he ever wrote. He had shown me passages as he was writing, and as soon as it was finished he gave me the complete manuscript, asking my opinion as to whether he should publish it. There was no doubt in my mind that he should. But, as Dannie knew, I was on the point of ending my association with Anova Books, so there was no real possibility of my publishing his book, much as I would have loved to. However, Tony Whittome, Dannie's loyal long-time editor at Hutchinson, took it and it was a big success – a bittersweet success, Dannie always felt, given its genesis. Following its publication and the remarkable reviews and coverage it received (which included both newspaper and radio serialisations), letters poured in to Dannie from people who had also been bereaved, telling him how much they had identified with his feelings and thanking him for the help his book had given them.

Gradually, Dannie started to regain his vitality, though the shadows always hung over him. We tried hard to get him to join us in France, but he wouldn't leave home. He and I sometimes went to a local deli we both liked where we enjoyed a salt beef sandwich together, as we used to when he was working near our office in town. On one of our visits, Dannie suddenly confided, 'It would have been our wedding anniversary tonight,' and as I started to say how privileged I felt to be spending that evening with him, he said quietly, lightening the mood, 'I'll tell you one thing. If Joan had been here, the evening would have ended differently!' We went home like two schoolboys, smiling.

*   *   *

Leaving Anova, as I did in August 2006, meant leaving our own company, Robson Books, behind, and for me it was a highly charged, emotional time. In some ways I felt ashamed, feeling I was betraying so much and so many, but the reality was that in the circumstances it was time. In my last hour in the small office I inhabited, which had come to seem like a cell, I looked around the shelves and was reminded of the many parts of my life contained within the covers of other people's books – none of them strangers, many of them friends. Alan Coren's name stared from so many of them that on an impulse, feeling blue, I dialled his number, trying to rein back my escaping emotions. We talked about future books in my new home, wherever that was, and he made it clear that he would always want me to be his publisher. (Alan could be tough, but he was also kind and loyal.) We also talked about getting the rights back for earlier titles, which we eventually did. Some years previously we had published an *Alan Coren Omnibus*, but he'd written so much since then that we decided we would work towards another 'Collected Coren' for the following year, as well as a new collection, and I left for the small drinks party Anova had sprung on me with Alan's cheering words in my ears. He had a rather romantic, old-fashioned attitude to publishing which chimed with my own. For him, publishing companies were 'Houses' and editors were 'Editors' with a capital E. I liked that.

Alan and Anne always spent the summer in the south of France, where they had a house, and it was there, perhaps bitten by an insect, that he contracted a terrifying flesh-eating disease called necrotising fasciitis. Anne, a doctor, had rushed him to the hospital in Nice but quickly got him back to England, where he remained very seriously ill in hospital for quite some time. I've never been sure how well Alan really was when he finally left hospital and started to write again, and to take part in *The News Quiz*, of which he was such a star. As well as making others laugh, he was able to laugh about himself and his illness, if wryly, as his *Punch* colleague and friend Michael Bywater recalled in an article in *The Observer*. In response to an invitation from Bywater, Alan had replied that he had this dreadful illness: 'All I lost was my left armpit,' he wrote. 'Got big hole now, perfect for carrying Walther PPK 9mm should Daniel Craig chuck in the sponge. Also got ulcerative co-litis, so, director, please note, scenes should not be longer than ten secs.' But he said he'd 'cork up' for the party and come. In that article Michael Bywater also gave a wonderful picture of Alan, the great *Punch* editor:

His word was law. Although theoretically a triumvirate with individual powers of veto, Coren made the running. I once made the mistake of writing a riff about a woman with a vibrator. He wouldn't have it. The joke was, he said, structurally illogical. I argued. He shouted. I argued some more. He shouted louder. Soon the entire editorial staff had gathered in the doorway of his office as he stood, legs akimbo, like some empurpled Mussolini, bellowing with righteous anger. I couldn't resist it and took another poke. Alan swelled to twice his normal size and went scarlet. Hitting a volume that can't have been heard since Soviet Russia set off the fifty-megaton Tsar Bomba, he declared that if I 'argued the fucking toss any more I am going to get aaanngryyyy'. There was a stunned silence, then a swell of applause, after which things returned to normal. Or as normal as they ever got.

When we had lunch together in a fish restaurant near his house in Primrose Hill (by which time I was fully established in my new 'House' in the guise of JR Books, of which more later), Alan certainly seemed to be driving at full throttle, his conversation as scintillating as ever. It was time, we both felt, for another book, and he started putting together what became his last one for us, *69 for 1* – the title Alan's, of course. In an email dated 1 June 2007 and timed at 13.26 he wrote, '69 for 1 – first time I've seen it written down. It looks good. Just came to me in a flash, a good sign in itself. Mail me back, ever A.' Then, at 17.30, came another email:

> It gets better. Not only 69 (my age) for 1 (me), not only the *soixante-neuf petit frisson* to catch the Waterstones browser, but also 69 pieces for one book – I just worked it out, 69 of my shorter pieces will come out at around 50,000 words – say 190pp. Cover price £69? Ever, Alan.

As the editor of a magazine that published the country's best cartoonists and employed top graphic designers, Alan always had his own ideas when it came to book jackets and he wasn't easy to please. I gave this to one of our favourite freelance designers, and he came up trumps, Alan emailing:

> I think Andy Wadsworth's cover rough is terrific – EXACTLY what I'd envisaged. In fact, I'd treat the rough as the finish, because it's so strong as it is. I really like the green on green lettering, as if cut in the turf, I like the brute force of the b/w scoreboard and the cheery blue sky behind it – all spot on. Ever, Alan.

As always he produced his word-perfect blurb, starting with a reference to his illness, then continuing in his usual knockabout way, obliquely referring to pieces in the book:

> Having taken up his pen again after contracting a rare illness, Alan Coren found that the world had changed little in his absence. Threatened by Josef Mengele's poisoned chickens, children still turned to Winston Churchill to save them from school dinners, Clark Gable snuggled, as ever, against the bristly chest of his lover Errol Flynn...

His blurb ended with the sentence: 'For that is the world in which Alan Coren, by a stroke of luck, lives.'

However, as the book progressed through the summer, I felt there was something odd. Alan spent an unusually long time checking the proofs, and didn't seem to be taking his normal care, more or less leaving it to our proofreader, and not wanting to double-check the revises. Also, in one phone call he said, 'Jeremy, whatever happens to me you will publish the book, won't you?' I somehow found the voice to reassure him.

What I didn't know was that he had been diagnosed with cancer, and his death followed very quickly, just as we were going to press. Awful though it was, we felt we had to change the tense of that last sentence in his blurb, and the word 'live' to 'lived'. Naturally, the papers were full of tributes to Alan's genius as editor, broadcaster, writer and humorist, for he was, in the words of the *Sunday Times*, 'the funniest writer in Britain today ... the undisputed guvnor'. A rather more personal tribute reached me in an email from Tom McCormack, whose St Martin's Press had published several of Alan's books:

> As you did, I appreciated his writing and his presence. I recall the gathering at your home with Alan, Harry Secombe and others as the paradigm of what wit and sophistication can bring to a dinner party ... and then the book party here at Central Park West. It was supposed to be cocktails and hors d'oeuvres and then a few of us were to go out to dinner. But nobody would leave! Luckily the caterer had brought platters of hors d'oeuvres the size of billiard balls, there was plenty left over, so sometime between nine and ten we had the platters out again and dinner was right here, munching on leftovers. Alan did indeed mean wonderful times wherever he went.

*   *   *

The saga that follows is one I find painful to revisit. Alan's funeral was at Hampstead Cemetery, just down the road from where the Corens lived for many years, not a Jewish place of burial but a tolerant and broad-church one, where Alan had long since reserved a space, rather fancying the thought of being in the eternal company of Marie Lloyd, one of the other colourful occupants. (He had, in fact, written two emotive pieces about 'the Queen of the Music Hall', enchanted to have discovered that she lay some two hundred yards from his home. 'Tonight,' he had written, 'I shall put on "A Little of What You Fancy", turn up the volume, and open the window for her to hear.') A rabbi officiated in what was a deeply affecting ceremony, and a great many people came to pay their last respects. Later, at the *shiva*, the customary Jewish prayers at the mourners' home, I chatted to Alan's very friendly son Giles and told him that when he, his sister Victoria and Anne felt ready, I would love to get together with them to work on the new 'Collected Coren', which Alan and I had been discussing and which I hoped they would consider editing and introducing. I mentioned it again on another occasion but refrained from pressing the case as I did not want to appear insensitive while feelings were still so raw.

It was at an informal supper in our kitchen that I brought up the book idea again to Anne Coren, and there was a pause before she said, 'Well, you will have seen Victoria's letter, I imagined you had asked me here to talk about it.' That certainly was not the reason we'd invited her – and in any case I had not received Victoria's letter. However, a copy came through our letter box early the next afternoon, Sunday. It was a long letter, in which Victoria explained that Canongate (her publisher) had written to her agent and made a substantial offer for a 'Collected Alan Coren'. She and Giles felt very bad about it, given our long relationship and family friendship, but they didn't want to put me in a position of having to compete, and hoped I'd appreciate that they wanted to do their best for their father, and so on.

They obviously wished to accept the offer, but wanted to know how I felt before responding. I realised it had been a difficult letter for Victoria to write and I read it several times before suggesting we meet to talk about it. Victoria had asked for my feelings and there was no hiding the fact that I was stunned by the prospect of someone who didn't even know Alan publishing his last book, after all we'd gone through together, and that – yes – I was hurt and saddened and it felt like a kind of betrayal, the more so since this was the book that Alan and I had planned together. I tried to take comfort in the thought that their father had received many such approaches over the years, and never once had he considered them.

Giles and Victoria came to the office and we discussed it at some length, and I ended up swallowing my feelings and offering to top the offer they'd had. But their minds were made up and they went with Canongate. They did, though, invite me to participate in the service of thanksgiving for Alan's life and work, which they'd arranged at St Bride's Church in Fleet Street – to read a piece of Alan's and say a few words 'to represent all those years of working together'. Naturally, I accepted.

Referring to the fact that the service was in a church, Victoria wrote, 'I hope you won't find it a bit peculiar.' They'd wanted, she said, a church reflecting her dad's Englishness, and St Bride's was perfect because it was near Bouverie Street, where he worked for all those years, and was considered a journalists' church. She went on to tell me that they 'were understanding and open-minded' about Alan 'being born Jewish'… I felt as if she wanted my approval, but it was certainly not for me to reason why or judge.

Everything was carefully planned and the timing extremely tight. I chose to read an autobiographical piece Alan had written for *My Oxford*, cut and trimmed to fit the timing, leaving a minute or so to lead in with a few personal words. Arriving a little early, Carole and I crept into a small café around the corner, where we found Sandi Toksvig, who was also speaking, with her partner. Sandi told me she'd never been so nervous in her life, and I felt that if *she* was nervous then I was entitled to be, too. We chatted for a few minutes then made our way to the church, which was already packed with many famous and familiar faces. I was given instructions to bow to the cross when I went up to speak (which, without meaning any offence, I could not do), and to be careful not to trip on the steps. I sat with Carole at the front, next to David Frost and his wife, waiting my turn. Following the bidding prayer and a hymn, Christopher Matthew spoke, and then, after some music and the reading of a Shakespeare sonnet, it was my turn. I made my way slowly towards the altar, tripped on the steps, winked at the large photograph of Alan that faced the congregation, and did my bit.

Shortly after, a copy of the Canongate book arrived in the post with a warm note from the Corens thanking me for my words at the service. The volume was handsome, but I didn't really need to open it, for it contained pieces we had published over the years with which I was well acquainted. However, for Alan's sake I put it carefully on the shelf where all thirty-six of his books that we'd published had place of honour. I felt they could hold their own.

I miss Alan, our walks on the Heath, the extraordinary excuses he'd come up with when he didn't want to go somewhere, the novels he never wrote (and perhaps never intended to). He and Anne might even have come with us again to our house in Normandy, as they did soon after we'd bought it, Alan falling asleep in the hammock in the garden after driving in an impossibly short time from Calais. And I would have liked him to be here when I started writing poetry again after so many years, for he was continually asking me when I was going to, and though he might have been critical, it would have been the critical voice of a friend. And perhaps he might have written that 'auto-biography' we'd contracted him for.

29

BLUES IN THE PARK

If the emphasis in this saga has shifted from poetry to publishing, it is for the not-so-simple reason that for a very, very long period the poetry had dried up – scribbled lines here and there from time to time, perhaps, but nothing focused on or followed through. There were occasional readings for special events – such as the tribute concert for the dazzling – if anarchic – saxophonist Joe Harriott. That was at the invitation of Michael Garrick, who wrote afterwards, 'It was quite like old times. "Blues for the Lonely" [a very early set-to-music poem of mine I'd recorded with Mike and Joe] sounded v. fine and somehow extremely appropriate.' Much more recently, in 2009, there had been a tribute concert at the Queen Elizabeth Hall for the trumpeter Ian Carr, where I joined with Michael again to read a poem he'd set to music and which we'd often performed with the remarkable Ian. In the years since our many concerts together, Ian had won a wide following as leader of the jazz-rock group Nucleus, and the hall was packed, with the veteran bassist Coleridge Goode sitting in the front row, and people queuing to pay their respects. As well as these, there were several events following Vernon Scannell's death – one at the ICA with various poets reading and Michael playing solo on a keyboard between poems, and another – a poetry and jazz gig – in Aylesbury, where Vernon had taught. 'A happy reunion, indeed,' wrote Michael in his autobiography, 'bringing us all together, Vernon, writer par excellence, now sadly missing. Forty-eight years ago, I was lucky enough to have been asked to contribute to the first of such evenings and we played to large audiences. For me,' he continued wistfully, 'it represented ideal circumstances for honest, intimate, and largely unexpected sharing of language of the heart.'

I sensed that Michael, always so positive, was trying to draw me back into the arena, but for all these excursions, my poetry cupboard remained bare as I continued to experience what I would jokingly refer to as 'the longest writing block in literary history'. For me, however, it was far from being a joke, and I kept thinking, 'One day, one day...' while staring at the jottings and scribbles I could no longer read. And then, one day indeed, like the first primrose after a hard winter, a line came and started playing in my head. I wrote it down quickly, before it faded. Then, to my surprise, another followed, and I set to work on it, compulsively, teasing the words out. After several days' struggle, there it was, a poem called 'Now and Then' which starts:

> I had opinions then on
> many things, strongly felt, or
> so I thought, and springing hotly
> from the tongue, unsought...

Another poem, 'Final Set', swiftly followed, drawing on the imagery of tennis, my boyhood passion, but acknowledging the passing years,

> I have to say
> The serves aren't what
> they were, the lobs
> fall short, the drives
> that grazed the lines
> now dent the net.
> The volley's limp, inept.

I was coming up to a 'special' birthday, and perhaps that was the 'now or never' stimulus I needed. Who knows? The ways of the muse are mysterious indeed. Carole arranged a party at home, and instead of the speech people were calling for, I read the two poems ('It's your birthday, your party, do what you f***ing like,' were the encouraging words of the irrepressible Ms Lipman). It felt good, I felt whole again.

* * *

It's always been a wonder to me, the way poems gestate, and how quite traumatic experiences may stare you in the face yet remain buried in the unconscious for many years, perhaps for ever. When my father died in 1990, I thought the poems would flow, for, as I have shown, he was a significant force in my early life. But they didn't.

We were on holiday in France when I got the news that he'd been rushed into hospital with a severe heart attack, the phone call that we all dread ('grief just a phone call away' as I later put it). I'd spoken to him on the phone only a few days earlier, when, quite calmly, he told me he'd been for all kinds of tests for his heart (for he suspected something) but had been given the all-clear. He'd had a debilitating stroke some years earlier, but never any heart problems. 'I think the specialists are wrong,' he told me, and sadly he was right, as he invariably was when it came to diagnoses.

Rushing to Nice Airport that early summer morning, as the sea eased in and out uncaringly, I'd managed to get on the first plane to London and sat hunched in the cabin, isolated as never before, staring blankly at the racing clouds, pencil in hand... but the lines that came to me were not my own, but those of Dylan Thomas: 'Do not go gentle into that good night'.

When, an eternity later, I finally reached University College Hospital, I ran down the corridors to the intensive care unit, feeling that every second mattered, to find my mother and my brother David sitting in pale silence around the bed where my father lay propped up, with tubes everywhere. Only the life-support system, I was quickly informed, was keeping him breathing, and they were all waiting for my permission to switch it off. My mother and brother had already given theirs.

I stroked my father's hand and spoke to him urgently, sure he could hear me, feeling like an executioner. 'Rage, rage against the dying of the light,' I wanted to tell him, but to no avail. My mother, still the good doctor's wife who'd cared for him heroically since his stroke, was telling me she'd always promised never to allow him to become a vegetable, and this was the moment of truth. She and my brother, quite a bit younger than me but far more in command of himself and the situation than I was, impressed on me that there was no real option. As a lifestyle coach, David's training had perhaps helped prepare him for this moment, though it is hard to imagine that anything really could. Two doctors, who suddenly appeared as if on cue, endorsed what they were saying. And so it came to pass. But it was some twenty-four years and only after my mother died and I began to go through their effects that the lines began to come, sparked by small things, details, as my mind began to filter them – his walking sticks and cloth cap hanging in the hall, his old accordion lying unwanted beneath the lonely piano, an old cigar box, his patients' medical details filed away confidentially in a cabinet. And those things led to memories of much earlier days, too, when he was a GP and I a young schoolboy, a time when he had a dispensary at the back of his surgery where he mixed his own medicines in giant oval jars similar to those used for gobstoppers in the local sweet shop, and I would watch him.

Finally, I picked up my pencil and started to write. Was it that life, and the reality of death when it faced you head-on, had been too potent, too real, for poems? I'd never thought so – indeed, I had imagined that poetry fed on them. In the end, as was to happen with my mother too, though more immediately, it did, yet not when I expected it to, and not in the way I'd expected. But is it not always the unexpected that produces the poetry? Here are the final lines of 'A Doctor's Call', one of the poems I finally wrote about my father:

> Then, fragile years later, on one indelible
> day, his own faltering heart finally gave way.
> Dismayed, I found myself surveying the drips
> and tubes and the frightening battery of
> machines they tried to save him with, and
> thought back to those bottled cures of his.
> Who knows, they may just have done the trick.

* * *

The publishing, meanwhile, continued. I was now working (as JR Books) within Laurence Orbach's Quarto Group and was shortly to join Iain Dale's Biteback (as the Robson Press). I should explain that part of the original Robson Books deal with Chrysalis prevented me from using my own name in the event of my leaving; but with my move to Biteback in mind, I managed to renegotiate this and reclaim my name, though it seemed sensible to vary its usage slightly to avoid confusion (at one London Book Fair all three of 'my' imprints were displayed, which confused even me!).

Iain and I got on well, part of the strength of this new combination deriving from the fact that our interests and tastes could not be more different – Iain being steeped in the political world with extensive contacts, as a result of which Biteback has become a leading political publisher. On top of this, the LBC radio programme he hosted every weekday with great aplomb and expertise had increased his reputation. My interests, as any reader of this book will know by now, lay in other directions. Poetry is something Iain is decidedly not interested in and he would reach for his metaphorical gun whenever it was mentioned (it became an open joke). However, in his second-in-command, James Stephens, Iain had a particularly able, literary-minded associate with wide publishing experience on whom he relied to an increasing extent, and a meticulous first-class editor in Olivia Beattie, who was particularly helpful to me when producing the final manuscript of my most recent book of poems, as she has been with this book. It made for a strong and friendly team.

I moved quickly to establish the Robson Press list alongside Iain's essentially political one, and I remain proud of many of the books we published. Some, by such authors as Peter Brookes, Ann Treneman, Bel Mooney and Frederic Raphael, I have already mentioned, but there were also some new departures, such as Ivan Fallon's widely acclaimed book on the financial crisis, *Black Horse Ride* (which came via Vivienne Schuster at Curtis Brown), and a book Ivan subsequently brought me, on which he had collaborated: *A Bazaar Life*, the autobiography of (Lord) David Alliance. It is the truly remarkable story of a man who came to this country from Iran as a penniless youth, sleeping rough on the streets, who became one of Britain's wealthiest and most charitable men, establishing a major business school in Manchester and being instrumental in the secret airlift of Iran's dwindling Jewish community to Israel. I enjoyed working, too, with the great Russian violinist Viktoria Mullova and the celebrated Chinese chef Ken Hom on their respective biographies. Viktoria, who had fled to the West in 1983 after winning the gold medal in the Tchaikovsky Competition, famously leaving her Stradivarius behind, played Bach for us at the launch of her book, and Ken cooked for us at his. No one can say that publishing does not have its savoury moments. It was also particularly gratifying to publish, quite recently, Alfred Brendel's collected essays and lectures, *Music, Sense and Nonsense*, already in its third printing.

The irrepressible Stanley Johnson was another author who kept the home fires burning with his wittily titled second volume of autobiography, *Stanley, I Resume*. I loved the opening, in which he describes being abandoned by his lady friend on his 50th birthday and deciding, since he was alone, to trim a large tree in his extensive country garden. Sitting on a branch, he attacked it with his chainsaw – and, in classic cartoon style, crashed with it to the ground. I suppose you could say, with regard to Boris, that the son never falls far from the tree.

Now, though, parallel with the publishing, was the poetry, as more and more poems arrived. I can't say the floodgates exactly opened, but there was a narrow door though which, with increasing frequency, I managed to seize them. I felt revitalised, and able at last to look Dannie Abse in the eye when he talked about a poem he was working on, though I was reticent about showing him what I was up to, feeling unsure and somewhat defensive. For me, writing poetry has always been an essentially private act, an experience which is mine alone, to be shielded from the eyes of others. Strange, then, you might think, to read them in public as I sometimes do, yet somehow once the poem is cold on the page, there is a kind of distancing which makes it possible, though it must be said there are certain very personal poems I would never be able to read in public, feeling too exposed, too vulnerable. I had felt that protectiveness about writing my poetry from an early age, however inept my early attempts, as my clever friends went to top universities and set out on their successful careers. Perhaps it was a kind of compensation for not having pursued a similar academic path, a way of making up for missed opportunities. However illusory, it seemed to build a wall around me, giving me a kind of secret strength which at that raw stage of my life I needed.

More good things were starting to happen. In March 2011, Michael Garrick phoned to invite me to the Guildhall School of Music Jazz Festival, which he was directing – not to read, but to listen to various poems of mine read by student actors, some to Michael's settings played by the school's star jazzmen, whom he had rehearsed carefully. There were also poems by some of the other poets who had taken part in our events over the years. It was in effect a student poetry and jazz concert, and took me back to when Michael and I had met. Unfortunately, I was away for the concert but went to the final rehearsal, which gave me the chance to chat to the performers and offer a suggestion or two. The standard was exceptional and it was a memorable experience.

By then, Michael had become a real force in the jazz world, and not only in that milieu, having worked a great deal with schools and choirs and composed such 'religious' works as his *Jazz Praises*, which he had developed from a number of shorter pieces, including his 'Wedding Hymn' (inspired by Dannie Abse's beautiful poem 'Epithalamion') and his 'Anthem', which I was surprised to read in his autobiography, *Dusk Fire*, had sprung from a poem of mine. *Jazz Praises* was performed in many churches, including St Paul's Cathedral. It was for his wide-ranging, educative, innovative work that he was awarded an MBE in 2010. As the never easy-to-please Humphrey Lyttelton wrote, 'Mike's inventiveness, his zest for musical exploration, is little short of uncanny.'

At one point I'd tried to effect a collaboration between Michael and the composer John Taverner, whom I had met through Nicholas

Snowman and the conductor David Atherton (Carole was actually roped in to bang a kind of cymbal at appropriate moments in the premiere of one of Taverner's pieces at the Queen Elizabeth Hall). In an undated letter Michael sent me after their first get-together, he wrote:

> Met John Taverner today. Fine fellow. We both felt the need of an extra-musical theme or backcloth for a joint work. For the time being we feel we could use jazz soloists in an orchestral setting, as 'cadenza players' (i.e. no jazz rhythm section) or portrayals of definite characters in a drama, e.g. Jonah, Archangels, Prometheus, and who else?! He's coming to the Phoenix on August 21st. Can you join him?

Sadly, despite several meetings and the initial enthusiasm on both sides, nothing came of what might have been an exciting venture. A real shame.

I realised that it was coming up to fifty years since the first 'Poetry and Jazz Returns to Hampstead' concert, and I discussed with Dannie and Michael Garrick the idea of an anniversary concert. They thought it a good idea so I approached the directors of Pavlova House, where the Hampstead Literary Festival largely took place, and they responded warmly to the idea of hosting it. Michael lined up Dave Green (bass) and Trevor Tomkins (percussion), and I started to think about the poetry element. It was a shock to realise that so many poetry and jazz stalwarts had passed away, but I had an idea. As well as inviting Dannie and Alan Brownjohn to read, we could still feature the poetry of other regulars. Accordingly, I invited Laurie Lee's daughter, Jessy, to read her father's lyrical poems; actress Celia Mitchell, Adrian Mitchell's widow, to read his fiery poems; and their daughter Sasha to sing. Thomas Blackburn's novelist daughter Julia and granddaughter Natasha agreed to read Tom's poems, and so on. It was to be a celebratory occasion. Michael and I were both excited at the prospect of bringing it all together once more. We worked carefully on the programme, and Michael, an excellent mimic, even opted to read some of Spike Milligan's comic verse to add a little jollity, and one or two of Vernon Scannell's war poems.

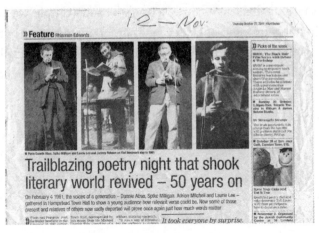

Fifty years on – the Hampstead and Highgate Express *features our anniversary concert.*

Then, on the day of the concert, I received an early morning phone call from Dave Green to say Michael had been taken into hospital for a heart bypass operation. I was stunned. Aside from my natural concern for Michael, who had apparently had heart problems for some time and had been dodging an operation, what about the concert? Should we cancel? Should we somehow struggle on? After all, tickets had been sold and some of the participants would already be on their way to London. But how could we carry on without Michael behind the piano, directing the music? However, he had told Dave Green that the show must go on, and Dave had sounded out a superb pianist, Barry Green, who was ready to step in, though he couldn't be there in time to rehearse, as he had an afternoon engagement. So, with Michael's insistent words in our ears, we decided to continue.

Barry arrived about half an hour before kick-off, and we quickly discussed things as the minutes ticked away. The expectant audience of course knew nothing about all this, and it fell to me to start by breaking the news and explaining a little of the historical background, and then we were off. It wasn't the evening we had worked for, but the audience seemed to enjoy it and it was better than we expected in the circumstances, Barry rising magnificently to the occasion, as did all the musicians and readers. The evening was even captured on film by the director David Cohen, who had brought a camera crew.

When I eventually got home I found two emails from Michael, the first sent at 5.30 that evening. 'Hope message reached you re sudden hospitalisation. Rang Dave yesterday and your office. Don't have your home number with me, but have just received my laptop. Sod's law is indeed alive and well.' The second email was sent a couple of hours later. 'Hope the gig was all OK – I bet it was. Musios are infinitely adaptable when needs be… Am I pissed off.' I replied at once, telling him how concerned everyone was, how much he'd been missed, and that although the concert had gone well enough it had not been the same without him. I ended, 'But I told the assembled throng about our meeting at the RFH and all you had done for P and J over the years, so you were there in spirit. Everyone was asking, "When is the next one?" So get well quickly and let's plan it. I hope everything goes smoothly with the op and look forward to cheering news.' He was quick to respond: 'Jeremy, am in Harefield Hospital: bypass tomorrow. Dave Green called in today and told me the gig was wonderful. Yes! Another! Dave reckoned the venue is perfect for jazz. Cheers – and thanks.' But it was not to be, and we were all shattered to hear that Michael had died during the operation.

Michael Garrick as I like to remember him. We did well over 300 concerts together.

*   *   *

The lead obituaries in the main national papers did him proud, but they were no substitute, as obituaries never are, for his live, vital presence. The *Telegraph* began:

> Michael Garrick, who has died aged 78, was a composer and pianist whose work extended well beyond the usual confines of jazz; in a career spanning more than 50 years he employed techniques from the genre to create music for choirs, string quartets, poems, symphony orchestras, and even the organ of St Paul's Cathedral.

The Times referred to his literary leanings 'that were later manifested in large-scale compositions', and to his 'intuitive ear for harmony and a sense of orchestral colour'. In terms of my own life, Michael's impact had been considerable, and I was pleased to be able to say so at the concert that his sons (themselves top-class jazz musicians) had arranged to follow the funeral, and at which musicians queued up to take part, among them Cleo Laine, whose husband, Sir John Dankworth (for whom Michael had started a jazz course at his music centre at Wavendon), had called him 'truly of world class'. At the funeral concert I read several poems, two to settings by Michael. We had met as enthusiastic young men and had formed a natural alliance. His settings for my poems were always sensitive and complementary, and even listening now to some of the recordings we made together, I marvel at his lyrical and rhythmical response to the words, and his ability to add a dash of humour where appropriate.

To mark the first anniversary of his death, a tribute concert was arranged at the Purcell Room in November 2012 as part of the London Jazz Festival, at which his sons played and invited me to read. I'd written a poem called 'Some of Those Days', which referred to a song made famous by Sophie Tucker, a favourite of my mother's, who used to sing it. At Mike's funeral concert, the fabulous Norma Winstone had sung a chorus from that number as a lead-in to my reading of the poem, and we'd planned to do it again at the Purcell Room. Norma had worked closely with Michael over the years and had sung at several poetry and jazz concerts, so it seemed appropriate. But for some reason she'd had to cancel and Jacqui Dankworth took her place, generously agreeing to learn the song and singing it slowly and movingly alongside my reading of the poem. It was to lead to fresh beginnings.

*   *   *

I now had some forty new poems. It was at the Hampstead Theatre, where Carole and I had gone to see Maureen Lipman in a play called *Old Money*, and were congratulating her on her performance over a drink in the foyer afterwards, that Mo suddenly said, 'Isn't it time you had a new book of poems? I'd be happy to do some readings with you to help promote it.' (Strangely, it was at the same theatre some four years earlier, when we'd gone to see her daughter Amy Rosenthal's engrossing play about D. H. Lawrence and his circle, *On the Rocks*, that, encountering Maureen in the foyer, she'd introduced us to her companion – Guido Castro. 'No need to introduce us,' Carole had responded, to Maureen's surprise. 'Guido is my cousin!' And what a lovely, cultured, gentle man he is, and how extraordinary that he'd entered Maureen's life and added an extra link to our already close friendship.)

It was a generous offer of Maureen's to read with me, but though I had the poems, finding a publisher was an altogether different matter. I would never, as I explained to Maureen, publish my own work, and while many years earlier I had been in the midst of the poetry world and publishing regularly in various poetry magazines, the years and editors had moved on. I was really starting all over again, and frankly didn't relish the thought of the rejections I would surely receive. Then, by a stroke of luck, I found myself in correspondence with Andrew Croft, a remarkable man whose publishing company, Smokestack, publishes only poetry – and poetry of a high quality and wide range with an international focus. Andy, himself a considerable poet, was 'committed' in a way that anyone with such an important but essentially uncommercial list would have to be. I floated the idea of a 'New and Selected Poems', drawing from my early books now long out of print, and adding new poems. Andy responded promptly, urging me to send the new ones, coming back with the exciting proposal that he publish an entirely new collection and think about my 'Selected' suggestion later. He explained that the Arts Council had shamefully withdrawn its grant and so he had to manage things carefully from a cash-flow point of view. This meant that, given the commitments he already had, he would not be able to publish my book for another couple of years, but if I was prepared to wait, he was game. His enthusiasm and positive response to the poems I'd sent him was all-important, and given that I'd already waited a great deal longer than that, I readily agreed. Some two years later, in September 2014, *Blues in the Park* was ready to be launched at the lovely Daunt bookshop in Marylebone High Street – containing not forty poems now, but over sixty. I couldn't have been more thrilled at the prospect, but there was a shadow over it all, and our world was about to be turned upside down.

* * *

Our friendship with Dannie Abse had remained as close as ever, and he and I had enjoyed reading together at another poetry and jazz concert, this time at the Hungerford Arts Festival at the invitation of Elizabeth Davis (formerly Rose), who organised the classy annual festival and is much featured in these pages from the time we worked together as editors of *The Goon Show Scripts* and then as Robson Books' first editor. While there was no Michael Garrick, the trio that had played at Hampstead agreed to participate, as did Dannie and Alan Brownjohn. At the ill-fated Hampstead anniversary concert, Adrian Mitchell's daughter Sasha had made a big impression singing and reading one of Adrian's poems to Michael's setting, so I invited her too. We drove to Hungerford together, and it was good to get to know her better and to chat about her father, who'd died in 2008 and to whom she had been very close. I had given many readings with Adrian but I had never really got to know him well (for which I blame myself). He projected a tough persona, and I guess I was a little shy of him, though he was always friendly and willing to join the fray from the first concert on. Indeed, he'd written to me warmly from Iowa in May 1964, where he was writer in residence and running a writers' workshop, saying, 'I'll be home in a month. Have written many poems … can I come back in the word circus? I miss it, man. So could you let me know what's happening? Hope all is well with you both and your book is doing well. Yes.'

It was good to hear about a softer, more private Adrian. He had become a hero of the left with such poems as 'Tell Me Lies About Vietnam', and had a loyal following. The large audience for his memorial concert at the Queen Elizabeth Hall, which Carole and I went to and at which a number of poets and musicians performed, attested to that. In the car, I played Sasha a recently released CD of a live poetry and jazz concert of ours at which Adrian had read. She hadn't heard it before, and listened intently, especially to a poem of Adrian's called 'Pal' which she was going to read to music at Hungerford, noting his pace, rhythm and emphasis.

At that stage of his life, Dannie was no longer alone. In 2008, he had given a reading at the annual Torbay Poetry Festival, and afterwards had signed a book for an 'attractive' lady and been struck by her sympathetic response to the poems he'd read (he had included several about Joan). Her name was Lynne Hjelmgaard. Next morning, by chance, they'd met again on Torbay Station, waiting for the train to London, and on the journey home he discovered that, though much younger than him, she was a widow with a family, and herself a published poet. They became partners, and Lynne – gentle, admiring, caring – brought comfort and love to Dannie's later years. As Dannie wrote in the final pages of a revised edition of his autobiography, *Good-bye Twentieth Century*, 'Joan had been my heartbeat, and still is, but my life of bereavement has changed too, has become, because of Lynne, more sunbright.' Lynne, for her part, has written about how the Torbay Festival changed her life, and how thankful she was to have gone there.

Lynne had been with Dannie at the Hampstead anniversary reading (her first taste of poetry and jazz) and was with him at Hungerford. It was a warm and friendly occasion; Dannie was in great spirits and read with his usual style and charm, and I could not have imagined it would be the last time we would read together. Nor could I have envisaged, when we met up one evening not very long after for our traditional salt beef sandwich (it was always either that or a local pizza), that it would be our last sandwich together. Dannie was in a buoyant mood, and very talkative. He'd had backache and a few niggling aches and pains, but had just received the results of various tests, which were all good, and he was gratified too, despite his strong socialist leanings, to have been awarded a CBE for services to poetry. In addition, he'd just finished reading all the entries for the prestigious Forward Poetry Prize, for which he was one of the judges. He had always appeared the maverick, the outsider, and I sensed he felt he was finally getting the serious recognition and respect that had in some way eluded him in certain quarters. Another reason for his upbeat mood was that, thanks to its intrepid artistic director, Leonie Scott-Matthews, the Pentameters Theatre in Hampstead had recently put on his *Pythagoras,* a play he'd written some years earlier and totally revised. And there had been an evening devoted to him at Jewish Book Week which I introduced and at which Diana Hoddinott read some prose extracts from his books alongside Dannie's own reading of his poems.

Dannie had seemed relieved to get out of the house for a few hours and chat, as BBC Wales were making a film about his life and work and had been interviewing him for much of the week, which was tiring; they had also interviewed me about Dannie just that day, spending quite some time going through and copying some of the many photos and posters I had. He was pleased to hear about that, but unusually anxious about the fact that they were planning to film a reading he was about to give with Lynne, and I think he found it helpful to discuss the poems he might read. I suggested to Dannie that it might be an idea to start with a story I'd heard him tell about the time he was reading at a rather formal event in Wales where he was given an overlong introduction by a local dignitary called Jones, who kept curtailing his surname to 'Abs'. Eventually, Dannie interrupted him, saying, 'Please do call me *Abse,*' emphasising the 'e', whereupon the chairman responded, 'Thank you, and you can call me Jonesy.'

Dannie had just finished reading his brother Leo's last, posthumous book, a psychoanalytically oriented biography of Daniel Defoe, and we went on to talk about the colourful, controversial Leo, who had died six years earlier, Dannie lamenting that he had never told his brother how much he admired him. I had never heard him talk that way about Leo, and I can't imagine Leo was the kind of man it would have been easy to say such things to (nor could I envisage him returning the compliment, though I know Leo greatly admired his brother's poems). Dannie had been particularly struck by the quality of Leo's writing and the remarkable range of his vocabulary. 'I've always prided myself on having a wide vocabulary,' said Dannie, 'but Leo's was far more extensive.' How amused the competitive Leo would have been to hear his brother say that! I gave Dannie an invitation for the launch of my book, and he took out his diary and noted the date, relieved that it didn't clash with a Cardiff City match. Nothing had really changed!

How distressing it was, then, to get a worried phone call some days afterwards from Robert Kirby, Dannie's devoted agent, asking if I knew what was wrong with Dannie. They'd had a lunch date which Dannie had cancelled, saying he was gravely ill. I sat in silence in my office, staring at the receiver, thinking back to our very recent dinner together. He'd looked so well, as vital and lively as ever, and I'd told him so. I hesitated, not knowing whether to phone him or not, and what to say if I did. After some minutes, I slowly dialled that number I knew so well. Dannie answered. 'I'm glad you phoned,' he said, before I could utter a word, 'I was going to phone you and Carole tonight.' He then went on to tell me he had cancer in a number of places, that it had spread and was terminal. He had opted not to undergo any treatment. 'Come round as soon as you can,' he added. 'I'd like to see you both.'

We needed no prompting and were there early that evening. Dannie sat in his usual armchair in the front room where he wrote, facing the television where he'd watched Cardiff City lose so many crucial matches. He spelt out the bleak news, saying (as we started to interject) that he knew treatment wouldn't work and that he was not prepared to put himself through it – a tough and brave decision for a doctor to make. He added that he was sorry he would be unable to make my book launch. How unimportant the book seemed in the context of this terrible news, but as it happened I had received the first copy that day, and I gave it to Dannie. Looking through it carefully, he asked me to sign it. He had already read most of the poems in manuscript. I remembered what he'd said about not having told Leo how much he admired him. I was not going to fail on that score with Dannie, and inscribed the book accordingly. He smiled, and leant forward so we could embrace.

We visited Dannie daily, and whenever the talk turned to poetry he visibly perked up. In fact, it was difficult to believe he was so ill. But after just a couple of weeks we got a call to say he'd weakened suddenly, and he died that night, on 28 September 2014, just six days after his 91st birthday.

After he'd gone, my mind was numb for quite some time but eventually I managed to write two poems for Dannie, the first rather raw one being set in the lovely Golders Hill Park near both our homes, where, amidst the peacocks and deer, he loved to walk – as Carole and I had done one fateful evening, thinking of Dannie close by and nearing the end. I called it 'Poet in the Park', and here is the middle section:

> Now, as the low September sun
> crowns the trees and the empty
> lawns gleam in the evening light,
> the silent park is like a stage set
> waiting for something to begin.
>
> But it won't.
> Amazed as we are by the beauty
> of it all, we know that nearby, in the
> book-lined room where you wrote
> and read and loyally watched
> that maddening Cardiff team of yours
> blow it yet again, and as light flickers,
> a final whistle is about to go.

*   *   *

I felt honoured when the family and Lynne asked me to read Dannie's powerful and emotive poem 'Last Words' at the funeral at Golders

Green Crematorium, after they too had read and spoken, and following the playing of a movement from Schubert's String Quartet in C
major, which Dannie loved. A week later, Cardiff City included a photo
and lengthy piece about him in the programme for their home match
against Nottingham Forest. There was also a tribute at half-time. And
the following spring the club planted a tree for him in Cardiff City's
garden of remembrance, the plaque saying: 'Dannie Abse. Acclaimed
writer and Bluebird'.

When I first met Dannie, I hadn't appreciated the depth of his passion for Cardiff City – his love of the Bluebirds must have run his
love of poetry pretty close! Nor did I then know that while a medical
student in London, a keen player himself at that time, he would return
to Cardiff in the holidays and train at Ninian Park; nor that on one
auspicious occasion the Cardiff manager, Cyril Spiers, invited him to
play for the reserves against Oswestry. Here is Dannie's rueful account
of what happened:

> On the day Oswestry turned up one short and Spiers asked me to play
> for them. So my dream of playing for City at home in front of 50,000
> didn't quite materialise – I played against City's reserves in front of 150!
> I missed a 'sitter' at the Grange End, and whenever I watched matches
> in future years from my seat in the stand, I would look at the goalmouth,
> remembering that miss, and hear Cyril Spiers shouting from the side –
> 'Now's your chance, son.'

I was invited to speak and read again on 25 March 2015 at a grand 'Remembering Dannie Abse' evening in the Great Hall of King's College
in the Strand. It was a moving and momentous occasion, with much
laughter as well as a few tears. There were readings and tributes by
a number of distinguished poets including the Poet Laureate Carol
Ann Duffy, her predecessor Andrew Motion, Alan Brownjohn, Elaine
Feinstein and Owen Sheers, as well as by Dannie's daughters and by
Lynne; there was a film of Dannie talking, music, and an entertaining
excerpt from his autobiography read by Diana Hoddinott. Dannie
would have been surprised and proud, as he would have been about

the Cardiff City tributes. He would also have enjoyed the pizzas afterwards with Lynne and his daughters and a few old friends. Yet it didn't seem real. We'd been close friends for over fifty years, he (and Joan) had helped form my early life and we'd shared so many experiences and happy times, stretching back to the historic Hampstead Town Hall concert in 1973. We'd swum in the sea at Brighton together like truant schoolboys before hurriedly changing to read at the university, and years later in the Sea of Galilee; we'd driven together up and down the M1 to read at this or that town; been together with Joan and Carole in New York, Princeton and Normandy; strolled together in Golders Hill Park, where the title poem of my new collection, *Blues in the Park*, was set and where Carole and I walked in silence when we knew he was approaching his end.

Dannie Abse pictured at Herod's Fortress, near Bethlehem, during our reading tour of Israel. So many memories over so many years.

In many ways Dannie had shown me what it meant to be a poet. For him – excepting Joan and his family, and despite his medical commitments – it was the be-all and end-all. The next poem was the all-important thing, and his standards were exceptionally high. I don't think I ever showed him a poem for which he didn't suggest changes or cuts, but it was done with positive intent, and he was the first to acknowledge that he could be wrong, that we all have our own rhythms and heartbeats. In the early days, I'd generally show him my latest 'masterpiece' (just as he would send or show me his new poems). One thing he taught me early on was that poems shouldn't be abstract, that images should always be concrete, exact. He maintained (and I heartily concur, despite our many public readings) that poems should be written for the page first and foremost, and not for reading aloud. Here are a few lines from a letter he wrote me in 1961, the year we met. I was twenty-two, and had just sent him a batch of poems – juvenilia, really. His criticism was gently couched:

> I like 'Strangers' though thought it was written more for reading aloud than for the eye. I mean sometimes an author will rewrite a poem on the page, changing end-stops of a line for his own convenience and breath. All this seems to me a kind of weakness. Lines should not begin and end in an arbitrary way – though heaven knows I've been guilty of this.

Again, he advises, in his careful way, 'To write in a given formal pattern brings the writer close to his poem as he is writing it. Words and the cadence of each word become magnified at the time of choice, and there are many choices and only one correct one.' He goes on to say, 'Poetry is certainly a fiction but it must appear to be real,' and, referring to a phrase in a particular poem, 'Some things will stay in the mind like your "ever present Pacifist newspaper-seller". I've heard his piping, fading voice in the grumble of traffic down Charing Cross Road. This is a concrete reference, corresponding to actual experience, which is why I like it.'

In all this he was nudging me, a very young would-be poet, in the right direction, and the fact that he took so much trouble when he hardly knew me is remarkable. He drew my attention to many poems and poets I hadn't yet encountered, not all English, and to books too. I remember being particularly captivated by Rilke's *Letters to a Young Poet*. But though poetry was lifeblood and breath for Dannie, once I had become involved in setting up my own publishing company there were conflicting loyalties and for me it could not be so all-consuming, given the organisation and responsibilities that publishing entailed. It is perhaps no great wonder that the writing dried up, while any creative energy and imagination I still possessed was absorbed into publishing and editing the work of others.

It always took Dannie about three years to write enough poems he was satisfied with for a new book. When I told him I had about sixty in my forthcoming collection, he was surprised, suggesting I should hold some over for the next volume, though when I pointed out that I hadn't written for an eternity and that this was the equivalent of some thirty years' work, he understood. He was wise, erudite, loved to laugh and had a rich store of entertaining anecdotes. He was always such uplifting company. As for Cardiff City, well, for some reason, I still feel a compulsion to check the results every week to see if they've won, and feel an uplift when they have. How thrilled Dannie would have been to see the Blues win their way back into the Premier League, as they did just a few months before this book went to press – though he would have been on tenterhooks for weeks as, in true Cardiff City style, they lost matches they should have won and everything was touch and go until the last ball of the season was kicked.

I remember Dannie once telling me – laughing as he did so – about some Orthodox rabbis who had knocked on his door, looking for a charitable donation, and going on to chide him for not belonging to a synagogue (they obviously hadn't read his poem 'Odd'). Finally, exasperated, as a last throw of the dice they had said, 'If you don't belong to a synagogue, you won't be able to have a burial,' to which Dannie had replied, the door already half-closed, 'I'm not going to die.'

If only that had been true.

30

PACKING MY BAGS

Strangely, the new beginnings for poetry and jazz hinted at in the last chapter were brought about unwittingly by the legendary opera singer Jessye Norman, whose autobiography I had just signed up. We'd been alerted to the fact that, while being an artist of true greatness, Ms Norman could be difficult and demanding – a real diva – so, apart from the expense of bringing her over from America, we felt it would be wise to steer clear of any promotional involvements. But fate dictated differently, thanks to another exceptional woman, Sally Dunsmore, who directs the Oxford and Blenheim Literary Festivals and for whom it seems nothing is too ambitious. I'd first met Sally when we accompanied Leslie Caron to Blenheim, where she'd entranced a large audience with stories of Paris and Hollywood and the films she'd starred in. Now Sally wanted to discuss the possibility of inviting Jessye Norman to Blenheim as the guest of honour at their black-tie dinner, always a grand affair. And while we couldn't even contemplate it, the resourceful and imaginative Sally somehow found a way, and Ms Norman came – behaving impeccably, I should add, and charming everyone – so much so that at Sally's invitation she came again the following spring to the Oxford Literary Festival.

However, it was while we were discussing all this over a drink, along with Sally's invaluable associate Tony Byrne, that the subject of poetry and jazz came up. Sally and Tony were intrigued by the history and, ever innovative, Sally proposed that I arrange one of our concerts at Blenheim to tie in with my new book of poems. Alas, there was no

Michael Garrick, and now, sadly, no Dannie Abse, so it could never be the same, but as I began to think about Sally's proposal I remembered Jacqui Dankworth's friendly collaboration in the tribute concert for Michael at the London Jazz Festival, and also Maureen Lipman's generous offer to read with me as and when I had a new book of poems published. If they were both willing to join me at Blenheim, I felt we could fashion an interesting programme, and so we did, closing the festival with a full-house concert in the glittering Orangery. The format for that concert was straightforward, the sophisticated Jacqui, accompanied by a superb trio, singing between groups of poems from my book, read by Maureen and me, with Maureen performing a couple of her own hilarious monologues.

Encouraged by the response, Sally followed up by inviting us to the Gibraltar Literature Festival, which she was then also directing. For this, Jacqui was joined by her husband, the American pianist/composer/singer Charlie Wood, who sings the blues as only someone born and bred in Memphis and steeped in the music can. The response was equally gratifying, the original venue having to be changed to a larger one to cope with the demand. (No self-delusion here – I quickly learned that the Lipman and Dankworth names work wonders, and for me it was sheer joy to read alongside them.) The new venue was to be the ballroom of the very original five-star hotel in which we were staying – a permanently moored ship. When I heard of the switch, I crept down one evening to have a recce and was more than a little alarmed at the size of the empty ballroom – no chairs, no piano, which made it seem even larger – and I remember conveying my fears to Maureen, who had just flown in with Guido. Extraordinarily, that concert venue too was sold out.

We all enjoyed the festival talks and our days on that historic island. For me, it was rather like going to the university I never went to as we lined up to attend one talk after another by eminent writers and scholars on subjects ranging from philosophy to Christianity, politics to music and history, and much else. It was a treat to stroll from lecture to lecture – A. C. Grayling's on 'Friendship among Friends' and Diarmaid MacCulloch's on 'Silence in Christianity' being among the most stimulating – before we too had to sing for our supper. Talking of singing reminds me of a lovely evening listening to the fabulous Patti Boulaye in a spectacular concert hall deep in the Gibraltar caves. We also enjoyed the nightly dinners, each directed by a celebrity chef, which were made especially memorable by the guests we were lucky enough to share a table with, such as John Julius Norwich, who regaled me with stories of Patrick Leigh Fermor, whose travel writings I was not as familiar with as he seemed to think I should be. An extremely friendly George Carey, the former Archbishop of Canterbury, was my near neighbour on another night, Sally sitting between us. He had been speaking at various Gibraltar schools about the importance of failure in life, and the publisher in me immediately rose to the surface, suggesting that this would be an excellent subject for a book.

On the last night, after our performance, we found ourselves on the same table as Ross King and Martin Kemp, two Leonardo da Vinci experts whose talks we'd been to. Despite her degree in art history (or perhaps because of it!) Carole was rather alarmed to find herself sandwiched between these two formidable scholars, but she needn't have worried since the last thing they wanted to talk about was Leonardo – or art. Indeed, Martin Kemp, emeritus professor of art history at Oxford University, was far more interested in discussing jazz, about which he was a knowledgeable enthusiast. He not only attended our Gibraltar concert but came again the following year when we appeared at the Oxford Festival, and he clearly enjoyed meeting Jacqui Dankworth and Charlie Wood, and also Maureen, who was at her best that night. He later told me that as well as enjoying the music and the poems, he had loved watching Maureen for her great sense of timing, which, as a frequent lecturer, he thoroughly appreciated.

Reading with Maureen has taught me things, too. She is a perfectionist and likes everything to be well ordered (which is not to say she doesn't improvise and inject humour as she goes along – she most certainly does!). When, sitting beside her on stage, with the fabulous Jacqui on my other side, who also never misses a beat, I fumble with papers or can't find my place in the book quickly, I rather feel I'm letting the side down. Almost all my other readings over the years have been a matter of waiting my turn, then coming on to read for fifteen or twenty minutes before exiting or sitting at the side of the stage out of the spotlight while others read. What we have now is a kind of continuous performance, and while I like to be as prepared as possible and hopefully professional, I'm not an actor playing a part, and I need a licence to be myself – to hesitate, think carefully, say a few words between poems. Maureen understands this and, of course, as well as performing her brilliant monologues, she is also 'performing' my poems – a fact that continues to thrill me. If there is humour to be found in a poem, she will tease it out in a way I never could, yet when she reads a serious poem, such as 'Vigil', you can hear a pin drop. Maureen chose to include it in the anthology *Poems That Make Grown Women Cry* and read it at the book launch at the National Theatre. Whenever she reads it, my eyes fill with tears, too. When we read a poem together, alternating verses, I experience at first hand the sense of timing Martin Kemp so admires, and note the way she changes the expression in her voice and on her face, and her visual projection of the lines. She may rue the day she volunteered to read with me, but I most certainly do not!

Returning to Martin Kemp for a moment, it was interesting to discover when talking to him that he'd been a protégé of the great art historian Ernst Gombrich, who had lived in the same road as us for many years, where Kemp had often visited him. He clearly had a great regard not only for Gombrich but for the great contribution remarkable Jewish refugees like him had made to the world of scholarship.

It seems to me that Sally Dunsmore's special gift is not only to attract such distinguished figures to her festivals, but to bring them together over drinks and dinners in a convivial atmosphere in which friendships and associations are formed. (I signed up Ken Hom after meeting him at Blenheim, and it was also there that I first met the novelist and poet Ben Okri, with whom I have since given several readings.)

If it now seems that publishing had begun to take a back seat in this story, that, to an extent, is true, but by no means entirely so. Interesting authors continued to come my way, none more timely than Paul

Gambaccini, with his exposé of the false accusations of paedophilia and the protracted police campaign against him. That important book came to me through Caroline Michel, after a lengthy negotiation which I often thought would falter simply because the author's impassioned text was overlong and Caroline wanted it reduced before letting me see it. She is always firm but fair and eventually we struck a deal that we were both happy with. I've always greatly enjoyed my dealings, conversations and lively lunches with the captivating Caroline, for as well as our mutual publishing interests, she is also switched on to the world of poetry, her former husband, (Lord) Matthew Evans, having been the MD and then chairman of Faber & Faber and thus the publisher of Ted Hughes, Sylvia Plath, Seamus Heaney and many other gilded names, so she knew them all. Indeed, I recall her telling me that when Ted published his revelatory *Birthday Letters* and wanted to escape the press, he and Carol had gone to stay with her and Matthew in the country. I discovered, too, that after university, where, unusually, she had studied Sanskrit, Caroline had worked for the literary magazine *Agenda*, to which I'd subscribed in my younger poetic years. Even Michael Winner once sang Caroline's praises to me, and praise from the intemperate Winner usually came in thimbles, if at all.

At that time, too, I found myself deeply involved in Freddie Raphael's tour de force memoir of his Cambridge days, *Going Up*. That period had, of course, been the inspiration for his famous television series, *The Glittering Prizes*. Publishing the erudite, pithy-penned Raphael is always a joy, and besides the books themselves the by-product of his emails from France is something I also relish – sharp, literary, entertaining and a real test of my vocabulary and knowledge – glittering prizes in their own way. However, as 2016 approached, I was feeling the tug of the poetry, the tug of starting to contemplate this book, and the tug of a close and growing family, and in February of that year I agreed with Iain Dale that come September I would stop working full-time for the company. I would continue as an editor-at-large, attending acquisition meetings and bringing books to the table – but, importantly, not going in to the office on a daily basis. It had been a five-year stint (indeed, for me, a fifty-year stint in all), and it was time,

I felt, to draw back. For all that, it seemed rather theoretical at first and way off in the future. Bel Mooney and Maureen Lipman both had attractive books scheduled for publication that September, which kept my mind focused on the present while I worked on these. There was also a remarkable book, *The Greatest Comeback*, by David Bolchover, I'd taken on about the Hungarian footballer Béla Guttmann, who survived the Holocaust and went on to become one of the most celebrated football coaches of the modern era, taking Benfica to European Cup glory in 1961 – a book that was to receive wide acclaim.

* * *

Inevitably, the end of September came. I emptied my drawers, packed up the books I wanted to take home, and began to clear the many thousands of emails that had accumulated on my computer. When I'd originally left my own company, Robson Books, to join up with the Quarto Group, I'd found it a deeply upsetting emotional experience. This was not at all like that, and when I finally left the office I felt quite calm about it, on the surface anyway, and on the way home I decided to stop off at Ossie's Barber Shop in Camden Town to have a long overdue haircut. I'd first met the amiable Ossie when he had a salon in Great Titchfield Street, near my old office. Old habits die hard. I always enjoyed chatting to him about Arsenal, and on occasion I'd bump into the newscaster Sir Trevor McDonald there, also an old Ossie regular, as I did that day. I knew from previous conversations that he'd been writing an autobiography for quite some time, and I asked him how it was going (old publishing habits die hard!). 'Still at it,' he told me, and while Ossie stood by his chair, waiting patiently for me to come under his scissors, Trevor told about the time he went to interview Yasser Arafat, a hair-raising story he was planning to write up that afternoon. It made a welcome distraction. Will he, I wondered, really get down to writing today after talking about it to me in such detail? Ossie's is a happy meeting place – Alan Bennett is another Ossie regular, as is Jonathan Miller – and I left in good spirits, and rather less dishevelled.

Iain had offered to throw a party for me, but I hadn't been able to face that: it would have been too final, and in any case I was still involved with the company, if in a more distant capacity, and the word 'retirement' was not something I wanted to hear. Iain and James generously allowed me to continue to use my office, and for some reason – force of habit? Inability to let go? A need to adjust gradually to the idea of no longer going into work every day? – I continued to clock in fairly regularly, even though I'd officially left. Then Carole and I went to our cottage in France, where I had an accident, tripping and landing eye-first on the large iron gates at the end of our path, knocking myself out for some minutes. It was nasty, and Carole rushed me to the nearest hospital, where they stitched the gash under my eye. I was lucky, declared the specialist I went to as soon as we got back to London. Slowly the closed eye opened, and gradually recovered. However, the accident seemed to have knocked some sense into me, for as well as looking as if I'd gone fifteen rounds with Muhammad Ali, I found myself no longer drawn to the office and began to write compulsively, every day. In fact, in the space of some five weeks I wrote seven poems and managed to slip them into my new book, *Subject Matters*, which was on the point of going to press. One was called 'Out for the Count' (the subject pretty obvious!), another 'Meditations on Giving Up Work', which starts:

> I walked away from a job today,
> perhaps my last, but who can say,
> and what had I lost as I stepped away?

And who *could* say? Some, I know, had been expecting me to start yet another imprint. (Jonathan Lloyd, witty chairman of the literary agency Curtis Brown, wrote: 'Congratulations. A slight pause and then another imprint?') And I suppose in some ways, like Fagin in the musical *Oliver!*, I was 'reviewing the situation'. I had authors – friends – I felt I was letting down, and there were tempting propositions, but as Carole said, it was time to start enjoying other things. Yet it was a strange feeling, being at home every day with time to a large extent my own. But was it? The office I'd had for those five years looked down over the Thames towards Parliament and Big Ben and I'd become obsessed with that clock. Now I'd finally escaped its gaze. In some ways it felt good… yet here is how my poem ends:

> Each day now is an adventurous one, and
> out of Big Ben's chilling sight I can smilingly
> claim all time my own. But not quite, I know,
> all too aware of that other ticking clock, even if,
> for the moment, I like to think it's stopped.

And, to refer to the opening lines of my poem again, what *had* I lost…? Well, I would be less than honest if I didn't record here my growing disenchantment with the publishing world, from which, or so it seems to me, the romance, such as it was, has to a large degree gone, everything now so impersonal. I would put it down to the obvious fact that I'd grown older, if I hadn't continued to be excited by every book I took on, every new author, seeing each one as a fresh adventure. But more and more in publishing these days it is the tail (the sales and accounts people) that wags the creative dog, with committees conferring on acquisitions, the days of lively reps with strong local contacts more or less over, Amazon demanding ever more wounding discounts and licking up the cream, while once-great booksellers like Waterstones order centrally, in mini-quantities, if at all. There are noble exceptions, of course, like Daunt's and the revitalised and expanding Foyles, but with fewer and fewer independent booksellers left, and book clubs and many supportive wholesalers gone, it's an uphill battle.

It's perhaps salutary that as I was putting the finishing touches to this book, Iain Dale should have announced that he was leaving Biteback to focus on his broadcasting and writing activities. From the conversations we'd had in recent months, I sensed that he too was growing frustrated and somewhat disillusioned by the state of things, though his achievements at Biteback were considerable. It will be fascinating to see how Andy McNab, who has come in to advise and oversee the company's future publishing programme, develops the list.

Looking back, I realise I was spoilt by having been for many years in the privileged position of being my own boss and able to seize tempting offerings; to act independently and decisively; to work with imaginative publicists who would pick up the ball and run with it, and with exceptional editors with whom I'd always confer. As with most small publishers, passion ruled, and for me it was always the authors who, for better or for worse, fired everything. Although it might seem as if authors are now thought of as 'product', whose books have to be turned around quickly, often with little or no time to work with them, to refine things, there are, I'm glad to say, energetic young literary agents and new publishers opening their doors. At my final Frankfurt of blessed memory I was delighted to come across the Mosaic Press, a small but distinguished company run by a cultured man called Howard Aster, whose wide tastes and interests are reflected in his list. He and I struck up an immediate rapport and a lasting friendship.

There's no dodging the fact that computers and new technology have revolutionised the old, slow, leisurely world of publishing. What with email, Facebook, Kindle, social media and the speed of it all, why, there's hardly time for a publisher's lunch (the Garrick Club must be feeling the pinch!). The days of hot-metal typesetting, galley proofs, faint carbon copies of manuscripts on flimsy paper, and lengthy communications and corrections by pigeon post seem such a long way in the past that I sometimes have to remind myself of how things were when I began. How did we ever get a book out, I wonder? Yet we did, and the packed book shelves that cover every inch of the walls of our house testify to that. Perhaps I should read them all again, for books are friends who've shared their experiences with you and need revisiting.

However, there won't be much time for that now as we enjoy the trips, visit the galleries, see the films we never had time for, travel and, most importantly, enjoy the family growing up around us. I might even take up the long-standing invitation from my brother David, an experienced sailor, to spend a few days sailing with him on the boat he keeps in Brittany. A good deal younger than me, he might even be able to haul me up the gangway!

Now Carole and I, with our parents gone, find ourselves in the front line, suddenly the Elders. All that said, and even though I realise that I may have spent many years looking in the wrong direction, I still haven't quite shaken off the guilty feeling that I should be working instead of driving our grandchildren to the various sporting and other activities they are involved in. But is this not a privilege, and a far more human and rewarding scene to contemplate as I sit at my desk trying to polish off poems, scribbling this memoir, recalling the recent launch (at Daunt Books again) of my book of poems *Subject Matters*, and a rather special reading at the Oxford Festival with Ben Okri? That was by candlelight before a log fire in the eighteenth-century lodgings of the Provost of Worcester, Professor Sir Jonathan Bate (Shakespeare scholar and biographer of Ted Hughes), who co-hosted the event with his delightful wife, the biographer Paula Byrne. Afterwards, we'd had the pleasure of joining them for a welcome glass or two of champagne in their elegant sitting room. With more readings and concerts to come with Maureen Lipman and Jacqui Dankworth, books to acquire for Biteback, poems to write, an invitation to appear in the Henley Festival, a return to Gibraltar, and the prospect of a *New and Selected Poems* from Smokestack in 2021, it is not such a bad future – in fact, it's very much like the early days of poetry and jazz. How ironic that as I write this, an article should have appeared in *The Times* headed 'Poets beat the drum for a new generation' and talking about young poets 'rejuvenating an art form that many had given up for dead'. It was, the article declared, 'reminiscent of what happened in the 1960s'. I smiled as I read it. Poetry returning to Hampstead or wherever, all over again. *Plus ça change...*

* * *

I had been set on calling this book 'Mr Fairbanks Is Packing His Bags', but people said (probably rightly) that it was too obscure, and that not everybody would have heard of or remember the legendary film star. But there was a story behind that title, and no writer likes to waste material, so here it is, the conclusion rather than the introduction to this saga it was originally intended to be.

But first, a few words about the debonair film star Douglas Fairbanks Jr, who was as swashbuckling off-screen as he was on, serving with great valour and distinction in the navy during the Second World War. Attached to the commando staff of (Lord) Louis Mountbatten, he'd been highly decorated, made an Honorary Knight Commander of the British Empire and awarded the Distinguished Service Cross. Thus in 1993 when Robson Books published his colourful war memoir, *A Hell of a War*, and he came to England to promote it with Vera, his glamorous young wife (his third), the Imperial War Museum offered to host a grand reception with all sorts of military top brass there, including the former Chief of Staff Lord Bramall, who had agreed to speak. The next day, there was to be a prestigious Foyles literary lunch at the Dorchester Hotel, hosted by Christina Foyle, with a roster of distinguished guests of honour.

The day before the launch – a Sunday, as I recall – we had arranged for Douglas to be interviewed at his hotel by the *Daily Mail*. He had agreed to the interview on one condition: there were to be no questions about the Duchess of Argyll or the 'headless man'. The Duchess, you may recall, had been involved in a scandalous front-page divorce case during which Polaroid photos were produced showing her dressed only in her signature three-strand pearl necklace and purportedly performing fellatio on a man whose head could not be seen and who could not, therefore, be properly identified – the so-called headless man. That man was widely thought to have been the dashing Fairbanks himself, though he had always denied it.

The interview took place, and all went well. There were no questions on that hot subject, and what's more the very charming Mr and Mrs Fairbanks seemed to like the interviewer. We had a few drinks and went on our way, mightily relieved. Then, very early the next morning, the day of the launch, I received a phone call at home from Mrs Fairbanks, whose opening salvo was, 'Mr Fairbanks is packing his bags.' Taken aback, I naturally asked why. 'Look at the *Daily Mail* and you will see why,' she responded indignantly.

Douglas Fairbanks and his wife join the family on the steps of the Imperial War Museum – Carole and Deborah on the left, Manuela on the right, me in the middle. I'm glad I persuaded him to stay.

Well, the journalist might not have asked the questions, but that had not stopped the paper from leading into the interview in true Fleet Street style with explicit details of the case, the supposed involvement of Douglas Fairbanks etc. This was a very big deal for a small publisher, and there was a lot at stake, so I fought valiantly to convince Mr and Mrs Fairbanks that it was not our doing and that I was every bit as distressed as they were, but that given the dignitaries who were planning to attend the launch that night, and the Foyles lunch next day, the publicity fallout would be terrible if they failed to turn up. Surely, I argued, the newspaper was best ignored and treated with the contempt it deserved.

Fortunately, they relented, medals were polished, and everything went ahead (I use the word advisedly) as if nothing had happened. I even have a signed book with the warm inscription, 'Thanks for a great visit, Douglas'.

As you can imagine, I did not ask Mr Fairbanks whether he was, indeed, the headless man, so I'll never know for sure. That same discretion had wisely intervened when I refrained from informing the young Prince Charles that my great-uncle Jack had had the privilege of circumcising him. Some parts just have to be kept private.

ACKNOWLEDGEMENTS

Over the years people have been urging, 'You really ought to write those stories down' to which I'd evasively reply, 'One day, perhaps.' As a publisher, I knew all too well how often this is flatteringly said to would-be writers by well-meaning friends, and how rarely those offerings see the light of published day, or indeed deserve to. But several rather special people were particularly encouraging, so as the balance of my life began to change – the publishing starting to take second place to the poetry, which had somehow revived after decades of silence – I began, in spare moments, to doodle. The letters weren't joined up at first, but as I began to think of themes and people who had been important to me in various areas of my life, the letters became words, the words became sentences, and – almost by their own volition – chapters began to form and grow... and grow.

The film-maker, author and publisher David Cohen was among the first to urge me to put pen to paper. He even rashly promised to publish my putative book under his own niche imprint. The seeds were sown. Then, most importantly, the literary agent Vivienne Schuster, with whom I'd enjoyed dealing over the years at Curtis Brown, took up the theme. It's not by chance that the dynamic and caring Vivienne had a cluster of classy, bestselling authors on her list, so when she said, 'Stop talking and start writing,' I began to take it seriously. Her constant encouragement, advice and friendship made me believe in the book and go on.

But, even then, I couldn't have done it without the help of Elizabeth Davies, who, as Liz Rose, was Robson Book's marvellous first editor – in at the start of it all. For some years Liz had been directing the Hungerford Literary Festival, and a couple of years ago, having invited me to read there, she too encouraged the idea of a memoir, my reflex response being, 'If I write it, will you edit it?' 'It's a deal,' she said, and over the following eighteen or so months Liz patiently read and commented on the chapters as I wrote them, correcting my many typos, pointing to repetitions and inconsistencies, adding my constant insertions and suggesting trims and areas where I could expand. My daughter Manuela was also heroic in this respect, selflessly and meticulously helping me over the last hurdles when Liz was temporarily unavailable.

I'm especially grateful to Chris Beetles for generously offering his wonderful Ryder Street gallery for the launch of this book.

I'm also indebted to Andy Croft, valiant publisher of the poetry imprint Smokestack Books, who liked my new poems enough to offer to publish them. The appearance of *Blues in the Park* in 2014, my first collection for many years, was a real tonic, as was the publication of its successor *Subject Matters* in 2017. It allowed me to return to the subject of poetry in this book without feeling the imposter I would otherwise have felt myself to be... and been. Then there was Maureen Lipman, our bestselling author over a number of books and years and a true friend, who not only volunteered to read with me from my new books at various festivals but asked continually about the progress of this one, even allowing me to steal some of her stories. And those festivals came about through another wonderwoman, Sally Dunsmore, who directs the Blenheim and Oxford Literary Festivals and also directed the Gibraltar Festival at that stage. It was Sally also who reignited the poetry and jazz concerts, though in a different format from the original Michael Garrick days.

My warm thanks to Sandra Parsons, literary editor of the *Daily Mail*, for the continuing and valued friendship and the many excellent deals we have done together; to her predecessor Jane Mays, with whom I dealt and was friendly with over many years; and to both Susie Dowdall, the *Mail*'s books editor, and Sally Morris, deputy literary editor, always extremely friendly and supportive.

Through all this, my wife, Carole, kept a watching but encouraging brief, reading and making valuable suggestions as the book grew, but never being censorious – not even when she read the early chapters covering the years before we met! In many ways, apart from those chapters, this is her story too, so I was relieved that her response was genuinely positive and glad that I was able to rekindle memories of many kinds for us both.

I'm also grateful to my daughter Deborah for filling in details of our Russian trip, and for recalling some of the 'twin' adventures she shared with her sister and other stories, and for her constant support; to Anthony Harkavy for his legal read of the manuscript, which became more than that as he brought a number of other things to my attention; to Maureen and Michael Joseph for their continued interest and encouragement; to Anne Hooper, Jeff Powell and Pete Brown for sharing their memories of the Regent Street Polytechnic; to Jeannette Kupferman for providing details of the Haberdashers' School review in which she appeared with her friend Pamela (Fiona) Walker; to Jeremy Morris for lending me his valued copies of *Skylark*, the Haberdashers' magazine and for his continuing friendship; to Keren Abse and Sacha Mitchell for their ready permission to quote letters I received from their respective fathers; to my cousins David Robson and Roger Seaton for details of my paternal great-grandparents and of our great-uncle Kurt (Zelma) Rosenberg, as well as to Margi and Leo Abelis for providing access to the Rosenberg family archives; to Michael Freedland for the excellent books and camaraderie over the years; to Marilyn Warnick, who apart from giving me the story about Robert Vaughan, bought a number of our titles for the *Mail on Sunday* over many convivial lunches; to Edward Gold for his vital role in getting the first readings going, and beyond; to Geoffrey Munn, whose masterly history *Wartski: The First Hundred and Fifty Years* provided valuable background information on my mother's side of the family (the Wartskis and the Snowmans), as did the *Camden History Review* (No. 31). I was also able to draw on the recollections of my mother, Charlotte, and grandmother Harriet, which I managed to record. Caroline Bloom generously gave me the two Wimbledon programmes to which I refer, and which were left to her by her mother, my much missed cousin Barbara. The memories of Wolfgang Foges by former Aldus Books stalwarts Bruce Robertson, David Lambert, Ross Macdonald, Douglas Hill and Felix Gluck, and in particular David Lambert's detailed account of the Aldus history, provided a valuable backdrop to my own personal experiences, for which I am most grateful. Another Aldus colleague, Joanna Jellinek, provided me with mementoes of her brother-in-law Felix Gluck, and was able to confirm various details, and Felix's son Dr Tim Gluck kindly provided the photo of his father that appears in the book. I was also glad to have been able to include Michael Bywater's brilliant evocation of Alan Coren as editor of *Punch* and am grateful to Bernard Kops for permission to quote from his poem 'Shalom Bomb'.

Regretfully, I never kept a detailed diary, but I do have cuttings from over the years, particularly with regard to the poetry and jazz concerts, and possess many letters from those who participated, which I was able to refer to – among them Dannie Abse, Laurie Lee, Ted Hughes, Stevie Smith, Lydia Pasternak Slater, Thomas Blackburn, Vernon Scannell and Adrian Mitchell. The remarkable Michael Garrick's autobiography, *Dusk Fire*, also reminded me of stories that had escaped my memory. In compiling the various anthologies I edited, I also found myself in friendly correspondence with a number of the poets involved, whose observations and contributions I have taken the liberty of drawing on briefly in discussing those books.

Apart from where specifically mentioned, virtually all the photos and pictorial material in this book come from my own archives, but I would like to thank the following for generous permission to include their photographs here: Gemma Levine, who covered a number of early Robson Books events; Roger Dixon, who covered the Muhammad Ali tour for us; KT Bruce for the pictures taken at the Oxford and Blenheim Festivals, for which she is the official photographer; Anna Ford and her daughter Katie Boxer for kind permission to include Mark Boxer's *Times* cartoon of Alfred Brendel; Peter Brookes for his generosity in giving me the cartoon that accompanies my poem 'The Cartoonist's Glasses'; Brian Davies for his photos from the Hungerford Festival; John Hopkins, who covered a number of readings, especially those for Centre 42, and gave me a number of exceptional photos taken at these for my personal use; my ex-Aldus colleague Ken Coton, who also covered many of our concerts and provided me with copies of his superb photos; Cecily Ben-Tovim for her arresting cover illustration for the Poetry Returns to Hampstead programme; Mark Lewisohn, Beatles expert, for photos he took at our Gibraltar concert, which he recorded; Michael Finberg for various party photos and kindnesses over the years.

I'm particularly grateful to my publisher – to my fastidious editor Olivia Beattie, who handled the ever-growing manuscript I handed over (and the many photos!) with skill and care; to Namkwan Cho, for his stylish jacket and design; to Iain Dale for wanting to publish my book despite the poetry; to Isabelle Ralphs, the company's lively and switched-on publicist; and to James Stephens, sales director and friend who virtually runs the company these days and whose great ability and initial enthusiasm drew me to Biteback when I was virtually committed elsewhere.

I owe a special thank-you to all the fine poets who participated in Poetry and Jazz in Concert over the years and helped to make it such a success. It was a privilege to read and share a platform with them, as it was with all the fabulous musicians who performed alongside us and added so much.

Finally, my warmest thanks to all those many authors who trusted us over the years with their work. Without authors, there can be no publisher, and that is something I've tried to remember right from the beginning.

INDEX